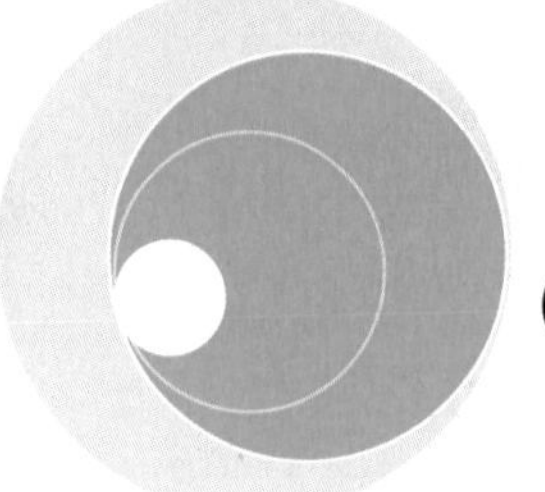

gateway science

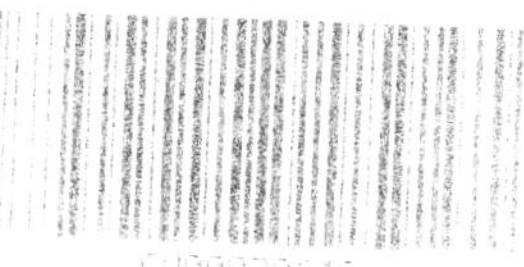

HIGHER

OCR Additional Science for GCSE

Ian Honeysett
David Lees
Averil Macdonald
Steven Bibby

Series Editor: Bob McDuell

www.heinemann.co.uk
✓ Free online support
✓ Useful weblinks
✓ 24 hour online ordering

01865 888058

Heinemann Educational Publishers
Halley Court, Jordan Hill, Oxford OX2 8EJ
Part of Harcourt Education

Heinemann is the registered trademark of Harcourt Education Limited

First published 2006

10 09 08 07 06
10 9 8 7 6 5 4 3 2 1

10-digit ISBN: 0 435 67524 9
13-digit ISBN: 978 0 435 67524 9

Edited by Bob McDuell
Designed by Wooden Ark
Typeset by Kamae Design, Cassington, Oxford
copy edited by Ros Davies

Original illustrations © Harcourt Education Limited, 2006

Illustrated by HL Studios
Cover design by Cooney Bains
Printed in the UK by Bath Colourbooks
Cover photo: © Getty Images
Picture research by Ginny Stroud-Lewis

Acknowledgements
The authors and publisher would like to thank the following individuals and organisations for permission to reproduce photographs:
Page 2, Corbis; 3, **T** SPL / J.C. Revy; **M** Eric Grave / Phototake Inc / OSF; **B** SPL / A. Barrington Brown; 6, Getty Images / PhotoDisc; 7, **T** NHPA / Andrea Bonetti; **B** Getty Images / Photodisc; 8, SPL / Steve Gschmeissner; 10, ?; 11, Harcourt Index; 13, The Advertising Archives; 14, **T** Getty Images / Photodisc; **B** Corbis / Bettmann; 15, T SPL / Du Cane Medical Imaging Ltd; **B** Pascal Goetgheluck / SPL; 17, Getty Images / Photodisc; 18, Getty Images / Photodisc; 19, Corbis; 22, SPL / Professor Miodrag Stojkovic; 23, **T** Corbis / Frank Young / Papilio; **B** www.mykoweb.com; 25, Corbis / Owen Franken; 26, **T** SPL / Cristina Pedrazzini; **B** Stone / Getty; 28, Chris Rogers / Corbis; 29, Corbis / James Darling / Reuters; 30, Art Directors and Trip; 31, **T** Roslin Institute / Phototake Inc / OSF; **B** Eyewire; 32, Getty Images / Photodisc; 38, Getty Images / Photodisc; 39, **T** Corbis; M Harcourt Index; **B** SPL / Dr Jeremy Burgess; 41, Richard Smith; 42, Art Directors and Trip; 43, Holt Studios International Ltd / Alamy (×2); 44, **L** Alamy Images / Phototake Inc; **R** Steve Gschmeissner / SPL; 46, Getty Images / PhotoDisc (×2); 47, **T** SPL / Volker Steger; **B** Art Directors and Trip; 49, **L** SPL / J.C. Revy; **R** SPL / Andrew Syred; 50, SPL / Martyn F. Chillmaid; 51, **T** Harcourt Index; **B** Mary Ellen Baker / Botanica / OSF; 52, cumulus; 53, Alamy; 54, SPL / Dr Jeremy Burgess; 55, Harcourt Education / Ginny Stroud-Lewis (×2); 58, Alamy Images / Andre Jenny; 59, **T** Stone / Getty; **B** Alamy Images / FLPA; 61, **T** Mary Clark / Alamy; **B** Harcourt Education / Ginny Stroud-Lewis; 62, T Harcourt Index; **B** Corbis / Joe McDonald; 63, **T** Corbis / Corbis Sygma; **B** Harcourt Education / Ginny Stroud-Lewis; 64, **T** Hybrid Medical Animation / SPL; **B** Robert Pickett / Corbis; 65, Harcourt Education / Ginny Stroud-Lewis; 66, Alamy Images / Hugh Threlfall / SPL; 67, Gary Braasch / Corbis; 68, SPL / Andrew McClenaghan; 69, Alamy Images / Elmtree Images; 70, **T** Dr Jeremy Burgess / SPL; **B** SPL / Michael Abbey; 74, SPL / Andrew Lambert Photography; 75, **T** SPL / Dr Mitsuo Ohtsuki; **B** Art Directors and Trip; 78, Corbis / Ed Young; 79, **T** Alamy Images / Helene Rogers; **B** Corbis / Bob Krist; 81, SPL / Andrew Syred; 82, Alamy Images / Ange; 83, Harcourt Education / Ginny Stroud-Lewis; 86, Art Directors and Trip; 87, T SPL; **B** Harcourt Education; 88, **T** Andrew Lambert Photography / SPL; **M** Harcourt Education / Trevor Clifford (×3); 90, Alamy Images / Peter Defty; 91, **T** Imagebroker / Alamy; **BL** Charles D. Winters / SPL; **BM** Andrew Lambert Photography / SPL; **BR** Andrew Lambert Photography / SPL; 92, Andrew Lambert Photography / SPL; 94, **T** Archimage; **BL** Corbis / Reuters; **BR** Harcourt Education / Ginny Stroud-Lewis; 95, **T** Corbis / Bettmann; **B** Harcourt Index; 96, Science and Society; 97, Adam Hart-Davis / SPL; 98, Corbis / Sygma / Parrot Pascal; 99, **T** Harcourt Education / Ginny Stroud-Lewis; **B** Alamy Images / J. Schwanke; 101, Andrew Lambert Photography / SPL (×3); 102, **T** Alamy Images / Jeremy Horner; **B** SPL / Astrid & Hanns-Frieder Michler; 103, Reed International Books, Australia; 104, **T** Leslie Garland Picture Library / Alamy; **B** Corbis; 105, Getty Images / PhotoDisc; 106, Corbis; 110, Getty Images / Photodisc; 111, **T** Getty Images / PhotoDisc; 111, **B** Greenshoots Communications / Alamy; 113, Martyn F. Chillmaid / SPL; 114, SPL / Martyn F. Chillmaid; 115, Getty Images / Photodisc (×2); 117, Art Directors and Trip; 118, Alamy Images / David Lyons; 119, T Alamy Images / Paul Glendell; **B** Alamy Images / DY Riess MD; 121, SPL / Robert Brook; 122, **TL** SPL / Andrew Lambert Photography; **ML** Corbis / Andrew Brookes; **BR** Art Directors and Trip; 123, **T** Corbis; **B** Corbis / Hulton-Deutsch Collection; 125, **T** Alamy Images / Photofusion Picture Library; **B** Photo Courtesy of Terra Nitrogen (UK) Limited; 127, **T** SPL; **B** Harcourt Education Ltd; 128, **T** Corbis; **B** Corbis / Wolfgang Kaehler; 130, Art Directors and Trip; 131, Corbis / Bettmann; 133, **T** Scott T. Smith / Corbis; **B** Erich Schrempp / SPL; 134, Frank Trapper / Corbis; 135, T Frank Trapper / Corbis; **B** Dr Peter Harris / SPL; 137, Dr Peter Harris / SPL; 138, Harcourt Education / Ginny Stroud-Lewis (×2); 139, **T** Alamy Images / Greenshoots Communications; **B** WaterAid / Jon Spaull; 141, SPL / Novosti Press Agency; 142, SPL / Robert Brook; 146, TBC; 147, Corbis; 148, TBC; 150, NASA Headquarters – Greatest Images of NASA (NASA-HQ-GRIN); 151, **T** picturesbyrob / Alamy; **B** Alamy Images / David Wall; 154, NASA (×2); 155, Getty Images / PhotoDisc; 158, TBC; 159, **T** Corbis, **B** Realimage / Alamy; 162, Harcourt Education / Tudor Photography; 163, **T** Corbis; **B** Corbis / Don Mason; 164, Motoring Picture Library; 165, Alamy Images / Paul Doyle; 166, Corbis / Ted Soqui; 167, **T** David Woods / Corbis; **B** Alamy Images / David Crausby; 168, Alamy Images / Eliane Farray-Sulle; 169, Joe Fox / Alamy; 170, Alamy Images / Travelbox; 171, Corbis / Joe McBride; 173, Schlegelmilch / Corbis; 174, Photos.com; 175, Corbis; 177, Art Directors and Trip; 178, Kelly-Mooney Photography / Corbis; 182, Getty Images / PhotoDisc; 183, **T** SPL / Andrew Lambert Photography; **B** Harcourt Education / Ginny Stroud-Lewis; 184, Mediscan; 185, Corbis (×2); 186, Wolfson Electrostatics, University of Southampton; 187, Corbis; 188, **T** Dacorum Gold / Alamy; **B** Jean-Francois Cardella / Construction Photography; 189, **T** Honda; M Harcourt Education / Gareth Boden; B Corbis; 190, SPL; 191, **T** Harcourt Education / Gareth Boden; **B** Cn Boon / Alamy; 192, Andrew Lambert Photography / SPL; 193, **T** Sheila Terry / SPL; **B** imagebroker / Alamy; 194, University of Southampton; 195, Getty Images / PhotoDisc; 198, Corbis, 199, Alamy; 201, John Greim / SPL; 202, Mediscan; 203, Alamy Images / Worldwide Picture Library; 206, Getty Images / Photodisc; 207, Harcourt Education / Jane Read; 208, Ian M Butterfield / Alamy; 209, Chris Priest / SPL; 210, Alamy Images / Imagina Photography; 211, Alamy Images / David Robertson; 213, T Bettmann / Corbis; B Corbis / Karen Kasmauski; 214, Corbis;

The authors and publisher would like to thank the following individuals and organisations for permission to reproduce copyright materials: 21, **TL** Relative rates graph for the human body, - Advanced Biology Principles and Applications by Clegg and Mackean, published by John Murray / **BR** Growth curves for boys head size and weight - Child Growth Foundation; 82 Bromine extraction from water, www.amlwchdata.co.uk/copperkingdom/aoc.htm; 96 Hoffman Voltameter - Letts GCSE Classbook Science by D Baylis, published by Letts Educational Ltd; 128 **B** Action of detergent - Chemistry Nuffield Co-ordinated Sciences, published by Longman; Water purification diagram - IGCSE Chemistry by Earl and Wilford, published by Hodder Education; 142 Reservoir capacity in England and Wales 2004/2005 - www.environment-agency.gov.uk.

Every effort has been made to contact copyright holders of material reproduced in this book. Any omissions will be rectified in subsequent printings if notice is given to the publishers.
Tel: 01865 888058 www.heinemann.co.uk

Introduction

This student book covers the Higher tier of the new OCR Gateway Science specification. The first examinations are in January 2007. It has been written to support you as you study for the OCR Gateway Additional Science GCSE.

This book has been written by examiners who are also teachers and who have been involved in the development of the new specification. It is supported by other material produced by Heinemann, including online teacher resource sheets and interactive learning software with exciting video clips, games and activities.

As part of GCSE Additional Science you have to do a Skills Assessment. This involves a Research task, a Data task and an assessment of your practical skills made by your teacher. You will find out more about these on pages 218–223.

If you are following this Additional Science course, you will either have completed or be progressing towards the Science Core GCSE award. The emphasis of Core Science is on how science affects our everyday lives. For Additional Science the emphasis changes – it is more about the work of scientists, both in the past and today. You will cover topics such as atomic structure, genetics and some quantitative Physics. It will provide you with the experience you need to start AS courses in Biology, Chemistry and Physics.

The next two pages explain the special features we have included in this book to help you to learn and understand the science, and to be able to use it in context. At the back of the book you will also find some useful tables, as well as a glossary and index.

About this book

This student book has been designed to make learning science fun. The book follows the layout of the OCR Gateway Additional Science specification. It is divided into six sections that match the six modules in the specification with two for Biology, two for Chemistry and two for Physics: B3, B4, C3, C4, P3, P4.

The module introduction page at the start of a module (e.g. below right) introduces what you are going to learn. It has some short introductory paragraphs, plus 'talking heads' with speech bubbles that raise questions about what is going to be covered.

Each module is then broken down into eight separate items (a–h), for example, B3a, B3b, B3c, B3d, B3e, B3f, B3g, B3h.

Each 'item' is covered in four book pages. These four pages are split into three pages covering the science content relevant to the item plus a 'Context' page which places the science content just covered into context, either by news-related articles or data tasks, or by examples of scientists at work, science in everyday life or science in the news.

Throughout these four pages there are clear explanations with diagrams and photos to illustrate the science being discussed. At the end of each module there are three pages of questions to test your knowledge and understanding of the module.

There are three pages of exam-style end of module questions for each module.

The talking heads on the module intro page raise questions about what you are going to learn.

The numbers in square brackets give the marks for the question or part of the question.

The bulleted text introduces the module

This box highlights what you need to know before you start the module.

Context pages link the science learned in the item with real life.

This box highlights what you will be learning about in this item.

General approach to the topic

Question box at the end.

Some amazing facts have been included – science isn't just boring facts!

Questions in the text make sure you have understood what you have just read.

When a new word appears for the first time in the text, it will appear in bold type. All words in **bold** are listed with their meanings in the glossary at the back of the book.

Clear diagrams to explain the science.

Examiner's tips are included to help you do better in your exams.

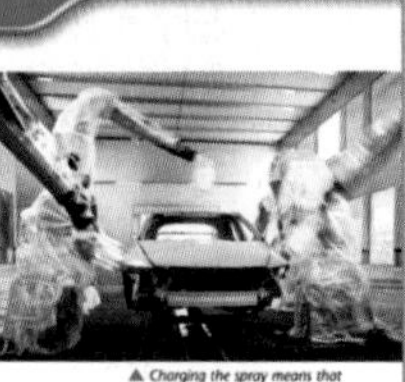

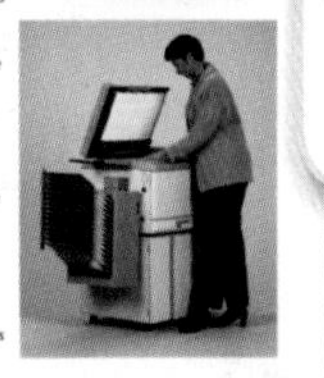

The keywords box lists all keywords in the item.

Contents

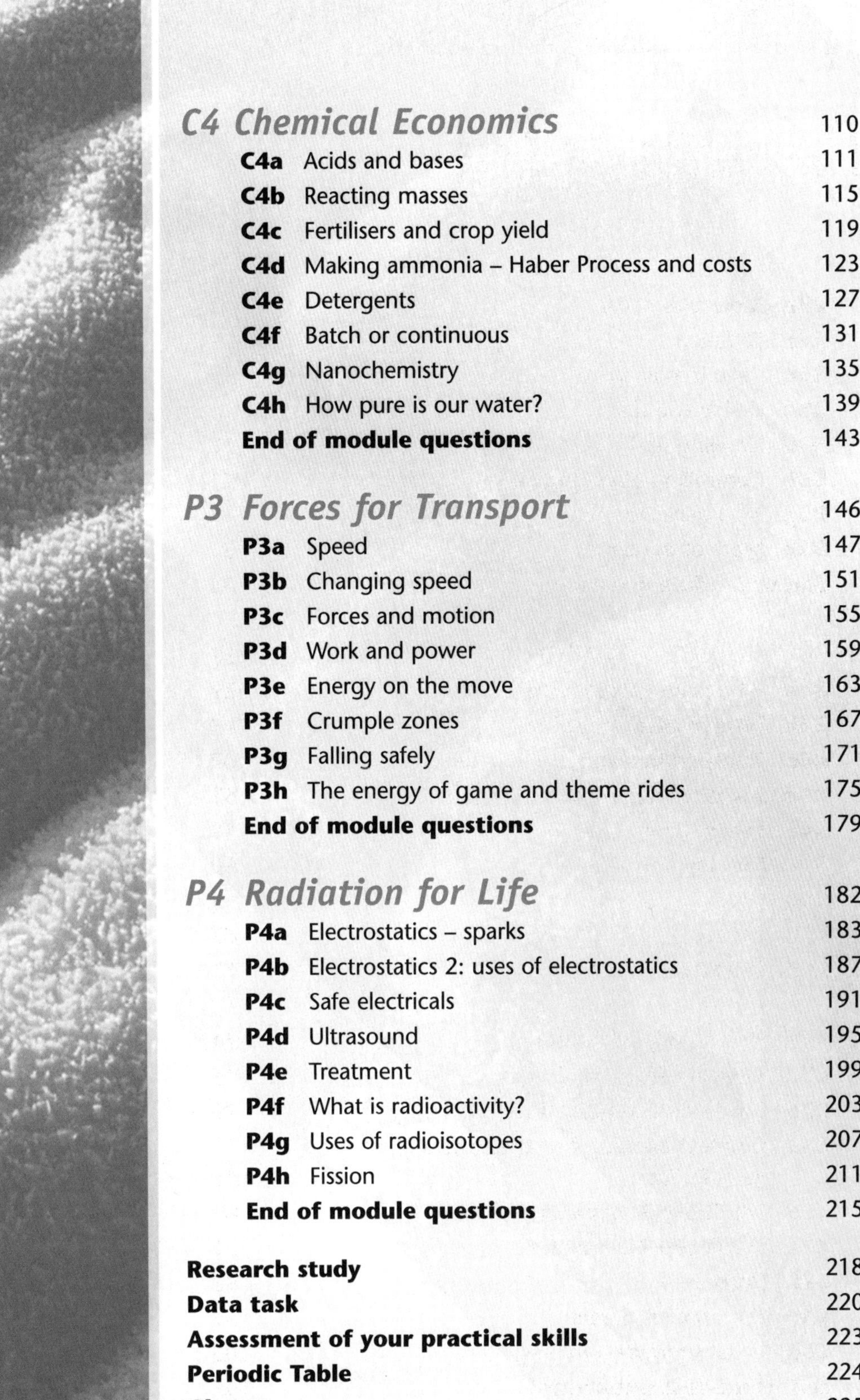

B3 Living and growing

- Every day, newspapers contain articles about new breakthroughs in genetics. They include stories of how scientists are going to produce new organisms by manipulating genes.
- All this is possible due to the discovery of the structure of DNA and how it acts as the genetic code.
- Life on our planet ranges from the smallest single-celled organisms to massive organisms made of millions of cells. Although there are advantages to being larger, these cells need organising and transport systems are needed to move substances around them.

I read in the papers that scientists can now make identical copies of any animal by cloning them.

I'm not sure that cloning would make identical copies of a person. Surely how we are brought up is just as important as our genes.

I don't agree with cloning people but it must be useful to be able to clone animals.

What you need to know

- About the reproductive system and the breathing system.
- What plants need so that they can make their own food by photosynthesis.
- The importance of proteins in the body.
- The structure of plant and animal cells.

Building blocks for organisms

In this item you will find out

- where respiration takes place in cells
- about DNA and DNA 'fingerprints'
- the function of enzymes and how they work

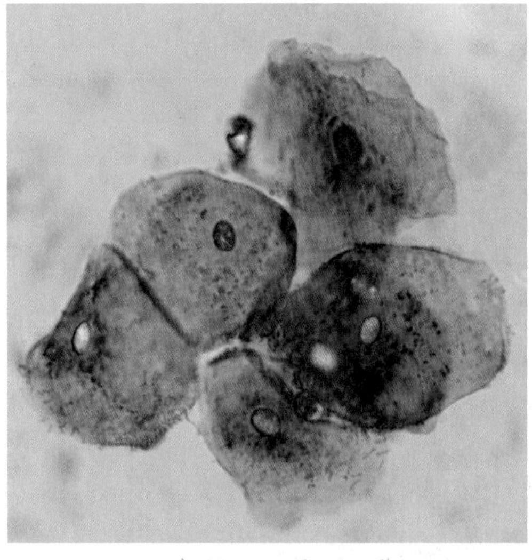

▲ *Human cheek cells*

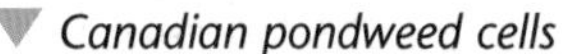

▼ *Canadian pondweed cells*

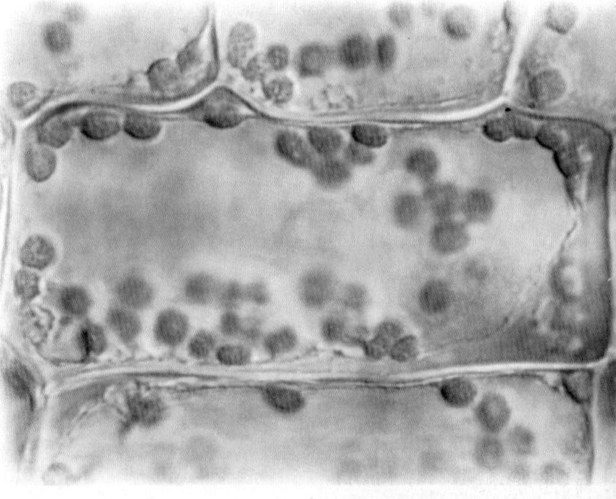

All living organisms are made up of cells. Using the naked eye we can see detail down to about the size of 0.1 mm. Cells are smaller than this so it is necessary to use microscopes to study them.

The first person to see cells was a British scientist called Robert Hooke in 1665. He looked at cork under the microscope and saw little boxes. He called them cells because he thought that they looked like the rooms where monks slept.

As microscopes improved, more and more detail could be seen in cells. You have probably used a light microscope to look at cells and seen images like the cells in the photographs.

a **What structures can you see in these cells?**

By using a light microscope, we can see objects as small as 0.002 mm clearly. About 50 years ago a new type of microscope was developed called the electron microscope. This could show even more detail in cells – down to about 0.000 002 mm.

Although this is small enough to see much of the detail in cells, this is still not small enough to see individual atoms. Scientists had to find other ways of investigating the molecules that are found in cells. One of these molecules is DNA.

Two scientists, James Watson and Francis Crick, used images obtained by firing X-rays at a crystal of DNA. They used these data to work out the structure of the DNA molecule in 1953.

Amazing fact

DNA is made of molecules called bases which are about 0.000 000 34 mm wide.

▲ *Watson and Crick*

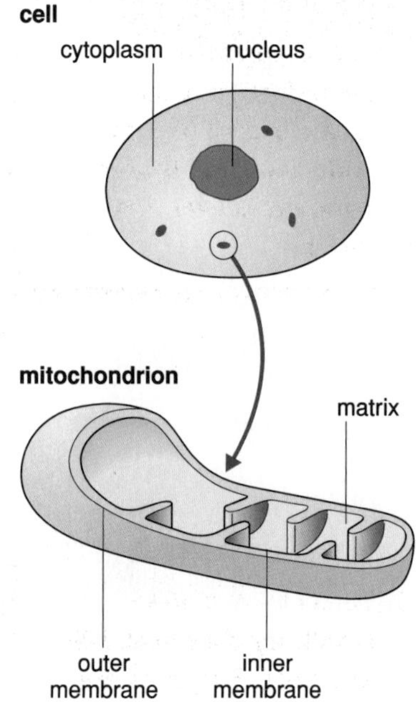

▲ *Inside a mitochondrion*

Inside cells

It is now possible to look more closely at the cytoplasm of animal cells. Using the electron microscope, the detail of structures such as mitochondria can be studied.

Mitochondria contain enzymes that carry out the final stages of respiration and this provides all the energy for life processes.

Why do you think the inner membrane of the mitochondrion is so folded?

Making proteins

We have known for a long time that the nucleus of the cell is the control centre. It regulates the activities of the cell by controlling which proteins the cell makes (protein synthesis). We now know that DNA is present in the nucleus of every cell where the code is kept. So, it is likely that DNA contains the genetic code.

Suggest what the functions of these proteins might be?

Each different protein is made up of a specific chain of amino acids. This determines the shape of the protein and how it works. So, DNA must code for the order of the amino acids.

We get the amino acids that are used by the cell to make proteins from our food. Some foods do not contain a very wide variety of amino acids. Fortunately, some amino acids can be converted into others in the liver (transamination) but essential amino acids must be obtained from our diet.

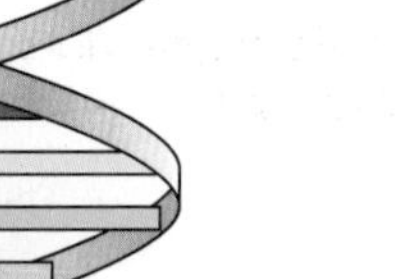

▲ *The structure of DNA*

Structure of DNA

Watson and Crick found that DNA was made of two strands of organic bases twisted up to make a spiral or a **double helix**. There are four different bases, known by the letters A, T, G and C. Pairs of these bases form cross links that hold the two chains together. Base A always pairs up with T and base G always pairs up with C. This is called **complementary base pairing**.

The order of the bases codes for the order of amino acids in each protein. Each amino acid is coded for by a sequence of three bases. This is shown in the diagram below.

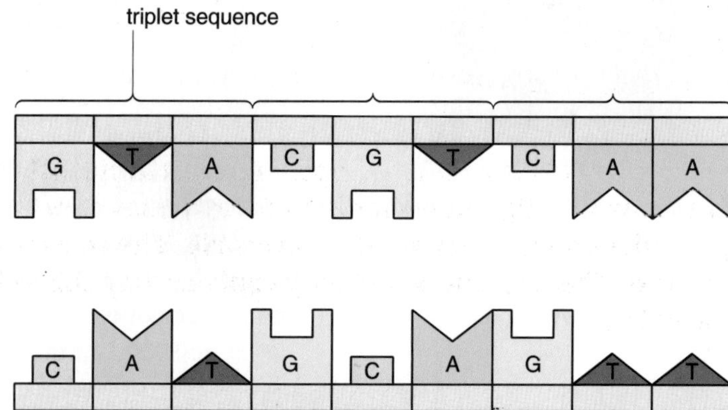

▲ *Strand of DNA showing detail of bases*

The whole base sequence that codes for one protein is called a gene. Each protein has its own number and sequence of amino acids, which means that each protein has a different shape and function.

Before cells divide, the DNA copies itself (DNA replication). The two strands of the DNA molecule can unzip and come apart to form single strands. As each part of the strand becomes unzipped, new bases can move in to form a double strand again by complementary base pairing. At the end of the process there are two complete double strands of DNA. Because the bases can only fit together in certain ways, both double strands of DNA are exactly the same. When the cell divides each copy of the cell has the same DNA.

Amazing fact

Even though a cell is less than 0.03 mm wide the DNA that it contains is over 1 m long!

Enzymes

Enzymes are one of the most important types of protein produced by all cells. Enzymes are biological catalysts. This means that they speed up the rate of chemical reactions in living cells, such as respiration, photosynthesis and protein synthesis.

All enzymes also share the following characteristics:

- they have an optimum temperature and pH where they work best
- each enzyme will only work on a particular reaction.

These properties of enzymes can be explained by looking at how they work. The chemical that is reacting (the **substrate**) fits into an area on the enzyme called the **active site**. The reaction then takes place. The enzyme and the substrate are like a lock and key. This explains why enzymes are specific to a substrate and a reaction.

Examiner's tip

Don't say that heat *kills* enzymes. Enzymes are not alive.

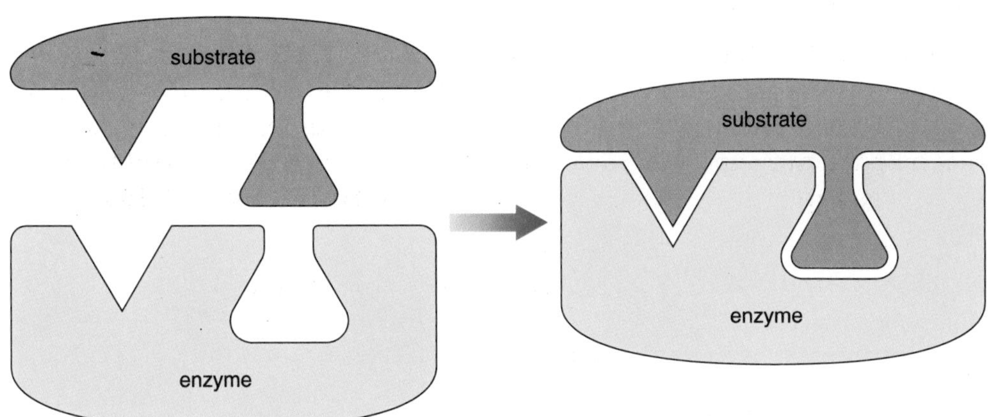

An enzyme fits into a specific substrate

Most enzymes work best at body temperature and at the pH of the organ in which they work. High temperatures and extremes of pH will change the shape of the enzyme's active site irreversibly. The enzyme is said to be **denatured**. The lock and key theory explains why this will stop the enzyme working.

Keywords

active site • complementary base pairing • denatured • double helix • mitochondria • substrate

Making a DNA fingerprint

Dr Rachel Wong works in a laboratory that deals with DNA testing. Although most of our DNA controls protein synthesis, some does not. This non-coding DNA is unique to each person and so can be used to identify an individual. It is called a DNA 'fingerprint'.

'Whenever I create a DNA fingerprint I go through several stages,' she says. 'The DNA is isolated and extracted from blood cells. Then it is cut into fragments using a special enzyme.

The DNA fragments are separated into bands during a process called electrophoresis. The bands are now embedded in gel but we can't see them. This band pattern is then transferred to a nylon membrane.

A radioactive DNA probe is added which binds to the bands of DNA. The extra radioactive DNA probe is washed off.

When the nylon membrane is X-rayed the radioactive DNA probe shows the pattern of the DNA fingerprint. This fingerprint can then be compared with another fingerprint.'

Rachel has just finished preparing the DNA fingerprints of a man, a woman and two children.

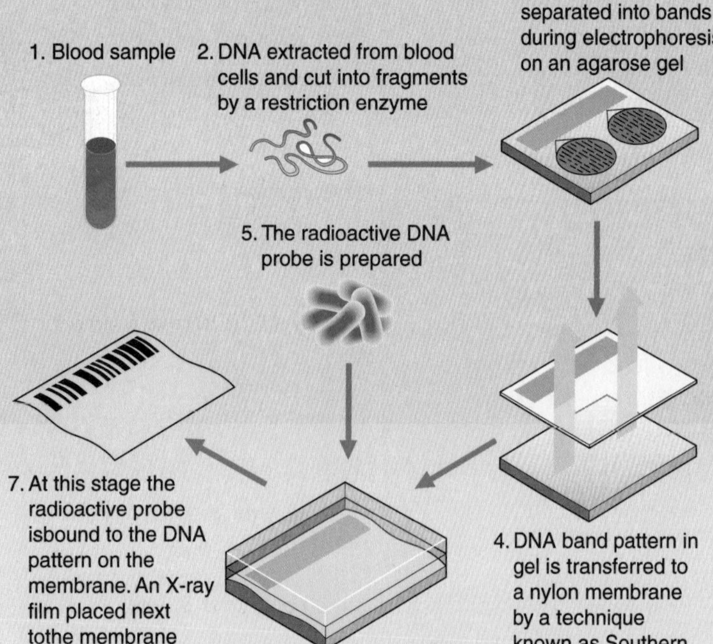

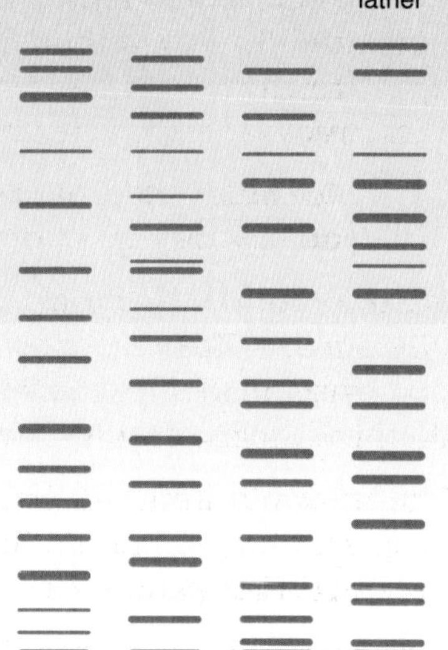

Questions

1 Why do you think a radioactive DNA probe is added before the DNA band pattern is exposed to an X-ray film?

2 Which of the children could be the offspring of the woman and the man?

3 What would the genetic fingerprint of identical twins look like?

4 Describe one other possible use of genetic fingerprinting apart from proving relationships between people.

Spreading far and wide

In this item you will find out

- how diffusion happens
- the importance of diffusion in animals
- how diffusion occurs in plant leaves

▲ *A female great peacock moth*

One morning in May during the 1870s, the French scientist Jean-Henri Fabre was pleased when a female great peacock moth emerged from a cocoon on a table in his laboratory-study.

He put her under a wire cage and left her to spread her wings to dry. That evening Fabre was amazed as dozens of male great peacock moths floated in through the open doors and windows of his house. Over the following week Fabre caught more than 150 male moths. No matter where in the house he moved the female, the male moths headed directly for her. 'What was attracting them?' he wondered.

Over the next several years Fabre carried out many experiments to learn the moths' secret. Eventually he concluded that, even though humans could not detect it, the female moth must release a smell that is very attractive to the opposite sex of her species.

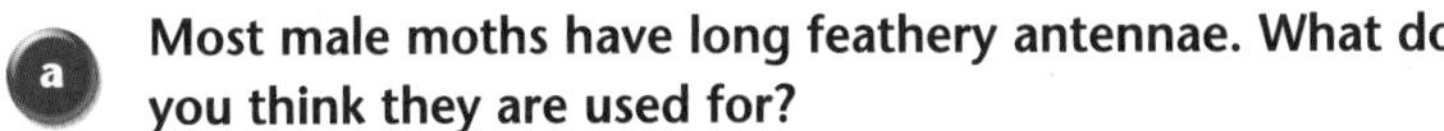

a **Most male moths have long feathery antennae. What do you think they are used for?**

We now call the chemicals that the moth was producing pheromones. They are produced by many animals and can attract mates from many kilometres away. But how do these chemicals travel such long distances in the air?

The answer is diffusion. Diffusion allows many chemicals to spread through the air. Insects are attracted to flowers by scent diffusing into the air.

Diffusion is also important inside the bodies of animals and plants. Many substances rely on diffusion to enter and leave the body and its tissues.

▼ *This insect is attracted by the flower's scent*

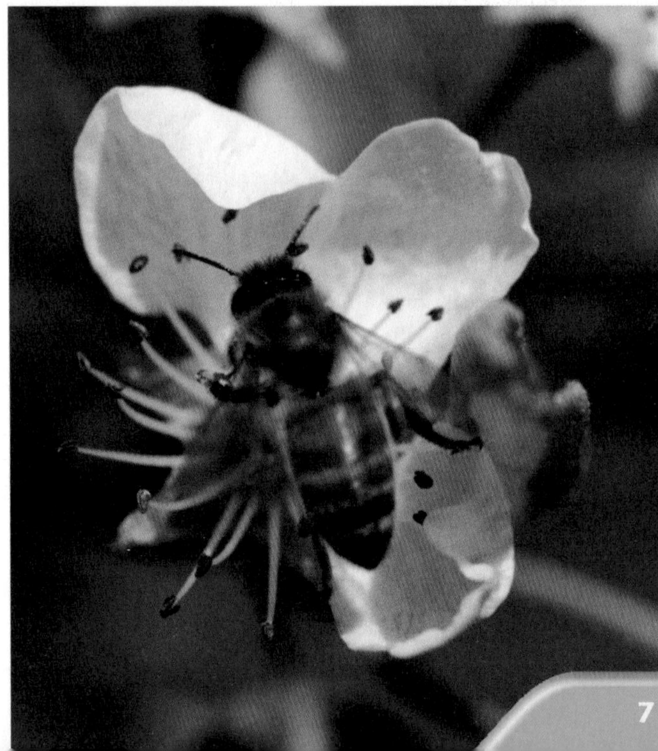

What is diffusion?

Diffusion is described as the net movement of a substance from an area of high concentration to an area of low concentration. It works because individual particles are constantly moving about at random and so they tend to spread out.

urea
carbon dioxide
minerals
oxygen
amino acids
glucose

▲ *What cells gain and lose*

A plant or animal cell will lose waste products and gain useful substances by diffusion through the cell membrane. This is shown in the diagram on the left.

The rate of diffusion of a substance can be made faster by:

- decreasing the distance the substance has to diffuse
- increasing the difference in the concentration between the two areas (the **concentration gradient**)
- making the surface area through which the substance has to diffuse larger.

b **How can the surface area of a cell membrane be made larger?**

Diffusion in animals

Substances can pass in and out of cells by diffusion and this allows animals to exchange substances with their surroundings.

In the small intestine, small digested food molecules are absorbed into the bloodstream by diffusion. The inside of the small intestine is long, permeable and covered with finger-like projections called **villi**. They are further covered by smaller projections called **microvilli**. Both the villi and the microvilli increase the surface area, speeding up absorption. The villi have a good blood supply as they contain lots of blood vessels. The food molecules can be taken away after being absorbed into the blood by diffusion.

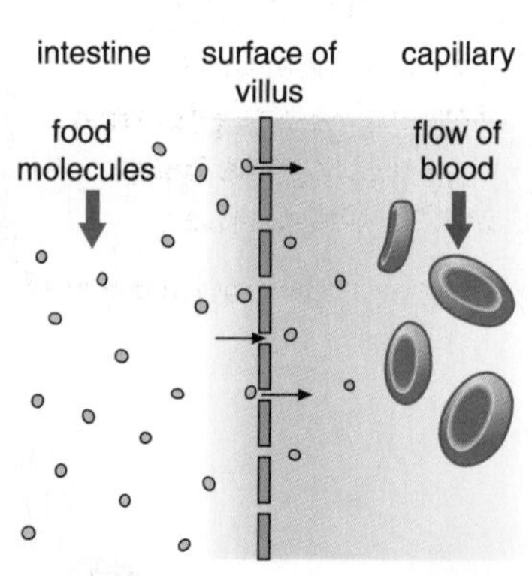

▲ *Food molecules are absorbed into the blood by diffusion*

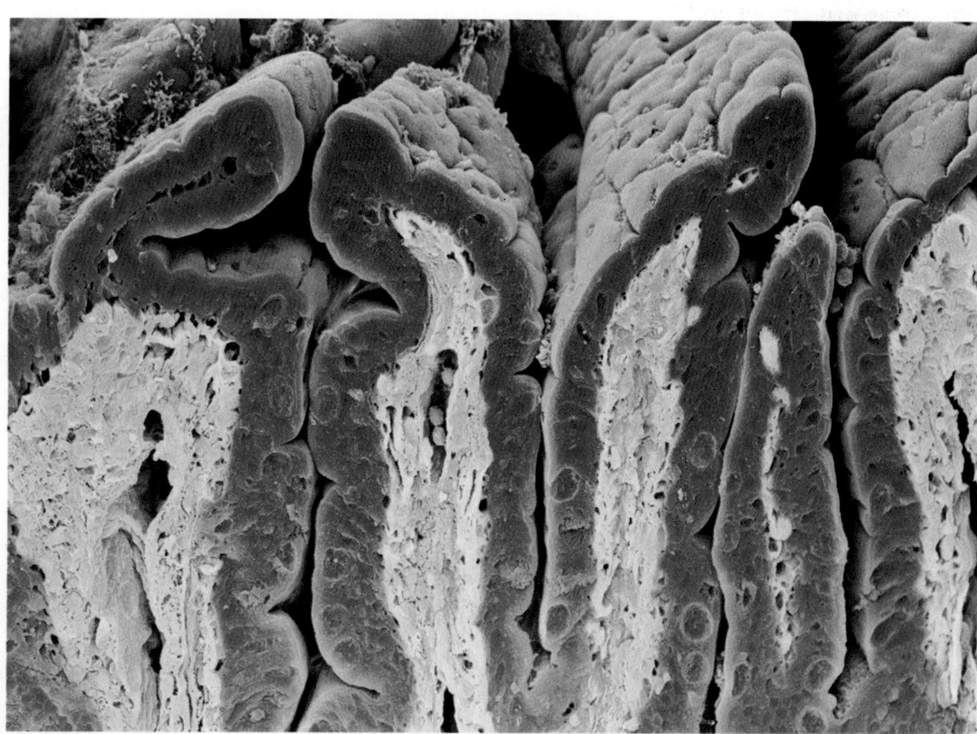

Villi inside the small intestine ▶

c **Why do you think it is important to keep removing the food molecules that have entered the villi?**

In the lungs, oxygen diffuses into the bloodstream and carbon dioxide diffuses out. This happens in small air sacs called **alveoli**. There are millions of these alveoli so that the total surface area is enormous. Like the villi, their walls are permeable and very thin (only one cell thick) so that the gases do not have far to diffuse. They also have a moist lining and a rich blood supply.

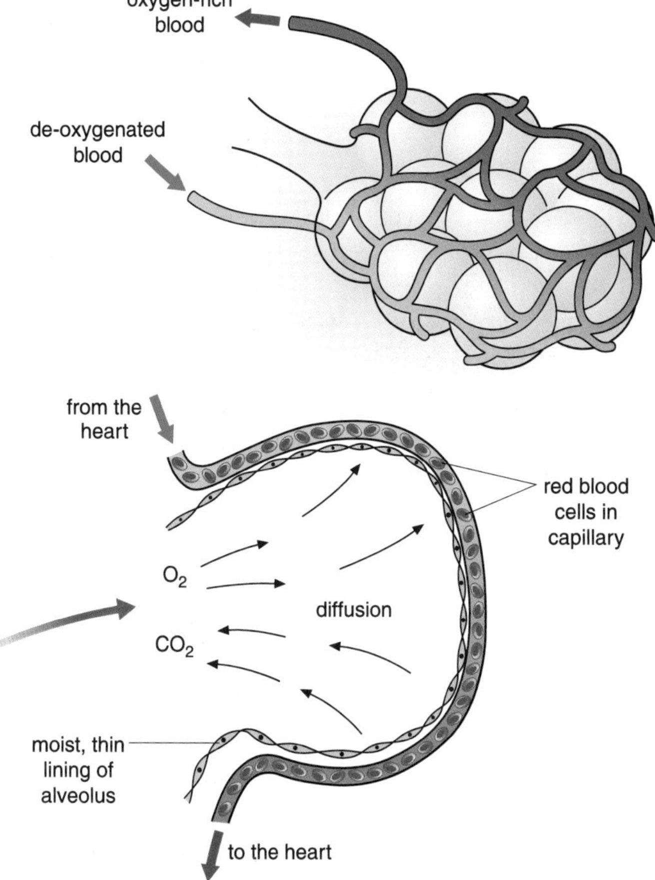

▲ *Diffusion in alveoli*

A **fetus** needs food and oxygen while it is growing – it gets them from its mother. In return, carbon dioxide and other waste products pass to the mother. Early in pregnancy the embryo grows a structure called the **placenta**. This is a disc of tissue that is attached to the wall of the uterus. All of these substances diffuse across the placenta. The placenta has projections called villi that increase the surface area for diffusion.

Diffusion is also important in the nervous system. One neurone is not directly connected to the next – there is a small gap. This is called a **synapse**. When a signal reaches the synapse, chemicals called **transmitter substances** are released and diffuse across the gap. This will set off a signal in the next neurone.

 **If all neurones in the body were directly connected, what would happen if one was stimulated?**

Examiner's tip

Remember the placenta is grown by the baby not by the mother.

Diffusion in plants

In plants, oxygen and carbon dioxide diffuse in and out through the leaves. Leaves are specially adapted to allow gases to diffuse in and out. They have thousands of microscopic pores called stomata on the underside, and the thin but flat shape of the leaves gives them a large surface area. Inside the leaf are air spaces that allow the gases to diffuse. All of these features increase the rate of diffusion of oxygen and carbon dioxide.

 **What processes produce oxygen and carbon dioxide in the plant?**

 **How will the diffusion of these gases differ at night compared with during daylight?**

As the stomata let gases diffuse in and out of the leaf, they will also allow water molecules to diffuse out. Plants lose large amounts of water from their leaves by this evaporation. This means they have to take up water from the soil in order to replace the water that is lost.

Keywords

alveoli • concentration gradient • fetus • microvilli • placenta • synapse • transmitter substance • villi

Sugar and eggs

Angus is carrying out an experiment to show diffusion of water molecules across the membrane of an egg. He removes the shell of an egg with ethanoic acid, leaving the membrane of the egg plus the white and the yolk. An egg contains lots of water so it is an area of high concentration of water.

He places the egg in a sugar solution which is made of pure sugar with only a small amount of water in it. This means the sugar solution is an area of low concentration of water.

After the egg has been in the syrup for about an hour, Angus can see a layer round the egg in the syrup. The water molecules inside the egg have diffused through the membrane into the syrup and this layer is an area where the water concentration of the syrup has increased.

After 36 hours, most of the water in the egg has moved into the sugar solution. Only the yolk and the egg membrane are left. The water molecules have moved from the area of high concentration to the area of low concentration until the water concentration in the egg and in the syrup is almost equal.

Before

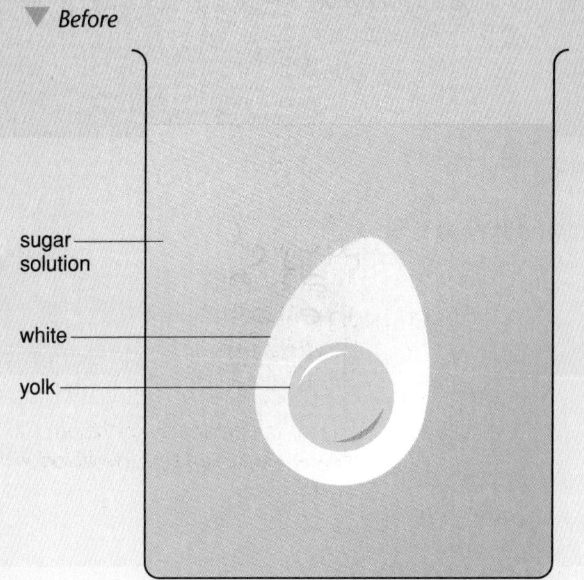

After 36 hours

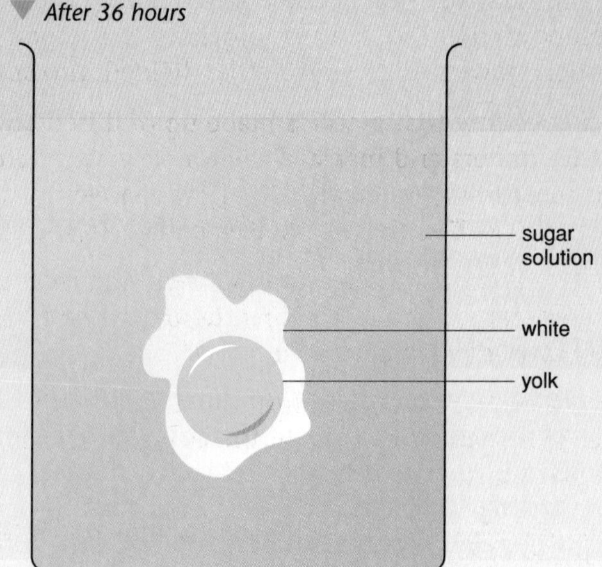

Questions

1 Why is the shell of the egg removed with ethanoic acid?

2 Why does a layer form round the egg after an hour?

3 After 36 hours the only parts of the egg left are the yolk and the membrane. What does this tell you about the egg white?

4 This experiment was carried out at room temperature. Suggest what would happen if the egg and the sugar solution were heated.

Blood is thicker than water

In this item you will find out

- how blood cells are adapted for the job they do
- how the heart and blood vessels move the blood
- about the problems of replacing hearts

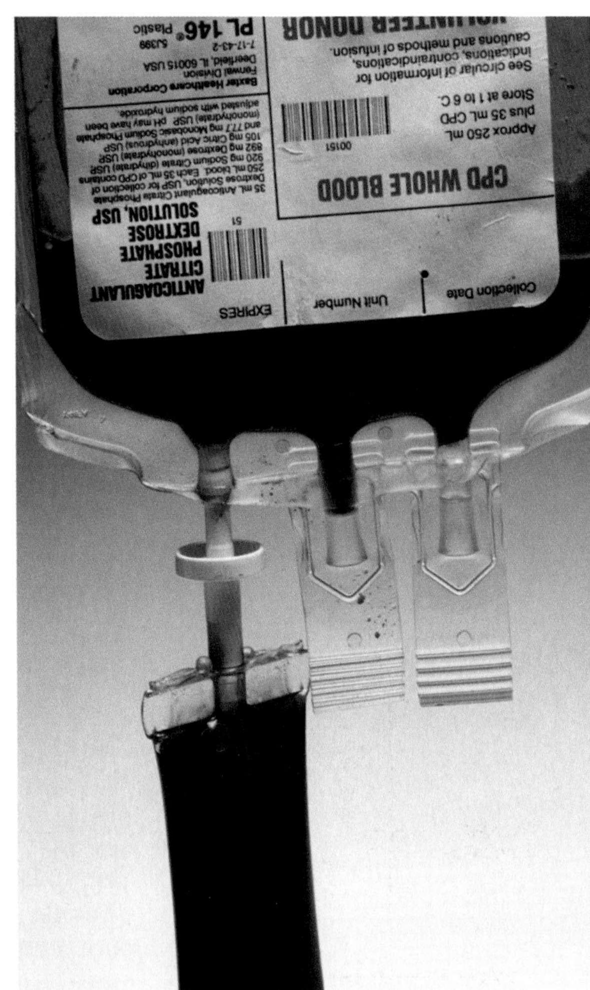

Our understanding of blood means we can give people blood in emergencies

For thousands of years people have realised the importance of blood to life. People used to believe that blood contained mystical powers and could not be divided into smaller parts.

We now know that blood is made up of different components and we understand many of the functions of the different parts. This means that we can predict how changes in the blood can affect us. Doctors can also make changes to the blood.

The blood contains three types of cells and they all carry out different jobs. The most numerous are the **red blood cells**. They carry oxygen around the body.

A red blood cell is shaped like a small disc with a dent in each side. This shape is called a biconcave disc. This is shown in the diagram on the right.

Red blood cells

Many features of a red blood cell make it well adapted for the job of carrying oxygen around the body:

- they are small cells so they can fit through the narrowest blood vessels
- they contain a red protein called **haemoglobin** which carries the oxygen around the body
- their small size and biconcave shape gives them a large surface area/volume ratio so that they can lose or gain oxygen more quickly
- they don't have a nucleus so that more haemoglobin can fit in.

At the lungs the haemoglobin combines with oxygen. This forms **oxyhaemoglobin**. When the red blood cells reach body tissues the oxyhaemoglobin releases the oxygen.

Amazing fact

Every cubic millimetre of blood contains about five million red blood cells.

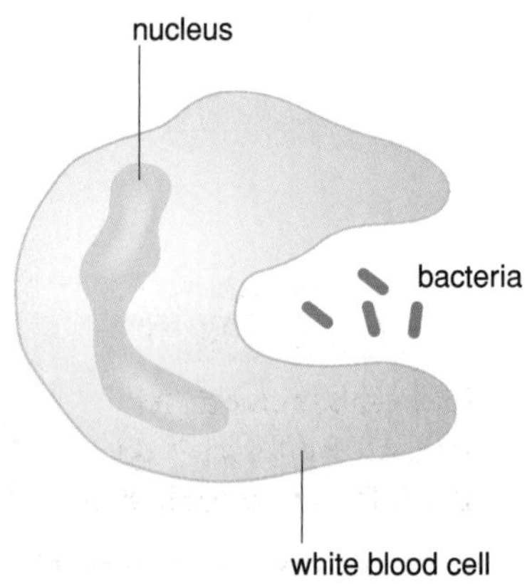

▲ White blood cells attack bacteria

White blood cells and plasma

The blood also contains **white blood cells**. They are twice as large as red blood cells and there is one white cell to every 500 red cells. They engulf and destroy disease organisms. To allow them to do this they can change shape so that they can squeeze out of the blood vessels and surround the invader.

All the cells are carried around the body by the liquid part of the blood called **plasma**. Plasma is mostly water but it also contains hormones, dissolved food, antibodies and waste products.

The pipework of the body

The blood is carried around the body in blood vessels. There are three types of blood vessels: **arteries**, **capillaries** and **veins**. Arteries carry blood away from the heart and veins carry blood back to the heart. Capillaries join arteries to veins and it is here that substances can be exchanged with the tissues.

vein
artery
heart
organ
capillaries

▲ Different types of blood vessel

The three types of blood vessels are each adapted for their particular function:

- arteries have a thick, muscular and elastic wall because the blood is under higher pressure than blood in the veins
- veins have a large lumen to reduce resistance to flow, and valves to prevent the blood flowing back because it is under low pressure
- capillaries are permeable so that substances can be exchanged with the tissues.

How the heart works

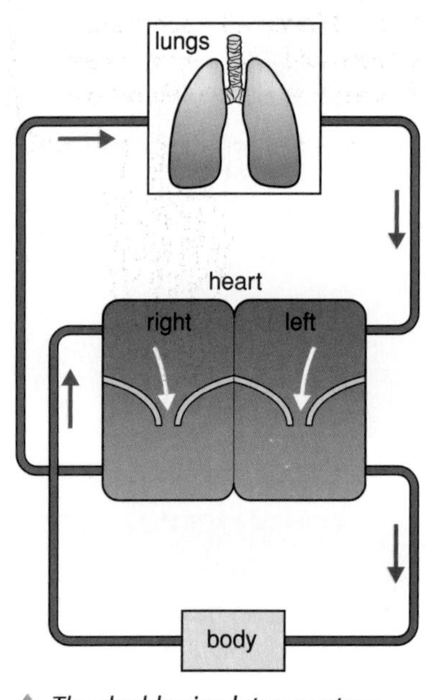

▲ The double circulatory system

Mammals have **double circulation**. This means that the blood has to pass through the heart twice on each circuit of the body. Deoxygenated blood is pumped to the lungs and the oxygenated blood returns to the heart to be pumped to the body. The advantage of this system is that the pressure of the blood stays quite high and so it can flow faster around the body.

Because of the double circulation the heart is actually two pumps in one. The right side pumps the blood to the lungs. The left side pumps it to the rest of the body.

The heart is made up of four chambers. The top two chambers are called **atria** – they receive blood from veins. The bottom two chambers are **ventricles** – they pump the blood out into arteries. The top two chambers, the atria, fill up with blood returning in the **vena cava** and **pulmonary** veins. The two atria then contract together and pump the blood down into the ventricles. The two ventricles then contract, pumping blood out into the **aorta** and pulmonary arteries at high pressure.

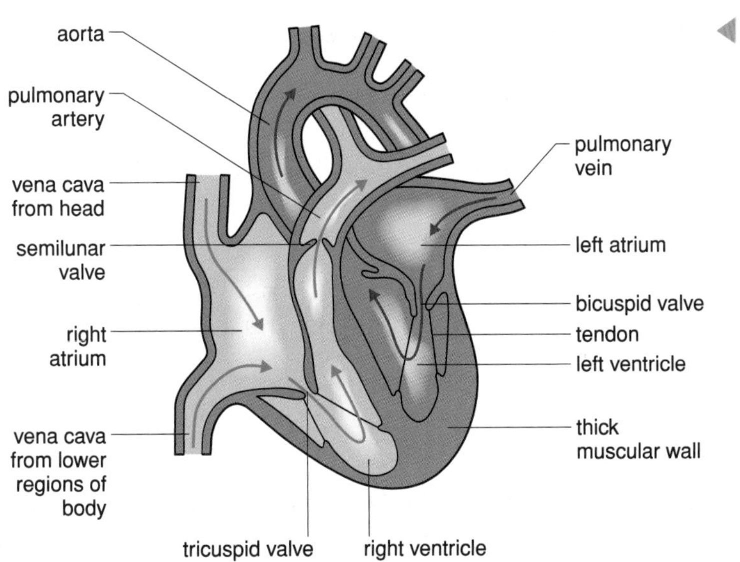

Inside the heart

Examiner's tip

Remember the right side of the heart is on the left as you look at it.

The muscle wall of the left ventricle is always thicker than that of the right ventricle. This is because it has to pump blood all round the body compared with the short distance to the lungs.

In the heart are two sets of valves. The function of the valves is to prevent blood flowing backwards. In between the atria and the ventricles are the **bicuspid** and **tricuspid** valves. These valves stop blood flowing back into the atria when the ventricles contract. The pressure of blood closes the flaps of the valves and the tendons stop the flaps turning inside out. There are also **semilunar** valves between the ventricles and the arteries.

Keywords

aorta • artery • atrium • bicuspid • capillary • cholesterol • double circulation • haemoglobin • oxyhaemoglobin • plaque • plasma • pulmonary • red blood cell • semilunar • tricuspid • vein • vena cava • ventricle • white blood cell

Too much fat?

Most people now realise that too much fat is bad for the heart. It is not all types of fat but two main types, saturated fats and **cholesterol**. Large amounts of these fats in the diet can cause cholesterol to build up in arteries. This happens over a long time and may form a blockage called a **plaque**. This may reduce or even stop blood flow and damage the heart. If the heart is badly damaged then the whole heart may need to be replaced.

Cholesterol build-up in an artery

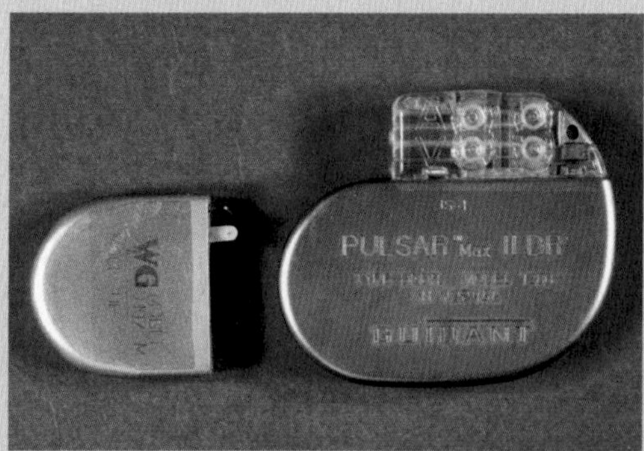

▲ A heart pacemaker

Replacing hearts

Derek Jones has been having problems with his heart for a couple of years. His doctor has sent him for some tests and the results have just come back.

'As we thought, your heart is beating irregularly. Also, your bicuspid valve is not working properly,' says Dr Galloway. 'We have two choices. We could fit you with an artificial pacemaker and an artificial valve. The pacemaker will regulate your heartbeat. Alternatively, we could give you a human heart from a donor.

'If we use a pacemaker and a valve, they are available now. However, there are problems with mechanical replacements. The pacemaker will need a battery to supply it with power which will need to be replaced regularly. Also, some people have bad reactions to the materials used to make the artificial parts. It is also difficult to get parts in the right sizes. It is harder for a pacemaker to change its rate during exercise than it is for a real heart.'

'What about a human heart?' asks Derek.

'Well, we can wait for a human donor heart to become available but there is a lack of donors. Once a heart is found we need to make sure that it is the correct size, age and tissue match for you. Even after successful surgery, you will need to take drugs to stop you rejecting your new heart.'

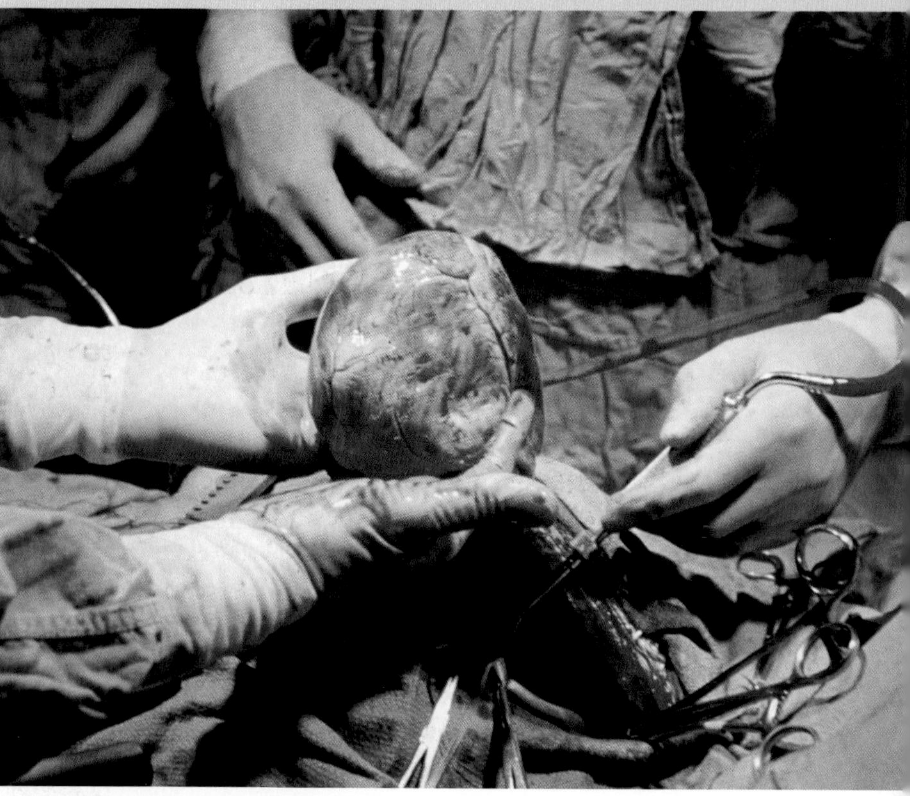
▲ Heart transplant being carried out

Questions

1. Why do you think the bicuspid valve not working properly in Derek's heart is a problem?
2. What does a pacemaker do?
3. What are the disadvantages of being fitted with a pacemaker?
4. At present many more people are given pacemakers than heart transplants. Why do you think this is the case?

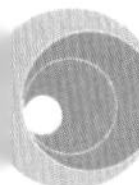

Cell multiplication

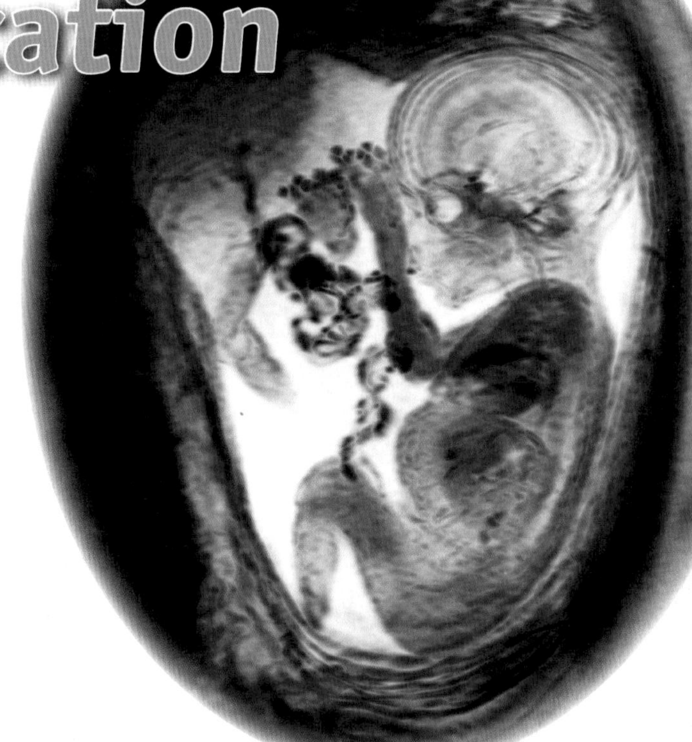

▲ *The number of cells in this fetus is increasing all the time*

In this item you will find out

- how organisms produce new cells for growth
- the advantages to an organism of being multicellular
- how organisms produce sex cells for reproduction

We all know that every organism is made up of cells – in the case of humans, a very large number of cells. One major question that scientists have asked for hundreds of years is where do all these cells come from?

Although sperm were first seen under the microscope in 1670, it was over 200 years before their role in fertilising the egg was understood. For a long time scientists thought that the sperm carried all the information needed to make a baby.

It was over 50 years later that scientists saw eggs under the microscope.

a **Why do you think scientists saw sperm before eggs even though eggs are much larger?**

When sperm were first seen fertilising eggs, scientists realised that both the eggs and the sperm must carry important information. However, they did not know how.

When chromosomes were seen in the nucleus of a cell, scientists realised that they must carry the genetic information for the new organism. This work made scientists wonder how cells divide to make eggs and sperm, and how the joining of these two cells can produce an organism made of millions of cells. Once these questions were answered, scientists could use this information to manipulate reproduction in many different ways. Scientists are now wondering if they can use knowledge about cell division to find answers to other problems, such as how to stop people growing old.

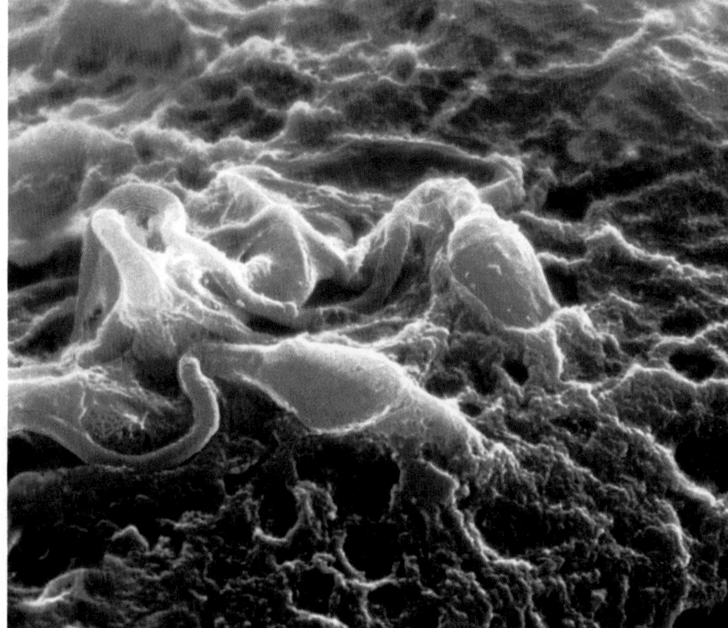

A sperm fertilising an egg ▶

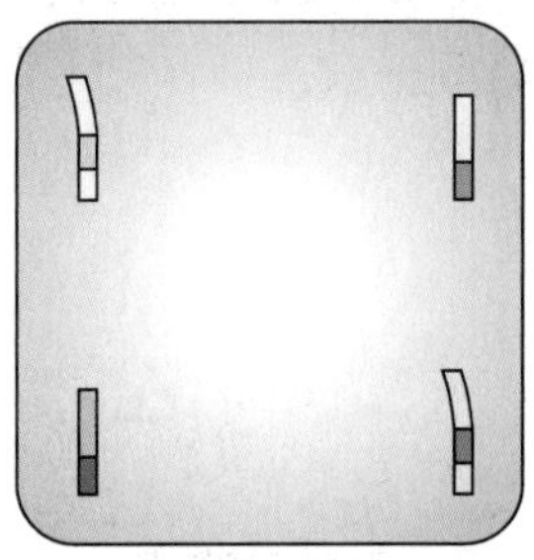
a cell has four chromosomes, two pairs

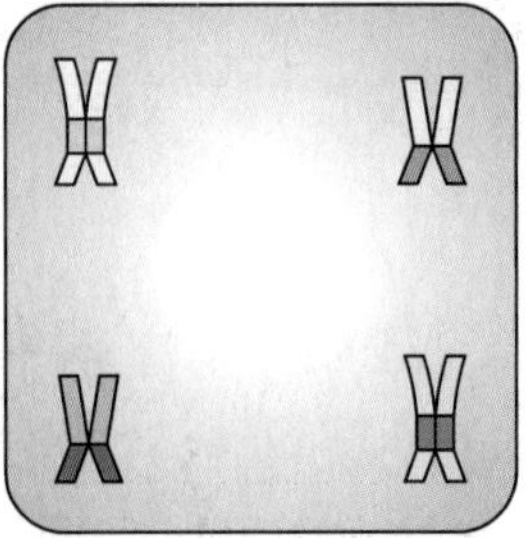
chromosomes are copied

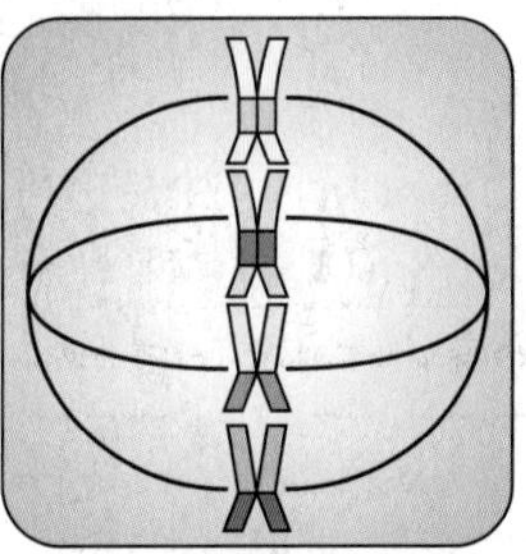
chromosomes form one line down the centre of the cell

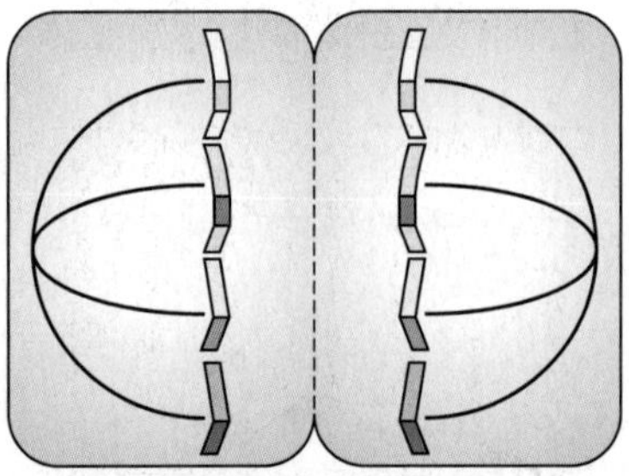
one copy of each chromosome moves to the opposite pole of the cell

▲ *Mitosis*

Cell division for growth

In order for an organism to increase in size or grow, its cells can become larger. However, there seems to be a limit to the size of cell a nucleus can control. Most growth involves cells dividing so that they can increase in number. The type of cell division that is used for growth is called **mitosis**.

In the body cells of mammals, the nuclei contain two copies of each chromosome. They are said to be **diploid**. In humans there are 23 pairs in each body cell making 46 chromosomes.

In mitosis the chromosomes are copied and the copies stay joined together. The chromosomes then line up down the middle of the cell. The copies of the chromosomes are then pulled apart to opposite ends or poles of the cell. When the cell divides into two, each new cell gets a copy of each pair of chromosomes, so they are genetically identical and still diploid.

Multi-cellular v unicellular

There are many advantages to being **multi-cellular**. It allows an organism to have different cells specialised to do different jobs. This is called **differentiation** and makes the cells more efficient. An organism can also become larger and more complex. This means that it can protect itself more easily. Lots of small cells also have a larger surface area than one large cell and so more materials can move in and out of the cells.

b **Many factories have differentiation in the jobs that their workers are trained to do. What can happen to the factory if a particular worker is not able to work?**

c **What is a possible disadvantage of differentiation in the body?**

Cell division for reproduction

Some organisms can reproduce by splitting into two, but this produces identical offspring. This is because their cells are all made by mitosis. Another type of reproduction is sexual reproduction. This involves sex cells (**gametes**) combining at **fertilisation** to form a **zygote**.

The sex cells, the sperm and eggs, have half the number of chromosomes of a normal body cell. In humans, the sperm and eggs each have 23 chromosomes instead of the usual 46. They are said to be **haploid**. This means that when the sperm and the egg join, the number of chromosomes becomes 46 again and the zygote has the diploid number of chromosomes. This is shown in the diagram on the right.

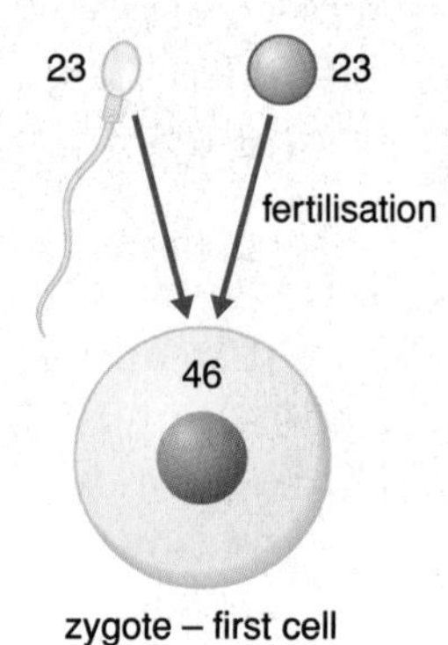

▲ *Gametes combine to form a zygote*

Examiner's tip

Because the words 'mitosis' and 'meiosis' are so similar make sure you spell them properly.

The type of cell division that makes gametes is called **meiosis**. This results in each gamete having a different combination of genes. Also, during fertilisation, any sperm can fertilise any egg. This means that the zygote can have any one of a number of possible combinations of genes. This explains why all organisms look different and how meiosis introduces variation into a species.

Before cell division each chromosome is copied. Pairs of chromosomes line up side by side. Each member of the pair is then pulled apart and they move to the opposite ends or poles of the cell. The cell then divides and then each chromosome divides and is separated. The cell then divides again to produce four cells. Each cell contains half the number of original chromosomes.

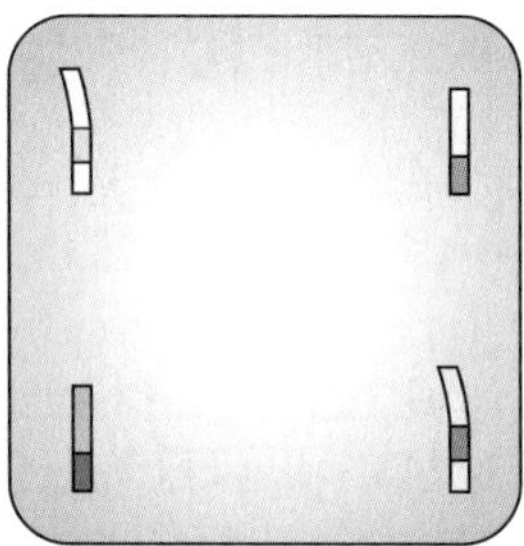

A cell has four chromosomes, two pairs

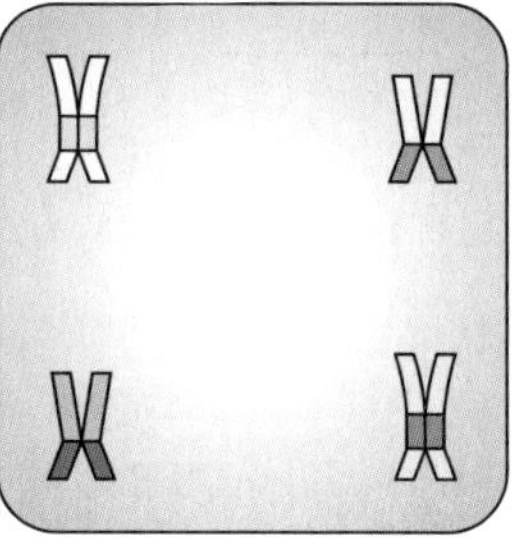

chromosome are copied

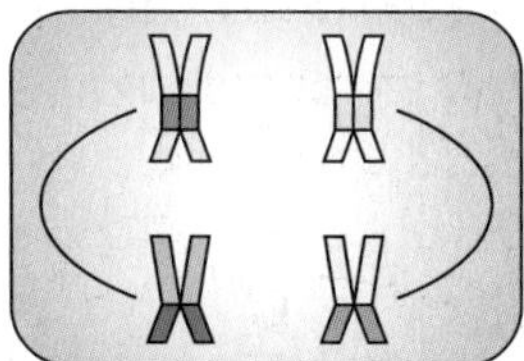

chromosome pairs line up side by side

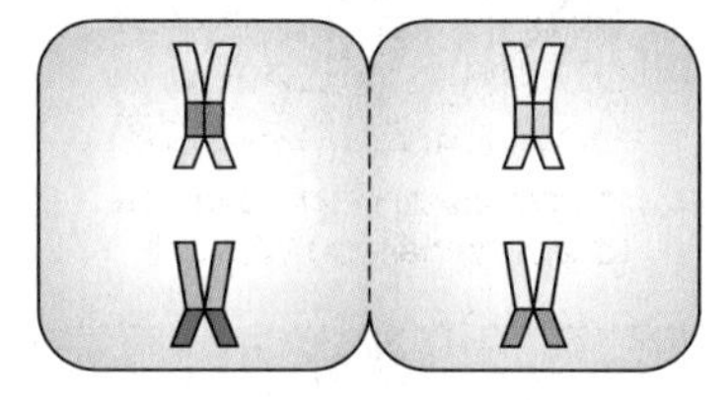

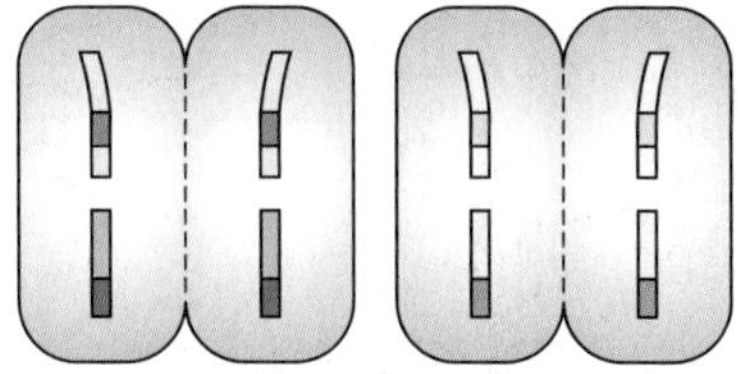

the copies split to produce four cells, each containing half the original number of chromosomes

▲ *Meiosis*

Sperm

Sperm cells have adaptations that allow them to carry out their function:

- they have lots of mitochondria to provide them with energy
- they have an **acrosome** which is a sac containing enzymes that enable them to digest the egg membrane and get into the egg.

d **What is the job of a sperm cell?**

e **Why does it need lots of energy?**

▲ *Sperm cells*

Keywords

acrosome • differentiation • diploid • fertilisation • gamete • haploid • meiosis • mitosis • multi-cellular • zygote

Can we live forever?

As we age, our bodies get worse at repairing damage to our tissues and replacing cells that have worn out. This is what getting old is all about. Even if doctors can stop us catching diseases, we cannot live forever because our bodies just wear out.

Scientists are now looking at why this is. Every time our cells divide, our genetic material or chromosomes have to copy themselves. It appears that our chromosomes have a 'protective cap' on their ends, just like shoelaces have plastic caps. These caps are called telomeres. Every time a cell divides these caps get shorter. When they reach a certain length the cell cannot divide any more. The person is getting old.

Scientists have now found that the cells that make the sex cells have an enzyme called telomerase. This repairs the telomere so that the sex cells have a full-length cap on their chromosomes.

The interesting question now is: 'Could all cells be made to produce this enzyme and make us live forever?' Some cells do have this ability, but the problem is they are cancer cells.

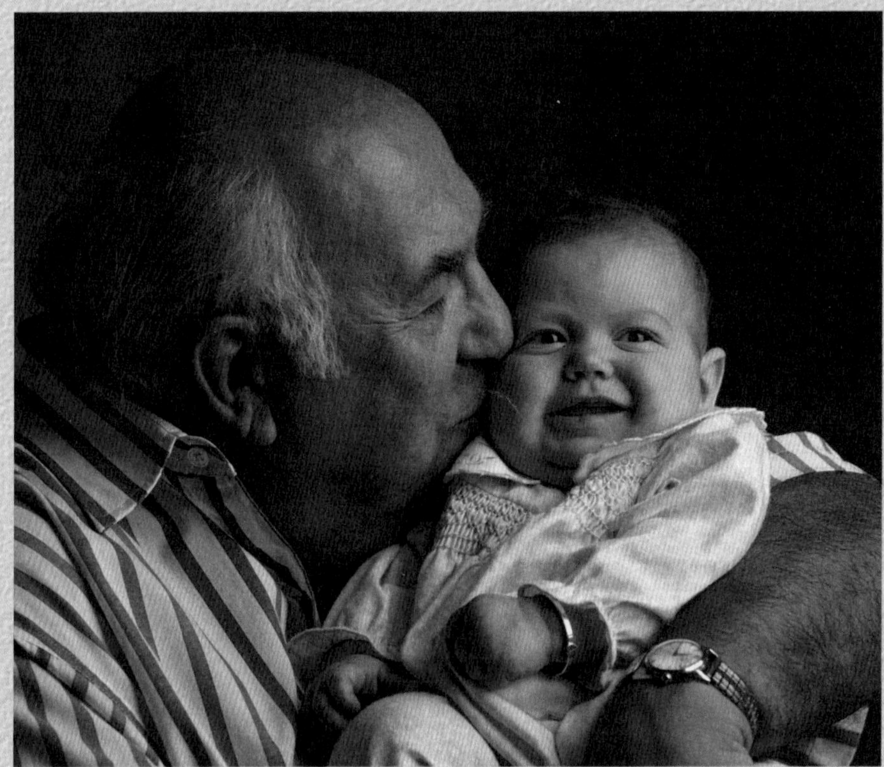

Questions

1 What is the name of the type of cell division that makes new cells for growth?

2 Why is it important that the chromosomes copy themselves exactly in this type of cell division?

3 A person receives a heart transplant from a much older person. Why is the discovery of telomeres rather worrying for this person?

4 Cancer cells have the enzyme telomerase. What can cancer cells do that normal body cells cannot do?

5 If we can only live for a certain maximum number of years, why do you think the average age that people live is increasing?

Growth spurts

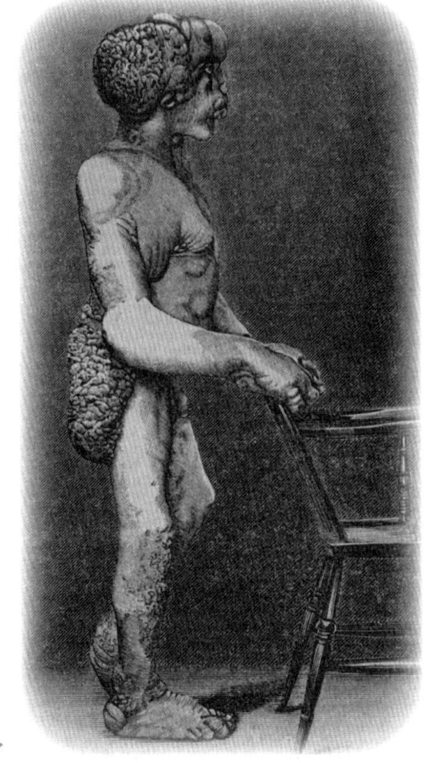

John Merrick

In this item you will find out

- the differences between plant and animal cells
- how plants and animals grow
- how cells become specialised

In 1862 a boy called John Merrick was born. As with any other baby, it had taken about 9 months for a fertilised egg to grow into the millions of cells that made up his body. This process involves not only cell division but cells becoming specialised for different jobs.

After John Merrick was born the process of growth continued in his body. However, before the age of two it was clear that something was wrong. Different parts of his body started to grow at an incorrect rate. This led to deformities over most of his body. He became known as the Elephant Man.

Extreme cases like that of John Merrick show how it is important it is for the process of growth to be carefully controlled by the body.

Growth problems rarely cause problems on this scale. However, after a human baby is born it is regularly checked to make sure that it grows and develops at the right rate. All babies develop at different rates but there are guidelines that show the range that is considered normal. The diagram on the right shows a chart used to plot the weight and head size of a baby boy.

Parents are encouraged to plot their baby's figures on the graph. It is quite usual for a baby's line, when it is plotted, to go across one of the lines on the graph. But if it drops suddenly this may be a sign of disease or growth problems.

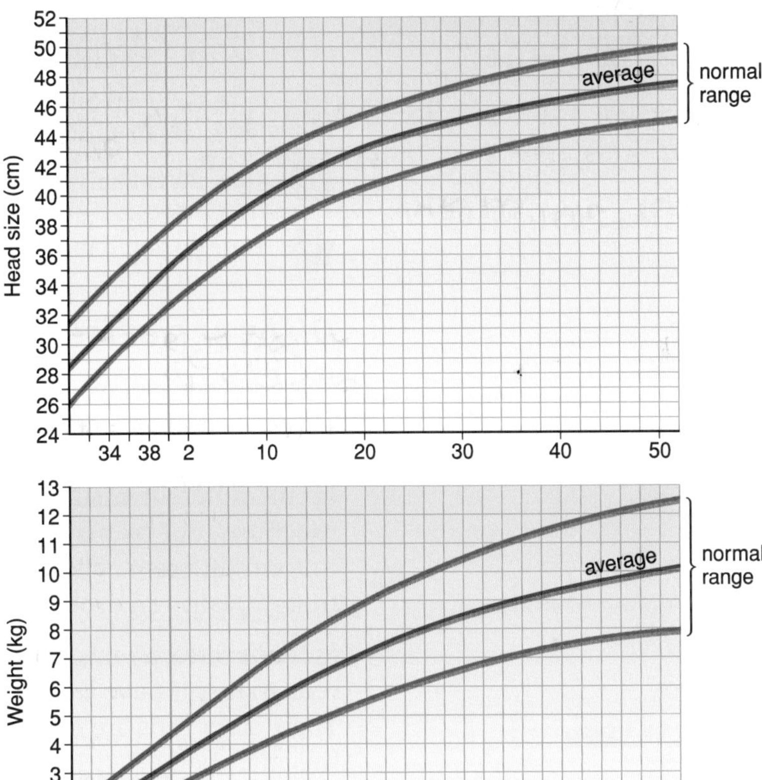

a **Different graphs are used for boys and girls. Why do you think this is?**

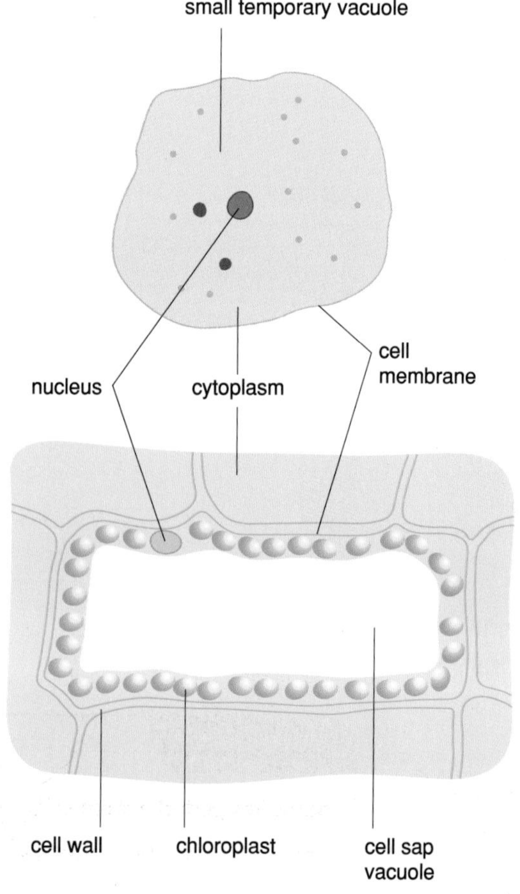

▲ *Animal and plant cells*

Plant and animal cells

Plant and animal cells both contain certain important structures. These include the cell membrane, cytoplasm and nucleus.

There are, however, important differences. Only plant cells have:

- chloroplasts to absorb light energy for photosynthesis
- a cell wall to help support the plant
- a large vacuole that stores cell sap and also provides support.

Growth in plants and animals

Both plants and animals increase in size or grow during their lives. They do this by a combination of making new cells and by the new cells enlarging. However, there are some differences between growth in plants and animals.

Most animals tend to stop growing when they get to a certain size but plants can often carry on growing for the whole of their lives. Some plants can become very large indeed.

Plant cells also enlarge much more than animal cells after they have been produced. This is usually how plants gain height.

In plants, cell division tends to happen at the tips of roots and shoots. This means a plant develops a branching shape. In animals, cell division happens over the whole of the body.

b **How do animals and plants feed?**

c **How do you think their different shapes help them to feed?**

Differentiation and stem cells

Once new cells have been made by mitosis they take on different functions. This is called differentiation. In animals, the cells may become muscle cells, nerve cells, blood cells or any of the other types of cells that make up the different tissues and organs. In plants many cells take on different functions, but plants also keep a large number of cells that retain the ability to form different types of cells. You can show this because a small piece cut from a plant can grow into a whole new plant.

Modern research has shown that animals, including humans, do have some cells that still have the ability to differentiate. They are called **stem cells**. These stem cells are easy to find in the embryo but much harder to find in the adult body.

Growing babies

The length of time between fertilisation and birth is called the **gestation period**. During this time the zygote divides to form a ball of cells called an embryo. Once the embryo has formed all the organs and tissues of a baby, it is called a fetus.

Different animals have different gestation periods. The most important factor controlling this is the size of the animal. It takes about 22 months to grow a baby elephant but only about 3 weeks for a baby mouse!

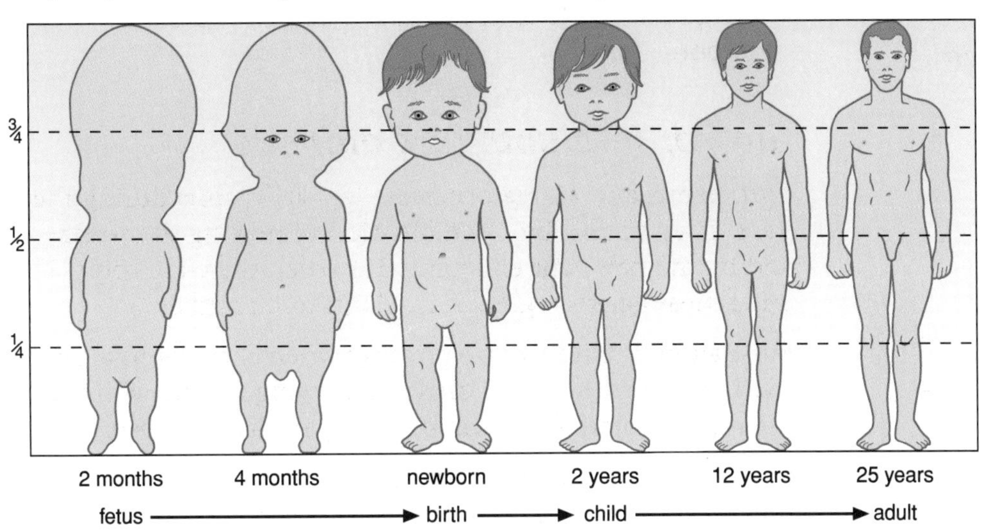

Keywords

gestation period • stem cells

Different parts of the same baby grow at different rates. The diagram above shows that the head and brain of an early fetus grow very quickly compared with the rest of the body. Later, the body and legs start to grow faster and brain and head growth slows down.

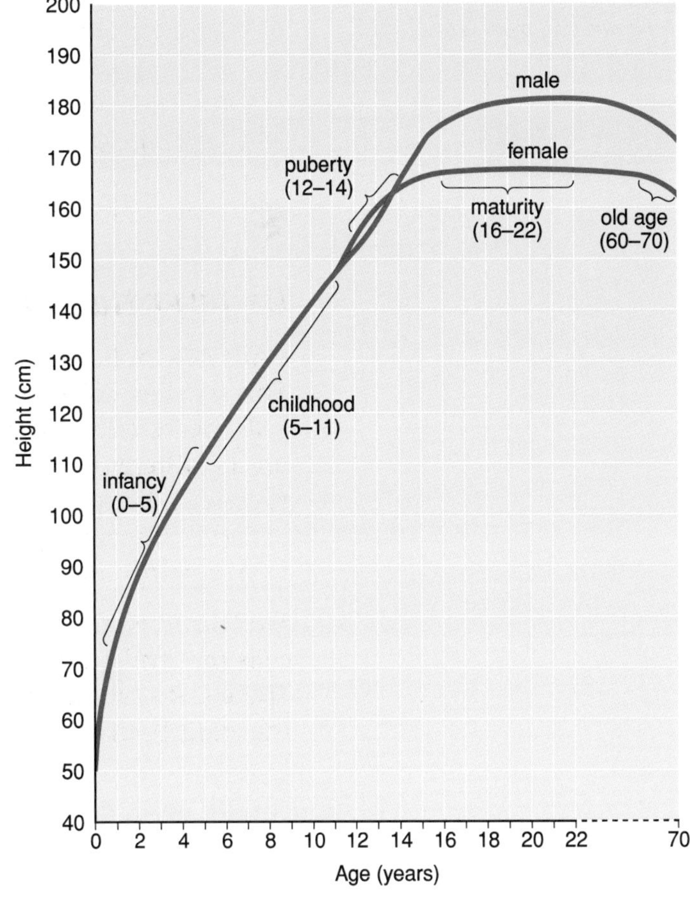

Growing up

Humans grow quickly or slowly at different times in their lives. The graph on the right shows how human growth changes over a person's lifetime. During infancy a child grows very quickly. This slows down slightly during childhood but there is a growth spurt during adolescence (puberty). Once a person reaches adulthood they stop growing.

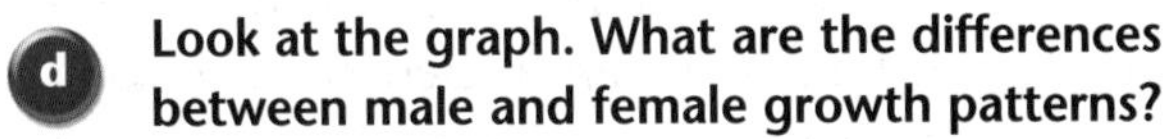

d **Look at the graph. What are the differences between male and female growth patterns?**

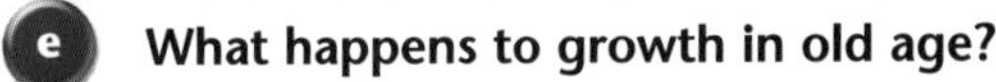

e **What happens to growth in old age?**

Uses of stem cells

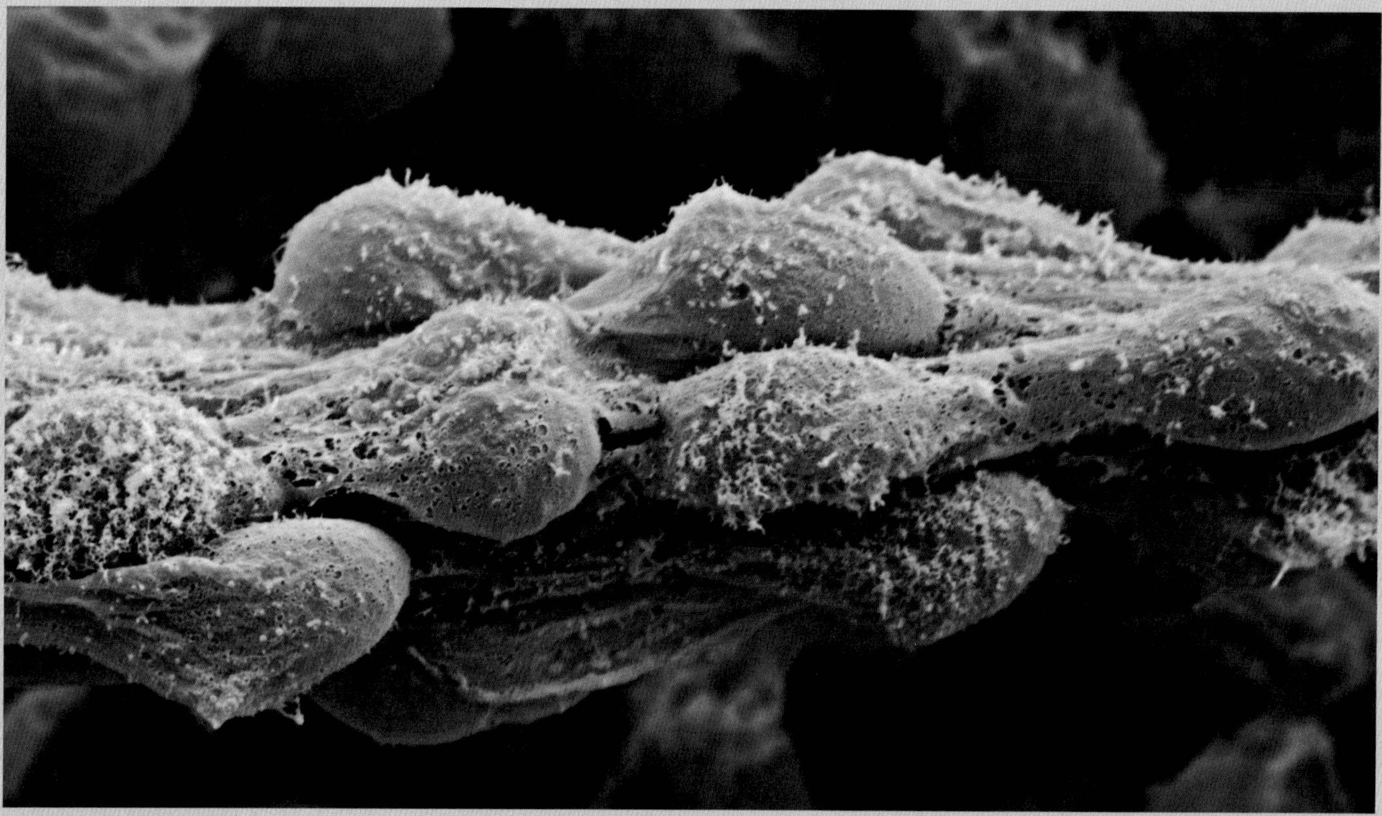

An embryonic stem cell

There are two sources of stem cells. They can be obtained from an early embryo or from an adult body. Stem cells can be identified in an embryo when it is only about 5 days old. These embryonic stem cells can develop into any of the 200 tissues of the body.

Stem cells from an adult body are harder to find and often they can only form a limited number of types of cell. One good source of these adult stem cells is the blood found in the umbilical cord after a baby is born.

The most useful stem cells are embryonic stem cells. However, the embryos are destroyed at an early stage in order to remove the stem cells. This is very controversial. Scientists believe that these cells could be used to cure a large number of different diseases, including diabetes and spinal cord damage.

Newspapers often have articles about stem cell use:

Mother becomes pregnant so that baby's umbilical cord blood can be used to treat ill brother

Scientists plan to produce embryos to cure paralysed man

Questions

1. Explain why embryonic stem cells are more useful to scientists than adult stem cells at present.
2. Discuss why some people may be against the use of embryonic stem cells as described in the newspaper headlines.
3. Scientists think that they will be more successful if the stem cell donor is closely related to the patient. Suggest why they think this.

Growing around corners

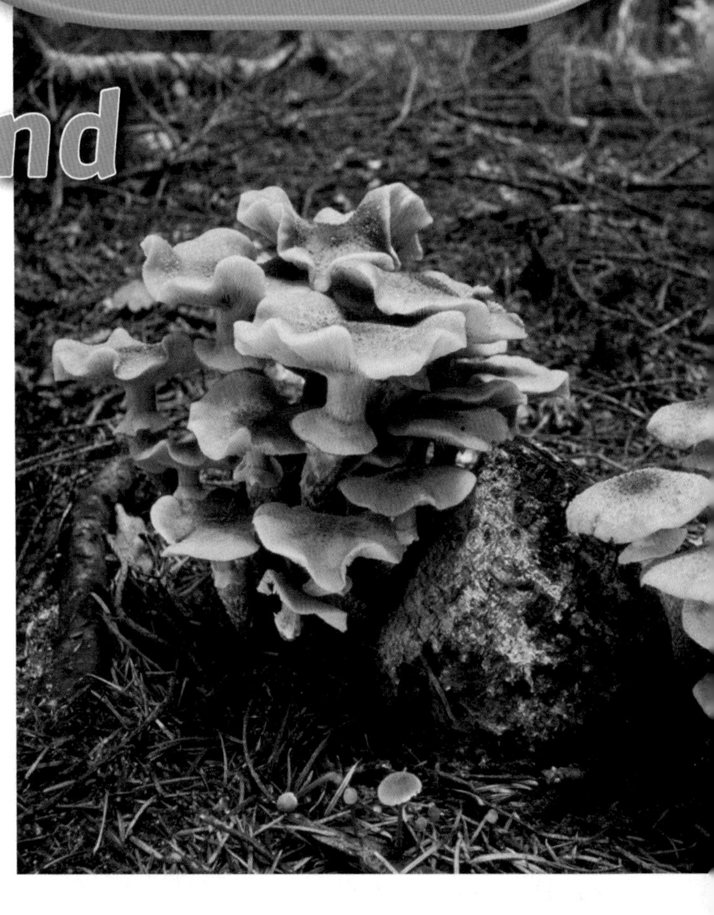

In this item you will find out

- that plant growth is controlled by chemicals called hormones
- how these hormones control plant responses
- how these hormones can be used to change plant growth

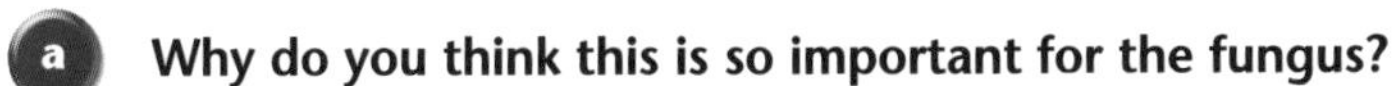

If you have ever seen mushrooms growing out of a dead tree stump then you may have noticed that they always grow out sideways but then bend upwards. You can see this in the photograph on the right.

Growing this way ensures that the cap of the mushroom, where the spores are released, is always horizontal to the ground.

a **Why do you think this is so important for the fungus?**

Scientists decided to investigate how fungi managed to grow in this way. On one of the Spacelab missions they grew fungi in the Spacelab where there was zero gravity. The fungi grew completely differently from the way that they normally grow.

b **How does their growth differ on the Spacelab?**

c **Suggest a reason for this difference.**

▲ *Fungi grown on Earth*

Scientists now know that this type of growth is also shown in green plants and is controlled by chemicals. These chemicals are produced in the plant. They control many aspects of the plant's growth and development such as:

- growth of roots and shoots
- seed germination
- leaf fall
- disease resistance
- fruit formation and ripening
- flowering time
- bud formation.

Scientists have identified many of these chemicals and can now produce artificial versions of them. These are available to gardeners and farmers.

▲ *Fungi growing in the Spacelab*

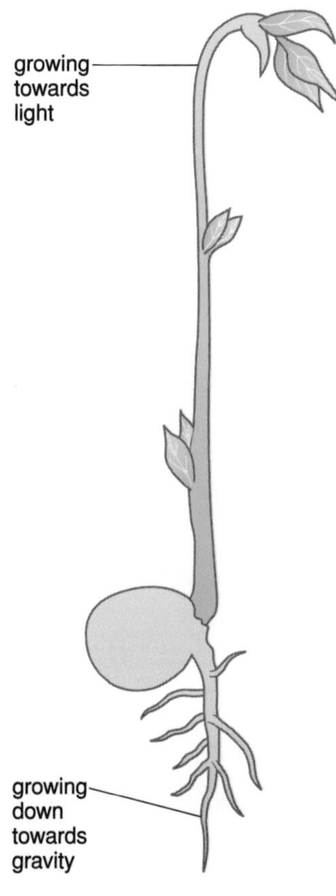

▲ *How light and gravity affect plant growth*

Responding to light and gravity

Like other living organisms, plants must be able to respond to changes in their environment. This is called sensitivity. Animals often respond to stimuli by moving about but plants cannot do this. They respond by growing in a particular direction. Plant growth movements that are in response to stimuli from a particular direction are called tropisms and the growth is called a tropic response.

Two of the most important stimuli that plants respond to are light and gravity. A response to light is called a **phototropism** and response to gravity is **geotropism**. Different parts of the plant will respond differently to these stimuli. This is shown in the diagram on the left.

Shoots grow towards light so they are positively phototropic. Roots grow towards gravity and so grow downwards. They are positively geotropic.

d **It is very important for the plant for the shoots to grow towards light. Why is this?**

e **Why is it also important that the roots grow towards gravity?**

When a seed starts to grow in the soil the shoot grows upwards. This happens even though it is in the dark. So, as well as being able to grow towards light, shoots must also grow away from gravity.

Stimulus	Growth response	
	Shoots	Roots
Gravity	away = negatively geotropic	towards = positively geotropic
Light	towards = positively phototropic	away = negatively phototropic

Experiments have shown that these growth movements are controlled by chemicals in solution that can move through the plant. These chemicals are **plant hormones**. The main plant hormone in these responses is called **auxin**.

How do tropisms work?

Over the past century many scientists have studied plants to try to work out how tropisms work. The results of their experiments show that:

- auxin is made in the tip of plant shoots and diffuses down the shoot
- the auxin then causes the shoot to grow
- in uneven light more auxin is sent to the shaded side of the shoot causing the cells to grow more and elongate so that the shoot curves towards the light.

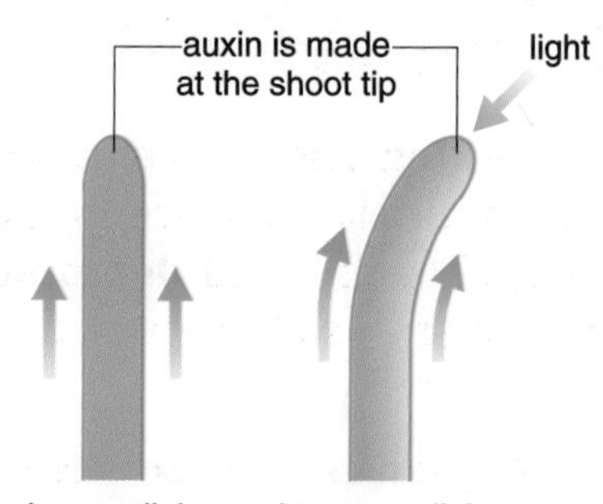

▲ *How plant auxin affects growth*

Uses of plant hormones

Scientists have developed many chemicals that are similar to auxin and other plant hormones. These can be used to aid plant cultivation and the effective production of food.

When they are sprayed on plants at high concentrations, they cause the plants to grow very quickly and die. Narrow-leaved plants such as grasses do not take up these chemicals and so the chemicals can be sprayed onto lawns. Because they will only kill the weeds, they are called **selective weedkillers**.

Other plant hormones encourage shoots to grow roots from their cut end. Gardeners use these hormones in **rooting powder** so that they can produce more plants by taking cuttings.

Plant hormones also control how quickly fruits ripen so they can be used to control fruit ripening – either slowing it down or speeding it up. This means that fruit such as bananas can be transported long distances and then be made to ripen at just the right time, ready to be sold in the shops.

Bananas picked before they are ripe

Seeds, flowers and buds all start growing at the best time of the year to give the plant the best chance to survive. If conditions are tough they will not develop. This is called **dormancy**. Plant hormones can be used to control this dormancy so that particular plants and flowers can be made available all year round.

f **Why is it useful to be able to transport fruit such as bananas before they are ripe?**

g **Why is it important for many flowers to open in the summer rather than in the winter?**

Keywords

auxin • dormancy • geotropism • phototropism • plant hormone • rooting powder • selective weedkiller

To bend or not to bend?

The diagrams below show three famous sets of experiments carried out by different scientists. They all experimented on young plant shoots to try to find out more about tropisms. Use these diagrams to answer the questions.

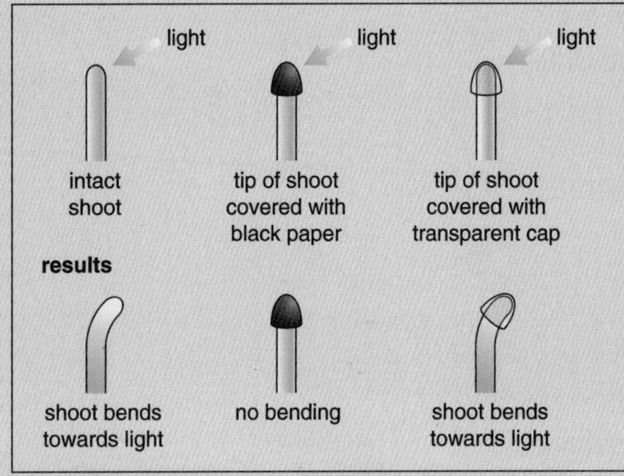

▲ *Experiments by Darwin (1880)*

light
light
light
tip removed
tip removed and replaced on impermeable block
tip removed and replaced on agar block
results
no bending
no bending
bends towards light

▲ *Experiments by Boysen-Jensen (1913)*

Darwin	English scientist Charles Darwin is famous for his work on evolution. He also carried out experiments on tropisms with his son Francis.
Boysen-Jensen	Peter Boysen-Jensen was a Danish plant biologist who became the first chairman of the International Plant Growth Association.
Went	Fritz Went was a Dutch biologist – he was the first to use the word auxin.

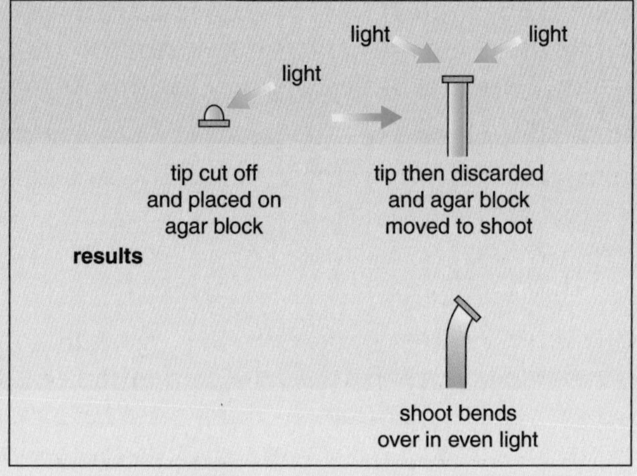

▲ *Experiments by Went (1928)*

Questions

1. Darwin's experiments showed where the light is detected in the plant. Explain how they show this.
2. Explain what conclusion Boysen-Jensen could make from his experiments.
3. The result of Went's experiment shows the shoot bending over although it is growing in even light. Explain why this is.
4. What would be a good control experiment for Went to have carried out?

Controlling the changes

Albino rabbits are the result of a mutation

In this item you will find out

- what causes mutations
- how selective breeding is used
- how genes can be moved from one organism to another

Most people have heard of the word mutation and may describe organisms that are unusual as mutants. But what is a mutation and what causes it to happen?

In many science fiction films, strange organisms are often produced by mutation. This is often caused by leaks of radiation or unusual chemicals. The mutant seems to take on a new form and always seems to be dangerous. Is this really what mutation is all about?

Amazing fact

Every time a human gene is copied there is less than a one in a million chance that a mistake will be made.

There is some truth in these stories. Mutations are in fact changes in the genes of organisms which can happen spontaneously. As a result, these changes can alter how an organism looks or behaves.

Most mutations are harmful to the organism and many will kill it. However, occasionally a useful mutation occurs. This can allow types of organisms to change and become more advanced. We are all mutants – without mutations we would not be here!

a **A mutation is more likely to have an effect if it occurs in a gamete. Suggest why.**

Scientists could use chemicals or radiation to try to change the genes of organisms by causing mutations. However, the results would be random. Instead, scientists use two techniques to change organisms. They are **selective breeding** and **genetic engineering**.

Selective breeding has been used for thousands of years to produce organisms with certain characteristics. Most of our strains of farm animals have been produced in this way.

Now genetic engineering is being used because it produces quicker results. Both of these techniques have their critics and people are worried that scientists have taken these processes too far.

Maize can be genetically modified

Examiner's tip

Don't get mixed up between 'selective breeding' and 'natural selection'. In selective breeding people decide which organisms will breed.

Mutations

Changes in the genes of an organism by mutation usually happen when the genes are copied before a cell divides. Under normal conditions, mutations usually happen at a very slow rate but the rate can be speeded up by:

- radiation such as X-rays or ultraviolet light
- certain chemicals such as the tar in cigarette smoke.

When a gene is copied, sometimes there is a change in the order of bases in the DNA. Since the order of bases codes for the proteins that a cell makes, this means that the cell may not be able to make the same proteins. This is why a mutation may change the cell and maybe the whole organism.

Selective breeding

If you look at all the different types of dogs that live today it is difficult to believe that they are all members of the same species. All the different types have been produced as a result of selective breeding. Two different breeds are shown in the photograph.

Some have been produced to be fast runners, others as guard-dogs and some as gentle pets. Selective breeding always works like this:

- two animals are chosen that have the characteristics that are wanted, such as speed
- these animals are allowed to mate – if they come from different breeds this is known as **cross-breeding**
- when the offspring are produced, the ones with the most desirable characteristics are chosen again and mated
- this happens for many generations until the animal with all the right characteristics is produced.

In this way humans have produced different breeds of dogs and champion racehorses.

Selective breeding can be carried out in the same way with plants. This means you can breed crop plants that are stronger, more resistant to disease or that are ready for harvesting earlier. This leads to improved agricultural yields.

Some people are worried that selective breeding uses organisms that are too closely related. This **inbreeding** can cause offspring to be born that have recessive abnormalities. It will also reduce the gene pool and there will be less variation in the population.

Why might less variation in the population be a problem?

Genetic engineering

One of the problems with selective breeding is that it takes a long time to produce the organism that is needed. However, scientists can now choose what characteristics an organism has by changing its genes. Genetic engineering involves transferring genes from one organism to another. This will produce an organism that has different characteristics.

Bacteria can be genetically modified to produce human insulin which can be used by diabetics to control their blood sugar levels. It is also possible to genetically modify crop plants, such as maize or wheat, so that they become resistant to frost damage, disease or herbicides.

c What is the advantage of making crop plants resistant to herbicides?

All of these examples of genetic engineering use a similar process. First, the scientists have to decide which characteristics they want to copy. Then the gene controlling these characteristics has to be found and isolated. The gene is cut out of the donor DNA using enzymes and is inserted into the host DNA again using enzymes. The host cell then copies itself (replication) including the new gene.

Keywords

cross-breeding • genetic engineering • inbreeding • selective breeding

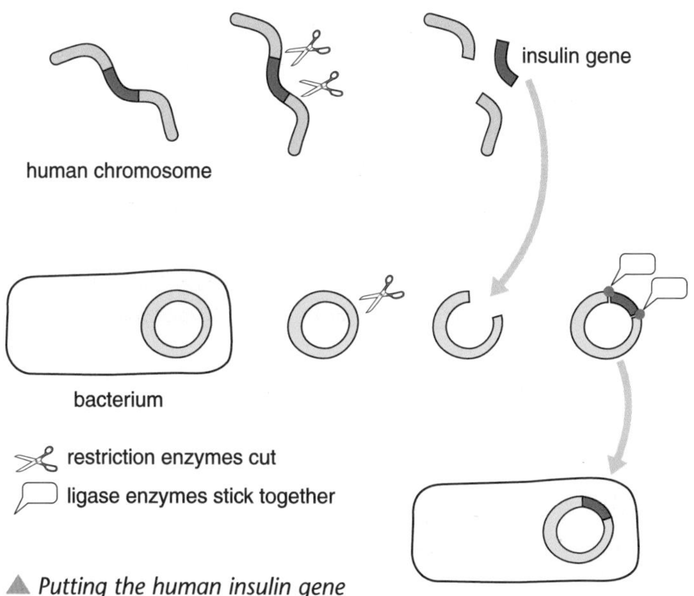

▲ *Putting the human insulin gene into bacteria*

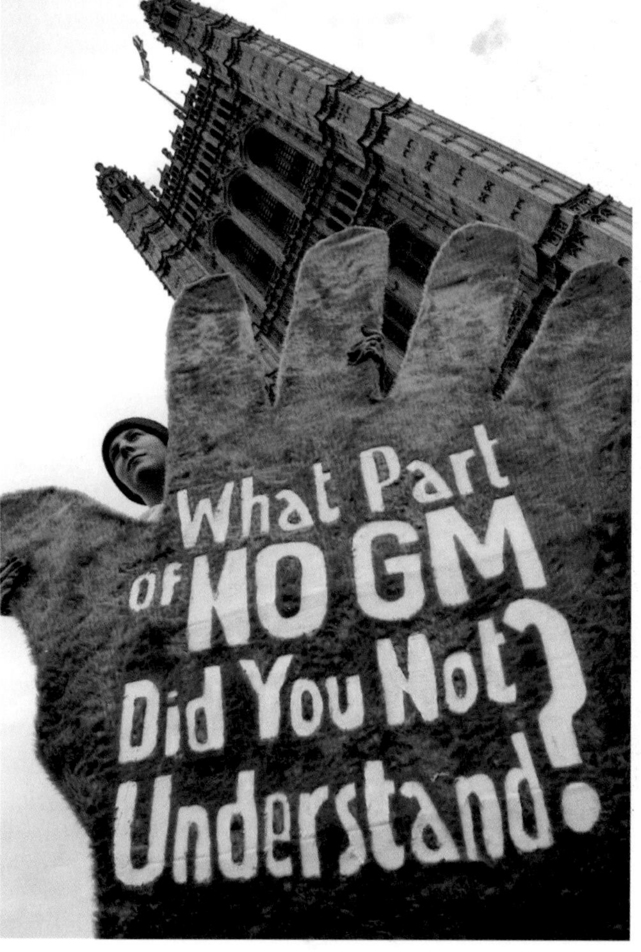

▲ *A protestor demonstrating against genetically modified crops*

Genetic engineering is useful because it produces new organisms quickly with the characteristics that we want. However, the new genes inserted into an organism may have harmful effects which the scientists were not expecting.

Some people are worried about this. They are concerned about eating food containing genetically modified crops and about the effects these crops will have on the environment.

d Why are some people worried about producing herbicide-resistant plants?

Golden rice solves a problem?

In many parts of the world people eat a lot of rice and not many vegetable or dairy products. This means they can become deficient in vitamin A. This can lead to problems with their eyes. The World Health Organization estimates up to 500 000 children go blind each year because of vitamin A deficiency.

Vitamin A deficiency can cause this disease

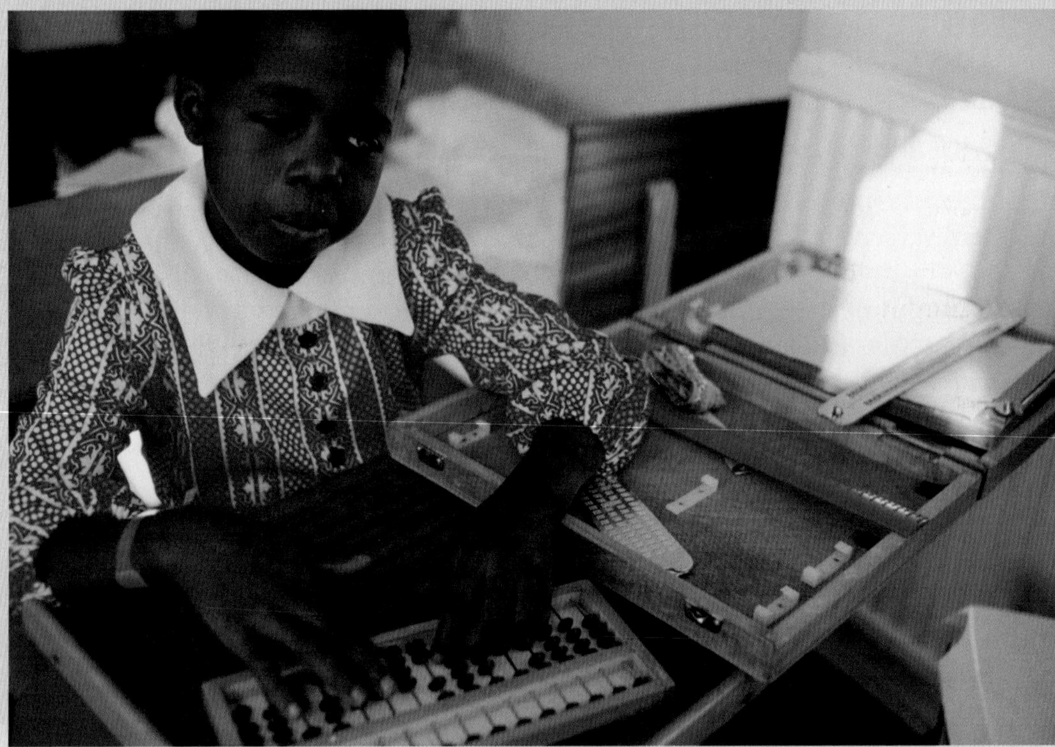

Vitamin A can be found in beta-carotene in carrots. Scientists have been able to take the genes from carrots that control beta-carotene production and insert them into rice. When people eat this genetically modified 'golden rice', they can convert the beta-carotene in the rice into vitamin A.

When the original strain of golden rice emerged from laboratories in Switzerland 5 years ago, it was hailed by some as an instant solution.

But not everyone believes golden rice is the best answer to Vitamin A deficiency. Some environmental groups say aiming for a balanced diet across the board would be a better solution. They point out that people who are deficient in vitamin A are also deficient in lots of other vitamins and minerals. They ask whether scientists are going to genetically modify a crop to solve each problem. They also say that not enough tests have been done on genetically modified crops.

Scientists have replied saying that for many years millions of pounds have been invested in improving people's diets but people are still suffering.

Questions

1. Describe briefly how golden rice can be made to produce beta-carotene.
2. Why do scientists think it is very important to produce this new rice?
3. Why are environmental groups against genetically modified rice?

Cloning around

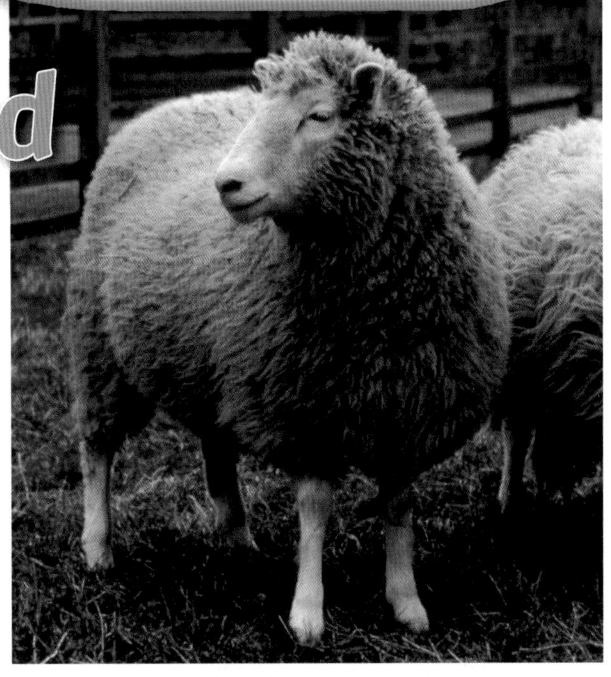
▲ Dolly the sheep

In this item you will find out

- how plants and animals can be cloned
- the advantages and disadvantages of using cloned plants
- some of the benefits and concerns of using cloning

A **clone** is a genetically identical copy of an organism.

A breakthrough in cloning animals happened in the 1970s when John Gurdon managed to clone a frog using the cell of an adult frog. The trouble was, nobody could successfully do the same experiment on a mammal – that is until Dolly the sheep was born in 1996. So it was over 20 years after Gurdon's work that scientists managed to produce a clone of a mammal from an adult body cell.

Now cats, dogs and horses have all been cloned. But why should scientists want to do this?

People can pay companies to make a clone of their favourite pet so that its genes will be preserved forever. Farm animals that have the characteristics the farmer wants can be cloned to make large identical herds.

Animals could also be genetically engineered so that they contain some human genes. They could then be cloned and used to produce useful human proteins such as insulin. They could also be used as a supply of organs for human transplants.

a **Why would a supply of animal organs for transplants be very useful?**

b **Why do you think it is better to transplant organs from animals that have human genes in them?**

Amazing fact

Each year over 3000 people have an organ transplant in Britain.

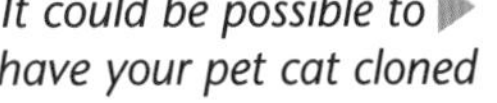
It could be possible to have your pet cat cloned ▶

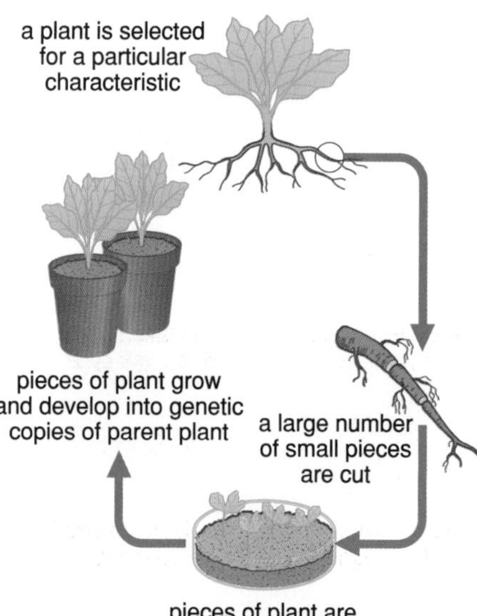

Cloning plants

Cloning is not new for gardeners. They have been using cloning technology for thousands of years. Some plants reproduce asexually and make clones of themselves. Many gardeners have used this process for centuries, but a more modern method uses **tissue culture**. This is useful because only a small quantity of tissue is needed rather than a large piece of a stem.

The scientists select a plant which has the characteristics that they want. They then cut the roots into lots of small pieces of tissue. The pieces of root are then grown in sterile conditions on a suitable growth medium. This is called **aseptic technique**. The pieces of plant grow into plants that are genetically identical to the original plant. This is shown in the diagram.

Producing plants by various cloning methods has some advantages and some disadvantages:

Advantages	Disadvantages
You know what you are going to get because all the plants will be genetically identical to each other and the parent.	The population of plants will be genetically very similar – there will be little variety.
You can mass-produce plants that do not flower very often or are difficult to grow from seeds.	Because the plants are all similar, a disease or a change in the environment could wipe them all out.

Examiner's tip

Remember that most plants, such as strawberry plants, can also reproduce sexually by producing flowers.

Cloning animals

Animals are much harder to clone than plants because, unlike plant cells, animal cells lose the ability to change into other types of cells (differentiate) at an early stage.

One way to clone an animal is to copy what happens in nature when identical twins are produced. An embryo is produced by a sperm fertilising an egg and then the embryo is split into two at an early stage. This is how cows can be cloned.

The scientists collect sperm from the bulls they have chosen. They then **artificially inseminate** selected cows with this sperm. When the embryos are large enough they are collected and split into two, forming clones. These embryo clones are implanted into cows which act as **surrogate** mothers and the calves are born normally. This process is shown in the diagram on the next page.

The problem with using this process to produce cattle is that you are never quite sure what you will get. Although the parent animals may be champion cattle, sexual reproduction is still involved. This means variation.

Dolly the sheep

Scientists tried for a long time to produce a clone of an adult mammal, without involving fertilisation. They succeeded in 1996 when a cloned sheep called Dolly was born.

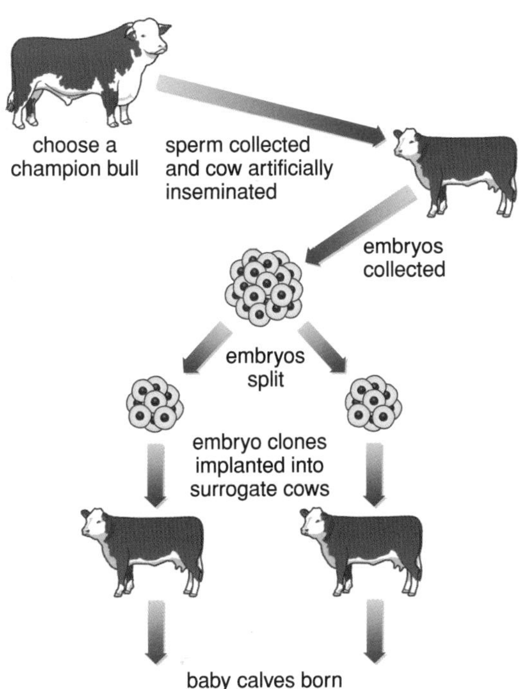

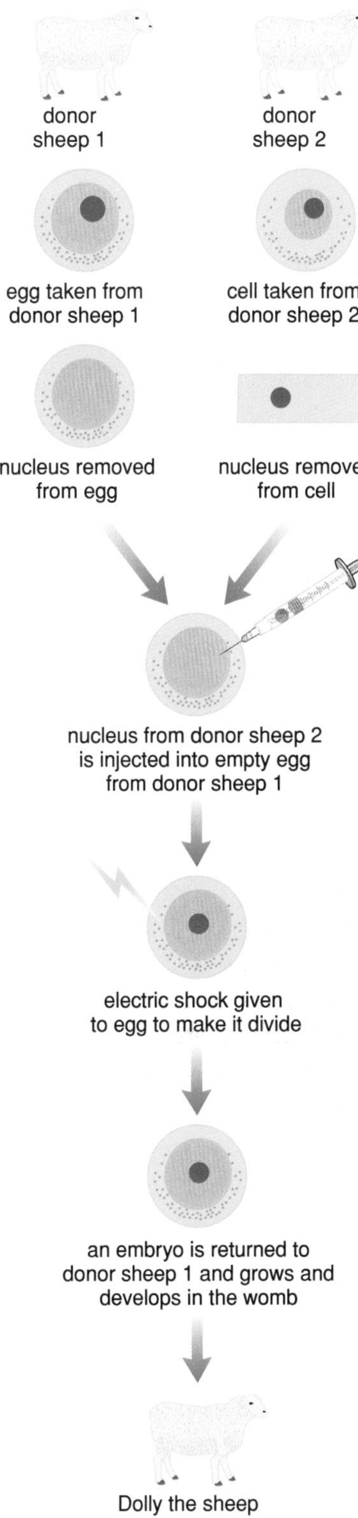

The scientists removed a nucleus from the egg cell of one sheep. They then replaced the egg cell nucleus with the nucleus from an udder cell from a second sheep.

As a result, the egg cell from the first sheep contained the nucleus and DNA of the second sheep. The egg cell was then implanted into the first sheep where it grew into a clone of the second sheep which had donated the udder cell. This is shown in the diagram on the right.

Should cloning animals be allowed?

Since Dolly was born in 1996, other animals such as pigs, cats, cows and horses have been cloned. Farmers might like the idea of having large herds of cloned prize-winning animals but some scientists believe that this could cause problems. If all the animals are genetically identical they could very easily be wiped out by a particular infection.

Using cloned animals as a supply of organs for human transplants would have important advantages but there are worries. Some people believe it is immoral and some are concerned that animal diseases could be spread to humans if this process was carried out.

However, there are other possible uses that are even more controversial. If animals such as sheep can be cloned then it should be possible to produce a cloned human embryo. This could be used in one of two possible ways:

- to extract stem cells at the embryo stage which could be used to treat illness (therapeutic cloning)
- to be implanted into a woman to produce a baby (reproductive cloning).

Keywords

artificially inseminate • aseptic technique • clone • surrogate • tissue culture

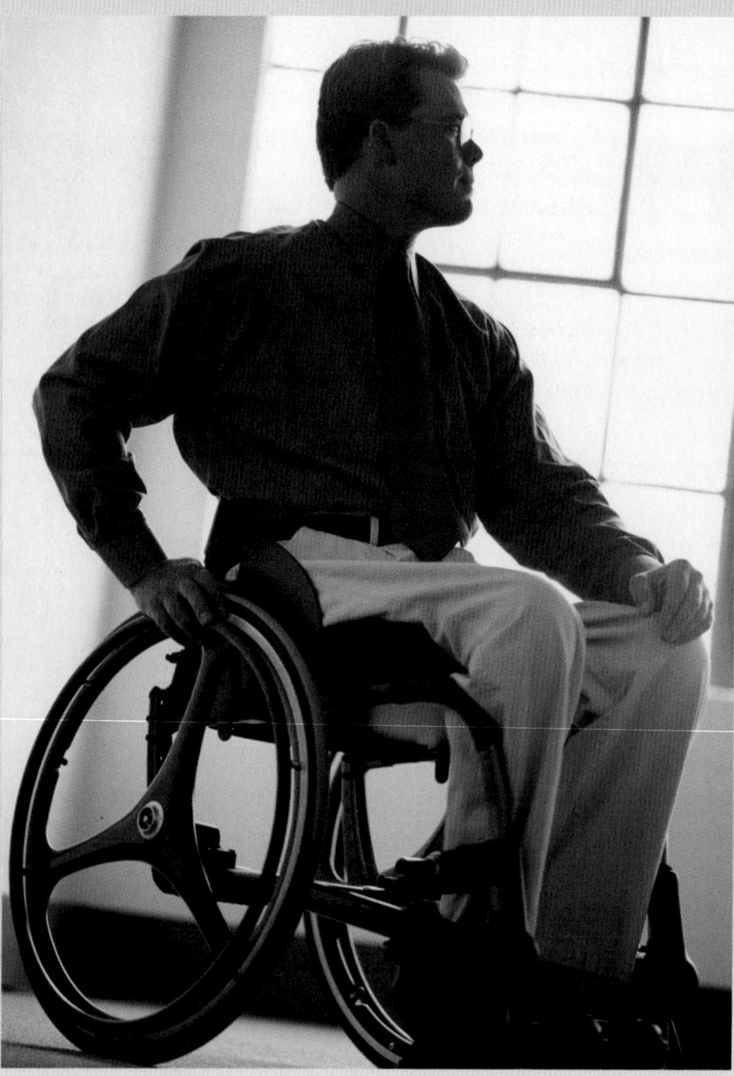

▲ Stem cell research may help spinal injury victims

Human clones

The ability to clone humans does have some medical benefits. It could allow an infertile couple to have a child. Many couples cannot have children naturally. There may be something wrong with the man's sperm or the woman's eggs. An Italian doctor, Severino Antinori, wants to offer cloning as a treatment for infertility. A couple could have a baby that was a clone of the man or the woman.

Scientists could also obtain a supply of stem cells which would be taken from a cloned embryo. The embryo would then be destroyed and the stem cells could be used to repair damaged tissues. This technique has already been tried for treating rats that had been paralysed due to injuries to their spinal cord. Scientists hope that it can be used to treat humans that have spinal cord injuries.

Recently, some families have asked scientists if they would take some cells from a dead or dying child. The cells could be used to create a clone of a child that had been killed in an accident or had an incurable disease.

However, there are ethical dilemmas associated with human cloning. Some people believe that all human cloning is ethically unacceptable. They feel that killing an embryo, even at an early stage, is taking a life. They also feel that a cloned child would not be a true individual, as it would have exactly the same genes as another person.

Questions

1. Why might a couple prefer to use cloning to produce a baby rather than use an embryo donated by another couple?
2. If a clone of a dead child is produced, do you think the clone would be identical to the dead person in all their characteristics? Explain your answer.
3. Some people seem to think that cloning is acceptable if it is used to produce a supply of stem cells. However, many more people are against the idea of reproductive cloning. Why do you think this is?

B3a

1 Where in a cell are mitochondria found and what is their function? [2]

2 Read the following statements about DNA.

Which statements are true?

A DNA controls the production of proteins.
B DNA consists of three chains wound together.
C The DNA molecule contains long chains of bases.
D DNA controls the production of amino acids.

[2]

3 The diagram shows a molecule of DNA being copied (replicating).

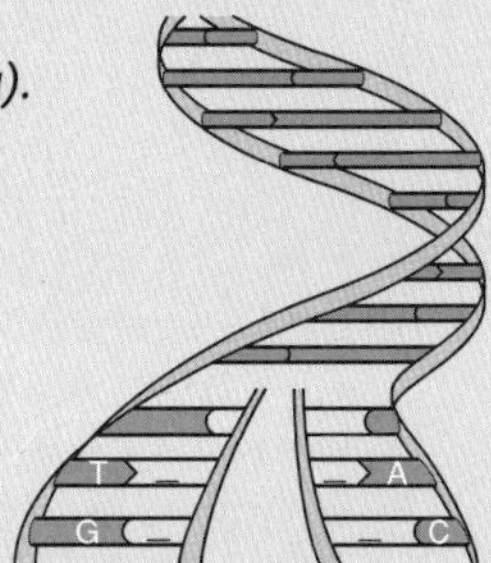

a How can you tell that the molecule is replicating? [1]
b What type of chemical do the letters on the diagram represent? [1]
c What holds the two strands of the DNA molecule together? [1]
d Copy and complete the diagram by writing a letter in each of the four spaces on the diagram. [2]
e Explain why the order of these letters in the DNA molecule is so important. [2]

4 The graph shows the effect of pH on three enzymes.

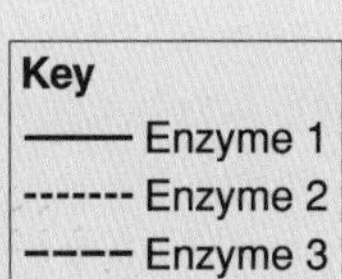

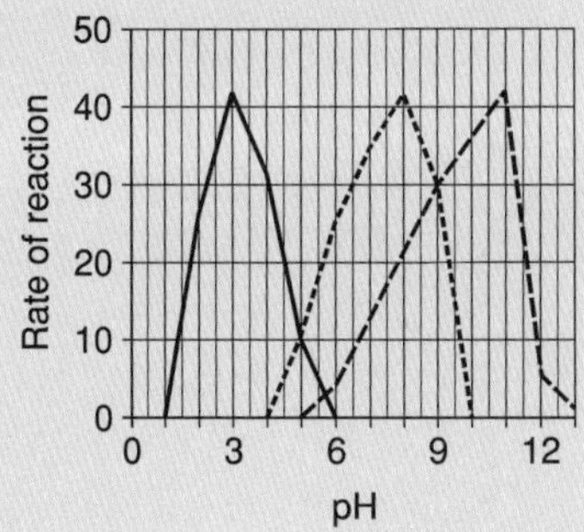

Enzyme	Optimum pH
1	3.0
2	
3	

a Copy the table (right) and use the graph to complete it. [2]
b Explain why enzyme 2 does not work above pH 10 or below pH 4. [3]
c Enzyme 1 is called pepsin. It breaks down protein. Explain why this enzyme can only break down protein and not starch or fats. [2]

B3b

1 The diagram shows part of an alveolus and a blood vessel.

a Where in the body are alveoli found? [1]
b Where on this diagram is the concentration of oxygen highest? [1]
c Explain how oxygen passes from the air in the alveolus into the blood. [3]
d Which way does carbon dioxide move? Explain why. [3]

2 Describe and explain three ways in which the alveoli are adapted for their job. [3]

3 Explain the functions of the following.

a microvilli in the small intestine [2]
b air spaces between spongy mesophyll cells [2]
c transmitter substances at the ends of neurones [3]

B3c

1 A table has been drawn to show some differences between arteries and veins.

Copy and complete the table by filling in the blank boxes. [6]

Feature	Arteries	Veins
direction of blood flow		
type of wall		
are valves present?		

2 Read the following information about some of the effects of smoking on the body.

Two parts of tobacco smoke that damage the body are nicotine and carbon monoxide. Nicotine dissolves in the liquid part of the blood and increases the heart rate and blood pressure. This can be particularly dangerous if there are plaques present in the arteries. It also makes the platelets too active which can be dangerous.

Carbon monoxide combines with haemoglobin to form carboxyhaemoglobin which does not break down.

a What is the name of the liquid part of the blood that nicotine dissolves in? [1]
b Explain how plaques form in arteries. [2]
c Suggest why it might be harmful if platelets become too active. [2]
d Explain how the combination of carbon monoxide with haemoglobin differs from the combination of oxygen and haemoglobin. [2]

B3d

1 *Explain why a sperm cell needs the following.*

a *many mitochondria* [2]
b *an acrosome* [2]

2 *The following diagram shows how sperms and eggs are produced. It also shows one sperm joining with one egg.*

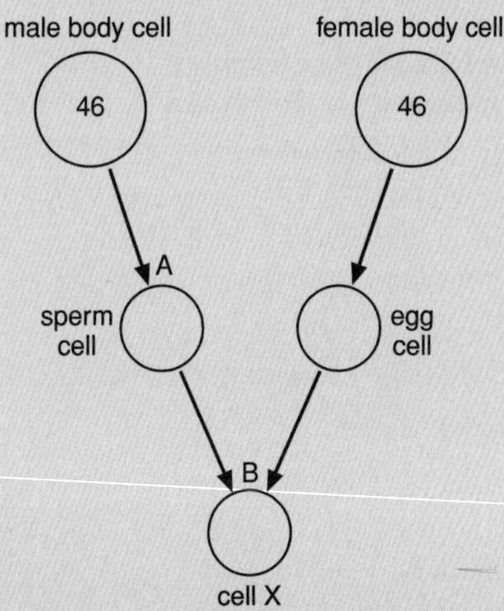

a *The body cells have 46 chromosomes. What is the number of chromosomes in:*
  i *the sperm cell*
  ii *the egg cell*
  iii *cell X?* [3]
b *The type of cell division shown at A makes gametes. What is the name of this cell division?* [1]
c *Process B shows the gametes joining. What is the name of this process?* [1]
d *What is the name given to the type of cell labelled X?* [1]
e *The gametes are said to be haploid. What does this mean?* [1]
f *Why is it important that the gametes are haploid?* [2]

3 *The diagram represents two animals. One is single celled and the other has eight cells.*

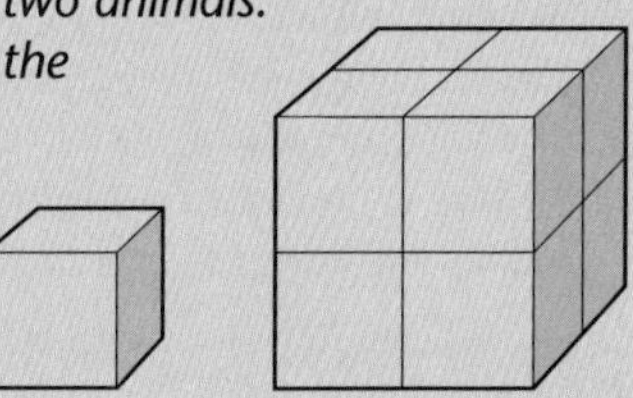

a *Each cell has dimensions of 1 × 1 × 1 unit. What is the surface area of each animal?* [2]
b *What is the volume of each animal?* [2]
c *Which cell has the smaller surface area : volume ratio?* [1]
d *Why is this a disadvantage to the cell?* [1]
e *If there are disadvantages for an organism if it becomes bigger then there must be some advantages. What are they?* [2]

B3e

1 *Make a list of the structures that are found in* ***both*** *plant cells and animal cells.* [3]

2 *Look at the diagram on page 21 showing the growth of different parts of the body.*

a *Approximately what fraction of the body length is the head at birth?* [1]
b *Why do you think that the main growth of the head happens before the main growth of the arms and legs?* [2]

3 *Read the following quote and answer the questions that follow.*

'People are always against new ideas such as using stem cells. Within a few years they will be used all the time to cure diseases. It is not that people object to using stem cells, it is where they come from that worries some people.'

a *What are stem cells?* [2]
b *How can they be used to cure diseases?* [2]
c *Why do you think that some people are worried about where they come from?* [3]

B3f

1 *The table shows some features concerning plant growth.*

Copy and complete the table by putting a tick or a cross in each box to show whether they are true of shoots and roots. [3]

Feature	Shoots	Roots
contain plant hormones		
show positive phototropism		
show negative geotropism		

2 *Read the following passage and answer the questions that follow.*

Plant hormones control how plants grow and so are often used in agriculture to alter plant growth. They might be used to change the rate that fruit ripens. This is particularly helpful with fruit such as bananas which have to be transported long distances. They can also be used as selective weedkillers because certain hormones will only kill the type of plants that have broad leaves.

a *Why is it helpful to change the rate at which fruit ripens?* [2]
b *What is a selective weedkiller?* [1]
c *Why can selective weedkillers be used on crops such as wheat and barley but not on tomatoes or lettuce?* [2]

3 The diagram shows two experiments on plant shoots.

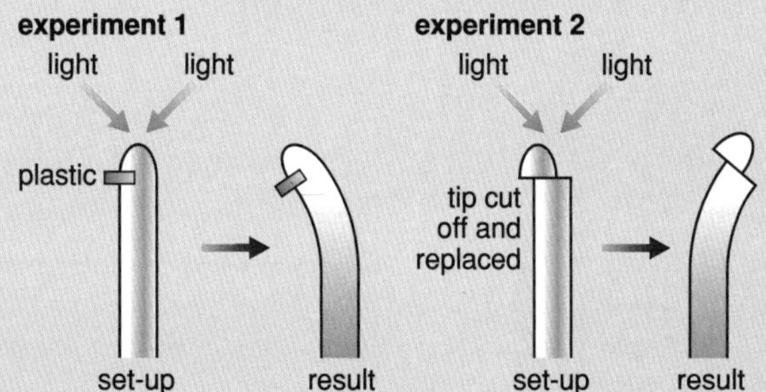

a What effect does auxin have on plant cells? [1]
b Explain why the shoot in experiment 1 bends to the left even though it is in even light. [3]
c Explain why the shoot in experiment 2 bends to the right. [3]

B3g

1 Copy and complete the following sentences.

A mutation is usually ___(1)___ to an organism and can be caused by it being exposed to ___(2)___ or ___(3)___ .

A more controlled way of changing the ___(4)___ of an organism is by genetic engineering. This is now used to make organisms such as ___(5)___ produce human insulin in large quantities. [5]

2 A type of cat has been bred that has very short front legs. These cats do not move around like normal cats but hop rather like kangaroos. This means that they cannot scratch with their paws or hunt animals.

a These cats have been produced by selective breeding. Explain the steps that would have been taken to do this. [3]
b Some people are keen to own these cats as pets. Others think that it is wrong to breed them. Describe the arguments that these two different groups of people might use. [4]

3 The diagram shows some of the stages in the production of human insulin by genetic engineering.

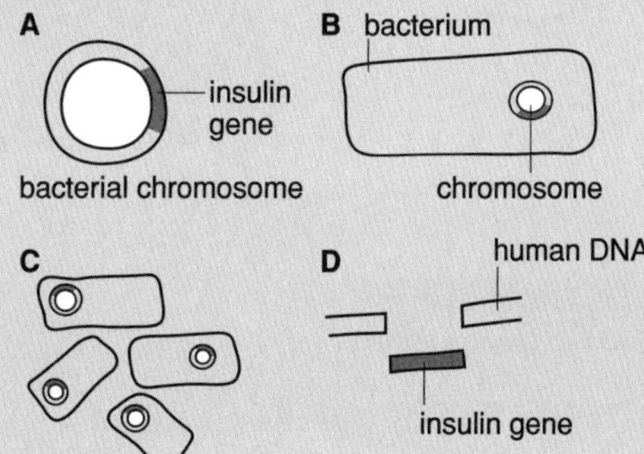

a Arrange the four stages in the correct order. [3]
b Explain what is happening at each stage. [4]
c Suggest why some people are unhappy about the transfer of human genes into other organisms. [2]

B3h

1 Which pairs of organisms are clones?

A two strawberry plants grown from runners
B identical twins
C two strawberry plants grown from seeds
D a brother and sister [2]

2 Clones can be produced by splitting up embryos produced from fertilised cows' eggs.

a Write down the stages A to E in the correct order. [3]
A cow artificially inseminated
B sperm collected from champion bull
C embryos collected from cow
D cloned embryos put into surrogate cow
E embryo split up
b Why do you think the farmers use a champion bull to provide the sperm? [2]
c What is a surrogate cow? [1]

3 Read the following passage about a gardener and answer the questions that follow.

George the gardener has a favourite geranium plant. He says that it is the same plant that was passed on to him by his father 30 years ago. Although it dies every winter he takes cuttings in the autumn and keeps them in a greenhouse for the next summer. This way he says he knows they will have attractive flowers.

a George says that his plant is the same plant that his father gave him thirty years ago. Why does he say this? [2]
b What does George do when he 'takes a cutting'? [3]
c How can George be so sure that the flowers will be attractive every year? [2]
d George has a whole flower bed full of these geraniums. Why does he have to be extra careful that they do not get a plant disease? [2]

4 Explain why the following statements are true.

a Cloning animals is much more difficult than cloning plants. [2]
b Tissue culture is a different process from taking cuttings. [2]
c It will not be easy to convince everybody that human cloning should be allowed. [2]

B4 It's a green world

- A walk in the country now is quite different from how it would have been 50 or 100 years ago. The fields are now much larger and farmers can use many different methods to increase their crop yields. These developments are possible because scientists now understand more about how plants produce their own food and grow.
- Leaves are very efficient in trapping sunlight. As well as sunlight, plants need water and minerals. The water may have to pass many metres up to the leaves from the soil.
- The minerals also come from the soil, and many are released from dead plant material. A study of how decay occurs can tell us a lot about how to stop the same thing happening to our food. All our methods of preserving food use this understanding.

I can't understand why anybody buys organic vegetables. They look just the same as the others but are much dearer.

I always buy organic vegetables and free range meat. I think that they are much safer to eat.

What you need to know

- Where diffusion occurs in plants.
- The word equation for photosynthesis.
- What a food chain shows.

Leaves for life

We can eat all these fruits and vegetables because of photosynthesis

In this item you will find out

- what are the main parts of a leaf
- how a leaf is adapted for photosynthesis

Leaves come in many different shapes, sizes and colours, but the main job of leaves is photosynthesis. This process uses the green chemical, **chlorophyll**, to trap sunlight and produce food for the plant. Directly or indirectly all life on our planet depends on this function of leaves to supply food.

While most leaves are green, many can vary in colour and may have different colours on the same leaf. So how can some leaves be yellow, orange or red if they all contain chlorophyll?

Chlorophyll is a mixture of different coloured chemicals. This can be shown using the process of chromatography. A leaf is ground up to release the chlorophyll and then the different coloured chemicals are separated on special paper.

All plants have the green chemical, but some have red or yellow coloured chemicals as well.

In some plants leaves do extra jobs. The Venus flytrap plant has special leaves that trap unsuspecting flies if they touch the hairs.

Venus flytrap

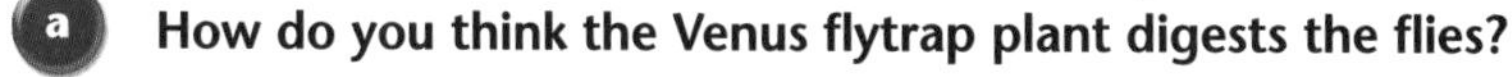

a How do you think the Venus flytrap plant digests the flies?

The leaves of the stinging nettle help to protect the plant. They have thousands of tiny hairs that are filled with poison. They break when touched and inject the poison into the skin.

b What advantages do these hairs give to the plant?

Amazing fact

A nettle called 'devil-leaf', which is found in Papua New Guinea, produces a poison that is so strong it has killed people.

Stinging nettle (magnified)

The reactions of photosynthesis

The process of photosynthesis is carried out by all green plants and some bacteria. It traps the energy from sunlight and uses it to make food in the form of a type of sugar called glucose. The plant can then convert the glucose into all the other chemicals that it needs to live and grow.

The raw materials that are needed for the reaction are carbon dioxide and water. Fortunately for animals, the waste product that is given off in the reaction is oxygen which they can use for respiration.

The structure of a leaf

Although leaves come in many shapes and sizes, they all have certain things in common.

The diagram on the left shows the external features of a leaf. You can see that it has a series of **veins** that spread throughout it. They carry water that has been absorbed by the roots to the cells of the leaf. They also transport away the glucose that is made by photosynthesis.

When you look at a thin section of a leaf under a microscope, you can see details of the cells inside.

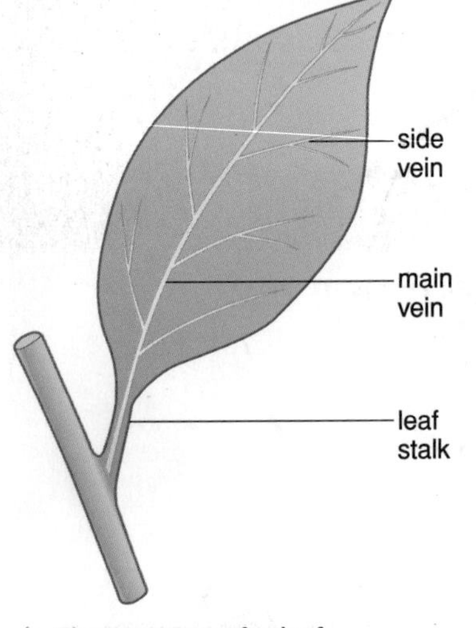

The structure of a leaf

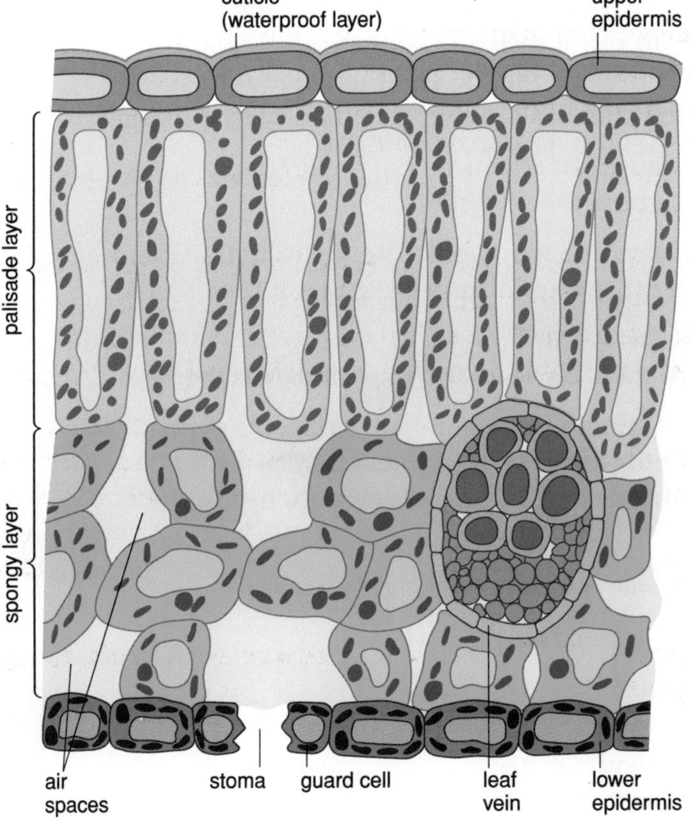

Inside a leaf

There is a waxy layer called the **cuticle** on the top of the leaf. Under the cuticle are different layers of cells. All the cells have a large central vacuole containing sap, as well as a tough cellulose cell wall. Some of the cells also have chloroplasts that contain the green chemical chlorophyll and so can carry out photosynthesis. The job of the chloroplasts is to absorb light energy.

Leaves efficiently absorb light energy

c **What do you think the waxy cuticle is for?**

d **Which types of cell contain chloroplasts?**

On the bottom of the leaf are pores called **stomata** which are opened or closed by **guard cells**.

Photosynthesis efficiency

Although some photosynthesis occurs in plant stems, it is the leaves that do most of the work. Leaves have evolved over millions of years to make them efficient at carrying out photosynthesis:

- they are broad so that they have a large surface area to absorb light energy
- they are very thin so that gases do not have far to travel
- they have a network of veins that support the leaf, and carry water in and glucose out
- they have stomata to allow gases to pass in and out by diffusion
- they have chlorophyll to absorb sunlight
- the air spaces inside the leaf mean that the leaf has a large internal surface area-to-volume ratio.

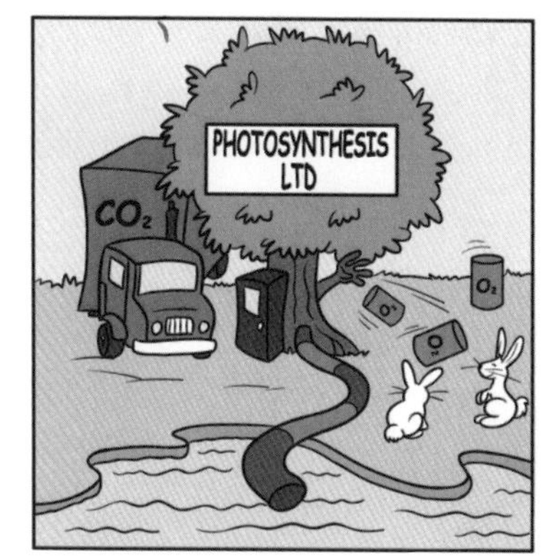

The top layer of cells, the **upper epidermis**, has no chloroplasts and so is transparent. This means that light hitting the leaf passes straight through to the **palisade mesophyll** layer. This is close to the top of the leaf and contains most of the leaf's chloroplasts. It is where most photosynthesis takes place.

The air spaces in the **spongy mesophyll** layer allow gases to diffuse between the stomata and the photosynthesising cells. Carbon dioxide diffuses in and oxygen diffuses out of the stomata. All the thousands of cells inside the leaf give a very large surface area for the absorption of carbon dioxide.

Apart from the guard cells, the cells of the **lower epidermis** do not contain chloroplasts.

Keywords

chlorophyll • cuticle • guard cells • lower epidermis • palisade mesophyll • spongy mesophyll • stomata • upper epidermis • veins

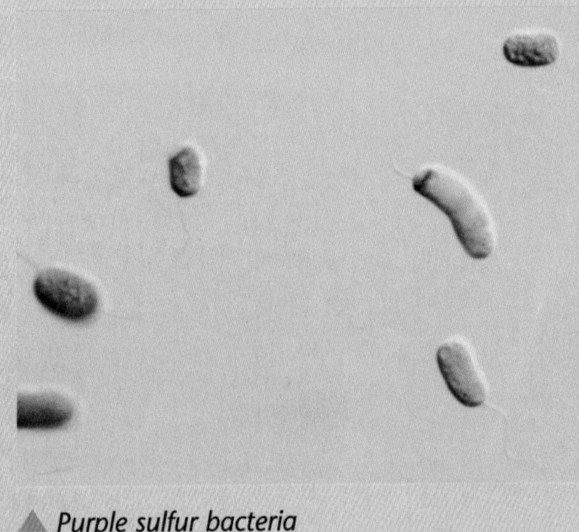

▲ Purple sulfur bacteria

Turning over a new leaf?

All life on our planet depends on the leaves of green plants trapping the energy from the sun for photosynthesis. Scientists are now trying to use this process to produce fuel that could be used instead of coal or oil.

Scientists got the idea from the first organisms to be able to use photosynthesis – these were tiny bacteria. They lived millions of years ago in warm springs that are often found near volcanoes. Very similar bacteria can still be found in warm water in places such as Yellowstone National Park in America.

Instead of using water (H_2O) for photosynthesis like plants do today, these bacteria use the gas hydrogen sulfide (H_2S). The bacteria use this gas as a source of hydrogen so that they can make glucose from carbon dioxide.

Some time later, one type of bacteria stopped using hydrogen sulfide as their source of hydrogen. They started to use water instead. This produced oxygen as a waste product instead of sulfur. This small change was vital to life on our planet. It also meant that plants could live in many more habitats.

Scientists hope to be able to build 'artificial leaves'. These will be made of metal but containing some of the chemicals found in the cells of plant leaves or bacteria. These chemicals will allow the 'leaves' to use the energy from sunlight to split hydrogen sulfide or even water. This would produce hydrogen and maybe oxygen that could be used as fuel.

An advantage of these leaves is that they will not fall off in the winter!

Questions

1. Purple sulfur bacteria and green leaves both carry out photosynthesis. Explain the differences between the photosynthetic process in each.
2. Write down the word equation that purple sulfur bacteria use for photosynthesis.
3. Why could organisms that used water rather than hydrogen sulfide 'live in many more habitats'?
4. The artificial leaves, like real leaves, are likely to be flat sheets. Why do you think they will be this shape?
5. Artificial leaves might use some chemicals from the cells of the leaf that are used in photosynthesis. Which cells do you think these are?
6. Suggest why scientists are keen to develop new fuels such as hydrogen and oxygen.

Looking at osmosis

In this item you will find out

- what osmosis is
- about transpiration
- how plants try to reduce water loss

Gardeners know that if they want to move a plant then it is much better to take a large amount of soil with the roots. This helps to prevent the roots being damaged. When the plant is replanted it must always be watered to stop it **wilting**. This water is taken up into the plant from the soil by the process of **osmosis**.

To keep vegetables and salad crisp, a cook will often put them into water. This means that they will take up water by osmosis and be prevented from becoming limp.

But why do plants wilt if they do not get enough water?

Water moves in and out of plant cells through the cell wall and membrane. When the vacuole of a plant cell is filled with liquid, the water pressure presses up against the cell wall. The cell is said to be **turgid**. The cell wall is inelastic and does not stretch so it supports the plant cell. This turgor pressure is very important in supporting plants.

When the vacuole does not have enough liquid in it, because the plant is losing more water than it is taking in, it cannot press up against the cell wall and there is not enough turgor pressure. The plant cells become **flaccid**. This means they collapse inwards and the plant wilts.

Both the inelastic cell wall and water are needed to support plants.

Sometimes the cells may lose so much water that the cell membrane may come away from the cell wall. This is called **plasmolysis**.

a **The cell wall is made of cellulose. What properties would you expect cellulose to have?**

▲ *This plant is wilting from lack of water*

▲ *This plant has plenty of water and its cells are turgid*

Amazing fact

The forces created by seeds taking up water can be so large that ships' holds carrying seeds have been split apart when the seeds took up water and swelled up.

What is osmosis?

Osmosis is a special type of diffusion. Plant cells are surrounded by a cell wall and a cell membrane. The cell wall is **permeable** and so lets quite large molecules through. The cell membrane is **partially permeable**. This means that small molecules like water can diffuse through but larger molecules cannot.

Osmosis is the movement of water from an area of high water concentration (a dilute solution) to an area of low water concentration (a concentrated solution) across a partially permeable membrane. Like all diffusion it happens because the molecules are constantly moving about at random.

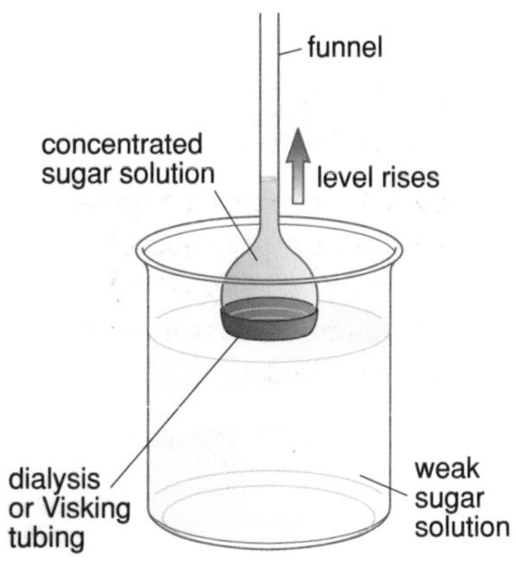

How osmosis works

You can see how this works by looking at the diagram.

Because there is less water in the concentrated sugar solution, water passes into it from the weak solution. The level of the concentrated solution rises up the funnel as its volume increases. The dialysis or Visking tubing acts as a partially permeable membrane.

If plant cells are placed in water they take up water by osmosis. Under a microscope the cells can be seen to swell up and then stop. The liquid inside the vacuole is an area of low water concentration and the water moves into the plant cells. When the plant cells have taken up enough water, the cell wall stops any more water from entering.

b **A plant cell with a vacuole containing cell sap equivalent to a 10% sugar solution is placed in a 5% sugar solution. Which way will water move by osmosis?**

Examiner's tip

When talking about osmosis it is best to talk about water concentration or sugar concentration. If you just say concentration the examiner might not know what you mean.

Animal cells and water

It is not just plant cells that take in water by osmosis – animal cells do too, but they behave differently from plant cells. When animal cells are surrounded by water they will take up too much water and burst. This is called **lysis**. The reason they burst is because animal cells do not have an inelastic cell wall to resist the pressure – they only have a cell membrane. In a concentrated solution, animal cells will shrink. This is called **crenation**.

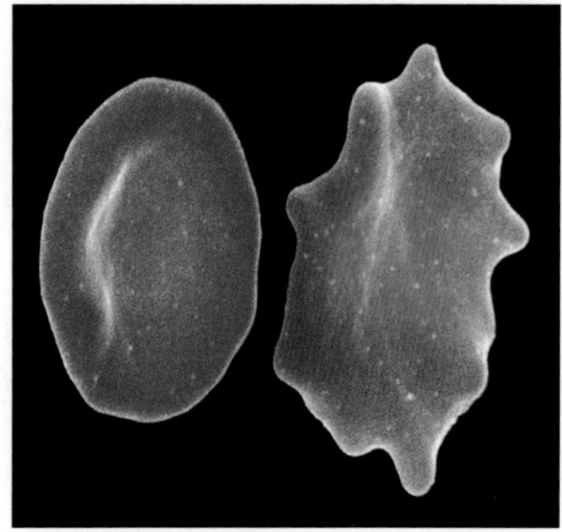

This cell has shrunk from too little water

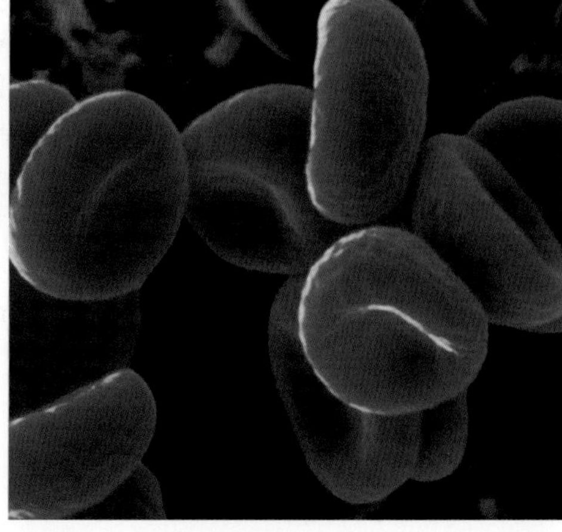

This animal cell has swollen from too much water

A balancing act

We have already seen that plant leaves are adapted for efficient photosynthesis. They are covered in thousands of small pores called stomata that allow gases to diffuse in and out of the leaf. However, if gases can diffuse in and out, then water molecules will also be able to diffuse out. This loss of water is called **transpiration**.

Water is taken up from the soil into the roots by osmosis. The younger parts of the roots are covered in fine projections called root hairs. They increase the surface area of the roots to speed up the uptake of water.

The roots grow from the tips pushing through the soil. Suggest why root hairs are only found on the younger parts of the root.

Although plants cannot stop losing water by transpiration, the flow of water to the leaves and into the atmosphere does help the plant in several ways:

- it helps to cool the plant down, rather like sweating in animals
- it provides the leaves with water for photosynthesis
- it brings minerals up from the soil
- it makes sure cells stay turgid for support.

Keywords

crenation • flaccid • lysis • osmosis • permeable • plasmolysis • partially permeable • transpiration • turgid • wilting

Cutting down water loss

Although transpiration has its uses, plants try to lose as little water as they can. They have a waxy cuticle on the top of the leaves which stops water leaving the leaf. They also only have a small number of stomata on the upper surface of the leaf. This cuts down on water loss because water is lost through evaporation from stomata when the sun's energy hits the leaf. Most of the energy hits the top of the leaf so if there are few stomata there then water evaporation is reduced.

Another way to reduce water loss is to close the stomata at night.

Why is it less important for stomata to be open at night?

The stomata are opened and closed in a clever way by the guard cells on either side of the pores. When there is a lot of light and water available, they take in water and become turgid. This causes the cells to bend and the pores to open. When light levels are low, or when there is little water available, the opposite happens and the stomata close. This is shown in the diagram on the right.

Plants that live in areas where there is not much water available may have fewer stomata.

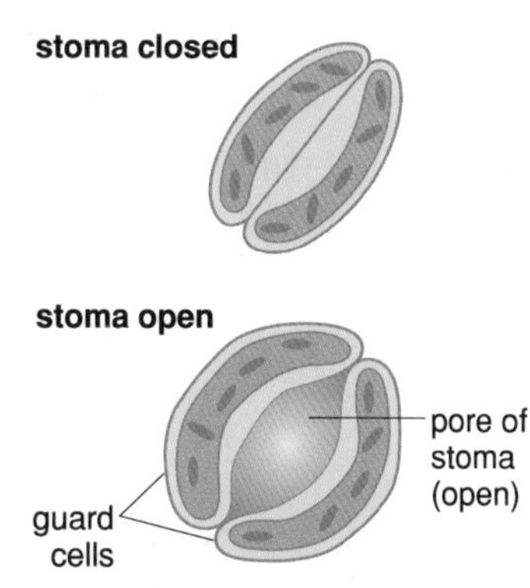

▲ *How guard cells control stomata*

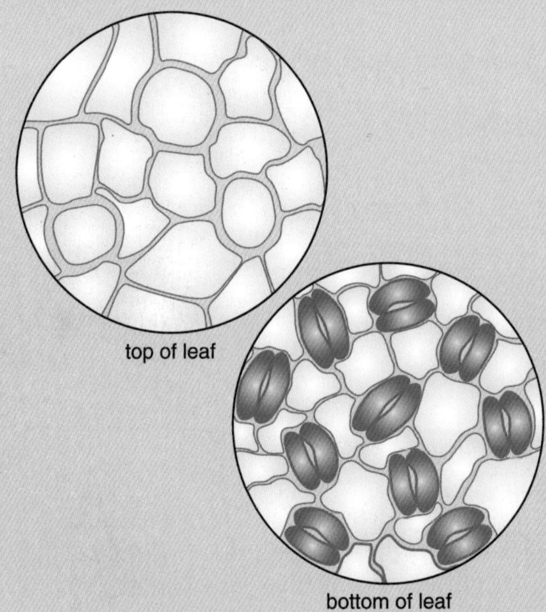

Counting stomata

Many scientists think that counting stomata can tell us a lot about where plants live. It may also tell us about conditions in the past.

It is quite easy to count stomata in the lab. A leaf is painted with a small amount of nail varnish which is peeled off once it is dry. This carries with it an imprint of the stomata. They can then be counted under a microscope.

This technique can be used to work out the number of stomata on each surface of different leaves. The results of an investigation into holly and oak leaves are shown in the table.

Type of plant	Number of stomata (mm^2)	
	Top leaf surface	Bottom leaf surface
holly	0	113
oak	0	340

▲ Oak leaf

▲ Holly leaves

Scientists have tried growing the same type of plant in atmospheres with different concentrations of carbon dioxide. They have then counted the number of stomata on the leaves of the plants. They have found interesting differences in the numbers of stomata that the plants develop.

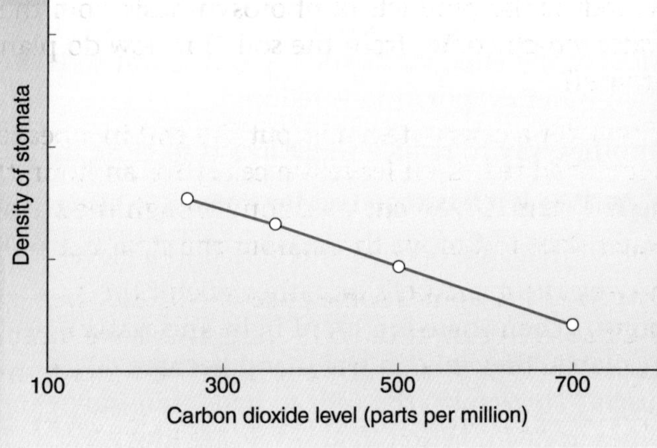

The scientists think that they might be able to use this discovery to find out about atmospheric carbon dioxide levels from many years ago.

Questions

1. Why is it necessary to make an imprint of a leaf to view under a microscope?
2. The area of the field of view shown in the diagram is 0.05 mm^2. What is the frequency of stomata per mm^2 on this leaf surface?
3. Why do you think the holly and the oak have all of their stomata on the bottom surface?
4. Suggest why the holly has fewer stomata than the oak.
5. Describe and explain the pattern shown by the graph.
6. Suggest how scientists could use these findings to estimate carbon dioxide levels from hundreds of years ago.

Xylem and phloem in action

In this item you will find out

- about xylem and phloem
- what alters the rate of transpiration

Small insects called aphids feed on the stems of plants by inserting their long, needle-like mouthparts straight into special cells in the stem. It is these cells that transport sugar around the plant. The aphids don't even need to suck – the sugar just oozes out.

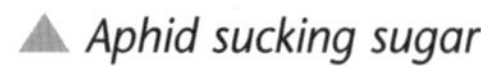

▲ *Aphid sucking sugar*

Plants transport many different substances both up and down their stems. As well as the products of photosynthesis from the leaves, there is also water which comes from the soil. But how do plants move these substances around?

If you cut a celery stem and put the end in a beaker of water which has been dyed red, then leave the celery for an hour, the water and dye move up the stem. If you cut a section through the stem, you will see that the water does not move throughout the stem but only moves in certain cells.

By giving the aphids some anaesthetic and then breaking them off, leaving their mouthparts in the cells, scientists have located the cells that move sugar. These cells are different from the water-transporting cells.

This can be confirmed if a plant is provided with carbon dioxide containing radioactive carbon. The plant will make radioactive sugar. When scientists take a section through the plant's stem the radioactive sugar can be detected. The sugar can be found close to the cells where the water is transported, but the sugar is in different cells. So plants transport different substances around in different ways.

a **The water containing the dye and the radioactive sugars are in different cells. Which direction is each moving in the plant?**

Amazing fact

A female aphid can give birth to 12 babies a day, every day!

▼ *Red dye travels up a celery stalk*

Xylem and phloem

The two different transport tissues in a plant are called **xylem** and **phloem**. In the diagram, you can see how they are arranged in the roots, stem and leaves of a **dicotyledonous** plant (it has two seed leaves).

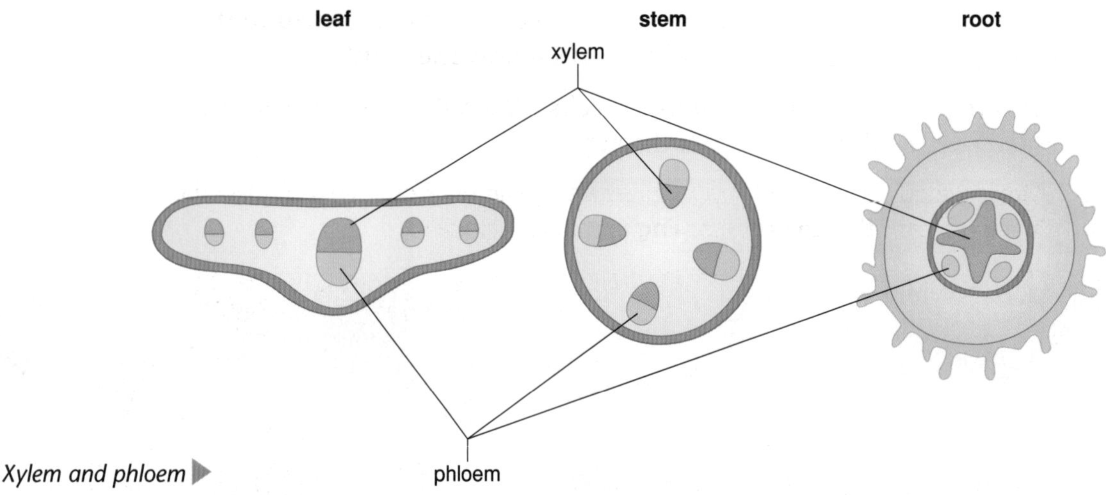

Xylem and phloem

Xylem transports water and dissolved minerals. The water and dissolved minerals are taken in by the roots and move up to the leaves and shoots where the water is lost in transpiration.

Phloem transports dissolved food substances (sugars) around the plant. Unlike the transport of water, the food may be transported up or down the stem. It may move from the leaves where it is made up to the tips of the shoots where growth happens. It may also be sent down the stem to storage organs such as swollen roots. This movement of food substances by the phloem is called **translocation**.

b **What is the sugar used for in the tips of the roots and shoots?**

The xylem vessels and phloem tubes run continuously from the roots to the stem and into the veins of the leaves. In the stem they are gathered together into collections called **vascular bundles**.

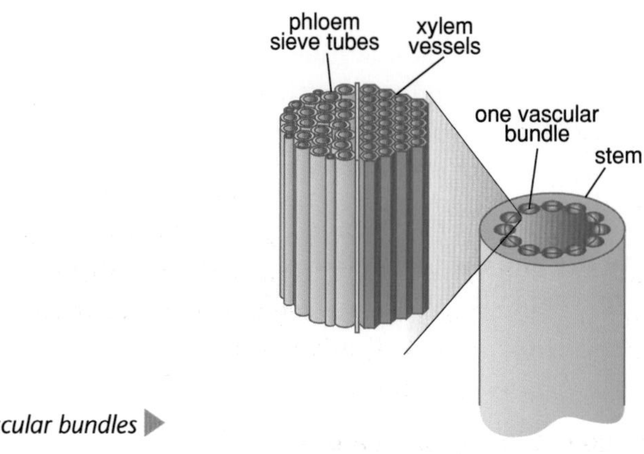

Vascular bundles

Specialised cells

The cells that make up xylem and phloem are specialised so that they can carry out their functions.

Xylem contains long thin tubes called vessels each with a hollow **lumen**. This means they are made from dead cells. The vessels are hollow so that water can easily pass through. Their cellulose cell wall is thickened to stop them collapsing and so xylem also helps to support the plant.

Phloem is made up of columns of living cells. The cells have holes in the end walls to allow the food to pass through.

c **Moving food through phloem requires a large amount of energy. Explain why it is important that the cells making up phloem are alive.**

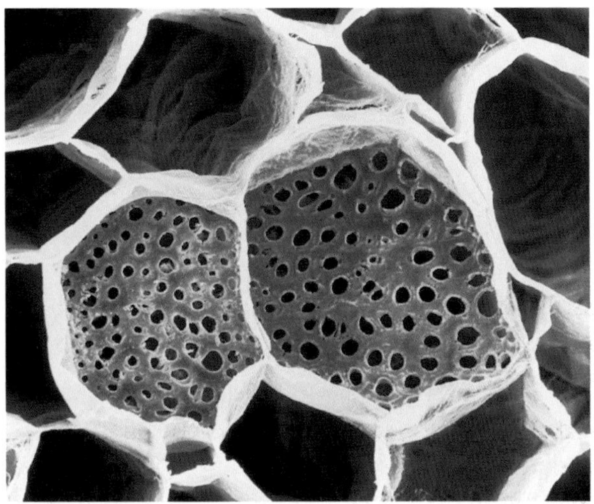

▲ *Phloem tubes*

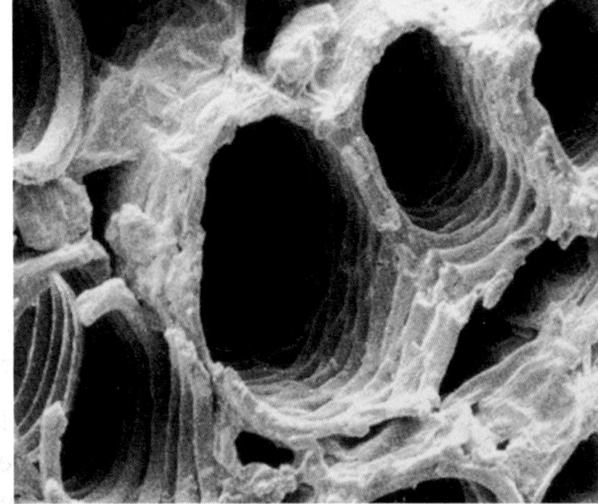

▲ *Xylem vessels*

Transpiration rate

As we have already seen, transpiration is the diffusion of water out of leaves through the stomata and its evaporation. When water is lost through the stomata, this creates a suction force that helps to pull more water up through the xylem vessels from the roots to the leaves.

The rate of transpiration is increased when:

- the temperature increases
- light levels increase
- it is windy
- it is dry and not very humid.

This is because, in warmer conditions, the water molecules have more energy and so evaporate faster. Also, an increase in light will cause more of the stomata to open and more water to diffuse out, while in windy conditions the water vapour in the air is blown away allowing more of it to evaporate. Finally, in dry conditions, the air holds fewer water molecules and so more water diffuses out of the leaf.

Suggest why gardeners do not dig up and transplant plants on a hot, sunny day.

Keywords

dicotyledonous • lumen • phloem • translocation • vascular bundle • xylem

Measuring water uptake

Dr Steven Okinwe is measuring water uptake by a leafy shoot using a device called a potometer.

He cuts off a leafy shoot from a plant underwater by holding the stem in a bucket of water. He then inserts it into the potometer underwater in a sink.

All the joints of the apparatus are greased to stop leaks and all air bubbles are removed.

As the shoot loses water, it draws water up from the capillary tube. The movement of the water along the capillary tube can be measured every minute. This can be done under different conditions.

His results are shown in the table.

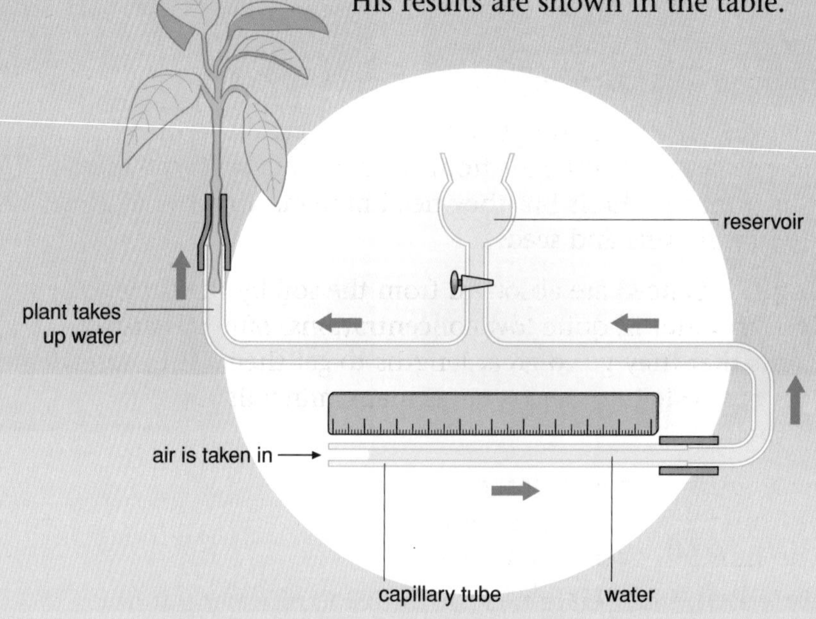

Conditions	Distance water moves from start position (mm)							
	0 min	1 min	2 min	3 min	4 min	5 min	6 min	7 min
leaves uncovered	0	3	7	10	14	17	20	23
top of leaves covered in grease	0	2	5	8	11	15	18	21
bottom of leaves covered in grease	0	1	2	4	6	7	9	10

Questions

1 Write down two of the precautions taken when setting up the apparatus and explain why they are necessary.

2 The apparatus does not measure water loss from the shoot but measures water uptake by the shoot. Why does the shoot take up slightly more water than it loses?

3 Plot the results on a grid. Use the same grid for all three conditions.

4 Explain the results of the experiment as fully as possible.

A healthy diet

▲ *Lichens consist of fungi and algae*

In this item you will find out

- what plants use minerals for
- what happens to plants if they lack minerals
- how plants take up minerals

Just like us, plants are in desperate need of **minerals** so that they can grow properly.

The difference between humans and plants is that we get our minerals from food but plants get their minerals from the soil. All plants can make their own food by photosynthesis but they need minerals in order to grow properly and produce flowers and seeds.

The minerals that plants need are absorbed from the soil by the roots. They are dissolved in water in quite low concentrations. Minerals are so important to plants that they go to great lengths to get them. They spread their root systems out wide in order to get as many minerals as possible from the soil.

Some plants recruit assistance in order to absorb minerals from the soil. Fungi are very good at taking up minerals even when they are in small concentrations. Some plants have fungi permanently attached to their roots. They spread out and take up minerals, passing some on to the plant. Lichens are combinations of fungi and single-celled algae. The fungi absorb water and minerals and share these with the algae.

Other plants that grow in soil which is very low in minerals catch insects and extract the minerals they need from them. They are often called carnivorous plants. They include the Venus flytrap, pitcher plants and sundews.

a **How do you think these plants catch insects?**

Amazing fact

Plants are usually said to respond slowly to stimuli but the Venus flytrap can shut its trap in less than 0.1 of a second.

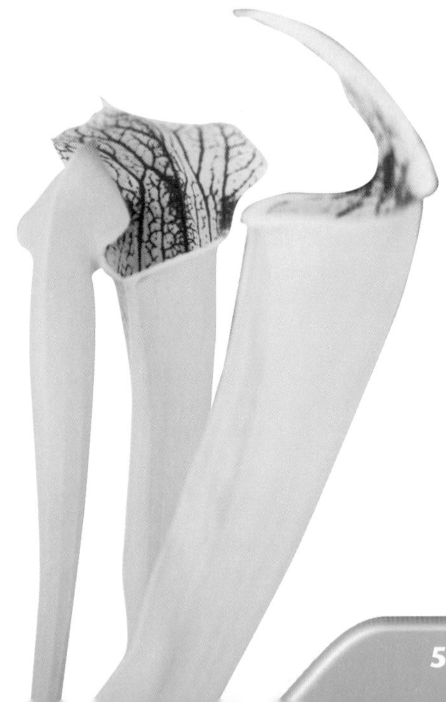

Pitcher plant ▶

Minerals

Plants can make sugars in photosynthesis using carbon dioxide and water. However, to turn these sugars into other important substances, such as protein and DNA, they need minerals. This is because sugars only contain the elements carbon, hydrogen and oxygen. Other chemicals that plants need contain elements such as nitrogen, phosphorus, potassium and magnesium. The table shows how plants obtain and use these elements.

Element required	Main source	Used by plants to produce
magnesium	magnesium compounds	chlorophyll for photosynthesis
nitrogen	nitrates	amino acids for making proteins which are needed for cell growth
phosphorus	phosphates	DNA and cell membranes to make new cells for respiration and growth
potassium	potassium compounds	compounds needed to help enzymes in photosynthesis and respiration

Examiner's tip

Do not call minerals 'food'. Plants make their own food by photosynthesis. They do not get food from the soil.

Mineral deficiencies

Just like people, if a plant grows without enough minerals it will not develop properly. This is called a **deficiency**. It is possible to demonstrate the effect of a lack of mineral by growing plants in solutions that are missing particular minerals. This is shown in the photograph below.

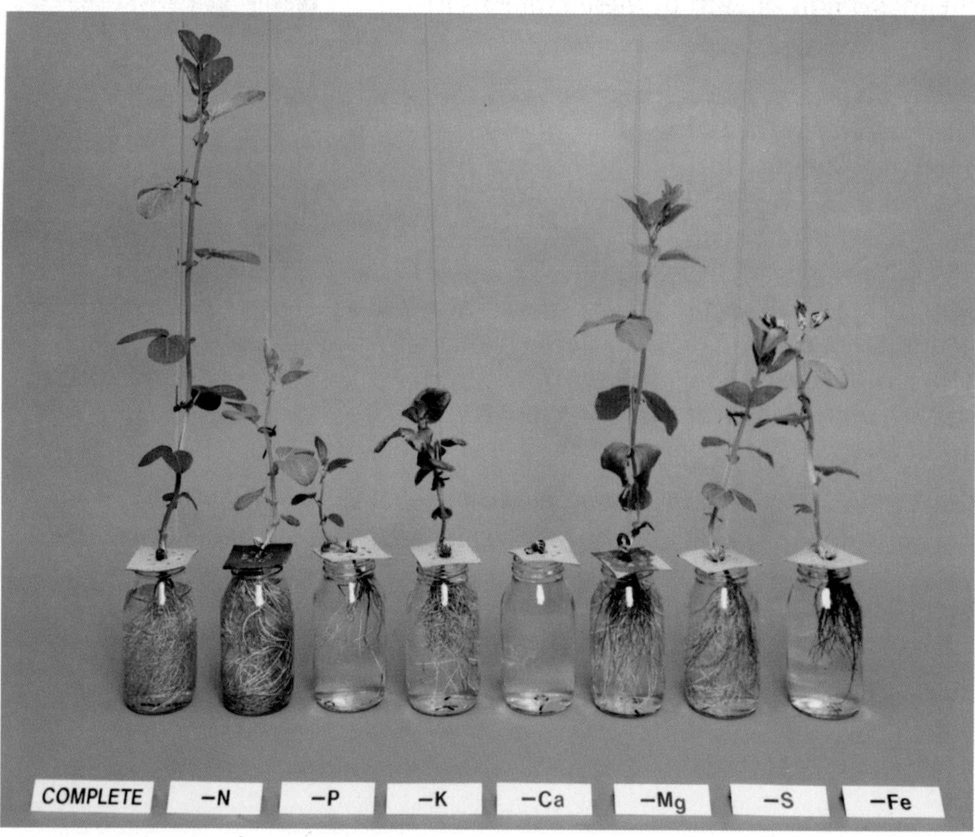

Bean plants with mineral deficiencies

Different mineral deficiencies can affect plants in different ways. Some of these are shown in the table.

Mineral	Effect of deficiency on growth
magnesium	yellow leaves
nitrate	poor growth and yellow leaves
potassium	poor flower and fruit growth and discoloured leaves
phosphate	poor root growth and discoloured leaves

b **Look at the two tables. Why do you think a lack of magnesium leads to yellow leaves?**

c **Suggest why a lack of nitrates lead to poor growth.**

Fertilisers

Farmers may add fertilisers to the soil to help their crops grow. These fertilisers contain various combinations of minerals, such as nitrates, potassium, magnesium and phosphate compounds. This is because some plants need more of one type of mineral than another.

The photograph shows a packet of fertiliser with an NPK value on it. This stands for nitrate, phosphate and potassium and tells the farmer the proportion of each of these minerals in the fertiliser.

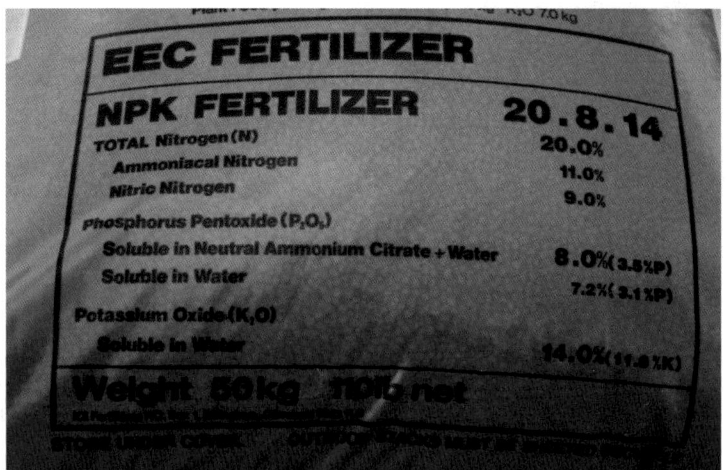

Different fertilisers contain different proportions of minerals

Absorbing minerals

The minerals that the plant needs are absorbed from the soil by the roots. They are dissolved in water in quite low concentrations.

The concentration of these minerals in the root hairs is much higher. This means that they cannot be taken in by diffusion. A process called **active transport** is needed. This process moves substances from low concentration to high concentration. This means that it moves substances against the **concentration gradient**. It requires the energy from respiration to do this.

Because active transport uses energy from respiration, roots need oxygen in order to take up minerals by this process. Farmers try to make sure that their soil is not waterlogged because this reduces the oxygen content of the soil.

d **Explain why there is likely to be less oxygen available to the plant roots in a waterlogged soil.**

Amazing fact

The water that a giant sequoia tree takes up in 24 hours contains enough minerals to pave five metres of a four-lane motorway.

Keywords

active transport • concentration gradient • deficiency • mineral

▲ Mycorrhiza help plants

The fungal helpers

Not many people have heard of mycorrhiza but about 95% of all plants have them. They are fungi that live attached to the roots of plants. They spread out in the soil and allow the plant to absorb minerals at a quicker rate. They can be seen in the photograph on the left.

It is thought that the mycorrhiza are particularly good at absorbing phosphates from the soil that plants find difficult to take up.

All this is theory but scientists have carried out experiments to test these ideas. Small plants were grown in normal soil and in soil that had been sterilised. The sterilising kills the fungi. After some time, the mass of the plants was measured. The mineral content of each group of plants was also measured.

The results are shown in the table.

Conditions	Dry mass of plant (g)	Mass of mineral in plant (mg)		
		Nitrogen	Phosphorus	Potassium
no fungi present	0.3	2.5	0.2	2.0
fungi present	2.8	37.5	4.0	36.0

Scientists have used this type of evidence to show that plants gain significantly from their relationship with the fungi. But as the famous saying goes 'there is no such thing as a free lunch' – the fungi must be getting something in return from the plant.

Questions

1. The mycorrhiza is a fine network of threads of fungus attached to the roots. Suggest how this helps the roots to absorb more minerals.
2. How much more nitrogen is there in the plants with fungi compared to the plants without?
3. Suggest how this helps to explain the improved growth rate of these plants.
4. It is thought that fungi are particularly good at absorbing phosphates. Does the experiment show any evidence for this?
5. The fungi may be getting something in return from the plant. Suggest what this could be.

Pass it on

Eating celery takes energy!

In this item you will find out

- about pyramids of numbers and biomass
- how energy flows through a food chain
- how we can use biomass

Plants can trap the energy from sunlight and use it to produce many products that are useful to us. Some products are used for food by animals although sometimes it can be difficult to make use of the energy trapped. For example, celery has energy trapped in its cells but it takes more energy to digest the celery than is released.

Other plants, such as the macadamia plant, produce material that is very high in energy. The nut of the macadamia plant contains almost 100 times more energy than celery but the nut is enclosed in the hardest shell in the world! Special nutcrackers are needed to break them open.

As well as using plant products for food, man also uses them for fuel.

Humans have burned wood for thousands of years but now there are many other ways that man is trying to use plants for fuel.

One idea has been put forward by a group of Japanese scientists. They want to build 100 vast nets that will float in the middle of the ocean. On the net will grow a quick-growing seaweed. The nets will then be towed back to land and the seaweed harvested. It will be dried and burnt to produce electricity.

a **Suggest one advantage of burning the seaweed for energy rather than burning coal or oil.**

A burning log fire

Amazing fact

An aircraft carrier travels about 5 cm on each litre of fuel.

Pyramids of numbers and biomass

You can see how organisms rely on each other for food if you draw a simple food chain like the one in the diagram below.

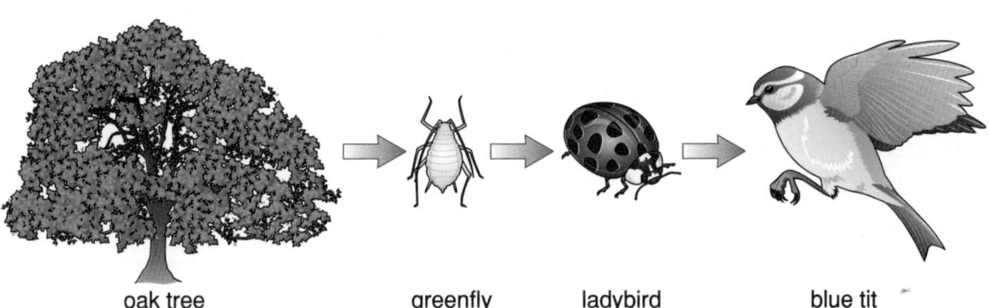

Examiner's tip

Don't confuse the words 'trophic' and 'tropic'. They mean different things.

In every food chain the first organism is the producer. This means that it can make its own food using the energy from sunlight. All the other organisms in a food chain are consumers. They need to take in food because they can't produce their own.

To give us more information about the numbers of organisms in a food chain you can construct a **pyramid of numbers**. The number of organisms at each stage in the food chain (**trophic level**) is counted. Each box in the pyramid is drawn so that the area represents the number of organisms.

The trouble with this type of pyramid is that it does not take into account the size of the organism. One oak tree takes up as much area as one greenfly!

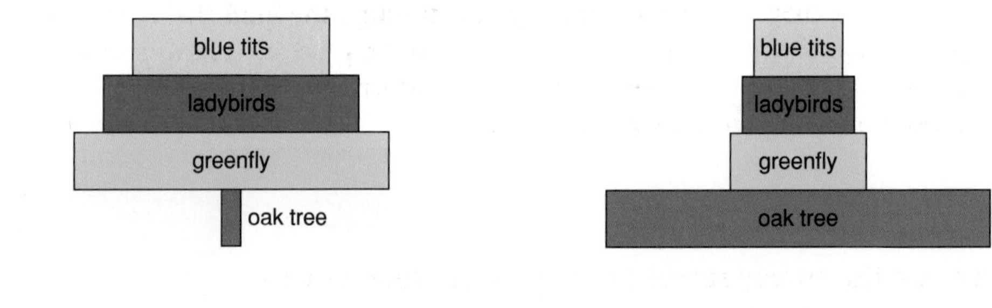

▲ *Pyramid of numbers*

▲ *Pyramid of biomass*

An alternative is to draw a **pyramid of biomass**. Biomass is the mass of living material of an organism. The mass of all the organisms at each level is measured and the boxes are drawn to show the mass at each stage in a food chain or web.

b **Why is the oak tree box much larger in the pyramid of biomass?**

c **Why do you think it is harder to get the information needed to construct a pyramid of biomass?**

Energy flow

Some scientists study the flow of energy through food chains. The energy enters the food chain when plants absorb sunlight. The producers trap some of this energy by photosynthesis and convert it into chemical energy in compounds such as glucose. This energy then passes along the food chain as each organism feeds on other organisms and takes in the compounds. This energy flow is shown in the diagram.

The diagram on the right shows that energy is leaving the food chain at each stage. This is because organisms give out heat that has been made in respiration. Some energy is also lost in material that is ejected from animals (**egestion**). This is food that has passed all the way through an animal and has not been digested.

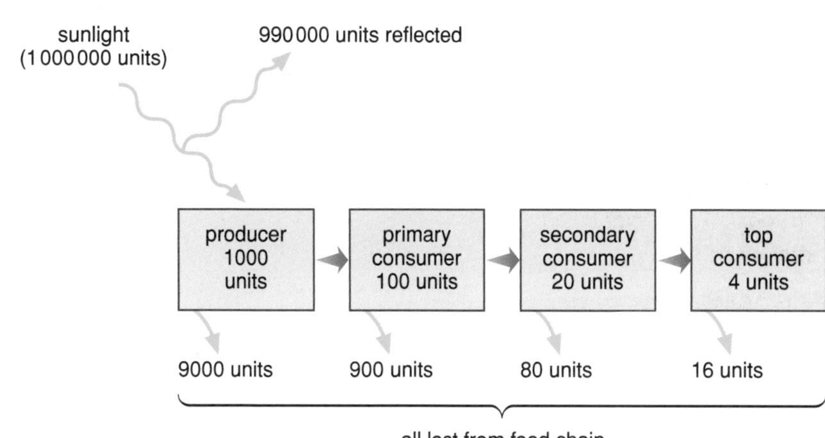

Energy flow in a food chain

The efficiency of energy transfer explains the shape of a pyramid of biomass. Due to energy loss, a larger mass of organisms is needed to support the level above. This results in a pyramid. The loss of energy also explains why food chains rarely have more than about five levels. Because of the energy loss at each stage, not enough energy is left to support any more levels.

Look at the diagram showing energy flow through the food chain. (i) What percentage of the energy is transferred from the producer to the primary consumer? (ii) What percentage is then transferred from the primary consumer to the secondary consumer?

Energy from biomass

We can use the energy stored in biomass in different ways:

- we can burn wood that comes from fast-growing trees
- we can produce alcohol by using yeast to ferment the biomass
- we can produce biogas which contains gases produced by bacteria fermenting the biomass.

All of these types of biomass are called renewable. This is because they can be produced at the same rate as they are used so they will not run out. **Biofuels** help countries that do not have reserves of fossil fuels so they do not need to import gas or oil. An added bonus is that when they are burned, the biofuels only release the same amount of carbon dioxide as is taken in to produce them. The carbon dioxide levels in the air should stay constant so there is no increase in air pollution.

Of course, the energy stored in biomass can also be used by humans or livestock by eating it, or we can grow the seeds into new plants to use as fuel.

Keywords

biofuel • egestion • pyramid of biomass • pyramid of numbers • trophic level

▲ Macadamia nuts

Nuts to energy

In Australia, the macadamia nut is in great demand for baking and sweet making. There are now more than 4.5 million macadamia trees growing in the country. The problem is waste. The nut has a very hard and thick shell. One factory can produce about 10 000 tonnes of waste shells each year.

There is also pressure from the Australian government to generate more energy from renewable resources. Strict penalties apply if businesses do not do this.

Now one company has come up with an answer that will solve both of these problems – burn the nutshells!

A nut company has teamed up with an Australian energy company and built a large power station. This will be powered by burning the nutshells. It should generate up to 9.5 gigawatt hours which is enough to power about 1200 homes. Some of the power will be used to supply the nut factory but the rest will be sold to the national grid.

It has been estimated that burning the nuts rather than fossil fuels will reduce carbon dioxide emissions by about 9500 tonnes each year. This is the same as taking 2000 cars off the road.

A spokesperson for the company said that if successful this idea could be used in a range of other industries, including peanut, timber, wheat and grain processors.

Questions

1 What is the problem with the macadamia nut industry?

2 The Australian government wants energy to be generated from renewable fuels. Suggest why the nutshells are considered to be a renewable energy source but coal is not.

3 Burning the shells releases carbon dioxide. However, burning the nuts rather than fossil fuels will cut down on the release of 9500 tonnes of carbon dioxide a year. How do you think this reduction of carbon dioxide is possible?

4 Suggest why the Australian government is so keen to reduce carbon dioxide output.

Food for everybody

In this item you will find out

- some of the advantages and disadvantages of intensive farming
- how plants can be grown without soil
- about organic farming

Traditional ploughing with oxen

Up until the last century farming methods had changed little for hundreds of years. Traditionally, farmers ploughed small fields using animals. Seeds were planted and crops harvested by hand.

In the last 500 years the world's population has doubled nearly four times. This increase in numbers has meant that there is a much greater demand for food.

This has resulted in major changes to farming methods. Crops are grown in large glasshouses and fish are bred in fish farms so that they grow much more quickly. Machinery has been developed to help the farmer. More and more chemicals are also available to farmers to use as fertilisers and to kill pests. This is known as **intensive farming**. This means trying to produce as much food as possible from a certain area of land and from the plants or animals that are farmed. In some areas crop yields have gone up tremendously because of intensive farming.

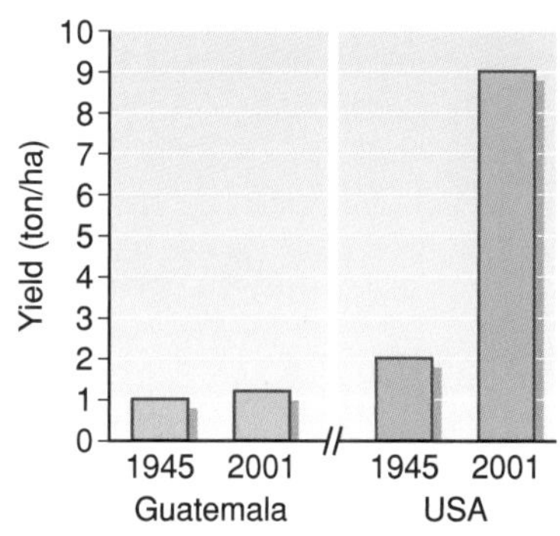

Crop yields in Guatemala and the USA

The graph on the right shows the yield of one crop, corn, in the USA and Guatemala. Intensive farming techniques are used in the USA but not in Guatemala.

a **How does the yield compare between the two countries?**

b **By using intensive practices, the USA has increased the yield of corn that is grown. By how much has the yield increased in 2001 compared with 1945?**

Battery farming involves keeping animals, such as chickens, in controlled conditions indoors. They are kept warm and their movements are restricted. This means that they will lose less energy as heat.

Some people think that raising animals in this way is unethical. Chickens, for example, have very little room to move around in and because they grow so quickly, their legs often cannot support their bodies.

Amazing fact

Sales of organic meat in the UK went up by 139% between 2001 and 2004.

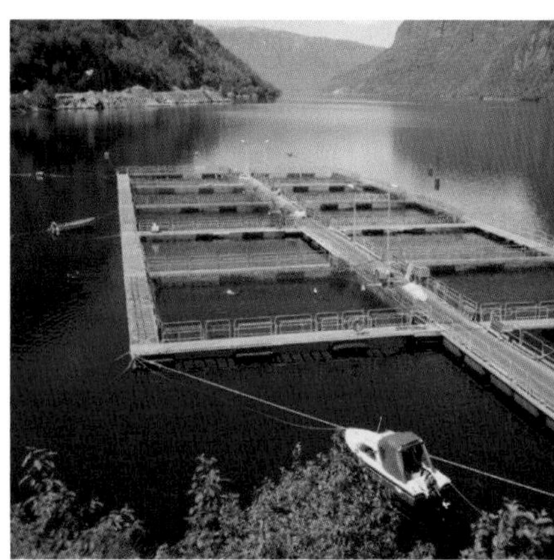
Fish can be intensively farmed

Energy efficient

Producing food by intensive farming improves the efficiency of energy transfer along food chains in several ways. Intensive farmers often use **pesticides**. These are chemicals that kill pests. Removing pests that eat part of the crop leaves more biomass and energy for farmers to harvest.

Farmers may also use herbicides to kill plants, such as weeds, in crop fields. This helps to prevent competition from the weeds and so the crops can more efficiently trap the energy from the sun.

c **Suggest three things that the crop plants and weeds are competing for.**

d **Why do you think farmers spray herbicide rather than weeding by hand?**

Damaging effects

Although using pesticides and herbicides has increased food production, there have been drawbacks.

Pesticides may harm useful organisms such as insect pollinators. They may also enter the bodies of organisms. As they do not break down, their concentration may build up in consumers higher up the food chain.

e **Look at the diagram on the left. Suggest why the fish do not die from the pesticide.**

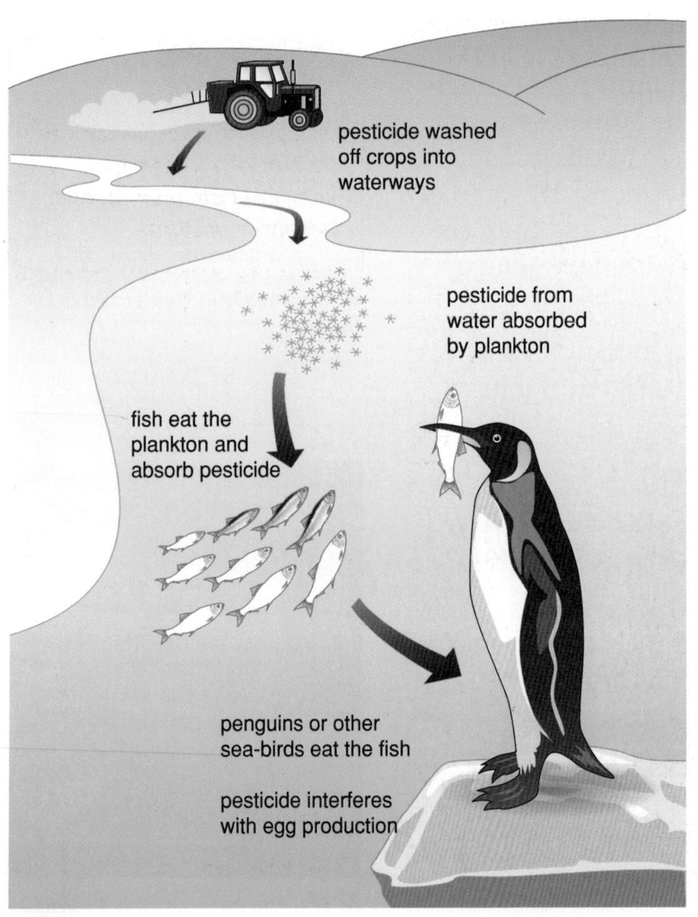

How pesticides travel up a food chain

Soil free?

Many farmers that use intensive farming grow plants in glasshouses. This helps to protect the plants from extremes of weather. Sometimes they are grown in soil but not always. The growing of plants without soil is becoming more popular in many areas.

This is known as **hydroponics**. Proper hydroponics means growing crops in water, but farmers may use an artificial soil. This technique may be very useful in areas where the soil is poor (or barren, as it is known), or for growing plants like tomatoes in glasshouses.

The disadvantages of hydroponics are that the plants are not supported by deep soil and you need to add fertilisers to the water or artificial soil. The advantages are that the mineral levels can be carefully controlled and you can control diseases by adding pesticides to the water so that they reach each plant.

No artificial additives

Due to the problems caused by intensive farming, lots of people think that plants should be grown without artificial fertilisers, herbicides or pesticides. This is called **organic farming**.

There are a number of alternative methods that organic farmers can use:

- animal manure and compost can be dug into the soil as fertiliser
- crops that can fix nitrogen in the soil, such as clover, can be grown
- crop rotation can be used so that the same plant is not grown in the same field each year and pests cannot build up in the soil.
- crops can be weeded by hand
- farmers can vary seed planting times.

All these methods may be more labour intensive but they reduce the need to use chemicals that some people believe may be harmful.

The success of organic farming may depend on people being prepared to pay slightly higher prices for their food. In the developed world this may be possible but in the developing world it may be harder to convince farmers that they should not use intensive methods.

▲ *Tomatoes growing in hydroponics*

Pest control

Instead of using pesticides and insecticides to control pests it is possible to use living organisms. This is called **biological control**. Often the organism used is a predator that eats the pest. For example, farmers growing crops in glasshouses can buy packets of spiders. These spiders are released in the glasshouse and they eat a pest called the red spider mite.

Care must be taken when biological control organisms are introduced because they may have effects on the food web. If they wipe out the pest completely then this may mean that other animals in the food web may starve and die out.

Sometimes the control organism or other animals may increase in numbers and become pests themselves.

◀ *A ladybird eats an aphid*

Keywords

battery farming • biological control • hydroponics • intensive farming • organic farming • pesticide

Prickly pear

Cane toad

You win some and you lose some

Many of the advantages and disadvantages of biological control have been learnt in Australia. This is because Australia has been an island for a long time and has an unusual selection of plants and animals living there. This means that any new organisms that are introduced can rapidly become pests. The first real success was controlling a plant pest called the prickly pear.

This plant grows naturally in countries such as Argentina but was introduced into Australia by man and soon spread. By 1925 it was completely out of control, spreading at the rate of half a million hectares a year.

In 1925 massive amounts of chemical poisons were used to try to kill the prickly pear but it was still spreading. The Australians had to do something so they introduced a caterpillar from Argentina called cactoblastis. After careful testing the caterpillars were first released in 1926. They started to eat their way through the prickly pears and within six years the plant was under control.

But there have been failures. Fresh from the prickly pear success, the Australians introduced 102 cane toads in 1935. The idea was for the toads to eat cane beetles, which were pests of sugar cane. The trouble was, the toads eat other food as well. They reproduce really quickly and produce poison from glands on their backs. There are now millions of the toads in Australia and they are still increasing in numbers, threatening native frogs.

Questions

1. What is meant by biological control?
2. Why do you think that the Australians looked in Argentina for a control animal for the prickly pear?
3. Why was cactoblastis tested before it was released?
4. Cactoblastis only eats prickly pear but the cane toad eats many different foods. What lessons do you think scientists have learnt from this?
5. Write down one advantage and one possible disadvantage of biological control using these examples from Australia.

To rot or not to rot?

▲ Otzi the iceman

In this item you will find out

- what affects the rate of decay
- the type of organisms that cause decay
- some of the methods used to preserve food

Plants and animals are all made from organic material. When this material dies it starts to break down or **decay**.

In September 1991, two people walking in the mountains near the border between Austria and Italy made an amazing discovery. Half buried in the ice was the body of a dead man. They thought that he had died recently of an accident or even murder. When people looked more closely at the body they found that he had a copper axe. They soon realised that this body was very old – in fact it turned out to be 5300 years old!

The preservation of the iceman is an extreme example. However, in the case of our food, most of it has to be preserved so that it can reach our tables without breaking down first. Prawns are a good example – they last 10 days if kept at 0°C, but only 2 days at 10°C.

All this shows that dead animals and plants break down very easily. Sometimes we want to speed up this process. A gardener wants dead plants to break down quickly to make compost so provides the best conditions for this by building a compost heap.

But in the food industry we want to slow down or prevent decay. This may involve controlling the temperature that food is kept at but there are many other methods. The aim is to make sure that the food does not deteriorate before we eat it.

▲ Seafood kept on ice at a fishmonger's

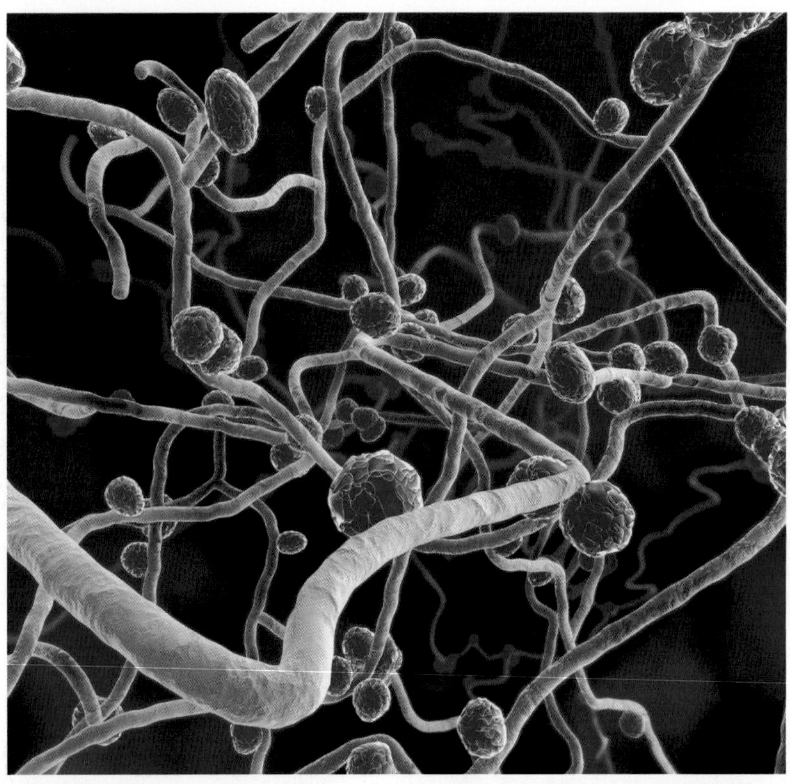

▲ *Fungus can break down dead organic material*

Organisms that cause decay

Organisms that break down dead organic material are called decomposers. They are very important because they allow chemical elements to be recycled. If decomposers did not do this all the chemical elements needed for life would build up inside dead organisms.

The two main groups of decomposers are bacteria and fungi. They release enzymes on the dead organic material and then take up the partially digested chemicals.

This type of feeding is called **saprophytic nutrition** and the bacteria and fungi are called **saprophytes**.

There are organisms that help the decomposers to do their job. Animals such as earthworms, maggots and woodlice feed on pieces of dead and decaying material (**detritus**). They are called **detritivores**.

Detritivores increase the rate of decay by finely breaking up material so it has a larger surface area. This means that it can be broken down faster by the decomposers.

a **Suggest why a piece of apple that has been dipped into disinfectant would decay faster than a piece that had not been treated.**

b **Suggest what effect temperature would have on the rate of decomposition caused by the saprophyte's enzymes.**

◀ *Worms are detritivores*

Rate of decay

In order for organic material to decay, several things need to be present: microorganisms, oxygen and water. Oxygen is needed for the aerobic respiration of the microbes, while water is needed to allow substances to dissolve and the chemical reactions of respiration to occur. It also needs to be warm enough.

The rate of decay can be changed if the temperature changes, or if there is a lack of oxygen or water. If it is too hot or too cold, too dry or lacking in oxygen, decomposition will not occur. This is because the respiration and growth of the microbes will be slowed down.

▲ *Pickling food helps preserve it*

Preserving food

The food that we eat is organic material and so is a target for decomposers to break down. To prevent this happening we use different techniques to reduce the rate of decay. This is called **food preservation**. Most food preservation techniques work by removing or altering one of the factors that the microbes need. Some examples are shown in the table.

Preservation method	Details of method	How decay is prevented
canning	food is heated in a can to about 100 °C and then the can is sealed	the high temperature kills the microorganisms; water and oxygen cannot get into the can after it is sealed
cooling	food is kept in refrigerators at about 5 °C	the low temperature slows down the growth and respiration of microorganisms
drying	dry air is passed over the food, sometimes, in a partial vacuum	microorganisms cannot respire or reproduce
freezing	food is kept in a freezer at about –18 °C.	microorganisms cannot respire or reproduce because their chemical reactions are slowed down
adding salt or sugar	food is stored exposed to a high sugar or salt concentration.	the sugar or salt draws water out of the microorganisms
adding vinegar	the food is soaked in vinegar	the vinegar is too acidic for the microorganisms preventing their enzymes from working

Amazing fact

After Lord Nelson was killed during the battle of Trafalgar, his body was brought back to England in a barrel of brandy in order to preserve it.

c **Why do you think that food still goes bad in a refrigerator?**

d **Suggest why salt or sugar draws water out of the microorganisms.**

Some of these food preservation techniques have been used for thousands of years. This was particularly important in hot countries where decay would happen rapidly.

Food can also be preserved by adding artificial chemicals or additives to the food. These chemicals are not popular with everybody. Some people say that they add unpleasant flavours to the food. Others claim that they have side effects on the body.

Keywords

decay • detritivore • detritus • food preservation • saprophyte • saprophytic nutrition

Astronaut ice cream

It is now possible to buy packets of ice cream that do not need to be kept in the freezer. This ice cream tastes just like ice cream except it is not cold.

It was developed for astronauts to take into space and uses the process of freeze-drying. The ice cream is made in the normal way by freezing the ingredients in order to change the water into ice. The machine then pumps out the air, creating a vacuum. This lowers the pressure inside the ice cream. If the ice cream is then slightly warmed, the ice turns straight into water vapour without becoming liquid. This is called sublimation. The water vapour is removed, leaving dry astronaut ice cream!

Freeze-drying is useful for a number of products as well for as making ice cream. This is because the food does not spoil so easily once it has been treated. It is also used to preserve certain medicines. Another advantage is that freeze-dried food is lighter. Freeze-drying will not prevent the food spoiling indefinitely because there is still a small amount of water in the food.

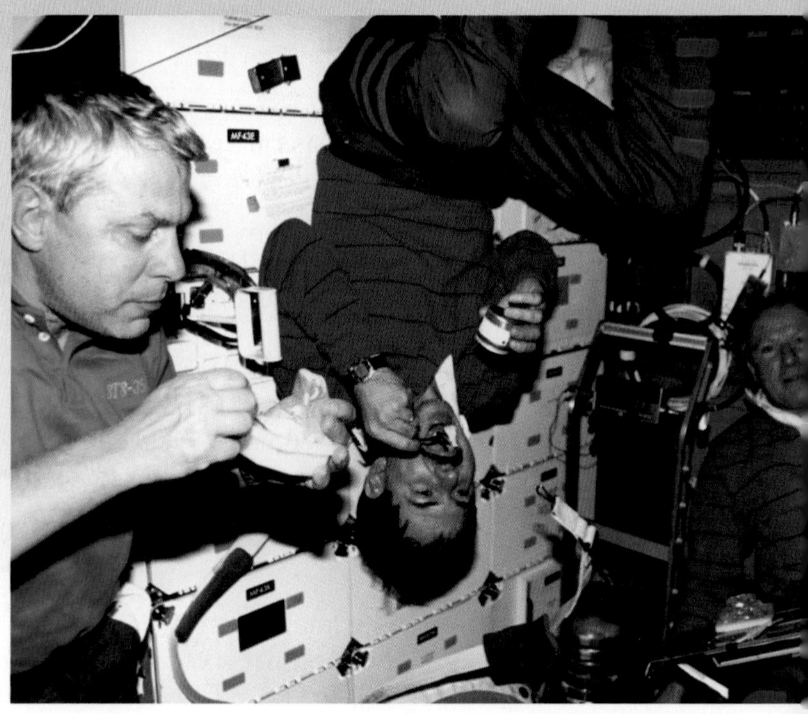

Questions

1. How is sublimation different from melting?
2. Why is food lighter once it has been freeze-dried? Why is this an advantage?
3. Suggest why food such as freeze-dried coffee is packed in airtight containers.
4. Explain why freeze-dried food will still spoil eventually.

Cycles for life

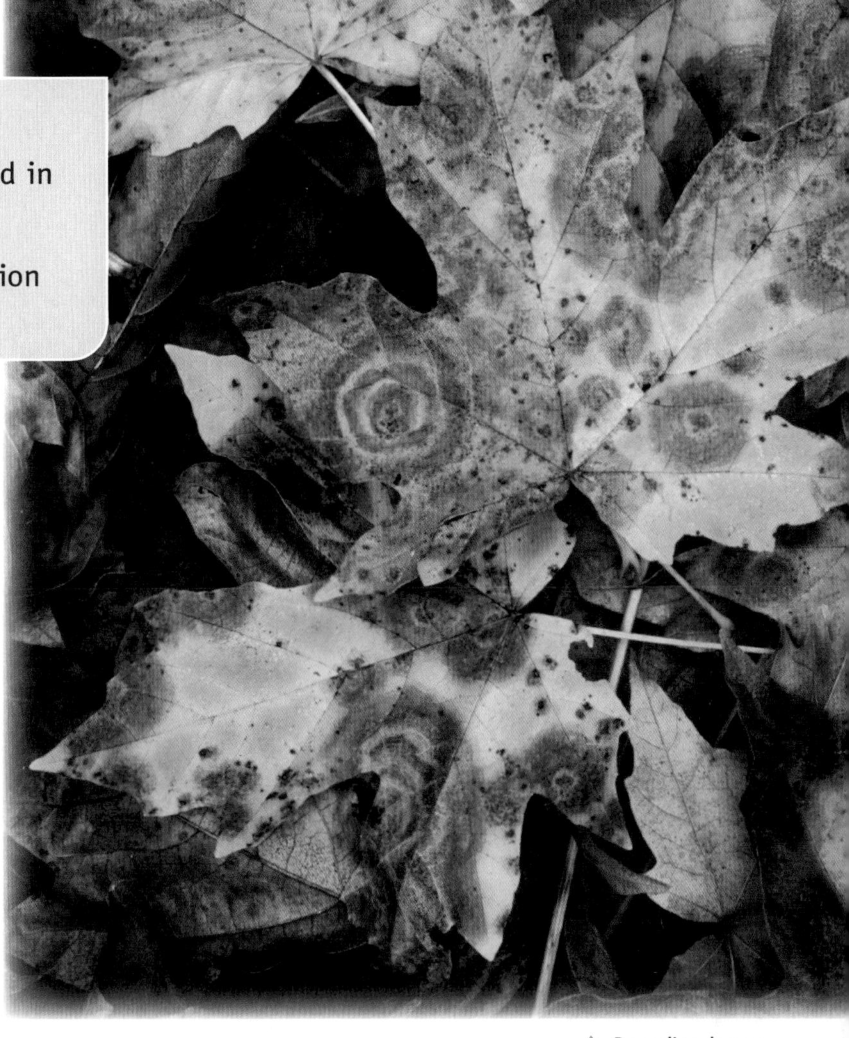

▲ Recycling leaves

In this item you will find out

- how carbon is recycled both on land and in the sea
- how nitrogen is recycled due to the action of bacteria

Recycling is becoming big business. Scientists have been getting very excited recently about a new development called nanotechnology. A nanometre is one thousand millionth of a metre and this is smaller than many atoms. Scientists now think that they can make structures about the size of 1–100 nanometres that can perform many roles. One important role that they are being designed for is to recycle minerals from many different materials.

a **Why do you think that scientists are under pressure to find ways of recycling materials?**

But humans are only beginners when it comes to recycling; bacteria and fungi have been in action for millions of years. Their job is to decompose dead plant and animal material and make all the chemical elements available again for living organisms. Without them, we would run out of carbon, nitrogen, oxygen and all the other elements that are needed for life.

Nitrogen often causes the largest problem for living organisms. Although we are surrounded by nitrogen it is not easy to use and it is desperately needed by plants. In 1909, the German scientist Fritz Haber developed a process to combine nitrogen from the air with hydrogen.

The ammonia that is produced can be turned into fertiliser for plants. Now about half of the nitrogen needed by all the plants grown in the world comes from the Haber Process.

However, providing all the energy needed for the Haber Process results in pollution, and so does the use of the fertilisers that are being produced.

Amazing fact

In every kilogram of soil there are about 5 g of living organisms many of which are microorganisms.

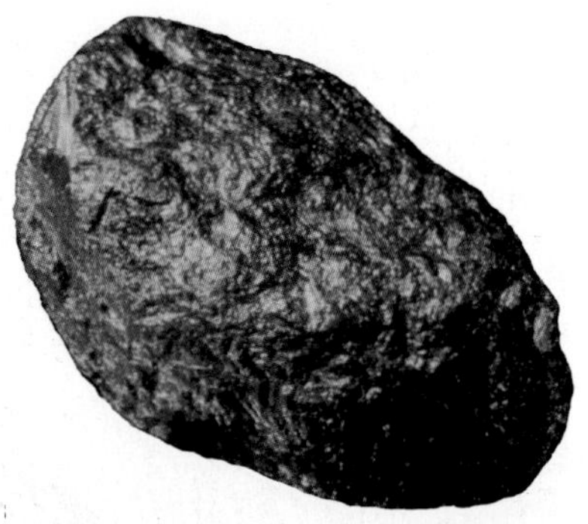

▲ Graphite is a form of carbon

The carbon cycle

The element carbon is the basis for all molecules that make up living organisms. Carbohydrates, proteins and fats all contain carbon. In nature, pure carbon is found as diamonds and graphite, but animals and plants cannot use this carbon.

The main source of carbon is carbon dioxide in the air but there is only one way that it can get into living organisms. This happens when plants photosynthesise.

This process traps the carbon inside carbon compounds and it is then passed from organism to organism along food chains or food webs. It returns to the air in carbon dioxide when plants and animals use the carbon compounds in respiration. This cycling of carbon is shown in the diagram.

The decomposers, bacteria and fungi in the soil, also release carbon dioxide when they use dead material for respiration.

Sometimes dead animals and plants do not decompose but over millions of years they are changed into fossil fuels. This process of fossilisation traps carbon in coal, oil and gas. Burning (combustion) of these fossil fuels releases this carbon again as carbon dioxide.

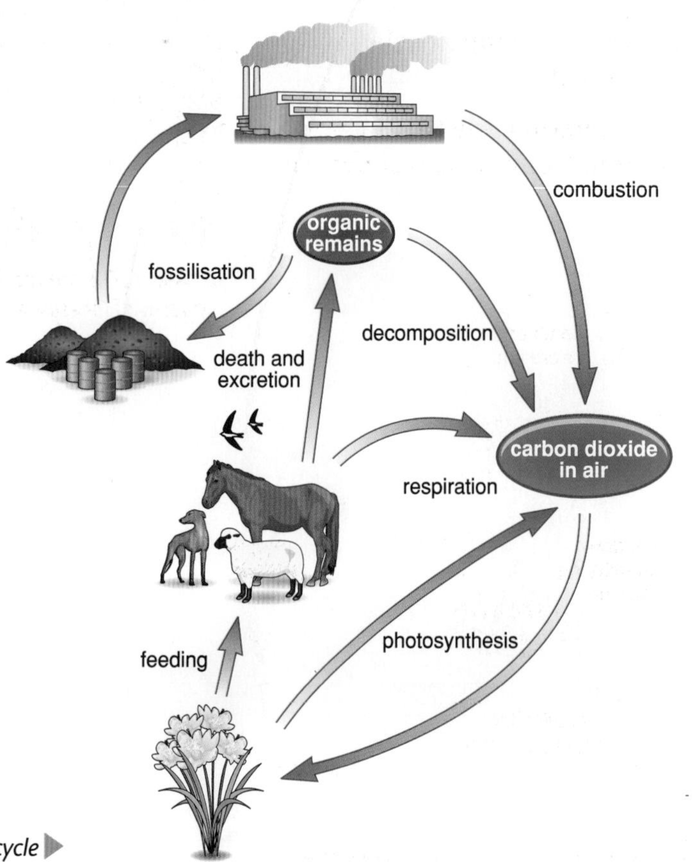

The carbon cycle ▶

Carbon in the sea

Carbon can also get locked up by organisms in the sea. Microscopic plants use carbon dioxide in photosynthesis and marine organisms use carbon to make shells. These shells are made of **carbonates**. When the organisms die the shells sink and get compressed at the bottom of the sea. They turn to limestone rock.

b **What do you think compresses the shells?**

Over the years this limestone rock can get worn away by weathering or more suddenly by volcanic activity. Carbon dioxide is released into the air and joins the cycle again.

▲ *These cliffs are made from chalk – a form of limestone*

The nitrogen cycle

Plants and animals are surrounded by air that contains 78% nitrogen but they cannot use it directly because it is too unreactive.

Plants take in nitrogen as nitrates through their roots and use the nitrates to make nitrogen compounds (proteins) for growth. This protein passes along the food chain or web as animals eat plants and other animals.

c **Explain why the quantity of nitrogen in the animals decreases along the food chain.**

Eventually all this trapped nitrogen is released when decomposers break down nitrogen compounds in dead plants and animals.

The nitrogen cycle is more complicated than the carbon cycle because four different types of bacteria are involved instead of just one. This is shown in the diagram below.

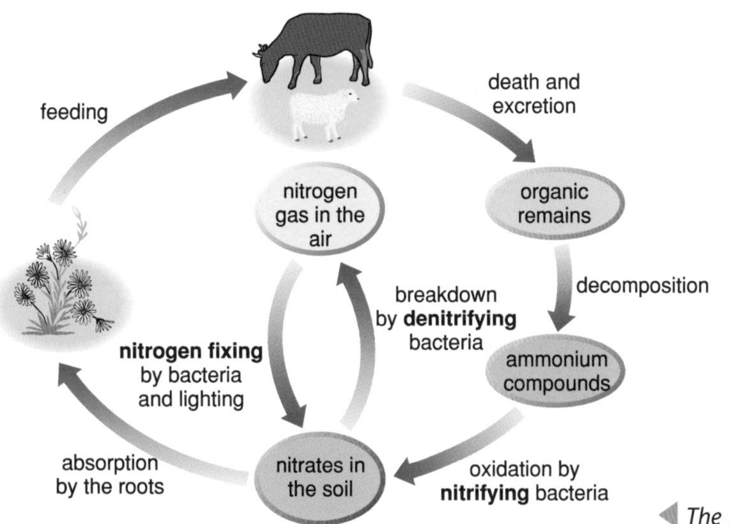

◀ *The nitrogen cycle*

Soil bacteria and fungi, acting as decomposers, convert proteins and **urea** into ammonia. This is poisonous to plants but **nitrifying bacteria** turn it into nitrates.

Denitrifying bacteria turn some of these nitrates into nitrogen gas. **Nitrogen-fixing bacteria** that live in the roots of plants of the pea family can make use of the nitrogen gas in the air and return it to the cycle. This is called fixing nitrogen. Lightning can also fix nitrogen.

d **Nitrogen is very unreactive. Why do you think nitrogen can react when there is a lightning strike?**

Keywords

carbonate • denitrifying bacteria • nitrifying bacteria • nitrogen-fixing bacteria • recycling • urea

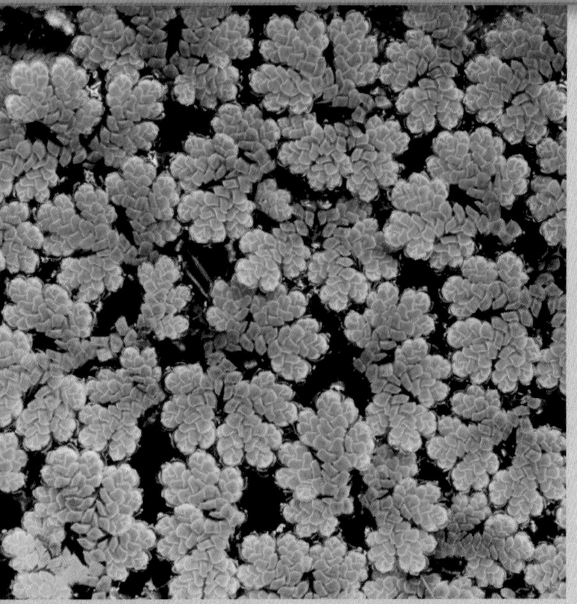

▲ *Azolla* fern

▼ *The bacteria that live in* Azolla *leaves*

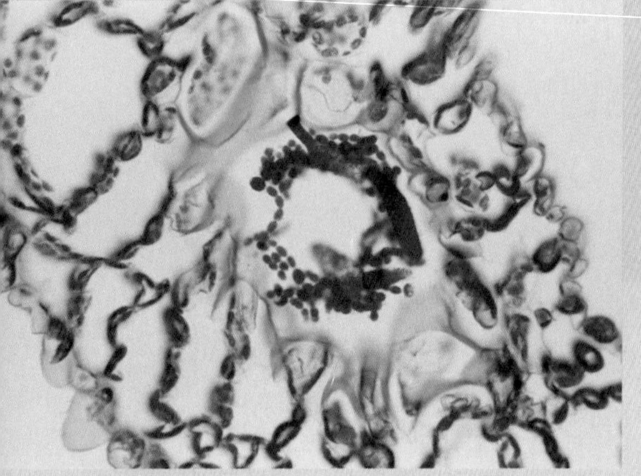

Feeding fish and rice

A little red fern is proving to be a very valuable plant for the Chinese. *Azolla* is a tiny fern that floats on the surface of lakes and rivers. The important thing is that the fern contains bacteria that live inside the leaves. These bacteria can fix nitrogen and so provide the fern with nitrogen-containing chemicals.

The Chinese have started to put this partnership to work in their rice fields. Rice is grown in large flooded fields. The Chinese also farm fish in the same flooded fields. This provides them with extra food and the fish eat the rice pests.

The problem is that there is not much food for the fish in the fields. This has been solved by adding *Azolla*. The fish eat the fern, which is rich in amino acids, and grow quickly. The fish also help the rice to grow by producing nitrogen-rich faeces that act as a fertiliser.

The yields that can be achieved are shown in the table.

Organisms growing in fields	Yield of organism from the field (kg/ha)	
	Rice yield	Fish yield
rice only	6930	–
rice and *Azolla*	8085	–
rice and fish	7656	150
rice, fish and *Azolla*	9324	350

Questions

1 The bacteria in *Azolla* fix nitrogen for the fern. What does Azolla make using use these nitrogen-containing chemicals?

2 Suggest what the fern gives the bacteria in return.

3 Construct a food web to include rice, fish, *Azolla* and rice pests.

4 The nitrogen in the fish faeces becomes available to the rice. Explain how this can happen.

5 Work out the total yield of fish and rice per hectare when they are grown without Azolla and when grown with *Azolla*.

6 What is the percentage increase produced by using *Azolla*?

B4a

1 The diagram shows a section through a leaf.

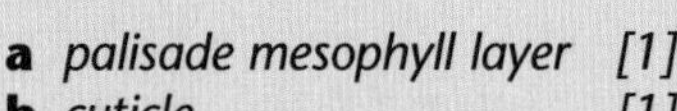

Write down the letter on the diagram that matches the following structures.

a palisade mesophyll layer [1]
b cuticle [1]
c a structure that supplies the leaf with water [1]
d a structure that allows gaseous exchange [1]

2 Explain how each of the following features help a leaf to photosynthesise.

a a broad shape [2]
b being thin [2]
c palisade cells with many chloroplasts [2]

3 A pupil wanted to investigate the properties of some leaves that he had collected from a tree. First he looked at a leaf. He noticed that it was greener on the top surface than on the bottom. He then dipped a leaf into hot water. He noticed that small air bubbles appeared on the bottom surface of the leaf but not on the top. He then wanted to look at the surface of the leaf but his teacher told him that he would need to make an impression of the surface rather than putting the leaf under the microscope.

a Use your knowledge of leaf structure to explain why leaves look greener on the top than on the bottom. [2]
b Where in the leaf does the air in the air bubbles come from? [1]
c Explain why there are only air bubbles on the bottom of the leaf. [2]
d Suggest why is it necessary to make an impression of the leaf to see details of the leaf surface. [2]

B4b

1 The diagram below shows two solutions in a glass beaker. They are separated by a partially permeable membrane. In compartment A there is a concentrated sucrose solution. In compartment B there is distilled water.

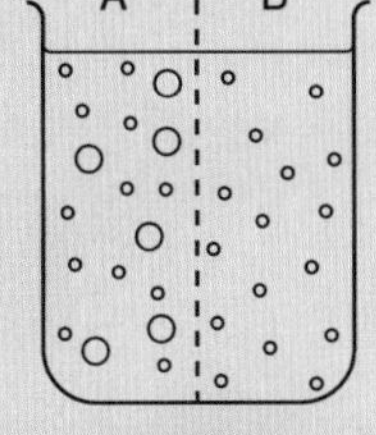

a Copy the diagram and draw an arrow to show which way the water will move. [1]
b What is the name of the process that causes the water to move? [1]
c The sugar molecules cannot move through the partially permeable membrane. Why is this? [1]

2 What is the difference between osmosis and diffusion? [2]

3 Explain why animal cells burst when placed in water but plant cells do not. [2]

B4c

1 Copy and complete the following sentences by entering a word or words in each of the lines.

In a plant stem the xylem and phloem are arranged in groups called __(1)__ . In the stem the __(2)__ is on the outside and the __(3)__ is on the inside of each of these groups. The xylem transports __(4)__ up the stem and the phloem transports __(5)__ in __(6)__ directions. The evaporation of water out of the leaves is called __(7)__ . [7]

2 The potometer shown on page 50 is used for another experiment. This time the leaves are not covered with grease but the experiment is carried out under different conditions. Some results are shown in the table.

Conditions	Distance water moved from start position in ten minutes/mm
normal lab conditions	30
with a kettle boiling in the room	25
with the kettle boiling and the lights off	20

a Explain why the water moves along the tube in the potometer. [2]
b Fully explain the results of this experiment. [5]
c Explain what would happen if the experiment was repeated with a fan pointed at the plant. [3]

3 Explain how the following tissues are adapted for the job that they do in a plant.

a phloem [1] **b** xylem [2]

B4d

1 Jane buys a packet of fertiliser to use on her garden. On the packet it says:

'This fertiliser contains all the minerals needed for your plant to grow. Simply dissolve in some water in a watering can and water the soil. Only use a small amount of the powder, plants are not used to too many minerals.'

a Why should water and a watering can be used to apply the fertiliser? [2]
b Why are plants not used to too many minerals? [1]
c Which mineral in the fertiliser would be needed for cell growth? [1]

2 *An experiment was carried out to investigate the effect of growing plants with different minerals available. The results are shown in the photograph on page 54.*

a *Suggest why each of the solutions in this experiment was made using distilled water and not tap water.* [2]
b *Which plant grew best and why?* [2]
c *What is the difference in colour between the nitrogen-free plant (–N) and the plant grown with all the necessary minerals (complete)?* [1]
d *What effects does the lack of phosphate (–P) have on the plant?* [2]

3 *The following apparatus can be used to see how fast plants take up minerals. The minerals are taken up by active transport. The graph shows how fast the minerals are taken up.*

plant
oxygen or nitrogen
solution containing minerals
Uptake of minerals
Time
+ oxygen
+ nitrogen

a *Why is active transport used to take up minerals?* [1]
b *What is the difference in the result when nitrogen is bubbled into the solution rather than oxygen?* [1]
c *Explain the difference in uptake when nitrogen is used rather than oxygen.* [3]

B4e

1 *Several animals live in a garden. The table shows what they eat.*

Animal	Food
snail	grass
rabbit	grass
mice	grass seeds

Animal	Food
fox	rabbit, mice
blackbird	snail

a *Which organism in the table is a producer?* [1]
b *Draw a food web for the organisms listed in the table.* [3]
c *Many tiny fleas live in the fur of the fox. Draw a pyramid of numbers for this food chain: grass plants → rabbits → fox → fleas* [2]
d *Draw a pyramid of biomass for the same food chain and explain why it looks different from the pyramid of numbers.* [3]

2 *The diagram shows energy being lost as it passes through a food chain.*

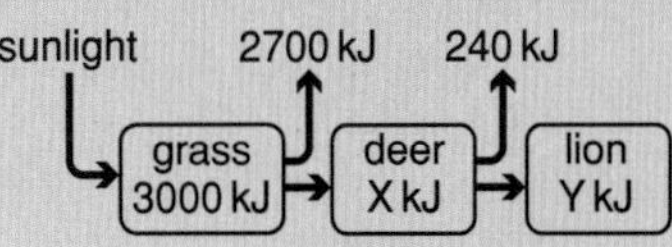

a *Calculate the amount of energy available to the deer for growth.* [1]
b *Calculate the amount of energy available to the lion.* [1]
c *What percentage of the original energy from the plant reaches the lion?* [2]
d *Name two ways in which energy is lost by the deer.* [1]
e *Use the information on the diagram to explain why food chains rarely have more than five levels.* [2]

3 *The diagram shows a process for converting biomass into a fuel called gasohol.*

corn extract → fermenter → alcohol → gasohol
yeast → fermenter
petrol → gasohol

a *Corn extract is the biomass that is placed in the fermenter. Where has the energy that is trapped in the corn come from?* [1]
b *Why is yeast added to the corn extract?* [2]
c *This process is used in countries such as Brazil. These are hot countries with long hours of sunshine. They do, however, have limited supplies of petrol. Explain why the use of gasohol as a fuel is ideal in countries such as Brazil.* [2]

B4f

1 *Tomato plants can be grown in glasshouses. They are often grown without soil.*

a *Why are tomatoes often grown in glasshouses?* [1]
b *What name is given to the method of growing tomatoes without soil?* [1]
c *Explain why these two methods mean that tomatoes can be grown in areas where they could not otherwise have been grown.* [2]

2 *A small red spider often feeds on the leaves of tomato plants. It is possible to control the red spider by releasing another type of spider called Phytoseiulus into the glasshouse.*

a *Suggest how Phytoseiulus controls the red spider.* [1]
b *What is the name given to this type of control?* [1]
c *Why is this type of control ideal for a greenhouse but less easy to use in a field?* [1]
d *Why must the owner of the greenhouse stop using pesticides when he uses Phytoseiulus?* [1]

3 *An organic farmer may use a range of different methods to try to increase his yield. Explain what is meant by the following methods and how they can increase yields.*

a *crop rotation* [3] **b** *manuring the soil* [3]

4 *Intensive farmers use a range of different methods compared to organic farmers.*

a *Suggest why battery farming can produce greater yields of meat from animals.* *[2]*

b *Why are some people against battery farming?* *[2]*

B4g

1 *Below are types of food preservation techniques and explanations of how they work. Link each technique with the explanation of how it works.*

1 freezing	*a microorganisms are killed by heat*
2 adding vinegar	*b temperature is too cold*
3 adding salt	*c pH is too low*
4 canning	*d microorganisms are dried out* *[?]*

2 *Different organisms are responsible for decomposing dead leaves. These are:*

- *earthworms, which may be about 5 mm in diameter*
- *small insects, such as maggots and woodlice, which may be 2–4 mm wide*
- *microorganisms which are smaller than 0.005 mm wide.*

A scientist decided to investigate how fast leaves decompose. He put leaves into three different bags and buried them in the soil. Each bag was made of nylon with different sized holes. Every two months he dug up the bags and measured how much of the leaves had disappeared.

Here are his results.

	Disappearance of the leaves/%		
Month	***Bag with 7 mm***	***Bag with 4 mm***	***Bag with 0.005 mm***
June	0	0	0
August	25	8	0
October	70	20	2
December	75	25	3

a *Which of the three types of organisms can get into each of the bags?* *[1]*

b *In which bag do the leaves decay the fastest?* *[1]*

c *Explain why the leaves decay at different rates in the three different bags.* *[4]*

d *How does the rate of decay change in November and December compared to July to October?* *[1]*

e *Explain this difference in rate.* *[2]*

3 *Many bacteria and fungi are saprophytes.*

a *What does a saprophyte feed on?* *[1]*

b *How does a saprophyte digest its food?* *[2]*

B4h

1 *The diagram shows part of the carbon cycle.*

carbon in the air
A
B
C
D
E
organic waste

a *Write down the name of the process represented by each of the letters on the diagram.*
Choose your processes from this list. You can use each process once, more than once or not at all.

decomposing **eating** **fossilising** **photosynthesising** **respiring** *[5]*

The carbon may get trapped in fossil fuels.

b *How does this happen?* *[2]*

c *How can this carbon rejoin the carbon cycle?* *[1]*

2 *Read the following passage about nitrogen and answer the questions that follow.*

Nitrogen is an important element for all organisms from grass to giraffes and pansies to pigs. All these organisms use nitrogen for growth. But they all have a problem. Although they are surrounded by plenty of nitrogen in the air, they cannot use it very easily. Animals rely on plants to get nitrogen from the soil. The plants absorb this nitrogen combined in minerals. The animals can then eat the plants!

a *What do animals and plants make from nitrogen that is so important for growth?* *[1]*

b *The article says that there is plenty of nitrogen in the air. What is the percentage?* *[1]*

c *Why is it so difficult for animals and plants to use this nitrogen?* *[1]*

d *What is the main mineral taken up by plants that contains nitrogen?* *[1]*

3 *The diagram shows part of the nitrogen cycle.*

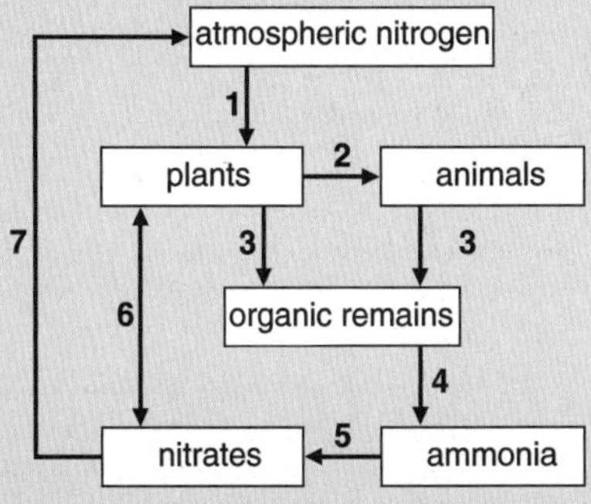

a *Write down the type of bacteria that carry out each of the processes 1, 4 and 5.* *[3]*

b *The bacteria carrying out process 4 are converting chemicals in organic remains into ammonia.*
Write down the name of one of these chemicals. *[1]*

c *Explain how lightning can play a role in the nitrogen cycle.* *[2]*

C3 The Periodic Table

- 200 years ago chemists knew that some elements have properties that are quite different from each other, while others have similar properties. But they could not see any logic or order to the properties of the elements.
- A Periodic Table of the elements was put together by Dmitri Mendeleev in 1869. He placed elements in order of increasing atomic mass. His brilliant idea was to leave gaps for elements that had not yet been discovered. Today we use a modern version of Mendeleev's Periodic Table.

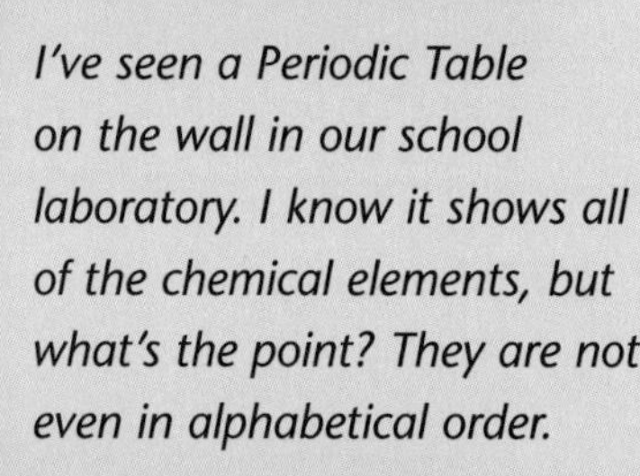

It's a way of putting the elements in order to show how they behave. It's all to do with the properties that each element has, and which elements have similar properties.

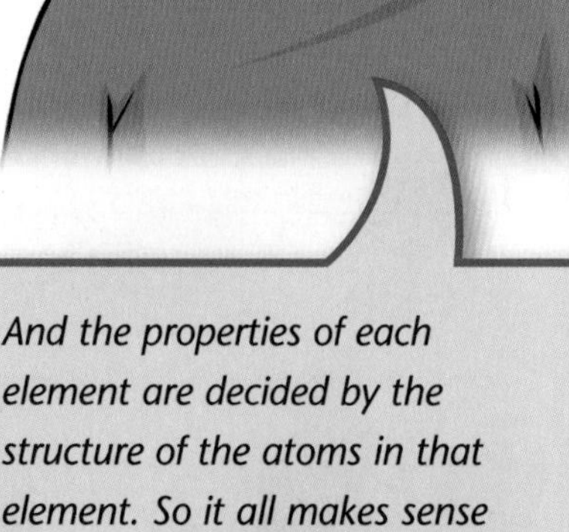

What you need to know

- All substances are made from elements.
- Elements are made up of atoms.
- Elements have different properties.

Atoms and elements

In this item you will find out

- about sub-atomic particles and their place in atoms
- the connections between atomic structure and the Periodic Table
- about the structure of isotopes

Have you ever seen an atom? You may think that atoms are too small to see, but using modern technology we can view images of some of the very largest atoms. The electron micrograph shows atoms in a crystal of uranium.

It is difficult to imagine how small atoms are. A 2 cm cube of iron contains about 600 000 000 000 000 000 000 000 iron atoms.

In the centre of an **atom** is the nucleus. This is where the **protons** are. **Electrons** are outside the nucleus, arranged in shells. Most atoms also contain **neutrons** in the nucleus.

These three sub-atomic particles have different properties.

Sub-atomic particle	Where found	Relative mass	Relative charge
proton	in the nucleus	1	+1
neutron	in the nucleus	1	0
electron	outside the nucleus	0.0005	–1

Because an atom has equal numbers of positive protons and negative electrons, the whole atom is neutral.

a **Electrons were discovered in 1887 and protons in 1911, but neutrons were not discovered until 1932. Suggest why it took longer for neutrons to be discovered.**

Amazing fact

About 2500 years ago the Greek philosopher Democritus proposed that the physical world consisted of atoms. He had no scientific evidence to support these ideas, which were discounted by Aristotle, the most influential man of this time.

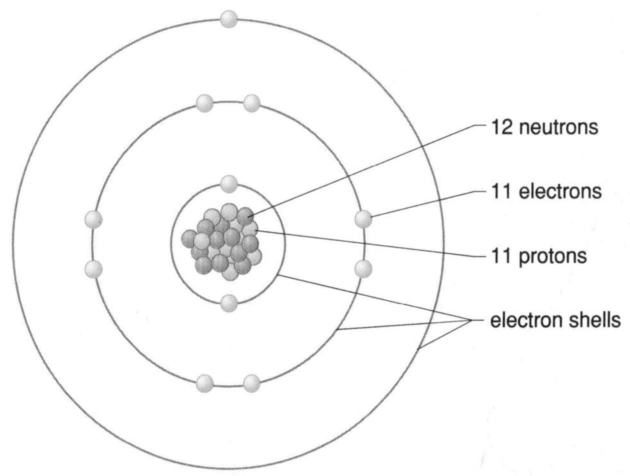

▲ *Inside a sodium atom*

Putting elements in order

Each element contains just one type of atom. Each atom in an element contains the same number of protons. This is called the **atomic number** of the element. It can also be called the **proton number**.

In the Periodic Table, elements are arranged in order of their atomic number.

These are the elements in the second row of the Periodic Table.

Element	Lithium	Beryllium	Boron	Carbon	Nitrogen	Oxygen	Fluorine	Neon
symbol	Li	Be	B	C	N	O	F	Ne
protons	3	4	5	6	7	8	9	10
electrons	3	4	5	6	7	8	9	10

The nucleus of an atom of beryllium contains four protons and five neutrons. If you add them together they come to nine. This is the **mass number** of beryllium. It can also be called the **nucleon number**. The mass number of an element is found by adding together the number of protons and neutrons.

Amazing fact

If a football was a hydrogen atom then its nucleus would be the size of a grain of sand yet account for most of its mass.

b **An atom of fluorine has 9 protons and 10 neutrons. What is the mass number of fluorine?**

Electron structures

As you found out earlier, electrons are arranged in shells around the nucleus of each atom. Each electron shell can hold a maximum number of electrons. The first shell can hold one or two electrons while the second and third shells can hold from one to eight.

When one shell is full, electrons start to fill the next shell. Since the number of electrons in a neutral atom is the same as the number of protons, the electron structures can be worked out from the atomic number of the element.

Some examples are given in the table.

Element	Symbol	Atomic number	Electrons	Electron arrangement
lithium	Li	3	3	2,1
carbon	C	6	6	2,4
neon	Ne	10	10	2,8
sodium	Na	11	11	2,8,1
chlorine	Cl	17	17	2,8,7
calcium	Ca	20	20	2,8,8,2

c **Use a Periodic Table to help you work out the electron structures of each of these elements:**

argon magnesium oxygen potassium silicon

Chemical shorthand

You can use a shorthand convention to give details of the sub-atomic particles in an atom. The diagram on the right shows the shorthand notation for an atom of carbon, which has six protons and six neutrons. The total number of protons and neutrons adds up to a mass number of 12.

$$^{12}_{6}C$$

▲ *Shorthand notation for carbon-12*

When atoms gain or lose electrons they form ions. Each positive charge indicates the loss of one electron from an atom. Each negative charge indicates the gain of one electron by an atom.

A sodium atom $^{23}_{11}Na$ has 11 protons, 11 electrons and 12 neutrons.

A sodium ion $^{23}_{11}Na^{+}$ has 11 protons, 10 electrons and 12 neutrons.

d **Work out the number of protons, electrons and neutrons in these particles:**

$^{14}_{7}N$ $^{19}_{9}F$ $^{27}_{13}Al$ $^{7}_{3}Li$ $^{35}_{17}Cl$ $^{24}_{12}Mg^{2+}$ $^{16}_{8}O^{2-}$ $^{27}_{13}Al^{3+}$

Isotopes

In each element every atom has the same number of protons. But in most elements some of the atoms have a different number of neutrons from others. Atoms of the same element with the same atomic number but with different numbers of neutrons, and so different mass numbers, are called **isotopes**.

Here is some information about the isotopes of carbon.

Isotope	Carbon-12	Carbon-13	Carbon-14
Atomic number	6	6	6
Mass number	12	13	14
Percentage of isotope	98.9	1.1	trace

Some isotopes, such as carbon-14, are radioactive. Over a period of time they decay to form other elements, becoming less radioactive as they do so.

From information in the table it is possible to work out the numbers of each sub-atomic particle in these atoms. For example, an atom of carbon-14 has six protons, so it must also have six electrons. It has 14 – 6 = 8 neutrons.

Use the numbers of protons, electrons and neutrons shown below to work out the identity of each isotope.

(i) 8 protons, 8 electrons, 10 neutrons

(ii) 19 protons, 19 electrons, 22 neutrons

(iii) 7 protons, 7 electrons, 8 neutrons

(iv) 92 protons, 92 electrons, 143 neutrons

Examiner's tip

The atomic number of an element tells you how many protons are in an atom, which is the same as the number of electrons. A positive ion will have fewer, and a negative ion more, than this number of electrons.

Keywords

atom • atomic number • electron • isotope • mass number • neutron • nucleon number • proton • proton number

New elements from old

▶ *This cyclotron was used to make the new superheavy elements*

Two new 'superheavy' elements were recently made by bombarding lead atoms with energy-packed krypton atoms at the rate of two trillion per second.

After 11 days, the scientists working at the Lawrence Berkeley National Laboratory, USA, had produced just three atoms of element 118. They each contained 118 protons and 175 neutrons in their nuclei.

The new atoms decayed almost instantly to element 116, which was also short-lived. But for that brief moment, they were the only three atoms of these elements ever to have existed on Earth.

In nature, no element heavier than uranium, with 92 protons and 146 neutrons, can normally be found. Scientists can make heavier ones by colliding two large nuclei together and hoping that they will form a new, heavier nucleus for a short time.

Synthetic elements are often short-lived but provide scientists with valuable insights into the structure of atomic nuclei. They also offer opportunities to study the chemical properties of the elements heavier than uranium.

Element 118 takes less than a thousandth of a second to decay by emitting an alpha particle. This leaves behind an isotope of element 116 which contains 116 protons and 173 neutrons. This element is also radioactive, alpha-decaying to an isotope of element 114. The chain of successive alpha decays continues until you get element 106.

Questions

1. How do scientists make elements heavier than uranium?
2. Why is it useful to make these elements?
3. For how long did the new element 118 last?
4. What happened to this new element?

Interesting ions

▲ *Food would be boring without salt*

In this item you will find out

- how to describe the formation of ions in terms of electron arrangement
- how to work out formulae for ionic compounds
- how to explain the properties of ionic compounds

In the time of the Roman Empire soldiers were often paid with salt. If you did a good job you were 'worth your salt'. We still use this expression today.

Can you imagine a world without salt? Not only would your potato crisps or chips taste odd, but lots of other things would be difficult to do.

Only about five per cent of the world's annual salt production ends up as seasoning at the dinner table. The vast majority is used in numerous commercial applications like manufacturing pulp and paper, setting dyes in textiles and fabric, and producing soaps and detergents.

Amazing fact

Over 5 million tonnes of salt are produced in the United Kingdom each year.

Sodium chloride is an ionic compound. This means that the sodium and chlorine are joined together by **ionic bonding**. When the compound is formed, the atoms form positive and negative ions.

There are lots of ionic compounds. Sodium chloride is just one example. Some other examples are sodium oxide, magnesium chloride and magnesium oxide.

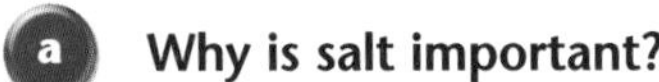

a **Why is salt important?**

b **Salt is mined as rock salt, a mixture of sodium chloride and grit. Many tons of rock salt are spread on roads during the winter. Suggest why this is done.**

▶ *Making soap*

Forming ions

Ions are atoms with a positive or a negative charge. Positive ions are formed when an atom loses one or more electrons.

A sodium atom loses one electron to form a sodium ion. Since one negative electron has been lost, and no positive protons have been lost, the ion has a single positive charge, Na^+.

When a magnesium atom forms an ion, it loses two electrons. This gives the magnesium ion a 2+ charge, Mg^{2+}.

Metal ions have positive charges. Non-metal ions have negative charges. A chlorine atom gains one electron but does not gain a proton. So a chloride ion has a negative charge, Cl^-. An oxygen atom gains two electrons to form an oxide ion, O^{2-}.

Atom or ion	Formula	Protons	Electrons	Electron arrangement
sodium atom	Na	11	11	2,8,1
sodium ion	Na^+	11	10	2,8
chlorine atom	Cl	17	17	2,8,7
chloride ion	Cl^-	17	18	2,8,8
magnesium atom	Mg	12	12	2,8,2
magnesium ion	Mg^{2+}	12	10	2,8
oxygen atom	O	8	8	2,6
oxide ion	O^{2-}	8	10	2,8

The table shows the way that the electron structures of some atoms change when they form ions.

When an atom forms an ion, it achieves a full outer shell of electrons, called a **stable octet**.

Metals atoms have one, two or three electrons in their outer shell. When they form ions all of the electrons in the outer shell are lost. The next shell, which is full, becomes the outer shell. Non-metal atoms have four or more electrons in the outer shell. They gain the correct number of electrons to fill this shell. Each ion has the same electron arrangement as a noble gas – for an oxide ion it is that of neon. The ion does not, however, have the same number of protons as the atoms of this noble gas.

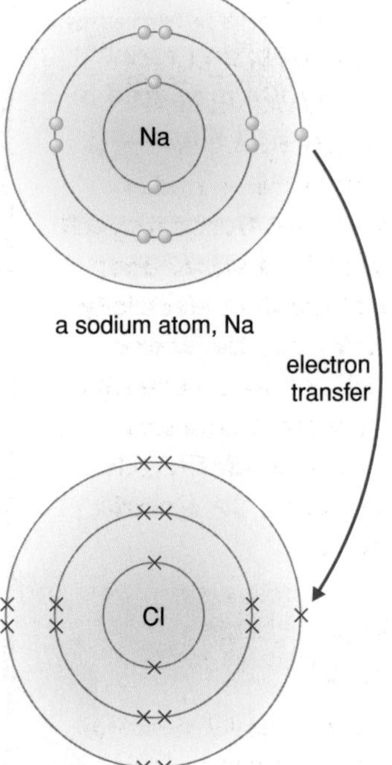

▲ *Transferring electrons in the formation of sodium chloride*

c **Why do atoms of different elements lose or gain different numbers of electrons to form ions?**

d **Work out the charges and write down the formulas for the ions formed from the following atoms:**

Li Al F Ca N K

Ionic bonding

An **ionic compound** is formed by transfer of one or more electrons from a metal to a non-metal. When sodium chloride is formed, each sodium atom transfers one electron to a chlorine atom. This forms a positive sodium ion, Na^+, and a negative chloride ion, Cl^-. These ions are then attracted to one another.

In the formation of the ionic compound magnesium oxide, both of the electrons lost from a magnesium atom are received by a single oxygen atom. This makes the ions Mg^{2+} and O^{2-}.

e **Draw a 'dot and cross' diagram, similar to those shown for sodium chloride and magnesium oxide, to show the transfer of electrons in the formation of magnesium chloride.**

f **Work out the electron structures and formulae of the ions in sodium oxide. Then find the formula for this ionic compound and draw a 'dot and cross' diagram to show how the compound is formed.**

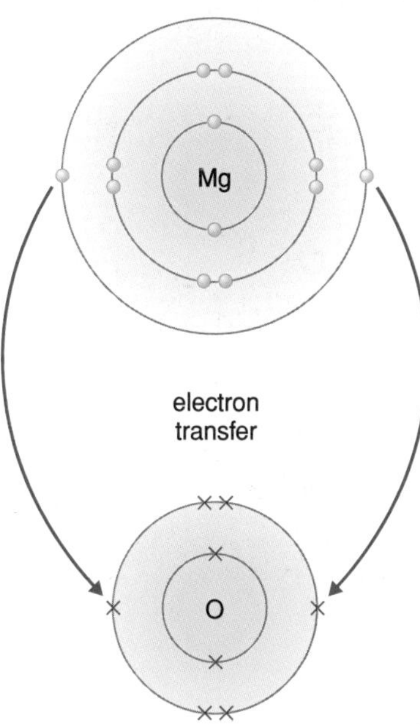

▲ *Transferring electrons in the formation of magnesium oxide*

More about salts

The ions in sodium chloride or magnesium oxide form a regular arrangement called a giant **ionic lattice**. This is held together because the positive ions are **electrostatically attracted** to the negative ions.

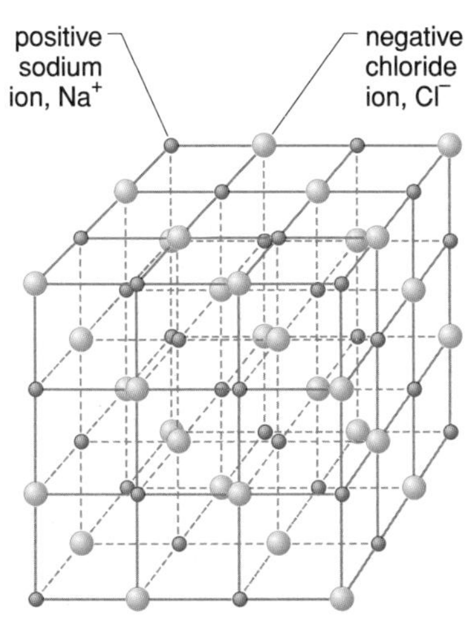

▲ *The arrangement of ions in a sodium chloride lattice*

▲ *Sodium chloride crystals*

Because of the strong electrostatic attraction between the ions in sodium chloride and magnesium oxide, a lot of energy is needed to pull the ions apart. This means that these compounds have high melting points.

Ionic compounds cannot conduct electricity when solid. This is because the electrons in the ions are firmly held – electrons cannot flow through the solid ionic compound to carry an electric current. Also, the strong electrostatic attraction between positive and negative ions prevents them moving to carry the current.

When sodium chloride or magnesium oxide is melted, the ions move apart and are able to move. This means that molten sodium chloride and molten magnesium oxide can conduct electricity.

The ions in sodium chloride or magnesium oxide are attracted to charges on water molecules so they are soluble in water. The ions separate when they dissolve so the solution conducts electricity. This is true of most ionic compounds.

g **Solid calcium chloride does not conduct electricity. Explain why.**

Examiner's tip

When an ion is formed by an atom losing or gaining electrons, the new electron arrangement has a full outer shell. When you draw a diagram of an ion, make sure the outer shell is full.

Amazing fact

Touching an electrical appliance or socket with wet hands may kill you! Pure water does not conduct electricity. However, tap water will conduct electricity because it contains dissolved ions which can carry the electric current.

Keywords

electrostatically attracted • ionic bonding • ionic compound • ionic lattice • stable octet

Beside the sea

Dr Sally Minto is a chemical engineer. She works at Amlwch on the island of Anglesey in North Wales where there is a factory that extracts the element bromine from seawater.

Bromine is a very poisonous and corrosive red-brown liquid. Bromine compounds are widely distributed on Earth but are normally found in low concentration. Dissolved bromide ions in seawater represent a considerable concentration of the element compared with sources on land.

Bromine is present in seawater at only 0.006 5% (65 parts per million). It takes 22 000 tonnes of seawater to make one tonne of bromine. The site at Amlwch has six large seawater pumps capable of pumping 500 000 000 gallons of seawater into the process every day.

The seawater is treated with chlorine which converts sodium bromide into free bromine by this reaction.

$2NaBr + Cl_2 \rightarrow 2NaCl + Br_2$

Bromine is a very volatile liquid which means that it easily vaporises into a gas. At Amlwch the bromine is literally blown out of the seawater using large fans.

fan
sulfur dioxide gas
acidified chlorinated seawater
seawater inlet
fresh water
seawater outlet
primary acid liquor
absorber packing
packing

▲ *Extracting bromine from seawater*

The bromine vapour is then condensed back into a liquid. From here the bromine can be purified and used to produce a range of useful products.

Bromine has a number of uses including the purification of water and the manufacture of dyes and medicines, fire retardants for plastics, and fumigants for killing pest infestations. Silver bromide is an important chemical in photographic film.

Questions

1 Write a word equation for the reaction that produces bromine from seawater.

2 Apart from the plentiful supply of seawater, suggest what other advantages there are for building a factory that makes bromine near to the coast?

3 Why do you think the concentration of bromine (as bromide ions) in seawater is higher than in any location on land?

4 Why is the extraction of bromine important to the chemical industry?

5 What precautions do you think Sally and the other workers at the Amlwch factory should take:
- **(a)** to ensure their own safety
- **(b)** to ensure the safety of people living on the island?

Bonding and beyond

▲ *Natural gas is methane*

In this item you will find out

- how non-metal atoms join by covalent bonding to make molecules
- why covalent molecules have specific properties
- how elements are grouped in the Periodic Table

When you turn on the fire or sit next to a hot radiator, do you think about the gas that lots of us use for our heating? Natural gas is the compound methane. This compound contains atoms of carbon and hydrogen, joined together by **covalent bonding**.

When an atom of a metal joins with an atom of a non-metal an ionic bond is formed. But when two non-metal atoms combine together, they share electrons to form a covalent bond. The atoms join to form a **molecule**.

Covalent compounds contain molecules with a number of different non-metal atoms joined together. A molecule of methane contains one carbon atom and four hydrogen atoms, so methane has the formula CH_4. Carbon dioxide, CO_2, and water, H_2O, are also covalent molecules. The diagram shows the formulas of some covalent molecules.

H—C(—H)(—H)—H
methane

O═C═O
carbon dioxide

H–O–H
water

H—H
hydrogen

Cl—Cl
chlorine

Some elements also have atoms joined by covalent bonds. For example, hydrogen consists of H_2 molecules and chlorine consists of Cl_2 molecules.

a **What are the states (gas, liquid or solid) of methane, carbon dioxide, water, hydrogen and chlorine?**

b **Water has unusual properties for a small covalent molecule. Use your answer to question a to suggest one unusual property.**

Amazing fact

Many small covalent molecules are gases with very low boiling points. Hydrogen has a boiling point of −253 °C. This is just 20 degrees above absolute zero, the coldest possible temperature.

Forming simple molecules

Each covalent bond involves the sharing of a pair of electrons, one electron coming from each atom. These 'dot and cross' diagrams on the right show the covalent bonds in hydrogen and chlorine.

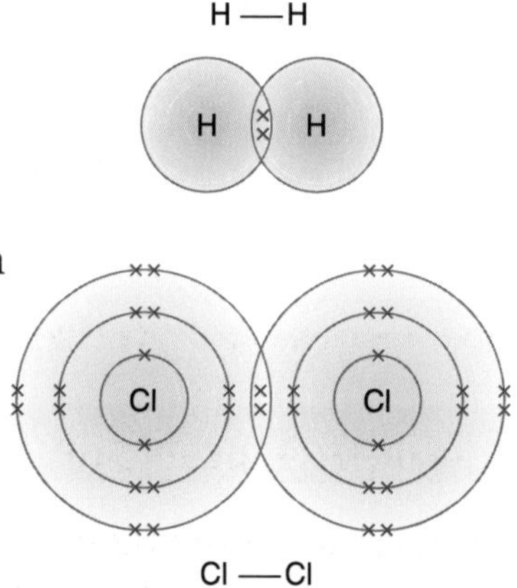

▶ *Covalent bonds in hydrogen and chlorine*

In the molecules of non-metal elements such as hydrogen and chlorine, two atoms from the same element share a pair of electrons in a covalent bond. One electron in this pair comes form each atom in the molecule.

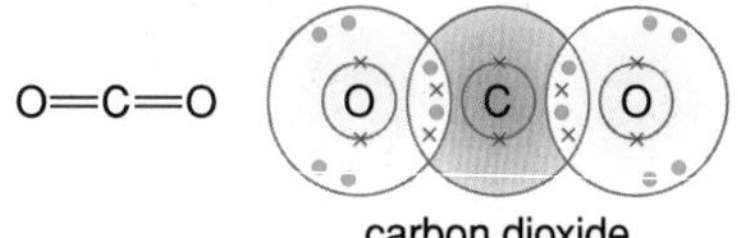

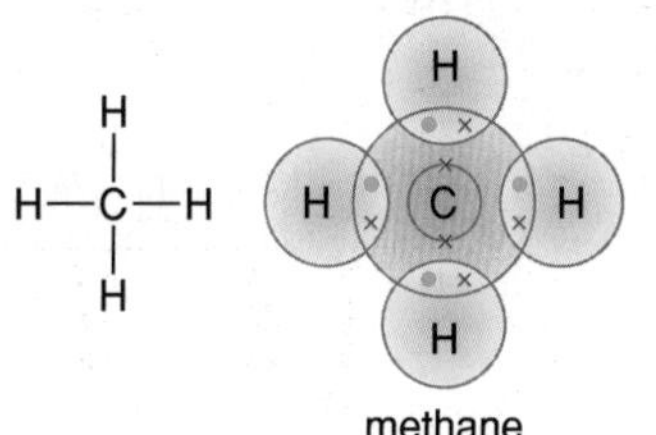

▲ *Covalent bonds in carbon dioxide and methane*

When non-metal elements form compounds such as carbon dioxide and methane, in each molecule of the compound atoms from different elements share pairs of electrons in covalent bonds. Again one electron comes from each atom that is sharing the pair of electrons.

By sharing pairs of electrons each atom has a full outer shell: a duplet (two electrons) for the first shell and an octet (eight electrons) for the second and third shells. This is the stable electron arrangement found in the outer shells of the noble gases.

Draw a 'dot and cross' diagram to show the covalent bonds in a molecule of water.

More about carbon dioxide and water

Covalent bonds are immensely strong and require a very large amount of energy to break them. However, the forces of attraction between molecules are much weaker. There is enough energy at low temperatures to break the weak **intermolecular forces** between most small covalent molecules.

This means that most simple covalent compounds have low melting points and boiling points and are gases or liquids at room temperature.

Covalent compound	Formula of molecule	Melting point (°C)	Boiling point (°C)
methane	CH_4	–183	–162
water	H_2O	0	100

Water is unusual in that it has higher melting and boiling points than most other covalent compound with small molecules.

Covalent molecules, such as water and carbon dioxide, are not charged particles. There are no ions or free electrons present in these compounds so they do not conduct electricity.

Examiner's tip

When drawing a dot and cross diagram of a covalent molecule, use the dots and crosses to show which electrons in the bonds are from which atom.

Here is the displayed formula for the covalent compound dibromoethane.

```
     Br  Br
     |   |
  H—C—C—H
     |   |
     H   H
```

d **How many atoms of each element are in a molecule of dibromoethane?**

Grouped together

The diagram on the right shows a shortened version of the Periodic Table.

The numbers across the top of the Periodic Table show the vertical **Groups** of elements. Group 1 contains the metals lithium to francium. Group 7 contains fluorine to astatine. Group 8 (sometimes called Group 0) contains helium to radon. The elements in each group have similar chemical properties.

The number of the Group that an element belongs to tells you how many electrons are in the outer shell of an atom of that element. All of the elements in Group 1 have one electron in the outer shell. All of the elements in Group 7 have seven electrons in the outer shell. All of the elements in Group 8 have eight electrons in the outer shell, except helium which has two. Going down a Group, each successive element has one additional complete shell to the element above it.

1	2	3	4	5	6	7	8
1 **H** Hydrogen 1							4 **He** Helium 2
7 **Li** Lithium 3	9 **Be** Beryllium 4	11 **B** Boron 5	12 **C** Carbon 6	14 **N** Nitrogen 7	16 **O** Oxygen 8	19 **F** Fluorine 9	20 **Ne** Neon 10
23 **Na** Sodium 11	24 **Mg** Magnesium 12	27 **Al** Aluminium 13	28 **Si** Silicon 14	31 **P** Phosphorus 15	32 **S** Sulfur 16	35.5 **Cl** Chlorine 17	40 **Ar** Argon 18
39 **K** Potassium 19	40 **Ca** Calcium 20	70 **Ga** Galium 31	73 **Ge** Germanium 32	75 **As** Arsenic 33	79 **Se** Selenium 34	80 **Br** Bromine 35	84 **Kr** Krypton 36
85 **Rb** Rubidium 37	88 **Sr** Strontium 38	115 **In** Indium 49	119 **Sn** Tin 50	122 **Sb** Antimony 51	128 **Te** Tellurium 52	127 **I** Iodine 53	131 **Xe** Xenon 54
133 **Cs** Caesium 55	137 **Ba** Barium 56	204 **Tl** Thalium 81	207 **Pb** Lead 82	209 **Bi** Bismuth 83	209 **Po** Polonium 84	210 **At** Astatine 85	222 **Rn** Radon 86
223 **Fr** Francium 87	226 **Ra** Radium 88						

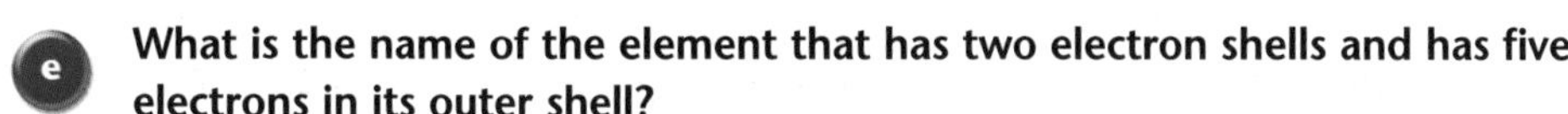

e **What is the name of the element that has two electron shells and has five electrons in its outer shell?**

f **To which Group does the element with the electron structure 2,8,4 belong?**

Periods

The horizontal rows of the Periodic Table are called **Periods**. The first Period contains only hydrogen and helium. The second Period contains eight elements, from lithium to neon. The third has another eight elements, from sodium to argon.

Each Period begins with an element in Group 1, with one electron in the outer shell, and ends with an element in Group 8, with a full outer shell. The number of the Period that an element is in is the same as the number of occupied shells in the atoms of that element. Magnesium is in Period 3 so an atom of magnesium has three shells of electrons.

g **In which Period does the element with the electron structure 2,8,5 belong?**

Keywords

covalent bonding • Group • intermolecular force • molecule • Period

A new Periodic Table

Chemistry students are used to seeing the modern Periodic Table.

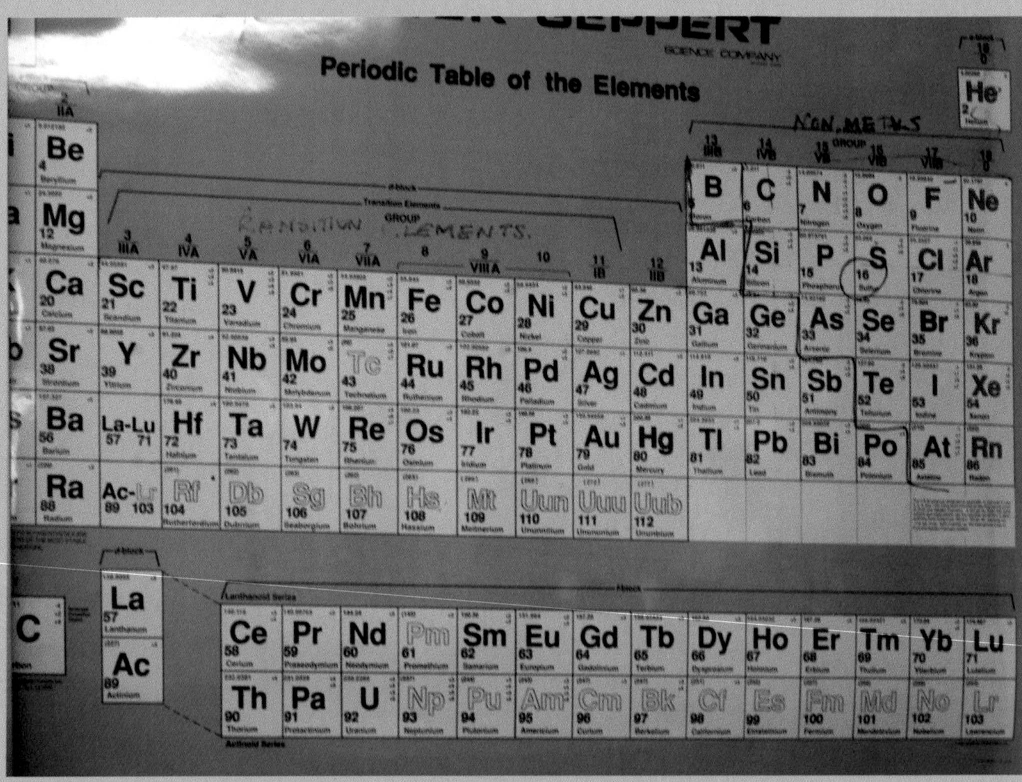

A new copy of the Periodic Table has been made for use by geology students. It shows how chemical elements are distributed in nature, sorting them by electrical charge rather than by numbers of protons and electrons.

The Earth's minerals consist mainly of charged elements, or ions. These behave differently from the original Periodic Table's neutral atoms. The new table groups ions with similar charge according to where they are found. Some elements appear several times with different charges. Sulfur appears four times.

Geologists know that a mineral's properties, such as melting point and solubility in water, depend on the size, charge and structure of its ions. It is possible to group ions according to their properties and occurrence on the Earth. Ions with similar chemical behaviour, and which are found in similar natural environments, can be put into the same group.

The new table has five families which represent minerals in the Earth's crust, the Earth's mantle, in solution in water, in the atmosphere and forming the basic nutrients of life.

Living things prefer ions with a single charge, like potassium in fertiliser and sodium in salt. Ions that can have more than one charge, like aluminium, can form resilient minerals that might be found in the Earth's crust or mantle.

Questions

1. What decides the Group that an element goes into in the modern Periodic Table used by chemistry students?
2. What decides how elements are grouped in the new geology Periodic Table?
3. Many of the compounds studied by chemists are covalent. Why would the geology Periodic Table cause problems for the study of covalent compounds?
4. In the new geology Periodic Table, sulfur appears four times. Explain why sulfur only appears once in the chemistry Periodic Table.

The alkali metals

▲ Distress flare

In this item you will find out

- how and why the metals in Group 1 react in a similar way
- how and why the reactivity in Group 1 increases down the Group
- how to use flame tests to identify Group 1 metal ions

The engine on your boat has failed and you are drifting towards dangerous rocks. How can you make sure that the lifeboat crew see and rescue you? One way is to set off a distress flare.

Distress flares are very bright. The light they give off is often a particular colour. Red indicates danger or 'stop'. Green indicates safety or 'go'.

What makes these flares different colours? Metal compounds are added to the mixture of chemicals in the flare. When the flare burns the very high temperature vaporises the metal ions. They absorb heat energy and re-emit it as light of a particular wavelength. This gives a colour to the flame.

In the laboratory this property of metal ions can be used to test for metals in compounds. A moistened nichrome wire is dipped into a solid sample of the compound containing the metal ion, and then put into a very hot Bunsen flame. The photograph on the right shows a **flame test** being carried out.

▲ Flame test

Light emitted by the metal gives the flame a colour. For example, each of the metals in Group 1 of the Periodic Table gives the flame a different colour.

The colour of the flame can then be used to identify the metal ion present in a compound.

Group I element	Symbol	Flame colour
lithium	Li	carmine red
sodium	Na	golden yellow
potassium	K	lilac
rubidium	Rb	red
caesium	Cs	blue

a **Suggest why different metals give different colours to the flame.**

b **Which metal may be used in a distress flare to indicate danger or 'stop'?**

The alkali metals

The elements in Group 1 of the Periodic Table are called the **alkali metals**. Three of the alkali metals are lithium, sodium and potassium.

The reactivity of the Group 1 metals increases down the Group, so lithium is the least reactive alkali metal. Reactions of these metals with water can be seen when a small cube of each metal is added to water in a trough.

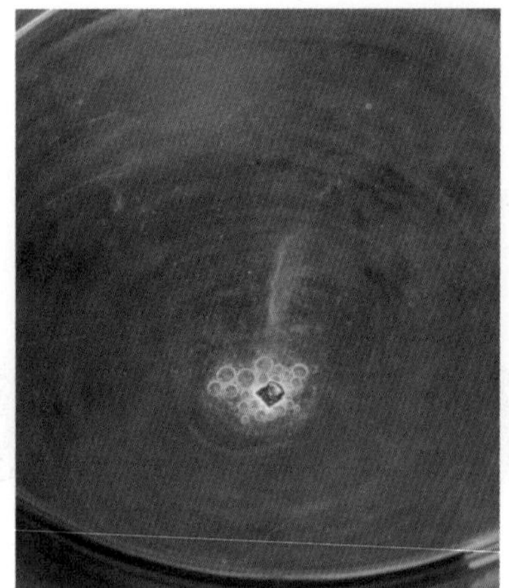

▲ Lithium reacting with water

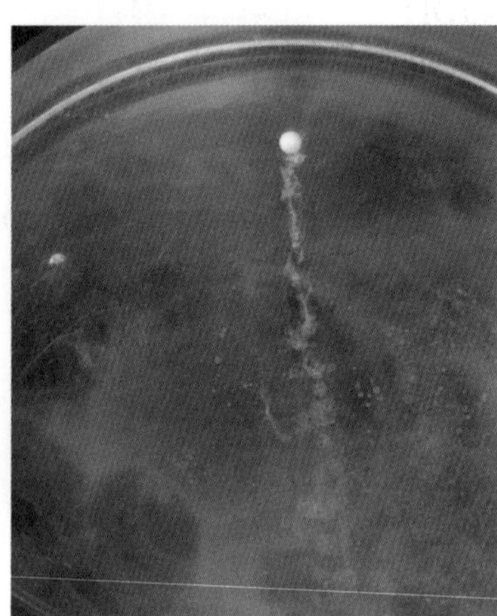

▲ Sodium reacting with water

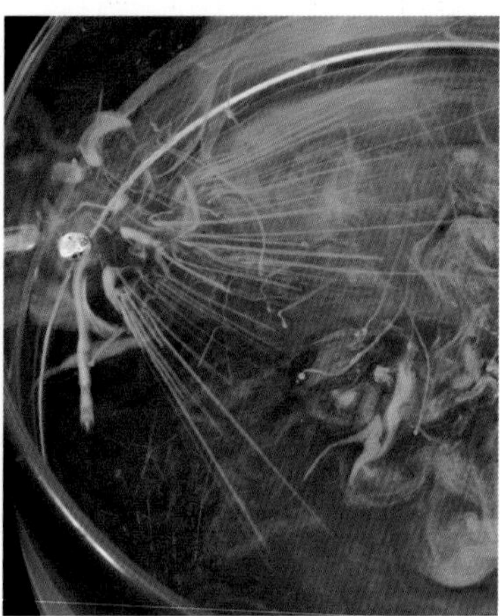

▲ Potassium reacting with water

The table shows observations made during this experiment.

Group 1 metal	Observations when the metal is added to water	Colour of Universal Indicator added to the water
lithium	• floats on the water • remains as a cube shape • fizzes slowly • disappears slowly	purple
sodium	• floats on the water • melts to form a ball of metal • fizzes quickly • whizzes around on the surface • disappears quickly	purple
potassium	• floats on the water • melts to form a ball of metal • fizzes furiously • whizzes around on the surface • burns with a lilac flame • disappears very quickly	purple

c What evidence does this experiment provide for the change in reactivity of the alkali metals down Group 1?

In each of the three experiments, water in the trough turns Universal Indicator purple. This shows that an alkali is formed during the reaction. This alkali is the metal hydroxide.

The fizzing in these reactions shows that a gas is given off. If you collect some of this gas in a test tube and put in a lighted splint, then the gas explodes with a squeaky pop sound. This shows the gas is hydrogen.

We can write symbol equations and word equations for these reactions.

$$2Li + 2H_2O \rightarrow 2LiOH + H_2$$
lithium + water → lithium hydroxide + hydrogen

$$2Na + 2H_2O \rightarrow 2NaOH + H_2$$
sodium + water → sodium hydroxide + hydrogen

d **Write a balanced symbol equation for the reaction of potassium with water.**

e **Rubidium is the next Group 1 metal after potassium. Use information from the table to predict how rubidium reacts with water.**

f **Write a balanced symbol equation for this reaction.**

Physical properties

Group 1 metals also show a trend in physical properties down the Group.

g **Predict the melting point and hardness of caesium, the metal below rubidium in Group 1.**

Group 1 metal	Melting point (°C)	Hardness
lithium	181	fairly hard
sodium	98	fairly soft
potassium	64	soft
rubidium	39	very soft

Group 1 metals and their electrons

The table on the right shows the arrangement of electrons in the first three Group 1 elements.

Group 1 element	Electron arrangement
lithium	2,1
sodium	2,8,1
potassium	2,8,8,1

The number of electrons in the outer shell of an atom determines how it will react. Each element in Group 1 has one electron in its outer shell. This means that Group 1 elements have similar properties.

When these atoms react each loses the one electron in its outer shell to form a positive ion. This loss of electrons is called **oxidation**.

For example, for sodium:

$Na \rightarrow Na^+ + e^-$

This ionic equation shows that an atom of sodium loses an electron during the reaction. This shows that the sodium atom has been oxidised. The next electron shell now becomes the outer electron shell of the ion. This shell is full, giving the ion a stable electronic structure.

As we move down Group 1, each successive element is more reactive. This is because it is easier for this element to lose an electron than the element above it in the Group. It is more easily oxidised.

Keywords

alkali metal • flame test • oxidation

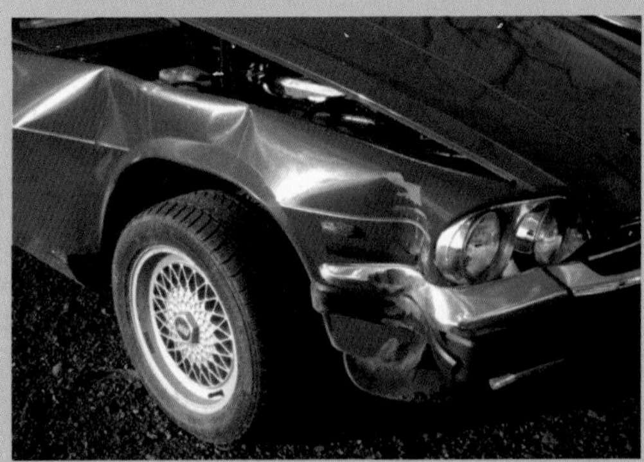

Investigating a 'hit and run' car accident

Police called to a 'hit and run' accident found shards of paint at the scene. They also found a damaged car not far from the scene.

Samples of paint from the scene and the car were sent to Dr Peter Brown, a forensic scientist. He used a technique called flame emission spectroscopy to analyse the paint.

When metal atoms are heated in a flame the energy they gain is given out as light. Each metal element gives out light of a characteristic colour or wavelength.

Although the colour of the flame as seen by the human eye can be used to identify which metal is present, this does not give a measure of the amount of each metal present.

The emitted light is analysed by a machine that can distinguish and measure light wavelengths far better than the human eye.

This is one of the most sensitive of all analytical methods. A few milligrams of a solid sample is usually enough for the detection of metallic elements present at a concentration of a few parts per million or less.

Here are some of Dr Brown's results.

Concentration in sample (ppm)		
Metal element	**Paint from scene**	**Paint from car**
barium	584	588
copper	1066	1072
lead	722	519
strontium	98	101

Questions

1. Suggest why it would not be good enough simply to compare the colour of the paint to see if the samples match.
2. Why did Dr Brown use flame emission spectroscopy instead of simply doing a flame test with a Bunsen burner?
3. Do Dr Brown's results prove that the paint came from the car? Explain your answer.

The halogens

The water in swimming pools is sterilised with chlorine

In this item you will find out

- how halogens react with alkali metals
- how the reactivity of halogens changes down the Group
- how to predict the properties of other halogens

Elements in Group 7 are called the **halogens**. These are very important elements with a variety of uses. Chlorine, fluorine, bromine and iodine are all halogens.

We use chlorine to sterilise the water used in swimming pools and supplied to the taps in our homes. It is also used in the manufacture of pesticides and plastics. Iodine is used to sterilise wounds. When painted onto a cut it prevents infection by bacteria.

As you can see from the photograph below, the elements in this group differ a great deal in their appearance.

Amazing fact

You need iodine in your diet to stay healthy. If you don't get enough iodine, your thyroid gland swells to form a goitre.

Chlorine, bromine and iodine

We can summarise the appearance of these halogens at room temperature in a table.

Halogen	State	Colour
chlorine	gas	green
bromine	liquid	orange-red
iodine	solid	grey

a **The appearance of these three halogens shows a trend going down the Group. Describe this trend.**

b **Fluorine is also a halogen. It is above chlorine in Group 7. Would you expect fluorine to be a gas, liquid or solid?**

c **Astatine is also in Group 7, below iodine. What colour would you expect astatine to be?**

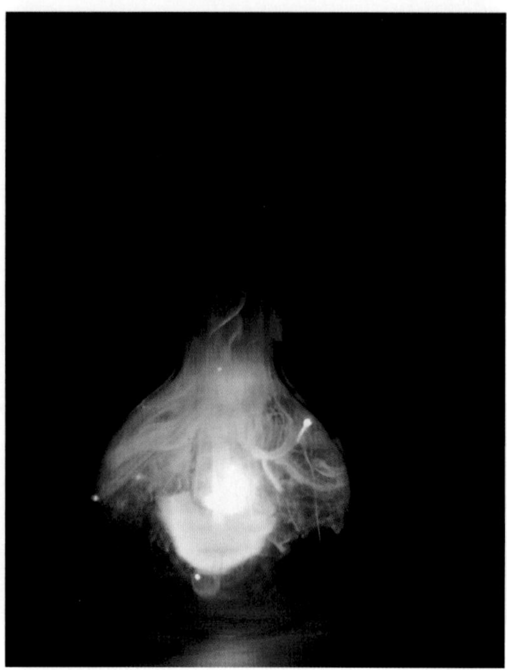
▲ Chlorine reacting with sodium

Halogens and alkali metals

The alkali metals react with the halogens to form salts called metal **halides**. For example, sodium reacts with chlorine to make sodium chloride (as in the photograph), with bromine to make sodium bromide, and with iodine to make sodium iodide. The other alkali metals react with halogens in a similar way.

d **What is the name of the alkali halide formed when potassium reacts with iodine?**

Here are symbol and word equations for the reaction between sodium and chlorine.

$$2Na + Cl_2 \rightarrow 2NaCl$$
sodium + chlorine → sodium chloride

e **Write a symbol equation for the reaction between sodium and bromine.**

f **Write a symbol equation for the reaction between potassium and chlorine.**

Reactivity of halogens

The reactivity of the halogens decreases down the Group. You can see this in the **displacement** reactions between halogens and metal halides. When chlorine gas is bubbled through a solution of potassium bromide, a red colour appears in the solution. This is the element bromine that has been displaced by the more reactive chlorine. The symbol and word equations for this reaction are shown below.

$$Cl_2 + 2KBr \rightarrow Br_2 + 2KCl$$
chlorine + potassium bromide → bromine + potassium chloride

A series of similar experiments gives the results in the table.

Examiner's tip

When working out the reactivity of elements, remember that in Group 1 reactivity increases down the Group, but in Group 7 reactivity decreases down the Group.

Halogen	Halide solution	Result	Halogen displaced
chlorine	potassium bromide	red solution	bromine
chlorine	potassium iodide	brown solution	iodine
bromine	potassium chloride	none	none
bromine	potassium iodide	brown solution	iodine
iodine	potassium chloride	none	none
iodine	potassium bromide	none	none

In these reactions a more reactive halogen displaces a less reactive halogen from a solution of its halide.

- Chorine displaces both bromides and iodides.
- Bromine displaces iodides.

g **Use information in the table to put the three halogens in order of reactivity, starting with the most reactive.**

h **Write a symbol equation for the reaction between bromine and potassium iodide.**

Predicting properties of halogens

Since the trend in reactivity of Group 7 elements goes from the top to the bottom, we can use results from the displacement reactions of chlorine, bromine and iodine to predict how other elements in the Group will react.

Fluorine is at the top of the Group, above chlorine. We can therefore predict that fluorine will displace chlorides, bromides and iodides. Fluorine is the most reactive halogen.

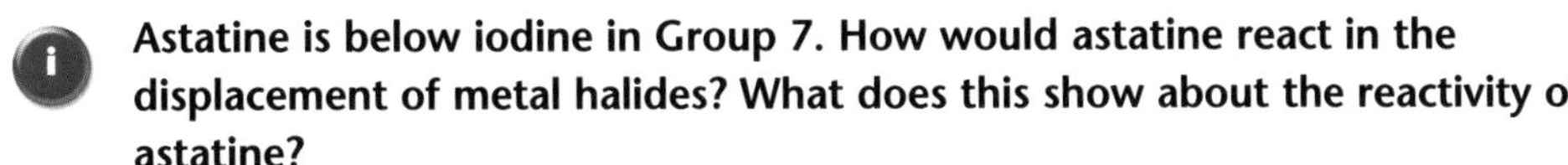

i **Astatine is below iodine in Group 7. How would astatine react in the displacement of metal halides? What does this show about the reactivity of astatine?**

Halogens and electronic structure

The halogens react in a similar way because they each have atoms with seven electrons in the outer shell. When these atoms react, each gains an electron to form a negative ion. The gaining of an electron is called **reduction**. The negative ion formed has a stable electronic structure. This is why the halogens all have similar properties.

For example for a chlorine molecule:

$Cl_2 + 2e^- \rightarrow 2Cl^-$

This ionic equation shows that each atom of chlorine gains an electron during the reaction. This shows that each chlorine atom has been reduced.

Halogen	Atom	Electron structure	Ion	Electron structure
fluorine	F	2,7	F^-	2,8
chlorine	Cl	2,8,7	Cl^-	2,8,8
bromine	Br	2,8,18,7	Br^-	?

j **Look at the table. What is the electronic structure of a bromide ion?**

As we saw earlier, the reactivity of the halogens decreases down the Group. The higher up the Group a halogen is the more reactive it is, and the easier it is for one of its atoms to gain an electron.

Keywords

displacement • halide • halogen • reduction

▲ Water treatment plant

Chlorine to the rescue

Cholera used to be a major health problem in the United Kingdom. An outbreak in 1882 killed 32 000 people.

Today, chlorine added to drinking water kills harmful bacteria and prevents the spread of waterborne diseases. Although chlorine is very poisonous, and was used as a weapon in the First World War, the low concentration in drinking water is harmless to humans. However, it is deadly to microorganisms.

The concentration of chlorine in tap water is less than that used in swimming pools. One reason for this is that we drink lots of tap water, so a higher concentration of chlorine could be harmful. We do not drink much of the water in swimming pools, so a higher concentration of chlorine is safe to use.

Cholera is still rife in many countries, such as India, where sewage is not adequately separated from drinking water sources, and chlorine is not added to water before it is pumped to houses. When travelling abroad it is important to make your drinking water safe.

The simplest way is to drink only bottled water. If water is purchased locally it is essential to ensure that the cap still has the manufacturer's seal, and the bottle has not been re-filled with contaminated water. Local water can be purified by boiling, adding iodine or adding chlorine. Silver-based tablets are also available from chemists and specialised travel equipment shops. These effectively kill bacteria in the water, making it safe to drink, though it may have an unusual taste.

▲ Well water can contain bacteria

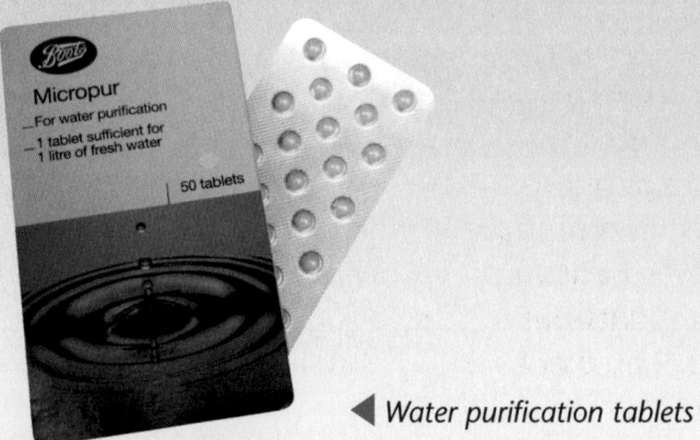

◀ Water purification tablets

Questions

1 Why is cholera no longer a problem in the United Kingdom?

2 Suggest how disease-causing organisms get into the water supply in countries such as India.

3 Describe two ways to avoid getting a disease from contaminated water.

Getting the metal

In this item you will find out

- what happens during the electrolysis of molten salts and solutions
- the products that can be made by the electrolysis of sodium chloride
- how electrolysis is used in the extraction of aluminium

Would you like to travel in an aircraft made of wood and string? Early aircraft used thin wooden spars, kept in place by strings or wires. This type of construction was light enough to be powered into the air by the engines in use at that time. The design was not very strong, and accidents were common.

▲ *Early aircraft*

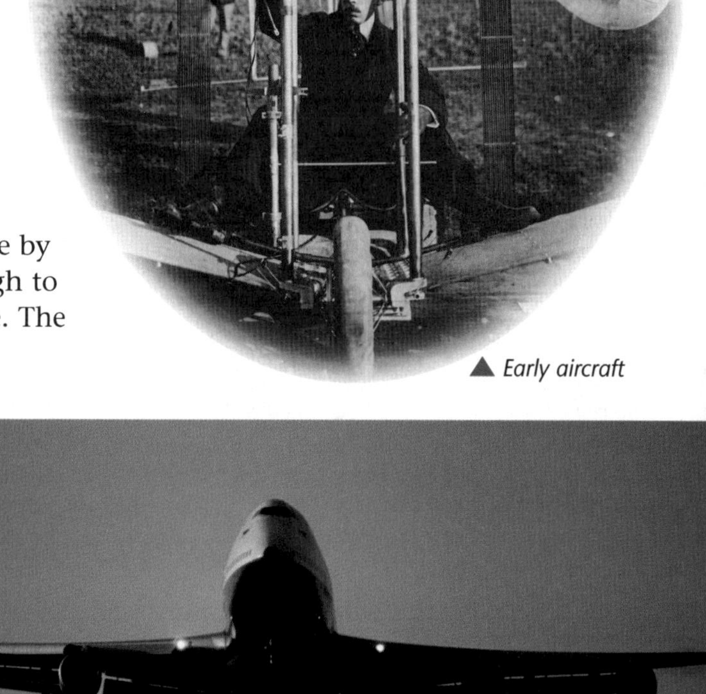

Modern aircraft are sleek, safe and comfortable. The body of a modern aircraft is made from Duralumin. This is a strong, hard, lightweight alloy of aluminium.

▲ *Modern passenger jet*

Although aluminium is a fairly reactive metal, it has a coating of aluminium oxide that prevents corrosion when it is exposed to the air. Aluminium is used to make greenhouse frames because it can withstand bad weather without damage to its surface. The oxide coating of aluminium can be polished to give an attractive, shiny appearance. This makes the metal a good choice for door handles.

Aluminium is more expensive than steel because you need to use large amounts of electricity to extract it from its ore. The industrial extraction of aluminium uses a process called electrolysis.

a **Suggest why aluminium is better than wood for making an aeroplane.**

b **Why is aluminium a better choice than steel (iron) for making a greenhouse frame?**

Amazing fact

Recycling aluminium uses only 5% of the energy used to make new aluminium. Each year over 12 million tons of aluminium is recycled, much of it from drinks cans.

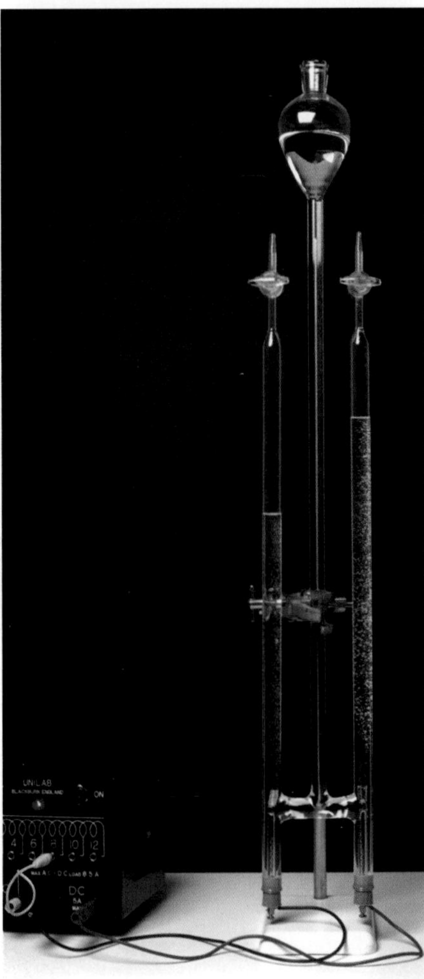

▲ Hofmann voltameter

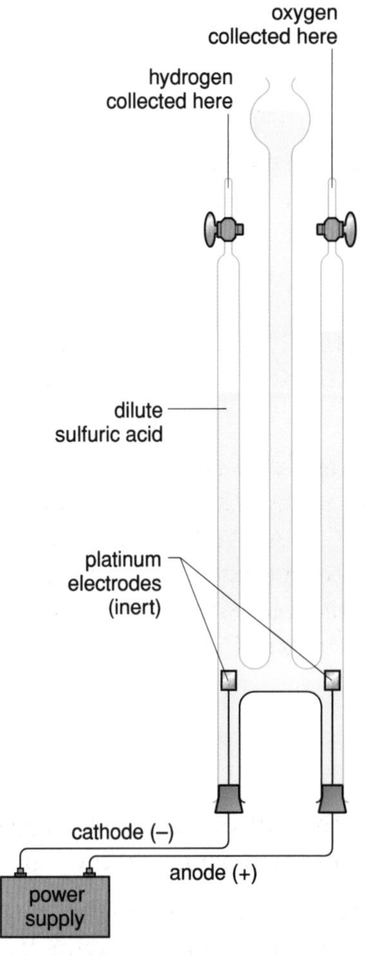

▲ Electrolysis equipment

Electrolysis of dilute sulfuric acid

In the laboratory electricity can be passed through an electrolyte of a dilute solution of sulfuric acid using a set of apparatus called a Hofmann voltameter. This is shown in the photograph and the diagram on the left.

Hydrogen and oxygen gases are released, and collected separately in the apparatus.

You can find out which gas is which by collecting them in test tubes and carrying out these tests:

- if the gas burns with a squeaky pop when a lighted splint is brought to the mouth of the test tube then the gas is hydrogen.
- if a glowing splint relights when it is lowered into the test tube then the gas is oxygen.

Electrode reactions

Sulfuric acid contains positive hydrogen ions, H^+, and negative sulfate ions, SO_4^{2-}. It also contains negative hydroxide ions, OH^-, from the water. Electricity is passed through the solution using platinum **electrodes**.

Since opposite charges are attracted to each other, the ions move to electrodes of opposite charge. Negative ions move to the positive electrode (anode) and positive ions move to the negative electrode (cathode). This is why negative ions are called anions and positive ions are called cations.

Hydrogen ions move to the cathode. Each hydrogen ion collects an electron from the cathode, becoming a hydrogen atom. Pairs of these atoms form molecules of hydrogen gas.

$2H^+ + 2e^- \rightarrow H_2$

Hydroxide ions move to the anode. As these ions give up electrons to the anode, oxygen gas is formed.

$4OH^- \rightarrow O_2 + 2H_2O + 4e^-$

Sulfate ions are not affected by the electrolysis, and remain in solution. The result of this electrolysis is therefore the decomposition of water into its elements.

$2H_2O \rightarrow 2H_2 + O_2$

The volume of hydrogen given off is twice that of the oxygen. How is this consistent with the overall equation for the electrolysis?

Extracting aluminium

Aluminium is found in the mineral bauxite which contains mostly aluminium oxide, Al_2O_3. Aluminium is extracted from purified aluminium oxide by electrolysis.

You can only carry out electrolysis using molten ionic compounds or their solutions in water. This poses a major problem for the extraction of aluminium, since a temperature of 2030°C is needed to melt aluminium oxide. This is a difficult and uneconomic temperature to maintain. Also, aluminium oxide is insoluble in water. This problem is solved by dissolving aluminium oxide in molten cryolite. This mineral has a melting point just below 1000°C.

carbon lining forming negative electrode
solid crust of electrolyte
carbon positive electrodes
insulation
molten electrolyte
molten aluminium

▲ *Electrolytic cell used in aluminium manufacture*

Aluminium and oxygen

In the electrolytic cell both the anode and the cathode are made of **graphite** which is a form of carbon. A cell is shown in the diagram on the right.

Positive aluminium ions, Al^{3+}, are attracted to the cathode which is the graphite lining of the electrolytic cell. Each aluminium ion gains three electrons from the cathode, forming an aluminium atom.

$Al^{3+} + 3e^- \rightarrow Al$

Molten aluminium forms and collects at the bottom of the cell. This is tapped off into moulds and allowed to cool to form solid ingots.

Negative oxide ions, O^{2-}, are attracted to the graphite anodes. Each oxide ion gives two electrons to the anode, forming an oxygen atom. Pairs of oxygen atoms join to form the molecules in oxygen gas.

$2O^{2-} \rightarrow O_2 + 4e^-$

The oxygen reacts with the graphite anodes, forming carbon dioxide. This means that the anodes have to be replaced frequently.

▲ *Ingots of aluminium*

Work out how many aluminium atoms and oxygen molecules are discharged from the solution for each 12 electrons that flow around the circuit.

You can see that electrolysis splits aluminium oxide into its elements.

$2Al_2O_3$	$\rightarrow$	$4Al$	+	$3O_2$
aluminium oxide	$\rightarrow$	aluminium	+	oxygen

Keywords

electrode • graphite

▲ *Paul Héroult*

Who got there first?

Two unknown young scientists, Paul Héroult and Charles Hall, simultaneously invented a new electrolytic process, which is the basis for all aluminium production today. They worked separately thousands of miles apart, and were unaware of each other's work. Both inventors discovered that if they dissolved aluminium oxide (alumina) in a bath of molten cryolite and passed a powerful electric current through it, then molten aluminium would be deposited at the bottom of the bath.

Charles Hall lived in the USA. On 23 February 1886, in the woodshed behind his family's home, he produced globules of aluminium metal by the electrolysis of aluminium oxide dissolved in a cryolite–aluminium fluoride mixture and repeated this experiment the next day for his sister Julia to witness. This achievement was the culmination of several years of intensive work on this problem.

Paul Héroult lived in France. His was a world of country folk and cottage industries. While a student at the École des Mines, Paris, he began working on the electrolysis of aluminium compounds. His father, Patrice, managed a small tannery, which Paul inherited. Paul used the tannery buildings for his experiments. His mother gives him her last 50 000 francs to acquire a dynamo to produce the electric current that he used in 1886 to produce aluminium.

On 9 July 1886, Hall filed a patent for his process. In July 1888 his application was found to be in interference with the application filed on 23 April 1886 by Paul L. T. Héroult. The Héroult process is essentially identical to the one discovered by Hall in the same year.

Héroult was the same age as Hall. For many years the two inventors battled in the courts to decide who had made the discovery first. Eventually an agreement was reached between the two inventors, who shared the legal rights to the process.

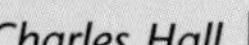

Charles Hall ▶

Questions

1. Hall and Héroult were unaware of each other's discovery. Suggest why this was not surprising in the year 1886.
2. It is unlikely that two scientists working on the same topic in the 21st century would be unaware of each other. Suggest why.
3. Both Hall and Héroult were amateur inventors, working with simple apparatus in makeshift laboratories. Most modern scientific advances are made in large university or industrial laboratories. Suggest why.
4. Suggest why the two inventors spent years arguing over who made the invention first.

Transition elements

▲ *Margarine is manufactured using a catalyst*

In this item you will find out

- about the properties and uses of transition metals
- about the properties of transition metal compounds
- how to identify transition metal ions

Margarine is made by the hydrogenation of vegetable oils. The addition of hydrogen to the molecules in the oils turns them from liquids to solids.

Ammonia is made by the Haber Process. Nitrogen and hydrogen combine under conditions of high pressure and high temperature.

What have these two important industrial processes got in common? They both use catalysts to speed up the reaction. A catalyst is not changed during the reaction, and so can be used for a long time before it needs to be replaced. The manufacture of margarine uses a nickel catalyst. The Haber Process uses a catalyst made of iron.

Amazing fact

Metal coins were not the first things to be used as money. The currency in China in the eighth century BC consisted of miniature farming tools.

Both nickel and iron belong to a large group of metals called **transition elements** or **transition metals**. These are found in a 'block' in the middle of the Periodic Table. Most of the catalysts used in industry are transition elements.

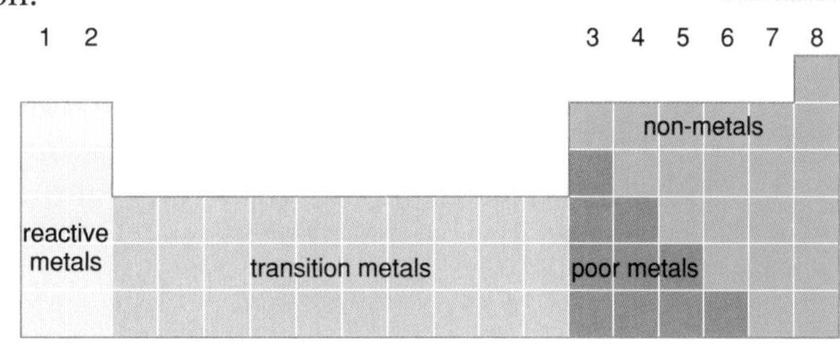

◀ *Where the transition elements are*

The transition metals have typical metal properties such as shiny appearance, conduction of electricity and conduction of heat. There are additional properties that are characteristic of most transition metals such as high melting point, high density, extreme hardness, low reactivity and coloured compounds.

Transition metals have many uses as pure compounds, but they are particularly useful when mixed in alloys.

▼ *This screw is made from transition metals*

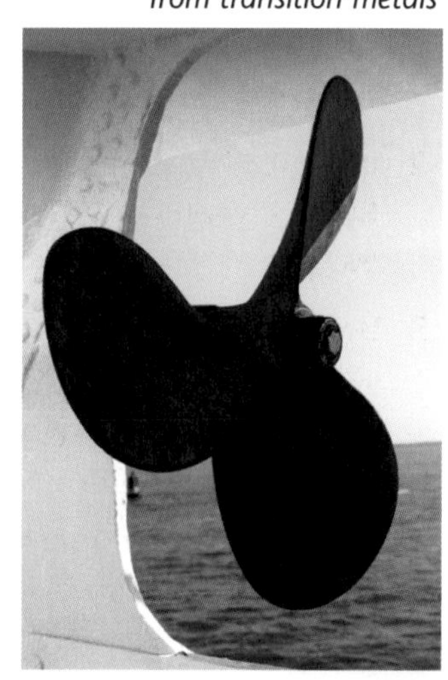

The screw in the photograph on the right is used to drive a ship. It is made from Monel, an alloy of the transition metals nickel and copper. It is extremely resistant to corrosion, even from seawater. Because of their durability, transition metal alloys are also used to make coins.

a **Write down the names and uses of three other transition elements that are not mentioned above.**

Transition metal compounds

The compounds of transition elements are often coloured. The table shows the colours of some of them.

Transition metal ion	Colour of compounds	Example
copper(II)	blue	copper(II) sulfate
iron(II)	light green	iron(II) nitrate
iron(III)	orange/brown	iron(III) chloride

▶ *Copper(II), iron(II) and iron(III) compounds*

Each transition metal gives a particular colour to most of its compounds. Copper(II) sulfate crystals are blue because they contain copper(II) ions.

 **What colour would you expect crystals of iron(II) sulfate to be?**

Thermal decomposition

Many transition metal compounds also show characteristic chemical properties. Thermal decomposition is a reaction in which a substance is broken down into two or more other substances by heat. Transition metal carbonates decompose when you heat them. In these reactions carbon dioxide gas is given off and a metal oxide is formed.

For example:

$$CuCO_3 \rightarrow CuO + CO_2$$
copper(II) carbonate → copper(II) oxide + carbon dioxide

$$MnCO_3 \rightarrow MnO + CO_2$$
manganese(II) carbonate → manganese(II) oxide + carbon dioxide

A test for the carbon dioxide gas given off is to bubble it through lime water. The lime water will turn milky.

Similar reactions take place when iron(II) carbonate and zinc carbonate are heated. In each of these decomposition reactions there is a colour change as the reaction takes place.

c **Write symbol equations for the thermal decomposition of iron(II) carbonate and zinc carbonate.**

Identifying transition metal ions

Precipitation is a reaction that produces an insoluble solid when two solutions are mixed. When you add sodium hydroxide solution to a solution of a transition metal compound, the metal ions and hydroxide ions form a **precipitate** of the metal hydroxide. The colour of this hydroxide can be used to identify the transition metal.

You can see the colours of copper(II), iron(II) and iron(III) hydroxides in the photographs below.

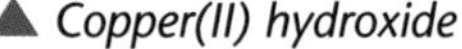

▲ *Copper(II) hydroxide*

▲ *Iron(II) hydroxide*

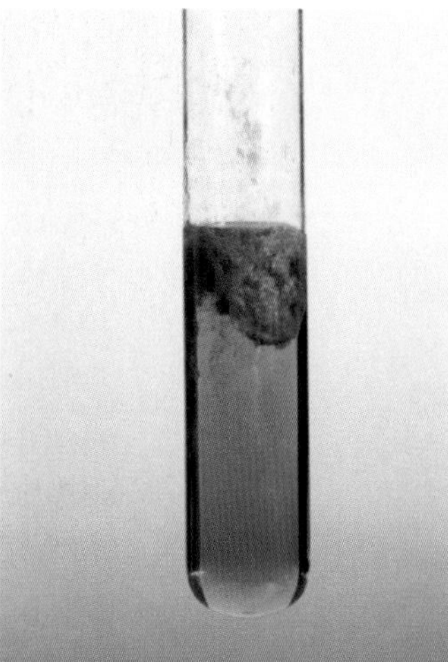

▲ *Iron(III) hydroxide*

Transition metal ion	Formula of transition metal ion	Colour of metal hydroxide precipitate
copper(II)	Cu^{2+}	blue
iron(II)	Fe^{2+}	grey/green
iron(III)	Fe^{3+}	orange

For the reaction between iron(II) ions and hydroxide ions, the symbol equation is:

$Fe^{2+} + 2OH^- \rightarrow Fe(OH)_2$

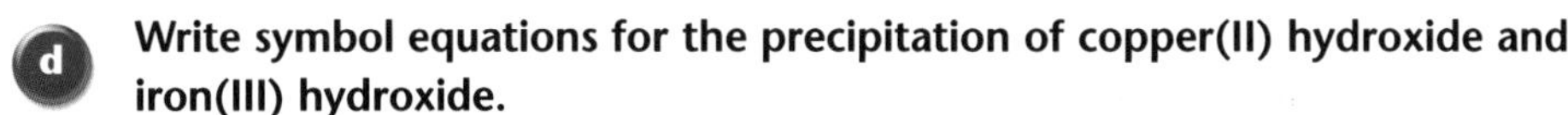

d **Write symbol equations for the precipitation of copper(II) hydroxide and iron(III) hydroxide.**

e **A student adds sodium hydroxide to a solution of iron(III) nitrate. Describe how the appearance of the solution changes as the sodium hydroxide is added.**

f **Write word and symbol equations for the reaction in question e.**

Keywords

precipitate • transition element • transition metal

▲ People in Tokyo often wear smog masks

Less exhausted

When petrol is burned in a car engine, the pollutant gases carbon monoxide and nitrogen monoxide are made. These are released into the air from the car exhaust.

Carbon monoxide is a very poisonous gas. It interferes with the transport of oxygen in the blood. As little as one per cent of carbon monoxide in the air can be fatal.

Nitrogen monoxide is also poisonous. It causes acid rain and city smog.

To reduce this pollution, every new car sold in the United Kingdom is fitted with a catalytic converter.

This contains the transition elements platinum and rhodium. These are very efficient catalysts for reactions that convert carbon monoxide and nitrogen monoxide into the less harmful gases carbon dioxide and nitrogen.

However, using a catalytic converter makes a car engine less efficient. The car will use more fuel to travel the same distance as a similar car without a catalytic converter.

Many catalysts, including platinum and rhodium, are 'poisoned' by small quantities of heavy metals such as lead. Cars fitted with catalytic converters must only use unleaded petrol.

Even when only unleaded petrol is used, the efficiency of the catalysts slowly decreases as the car is driven. Once a car is three years old, it has to be tested each year to see if the catalytic converter is reducing the concentrations of pollutant gases to a minimum standard. If too much carbon monoxide or nitrogen monoxide is detected in the mixture of gases from the car exhaust, the catalytic converter is replaced.

▲ Catalytic converter

Questions

1 Suggest why the efficiency of the catalyst decreases even though unleaded petrol is used.

2 Why do you think the efficiency of the catalytic converter is not tested until a new car is three years old?

3 The increase in the percentage of carbon dioxide in the air during the past century is a cause of global warming.
- **(a)** Suggest why the use of catalytic converters will not reduce global warming.
- **(b)** Why do you think using catalytic converters may increase global warming?

Metals

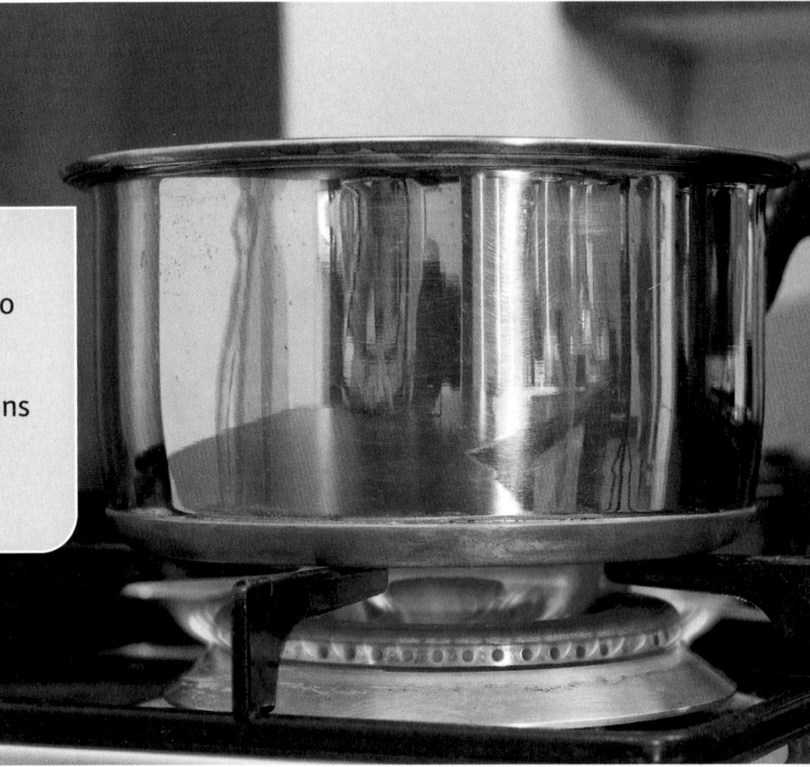

▲ *Saucepans are often made with copper bases*

In this item you will find out

- how the properties of metals are related to their uses
- how the nature of metallic bonding explains the properties of metals
- about superconducting metals

What properties should the materials used to make a saucepan have?

The material must be hard, durable, easy to shape, attractive, easy to clean, cheap to make, but most of all it must be a good conductor of heat. All metals are good conductors of heat, but not every metal would be good for making a saucepan. The alloy stainless steel has all of the qualities listed above, and is widely used to make saucepans.

Copper is a better conductor of heat than stainless steel, and some saucepans are made completely from this metal. But copper is a fairly soft metal so it is easily damaged. It also discolours in use and is not easy to clean. The ideal solution is to make a saucepan using stainless steel, but with a copper base.

Metals are used to make many articles. In each case a metal with the correct properties for the job is chosen.

Here are some examples:

- aluminium has a very low density and is used in the manufacture of aircraft frames
- tungsten is very hard and is used to make the sharp edges of cutting tools such as drills and saws.

a **Explain how a copper saucepan is in some ways better and in some ways worse than a stainless-steel saucepan.**

b **You can buy saucepans made from aluminium. What advantage would one of these saucepans have over a saucepan made of stainless steel?**

c **Suggest another product that aluminium would be suitable for, and explain your choice.**

Amazing fact

Over 17 million tons of copper metal are extracted from copper ores each year.

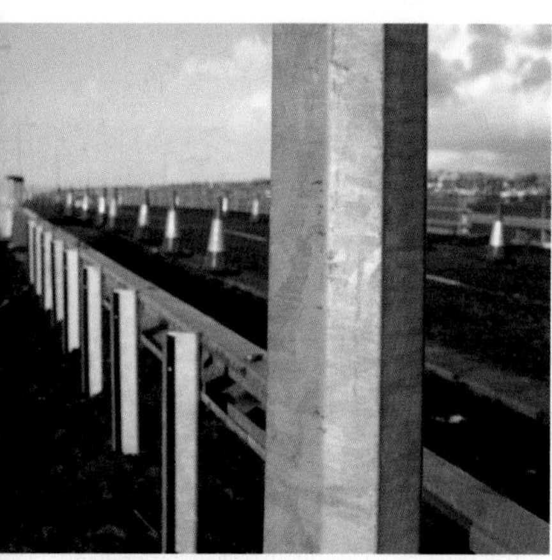
▲ You can see crystals on the surface of this post

Metallic bonding

Metals have a number of characteristic properties. Most are shiny (lustrous), hard, have a high density, high tensile strength, high melting and boiling points, and are good conductors of heat and electricity.

All metals are made of crystals. If you were standing close enough you could see crystals of zinc on the surface of the galvanised barrier in the photograph on the left. In these crystals, metal ions are held in a regular arrangement by very strong **metallic bonding**.

▶ Metallic bonding

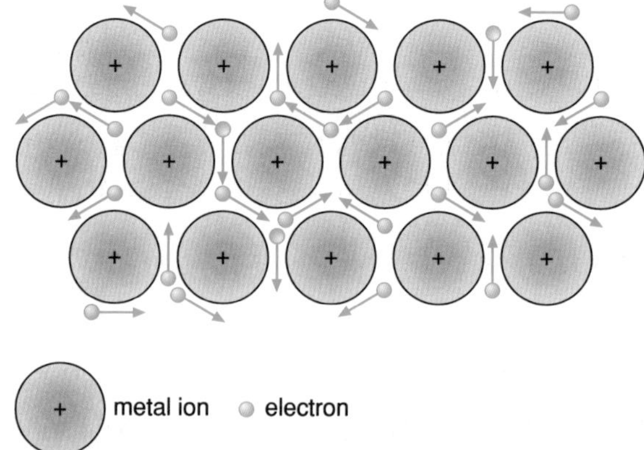

Positive metal ions are surrounded by a 'sea' of mobile negative electrons. Electrostatic attraction holds together the negative delocalised electrons and the positive ions very strongly. Because the particles are hard to pull away from each other, most metals are hard and strong. They also have high tensile strength, which means they do not easily break when pulled. These properties make iron, for example, a good material for the construction of road and rail bridges and car bodies.

Mixing metals to make alloys can give even more useful properties. Mixing iron with carbon to make steel increases its strength and hardness. Mixing copper with tin to make brass prevents corrosion.

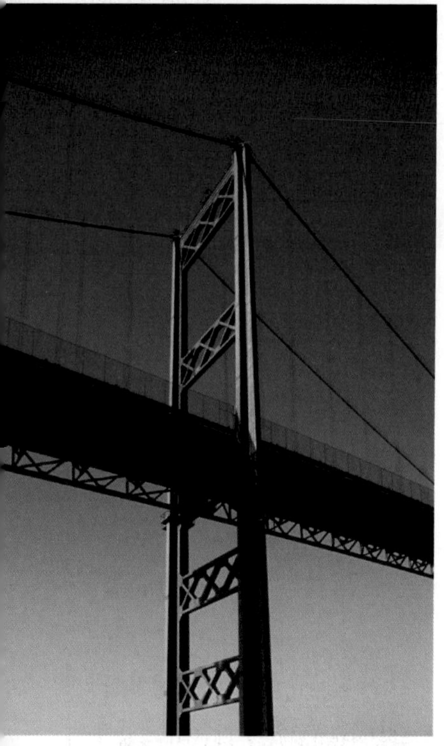
▲ Iron is good for making bridges

Melting and boiling points

Metal	Melting point (°C)	Boiling point (°C)
aluminium	661	2467
gold	1064	2807
tungsten	3407	5927
iron	1535	2750
Non-metal		
phosphorus	44	280
sulfur	113	445
iodine	114	185

As you've already found out, most metals have a high melting point and boiling point. Compare the data for some metals and some non-metals in the table on the previous page.

You can see that the metals have much higher melting and boiling points than the non-metals. This is because of the strong metallic bonds between the metal atoms.

To melt a metal the strong attraction between delocalised electrons and positive metal ions in the metallic bonding has to be overcome. This requires a lot of energy and so a high temperature. In a similar way, you also need a lot of energy to boil a metal so they have high boiling points.

▲ *Tungsten electric lamp filament*

The very high melting point of tungsten means that it can be used for the filament of electric light bulbs. It glows white-hot without melting.

There are, however, some metals that do not have a high melting point. Caesium melts if a glass tube containing the metal is held in the hand.

 **Suggest why some metals have a much lower melting point than others.**

Moving electrons

When metals conduct electricity, electrons move through them. Because the delocalised electrons are able to move easily through the regular arrangement of metal ions, metals are good conductors of electricity.

Because it is such a good conductor of electricity, copper is used for the wiring in houses. But even copper has some electrical resistance so energy is lost in heating up the wire.

Superconductors

At very low temperatures some metals, including mercury, lead and tin, can be **superconductors**. These conduct electricity with little or no resistance which means the electricity can move through them with no loss of energy. This is called loss-free power transmission.

Superconductors can be used to make super-fast electronic circuits and very powerful electromagnets.

One of the main problems with superconducting metals is that they only work at very low temperatures: about –269 °C. If we want to use them for practical purposes, we need to find a way to make superconductors work at 20 °C.

 **Why are low temperature superconductors not suitable for most practical purposes?**

Keywords

metallic bonding • superconductor

A superconducting future

The future of superconductors is bright and scientists are excited about superconductivity in a compound called magnesium diboride, MgB_2. This is because the temperature at which it has zero resistance is above what is normally expected for a superconductor.

It also has properties that other high temperature superconductors don't have. Normally these superconductors are brittle and hard to work with, which makes them hard to use for wires, but this new superconductor isn't like this. It's easy to bend and shape and it's cheap and plentiful. The amount of current it can carry is high and wires can easily be made out of it. This makes it ideal for industrial use. However, use of magnesium diboride for wires presents other problems, and further research is needed before commercial use of this superconductor is possible.

One of the main possibilities of superconductors being used in the future is in power lines. At present about 10% of the electricity we use is lost heating up the wires. The price of a superconductor has dropped so much that we may soon be able to afford to replace power lines with a superconducting wire.

The current carried by a superconducting wire is also much higher than that of a conventional copper wire. This means that a superconducting power cable could carry a lot more current than a conventional wire, with no loss of power transmission.

Superconductors could also allow for the development of magnetically levitated trains. Free of friction, they could glide along at high speeds using a fraction of the energy trains now use.

Questions

1 Magnesium diboride has zero resistance at a temperature above that normally expected for a superconductor. Why is this important?

2 What other useful properties does magnesium diboride have?

3 Why may the future use of superconductors in power transmission cables be a good idea?

4 What other applications of superconductors may be possible in the future?

C3a

1 Explain what is meant by the following terms:

a atomic (proton) number [1]
b mass (nucleon) number [1]
c isotope [1]

2 How are elements arranged in the Periodic Table? [2]

3 Copy and complete this table about elements and sub-atomic particles.

Element	Atomic number	Mass number	Number of protons	Number of electrons	Number of neutrons
lithium	3	7			4
	7	14	7	7	
aluminium		27	13		14
argon			18	18	22

[8]

4 The electronic structure of potassium is 2,8,8,1:

Use a Periodic Table to help you work out the electronic structure of the following elements:

a carbon [1] **b** fluorine [1]
c neon [1] **d** magnesium [1]

5 The table shows information about the isotopes of an element. Copy and complete the table, and name the element.

Mass number	Number of protons	Number of electrons	Number of neutrons
16	8	8	
17		8	9
	8	8	10

[4]

6 Aluminium, atomic number 27, was discovered by Hans Christian Oersted in Copenhagen, Denmark, in 1825. In 2001, a team of scientists working in Berkeley, USA announced the discovery of a new element with atomic number 118. The discovery of element 118 was later retracted after other scientists reported that they were unable to reproduce the results of the Berkeley team.

a Scientists around the world learned of the discovery of element 118 within hours of the announcement in 2001. The discovery of aluminium was not widely known for several years. Explain this difference. [3]
b Why is it important for the details of new scientific discoveries to be passed on to other scientists? [2]

C3b

1 Which statements about how sodium chloride conducts electricity are true?

A conducts electricity when solid
B does not conduct electricity when solid
C conducts electricity when molten
D does not conduct electricity when molten
E conducts electricity when in solution in water
F does not conduct electricity when in solution in water [3]

2 Explain how metal and non-metal atoms combine. Use ideas about electrons, ions and attraction in your answer. [3]

3 Draw 'dot and cross' models to show the ionic bonding in the following compounds.

a sodium chloride [3] **b** magnesium oxide [3]

4 Potassium ions have the formula K^+.
Aluminium ions have the formula Al^{3+}.
Chloride ions have the formula Cl^-.
Oxide ions have the formula O^{2-}.
What is the formula of each of the following compounds?

a potassium chloride [1] **b** potassium oxide [1]
c aluminium chloride [1] **d** aluminium oxide [1]

5 Use ideas about the structure of magnesium oxide to explain each of the following facts.

a Magnesium oxide has a high melting point. [2]
b Solid magnesium oxide does not conduct electricity. [2]
c Molten magnesium oxide does conduct electricity. [2]

C3c

1 Non-metals combine together by sharing electrons. What is the name given to this type of bonding? [1]

2 Copy and complete this table about Groups and Periods in the Periodic Table.

Symbol of element	Group number	Period number	Number of electrons in outer shell
Li		2	1
Cl	7	3	
Na	1		1
Ne		2	8
F	7		7
Ar	8	3	

[6]

3 Draw 'dot and cross' diagrams to show the bonding in the following molecules.

a hydrogen, H_2 [2] **b** methane, CH_4 [3]

4 Use ideas about forces between molecules to explain the following facts.

a carbon dioxide is a gas at room temperature [2]
b pure water does not conduct electricity [2]

5 The electronic structures of some elements are shown below.

To which Group and Period does each of these elements belong?

a 2,1 [1] **b** 2,8,8 [1] **c** 2,8,7 [1]
d 2,4 [1] **e** 2,8,2 [1]

C3d

1 **a** Describe two things that you **see** when a small piece of potassium is dropped into a trough of water. [2]
b Write word and symbol equations for this reaction. [4]
c Other elements in Group 1 react with water in a similar way. Use ideas about the electronic arrangement of these elements to explain why. [2]

2 A student carries out a flame test on a white powder. The flame has a lilac colour.

a Describe how this flame test is carried out. [4]
b Which Group 1 metal is present in the white powder? [1]

3 The table shows some of the properties of four Group 1 metals.

Group 1 element	Reaction with water	Melting point (°C)	Density (g/cm^3)
lithium	slow	181	0.54
sodium	fast	98	0.97
potassium	very fast	63	0.86
rubidium		39	1.53

Use information in the table to predict the following. For each one, explain your answer.

a The way that rubidium reacts with water. [1]
b Whether caesium will float on water. [1]
c Whether caesium will melt if held in the hand. [1]

4 The reactivity of the elements increases down Group 1. Use ideas about electronic structure and bonding to explain this. [4]

5 When an ion is formed from an atom of potassium, an electron is lost.

a Write a symbol equation for the formation of a potassium ion. [2]
b The formation of a potassium ion is described as an oxidation. Explain why. [2]

C3e

1 Potassium reacts violently when in contact with fluorine.

a Name the compound formed in this reaction. [1]
b Write word and symbol equations for this reaction. [2]

2 The table shows results of some experiments where a halogen was added to the solution of a halide.

Halogen	Halide solution	Result	Halogen displaced
chlorine	potassium bromide	red solution	bromine
chlorine	potassium iodide	brown solution	iodine
bromine	potassium chloride	none	none
bromine	potassium iodide		
iodine	potassium chloride		
iodine	potassium bromide		

a Copy the table and fill in the blank boxes to complete it. [6]
b Explain how these results show the trend in reactivity in Group 7. [3]

3 Predict and explain what you would see in each of the following.

a fluorine is added to a solution of potassium iodide [2]
b fluorine is added to a solution of potassium bromide [2]
c fluorine is added to a solution of potassium chloride [2]

4 The table gives information about some physical properties of three halogens.

Halogen	Boiling point (°C)	Melting point (°C)	Density (g/cm^3)
chlorine	−34	−101	1.56
bromine	59	−7	3.12
iodine	185	114	4.93

a Predict the density of astatine. [1]
b What is the state of astatine at room temperature? [1]
c Predict the boiling point of fluorine. [1]

5 **a** Write an equation to show the formation of a fluoride ion from a fluorine molecule. [2]
b Why is this called a reduction reaction? [2]
c Use this reaction to help you explain why the halogens have similar properties. [2]
d Use this reaction to help you explain the trend in reactivity in Group 7. [4]

C3f

1 During the electrolysis of dilute sulfuric acid a gas is given off at each electrode.

a Which gas is given off at the cathode? [1]
b Which gas is given off at the anode? [1]

2 *Aluminium is extracted by the electrolysis of aluminium oxide.*

a *What gas is formed at the anodes?* [1]

b *The anodes are made of carbon (graphite). Why do they need frequent replacement?* [1]

c *Write a word equation for the decomposition of aluminium oxide that takes place in this electrolysis.* [2]

3 *Write equations for the reactions that take place at the electrodes during the electrolysis of dilute sulfuric acid.* [6]

4 **a** *Aluminium oxide is dissolved in molten cryolyte to make the electrolyte used in the extraction of aluminium. Why is this used instead of just molten aluminium oxide?* [2]

b *Electrolysis is an expensive way to extract a metal from a mineral. Explain why.* [2]

5 *Write equations for the reactions that take place at the electrodes during the extraction of aluminium from aluminium oxide.* [6]

C3g

1 *Transition metals are often used as catalysts. Describe how one transition metal is used in this way.* [2]

2 *The table shows the colours of precipitates made when sodium hydroxide is added to some transition metal ions in solution.*

Transition metal ion	Formula of transition metal ion	Colour of metal hydroxide precipitate
copper(II)	Cu^{2+}	blue
iron(II)	Fe^{2+}	grey/green
iron(III)	Fe^{3+}	orange/brown

Sodium hydroxide solution is added to solution X containing a transition metal sulphate. A green precipitate is formed.

a *Name the transition metal compound in solution X.* [1]

b *Write a word equation for the reaction between the transition metal compound and sodium hydroxide.* [2]

3 *Many carbonates containing transition elements undergo thermal decomposition when heated. Carbon dioxide is given off and the transition metal oxide formed.*

a *What do you* **see** *when a transition metal carbonate is heated?* [2]

b *Write a symbol equation for the thermal decomposition of copper(II) carbonate.* [2]

4 *When sodium hydroxide solution is added to a solution containing a transition metal ion, a coloured precipitate is formed. What does this suggest about the solubility of transition metal hydroxides?* [1]

5 *Write a symbol equation for the reaction between iron(III) ions and hydroxide ions.* [3]

C3h

1 *Most metals have high melting and boiling points. Use ideas about the bonding in metals to explain these facts.* [2]

2 *Superconductors are better conductors of electricity than other metals.*

a *How does a metal conduct electricity?* [1]

b *Why do superconductors conduct electricity so well?* [1]

c *State two uses of superconductors.* [2]

3 *This table shows properties of some metals*

Metal	Electrical conductivity	Heat conductivity	Density (g/cm^3)
aluminium	good	good	2.70
copper	excellent	excellent	8.92
iron	good	good	7.87

a *Suggest why saucepans made from iron often have copper bases.* [1]

b *Why is house wiring made of copper instead of aluminium?* [1]

c *Why are the overhead power cables that stretch between pylons made from aluminium instead of copper?* [2]

4 **a** *Describe the bonding in a metal.* [2]

b *Use ideas about this bonding to explain why metals have high melting points.* [2]

c *Use ideas about this bonding to explain why metals are good conductors of electricity.* [1]

5 *What are the disadvantages of using superconducting metals?* [4]

6 *Scientists tested the hardness of a metal by measuring the force needed to produce a 3 mm deep dent in each of six samples.*

Sample number	1	2	3	4	5	6
Force/N	455	458	398	455	456	454

a *Suggest why the scientists tested six samples rather than one.* [2]

b *The scientists used their results to calculate an average. They did not include the result for sample 3 in this calculation. Explain why.* [2]

C4 Chemical economics

Today I saw a farmer spreading fertiliser on a field. He is using huge bags of the fertiliser. Surely they cost a lot of money, and I thought that using fertiliser was supposed to help farmers grow cheaper food.

Fertiliser is a bulk chemical. It is made in very large quantities and so can be made cheaply. Without cheap fertiliser farmers could not grow as much, so food would be more expensive.

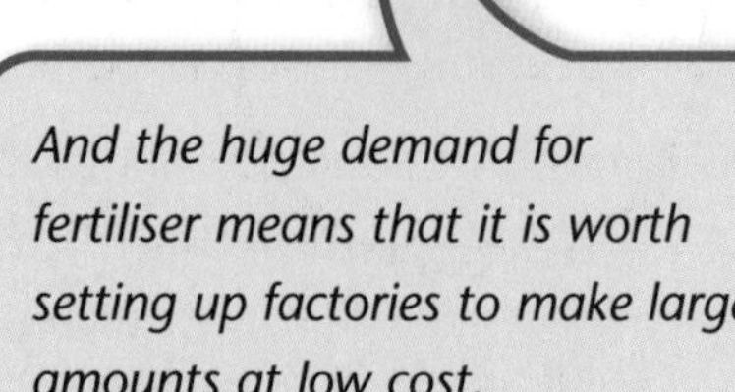

- During the past century the discoveries of chemists have changed the way we live. Methods have been found to extract metals such as aluminium from the Earth, new materials with exciting properties have been invented, and new ways of using well-known materials have been discovered.
- Millions of tons of commonly used metals, such as iron and aluminium, are produced each year. Reagents such as ammonia and nitric acid are made continuously to provide reactants for chemical processes. Vast quantities of fertilisers and polymers are manufactured.
- Other chemicals are needed in much smaller quantities and may be very expensive to make. Many of the new medicines invented by chemists each year are manufactured as they are required to treat diseases.

What you need to know

- Reactants are turned into products in a chemical reaction.
- Accurate measurements can be made using a burette or pipette.
- The use of techniques such as filtration, evaporation, crystallisation and chromatography.

Salt and acid please

▲ These fruits contain citric acid

In this item you will find out

- how acids are neutralised by bases, alkalis and carbonates
- how salts are formed during neutralisation reactions
- how to write balanced equations for neutralisation reactions

Citrus fruits like oranges, lemons and limes have a sharp taste. This is caused by an acid called citric acid that is contained in these fruits. Citric acid is a weak acid so it is safe to eat.

Vinegar is a solution of ethanoic acid, also called acetic acid. You can put a dilute solution of ethanoic acid on your food without harming yourself because it is also a weak acid. Boric acid is so weak it is even used in eye drops to treat infections.

But not all acids are weak and harmless. On 6 August 1949, John George Haigh was executed. He had been found guilty of murdering five people. He disposed of the bodies of his victims by dissolving them in sulfuric acid.

Haigh mistakenly believed that a corpse could be completely disposed of by using the acid. But his last victim's gallstones and false teeth did not dissolve as quickly as the rest of the body. This gave police enough evidence to convict Haigh.

Sulfuric acid is a strong acid. It is very corrosive and will attack many materials including skin and bones. Because of its corrosive properties, this acid is used to clean metal surfaces before they are coated with other metals by electroplating.

▲ Metal surfaces can be cleaned by sulfuric acid

a **Suggest why it is important to remove grease and dirt before the metal surface is coated with another metal.**

b **Suggest why some acids are safe to eat but others are not.**

The pH scale

We can measure how acidic a solution is by using Universal Indicator. When this **indicator** is added to a solution it changes colour to show the level of acidity. This is shown in the diagram.

pH	colour of Universal Indicator	
1	red	strong acids
2		
3		
4		
5	orange	weak acids
6	yellow	
7	green	neutral
8	blue	weak alkalis
9	blue-purple	
10	purple	strong alkalis
11		
12		
13		
14		

The acidity is shown by a number on the **pH** scale.

Describe a solution with pH 8.

Neutralisation

A **base** is a substance that neutralises an acid. Bases are solids but some dissolve in water to form an alkali, for example sodium hydroxide. A base always has a metal part, in this case sodium, and a non-metal part, in this case hydroxide.

When an alkali is added a little at a time to an acidic solution, the pH of the solution gradually changes from acidic to neutral to alkaline. When an acid is added to an alkali the opposite change takes place. Adding an alkali increases the pH. Adding more acid decreases the pH.

The reaction between an acid and an alkali is called **neutralisation**, and always makes a salt and water.

acid + base → salt + water

For example:

$$H_2SO_4 + 2NaOH \rightarrow Na_2SO_4 + 2H_2O$$

sulfuric acid + sodium hydroxide → sodium sulfate + water

Name of acid	Name of salt
sulfuric acid	sulfate
hydrochloric acid	chloride
nitric acid	nitrate

The name of the salt formed during a neutralisation reaction comes from the name of the metal in the base and the name of the acid.

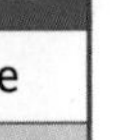

Write word and symbol equations for the reaction between hydrochloric acid and potassium hydroxide.

All acids in solution in water contain hydrogen ions, H^+. All alkalis in solution in water contain hydroxide ions, OH^-. When an acid is neutralised by an alkali, these two ions react to form water.

$$H^+ + OH^- \rightarrow H_2O$$

More about bases

Metal oxides and metal hydroxides are bases, and will neutralise acids. For example:

$$H_2SO_4 + CuO \rightarrow CuSO_4 + H_2O$$

sulfuric acid + copper(II) oxide → copper(II) sulfate + water

$$2HCl + Cu(OH)_2 \rightarrow CuCl_2 + 2H_2O$$

hydrochloric acid + copper(II) hydroxide → copper(II) chloride + water

e **Write word and symbol equations for the reaction between nitric acid and copper(II) oxide.**

f **(i) What salt is produced when magnesium hydroxide neutralises sulfuric acid?**

(ii) Write a balanced symbol equation for the reaction.

Ammonia, NH_3, is a base. When ammonia gas is bubbled into an acid a neutralisation reaction takes place.

$$NH_3 + HNO_3 \rightarrow NH_4NO_3$$

ammonia + nitric acid → ammonium nitrate

g **Write word and symbol equations for the reaction between sulfuric acid and ammonia.**

Acids can also be neutralised by carbonates. In this reaction as well as a salt and water, carbon dioxide gas is made. For example:

$$2HCl + CaCO_3 \rightarrow CaCl_2 + CO_2 + H_2O$$

hydrochloric acid + calcium carbonate → calcium chloride + carbon dioxide + water

h **Write word and symbol equations for the reaction between sulfuric acid and sodium carbonate.**

▲ *Calcium carbonate and hydrochloric acid reacting together*

Examiner's tip

When you have written a symbol equation, count up the number of atoms of each element on either side of the arrow. When the equation is balanced they are the same.

Amazing fact

Most indigestion remedies contain magnesium carbonate or calcium carbonate to neutralise excess acid in the stomach.

Keywords

base • indicator • neutralisation • pH

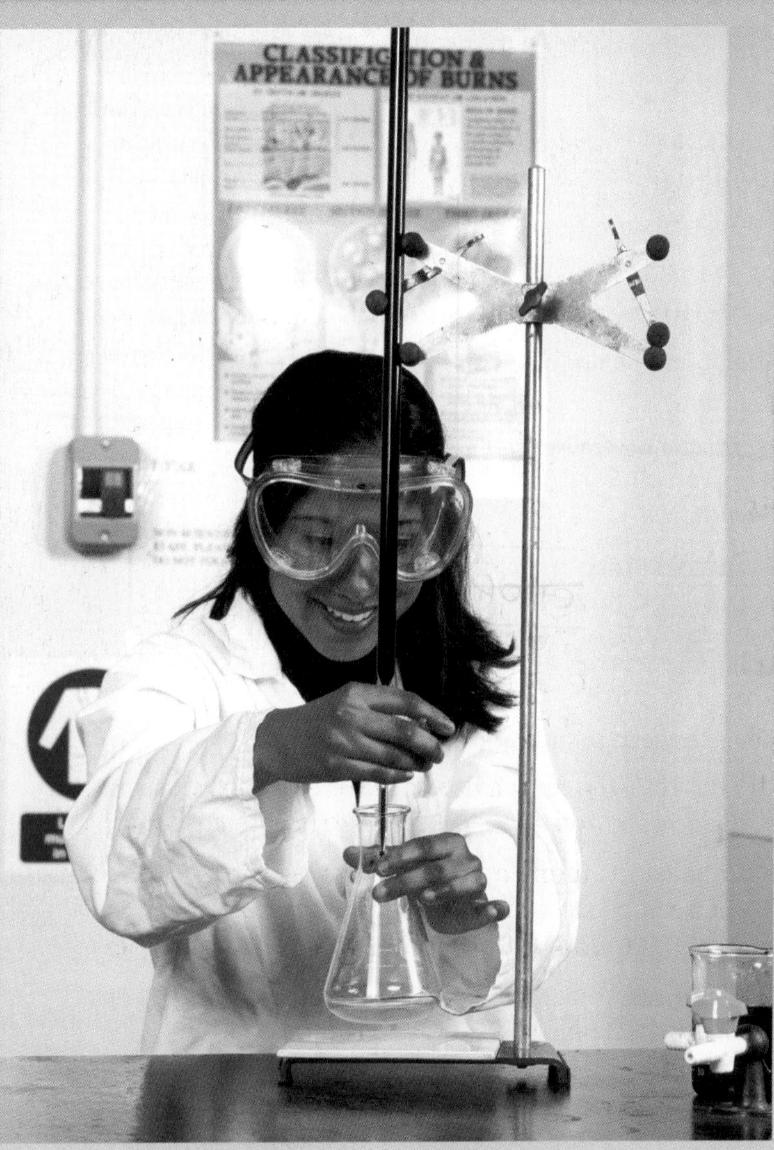

An acid test

Manjit works for a company that makes vinegar. She is a laboratory technician.

She measures the concentration of ethanoic acid in samples of vinegar.

For each sample she:

- accurately measures a volume of the vinegar sample
- adds a few drops of phenolphthalein indicator
- sets up a burette containing sodium hydroxide of known concentration
- adds sodium hydroxide from the burette into the vinegar
- swirls the liquid to make sure it is well mixed
- stops adding sodium hydroxide when the indicator changes to a pink colour
- notes down the volume of sodium hydroxide added.

Manjit uses phenolphthalein indicator. This gives a very clear colour change from colourless when the solution is acidic to pink when the solution is neutral.

She repeats the test until she has two results that are within $0.2\,cm^3$ of each other. She then takes the average of these results.

From the volume of vinegar used and the volume of sodium hydroxide added, Manjit can work out the concentration of vinegar in the sample.

Questions

1 Suggest why the company wants to know the concentration of ethanoic acid in its vinegar.

2 Why does Manjit use phenolphthalein instead of Universal Indicator?

3 Why does she stop adding sodium hydroxide when the liquid turns pink?

4 Why do you think she repeats her experiments until the results are in close agreement?

Disappearing act

▲ Forest devastated by fire

In this item you will find out

- why mass is conserved during chemical reactions
- how to work out the masses of reactants and products in a reaction
- how to work out percentage yield for a reaction

Every summer fires devastate large areas of forest.

Very little is left of the trees that once stood in the forest. Just a few charred stumps and some ash remain. What has happened to the wood in the trees that burned? Where have the many tons of mass gone?

Apart from water, most of the mass in the trees is made of carbon compounds. Only small amounts of other substances are present, for example, compounds of metallic elements. When the carbon compounds in the trees burn they produce carbon dioxide. This goes into the atmosphere, together with the water, which evaporates.

 **Suggest why when trees burn some of the mass remains as ash.**

None of the mass from the trees has been lost. The air has gained exactly the mass that has gone from the forest.

This idea can be demonstrated using a candle. Candle wax is a hydrocarbon. As a candle burns it gets smaller. The candle wax seems to disappear. The hydrogen in the hydrocarbon reacts with oxygen in the air to make water. In the hot flame, this water is formed as a vapour. Carbon in the hydrocarbon also reacts with oxygen, forming carbon dioxide. The water vapour and carbon dioxide go into the air.

In the apparatus on the right, the water and carbon dioxide are absorbed by soda lime (a mixture of sodium hydroxide and calcium hydroxide) in the tube. The mass of both the candle and the tube of soda lime are measured before and after the experiment. It is found that the soda lime gains more mass than that lost by the candle. The extra mass comes from oxygen in the air that has combined with carbon and hydrogen in the wax hydrocarbons to form carbon dioxide and water.

In a chemical reaction the mass of products is always the same as the mass of reactants.

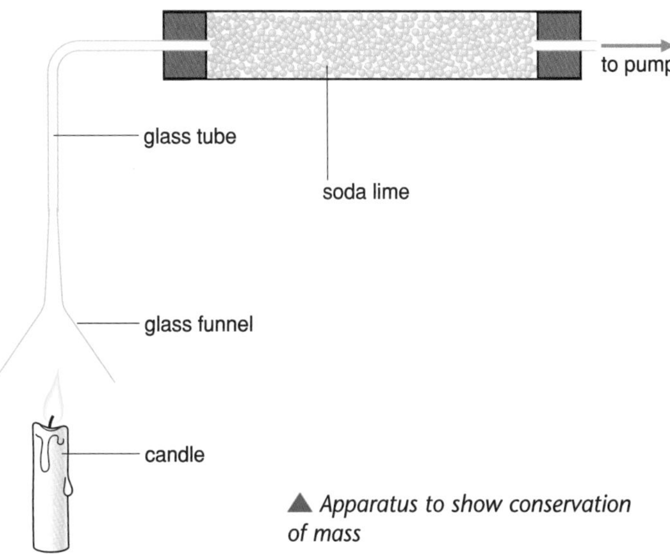

▲ Apparatus to show conservation of mass

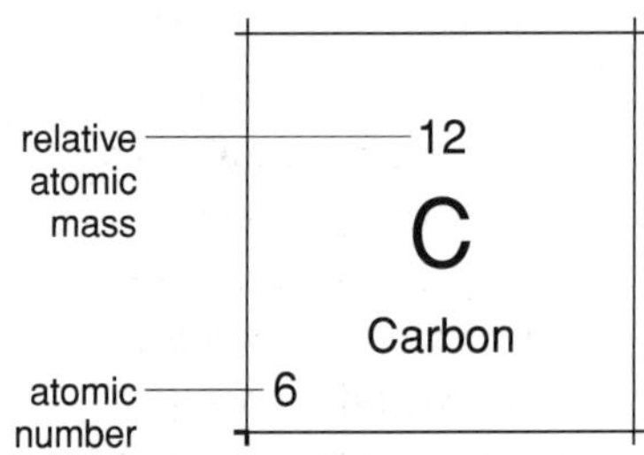

Relative formula mass

In the Periodic Table both the atomic number (proton number) and the **relative atomic mass** (RAM) are shown for each element as shown on the left.

Relative atomic masses are a way of comparing the masses of one atom of each element, using a scale of one atom of the isotope carbon-12 having 12 units of mass.

On this scale an atom of magnesium has a relative atomic mass (RAM) of 24, and an atom of hydrogen has a RAM of 1. This means that an atom of magnesium has the same mass as two atoms of carbon, or 24 atoms of hydrogen. This is shown in the diagram below.

Amazing fact

Atoms are very small. One gram of magnesium contains 25 000 000 000 000 000 000 000 atoms.

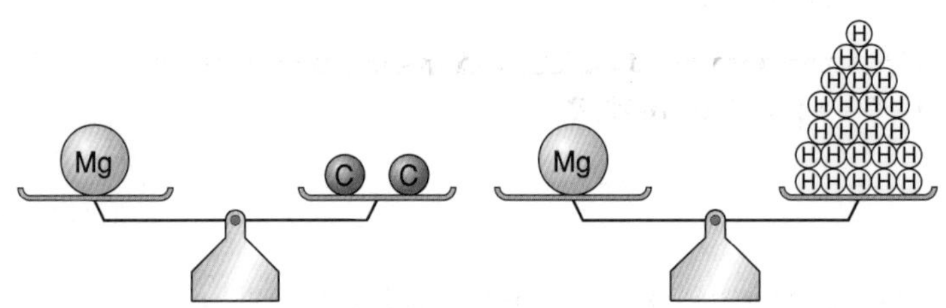

The formula of a compound tells us which atoms are joined together, and how many there are of each. We can use the relative atomic masses shown in the Periodic Table to work out the **relative formula mass** (RFM) of a compound. For example:

H = 1 O = 16 $H_2O = (2 \times 1) + 16 = 18$

The relative formula mass of water is 18.

Sometimes a formula includes symbols in brackets. When the RAMs of the symbols in brackets have been added together, they are multiplied by the number following the brackets.

For example, calcium hydroxide, $Ca(OH)_2$, has two hydroxide groups joined to one calcium atom.

Ca = 40 O = 16 H = 1 $Ca(OH)_2 = 40 + [2 \times (16 + 1)] = 40 + 34 = 74$

The relative formula mass of calcium hydroxide is 74.

Work out the relative formula mass for each of the following compounds.

CaO CO_2 Na_2O $MgCl_2$ $CaSO_4$ $Mg(OH)_2$

Mass of reactants and products

During a chemical reaction reactants are changed into products.

reactants → products
$2Mg + O_2 \rightarrow 2MgO$

A reaction involves a rearrangement of atoms into new compounds. No atoms are gained or lost, so the total mass of the reactants is exactly the same as the total mass of the products.

We can work out how much product is produced from a specific mass of reactant, or how much reactant is needed to make a certain mass of product. For this we use relative formula masses but with g, kg or tonnes as the units.

For example, how much magnesium oxide is made when 6.0 g magnesium burns in an excess (more than enough to react) of oxygen?

$2Mg + O_2 \rightarrow 2MgO$

2 × 24 = 48 g magnesium produces 2 × (24 + 16) = 80 g magnesium oxide

so 6 g magnesium produces $80 \times \frac{6}{48} = 10$ g

Examiner's tip

In a calculation, always show clearly how you have worked out your answer. If you make a small mistake and get the wrong answer, you can still score marks for the working.

c **What mass of magnesium oxide is produced when 16 g of magnesium is burned in excess oxygen?**

d **What mass of magnesium must be burned in excess oxygen to produce 16 g of magnesium oxide?**

▲ *Magnesium burning in a gas jar of oxygen*

Yield

Yield describes how much product has been collected. We can use relative formula masses to work out the maximum mass of product that can be made from the masses of the reactants used. This is called the **predicted yield**.

If we collect the product and weigh it, the mass we have is called the **actual yield**.

During the experiment some of the product is usually lost, so the actual yield is less than the predicted yield. We can compare predicted yield and actual yield by working out the **percentage yield**.

$$\text{percentage yield} = \frac{\text{actual yield}}{\text{predicted yield}} \times 100$$

For example:

In an experiment 11.5 g of sodium is reacted with an excess of chlorine.

The mass of sodium chloride made is 23.4 g. What is the percentage yield?

$2Na + Cl_2 \rightarrow 2NaCl$

2 × 23 = 46 g sodium produces 2 × (23 + 35.5) = 117 g sodium chloride

so 11.5 g sodium produces $117 \times \frac{11.5}{46} = 29.25$ g sodium chloride

$$\text{percentage yield} = \frac{23.4}{29.5} \times 100 = 80\%$$

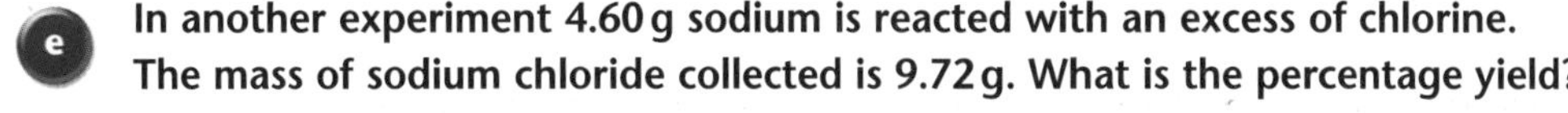

e **In another experiment 4.60 g sodium is reacted with an excess of chlorine. The mass of sodium chloride collected is 9.72 g. What is the percentage yield?**

Keywords

actual yield • percentage yield • predicted yield • relative atomic mass • relative formula mass

Keep on trucking

Bill drives a truck at a limestone quarry.

The quarrymen use explosives to blast the limestone from the quarry. A crane loads large boulders of limestone onto Bill's truck. Each truckload contains 15 tonnes of limestone. Bill drives across the quarry and tips this load into the crusher.

When the limestone is crushed, the smaller pieces of limestone are heated in a rotating furnace. Limestone is made of calcium carbonate. When heated, this decomposes to form quicklime, calcium oxide.

$$CaCO_3 \rightarrow CaO + CO_2$$

calcium carbonate → calcium oxide + carbon dioxide

A measured amount of water is added to this quicklime to produce slaked lime, calcium hydroxide.

$$CaO + H_2O \rightarrow Ca(OH)_2$$

calcium oxide + water → calcium hydroxide

Bill's friend Stan is in charge of the production of calcium oxide and calcium hydroxide at the quarry. Part of his job is to work out the yield of these products.

Questions

1. Work out the maximum mass of calcium oxide that could be made from each load of 15 tonnes of limestone that Bill tips into the crusher. For your calculation assume that limestone is pure calcium carbonate. This is the predicted yield.
2. The predicted yield is less than 15 tonnes. Where do you think the rest of this mass goes?
3. Stan says that the actual yield of calcium oxide from each truckload of limestone is 5.2 tonnes. Suggest why the actual yield for this reaction is less than the predicted yield.
4. Work out the percentage yield for the reaction.
5. What is the maximum mass of calcium hydroxide that could be made from 5.2 tonnes of calcium oxide?
6. The reaction produces calcium hydroxide with a percentage yield of 79%. What mass of calcium hydroxide is produced from each truckload of limestone?

Food for plants

In this item you will find out

- how fertilisers can supply the minerals needed by plants for their growth
- how fertilisers can be made
- some problems caused by using fertilisers

Have you ever seen a polluted river like the one in the photograph on the right? Dead fish float on the surface and the water has a very unpleasant smell.

Lots of chemicals can pollute rivers. One cause of pollution is the overuse of fertilisers. Farmers use fertilisers to increase crop yield. They replace **essential elements** that have been removed from the soil by the previous crop. They can also provide extra essential elements to help the crop to grow better. One of the main elements provided by fertilisers is nitrogen. This gets incorporated into plant protein and so increases growth.

But overuse of nitrogen-containing fertilisers can cause a type of pollution called **eutrophication**. This happens in several stages.

- rain water dissolves fertiliser and the solution runs off from fields into rivers
- the concentration of nitrate or phosphate in the river water increases
- microscopic water plants called algae use these nutrients to grow at a very fast rate, causing an **algal bloom**
- the dense growth of algae blocks sunlight from reaching water plants
- water plants die from lack of sunlight, and the algae also die as nutrients are used up
- bacteria feed on the dead plants and algae, and multiply rapidly, using up oxygen in the water
- without oxygen, fish and other water animals die.

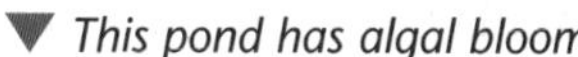
▼ *This pond has algal bloom*

a **Why do the water plants die when sunlight is blocked by algae?**

Most farmers are very careful to apply only the correct amount of fertiliser. They also check the weather forecast before spreading fertiliser, to make sure that there will not be heavy rain.

b **Suggest why farmers need to check the weather forecast before spreading fertiliser.**

Nutrients and plant growth

Plants need a number of chemical elements to grow well. These essential elements are contained in compounds called minerals. Plants get minerals from the soil. When crops are grown and harvested, the soil loses these minerals.

Unless the minerals are put back into the soil by adding fertilisers, future crops will not grow well. Fertilisers also provide extra essential elements, such as nitrogen, phosphorus and potassium, to help plant growth.

Plants take in water through their roots. Minerals are dissolved in this water. The minerals in fertilisers must be in compounds that dissolve (are soluble) in water. Plants can then take in the solution through their roots. You can see this in the diagram below.

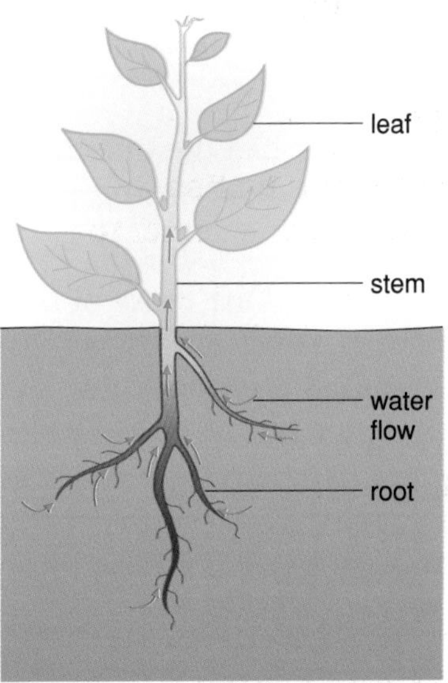

c How do minerals get to the leaves?

Plants use the nitrogen in fertiliser to make protein. When a fertiliser is used to provide more nitrogen, the plants grow faster and bigger. This increases the yield from the crop.

Ammonium nitrate, NH_4NO_3, is a good fertiliser because it contains a lot of nitrogen and is very soluble in water.

The uptake of minerals by a plant is also affected by soil conditions. If the soil is too acidic or too alkaline, plants may not take up as much of a mineral. Farmers may test a sample of soil using Universal Indicator before applying fertiliser.

d Suggest what farmers could do if the soil is too acidic?

Amazing fact

Fertiliser can be dangerous. On 21 September 2001, ammonium nitrate stored in a fertiliser factory in Toulouse, France, exploded. Thirty-one people were killed and over 2000 were injured.

Fertiliser calculations

The relative formula mass of ammonium nitrate can be worked out from the relative atomic masses of the elements.

relative atomic masses: N = 14   H = 1   O = 16

relative formula mass of NH_4NO_3 = (2 × 14) + (4 × 1) + (3 × 16) = 80

The percentage nitrogen in ammonium nitrate can then be calculated.

percentage nitrogen = $100 \times \frac{28}{80} = 35\%$

Ammonium nitrate contains a high proportion of nitrogen. A small amount of this fertiliser gives plants a lot of this essential element.

What is the percentage of nitrogen in the fertiliser sodium nitrate, $NaNO_3$?

Making a fertiliser

A fertiliser can be made by a neutralisation reaction. An acid and an alkali react together to make a salt. For example:

$$NH_3 + HNO_3 \rightarrow NH_4NO_3$$

ammonia + nitric acid → ammonium nitrate

The correct quantities of the acid and the alkali must be mixed. To do this, accurate volume measurements have to be made using a pipette and burette.

Suggest why accurate measurement of the amounts of acid and alkali is important.

The salt solution is evaporated to a smaller volume, then left to cool until solid crystals of the salt form. These crystals are separated from the remaining solution by filtration.

By using different acids and alkalis, different fertiliser compounds can be made.

▲ *Fertiliser bags*

Acid	Alkali	Fertiliser
nitric acid	ammonia	ammonium nitrate
sulfuric acid	ammonia	ammonium sulfate
phosphoric acid	ammonia	ammonium phosphate
nitric acid	potassium hydroxide	potassium nitrate

These salts can then be mixed to make a fertiliser that will provide plants with nitrogen, phosphate and potassium. This is often referred to as an NPK fertiliser.

Examiner's tip

Lime, calcium hydroxide, is often spread on fields to neutralise acidity, but it is not a fertiliser. Ammonium nitrate is a fertiliser because it supplies nitrogen for plant growth.

Keywords

algal bloom • essential elements • eutrophication

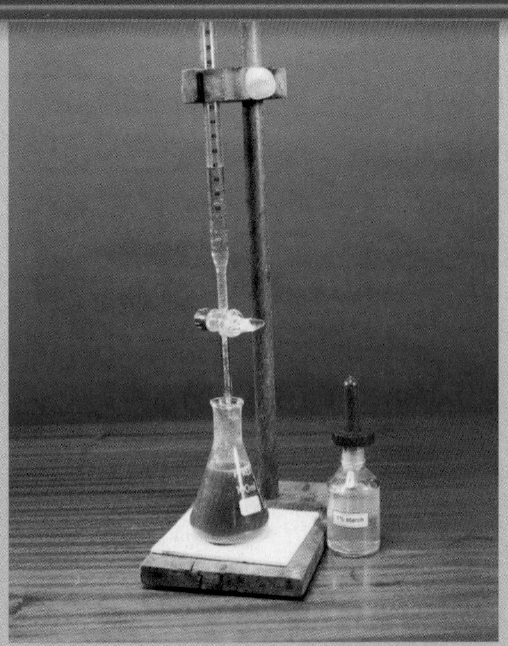

▲ Apparatus used for titration

Making potassium nitrate

Chris works in the laboratory of a chemical company. He makes a small quantity of potassium nitrate to test its use as a fertiliser.

He follows a procedure called a titration to make a solution of potassium nitrate.

He repeats this titration to get a second solution. He then makes crystals from the second solution.

Chris fills a burette with dilute potassium hydroxide solution.

He then uses a pipette to measure out a volume of dilute nitric acid into a conical flask.

To this nitric acid he adds a few drops of phenolphthalein indicator – this is colourless in an acidic solution but pink in a neutral solution. To the mixture in the conical flask he gradually adds potassium hydroxide solution from the burette.

Chris stops adding the potassium hydroxide when the indicator changes from colourless to pink, showing that all of the acid has reacted with the alkali. He notes down the volume of potassium hydroxide added from the burette, and throws away this first pink solution.

Then Chris measures a fresh sample of dilute nitric acid (the same volume as before) into a clean conical flask, but this time he does not add any phenolphthalein indicator. He adds to this nitric acid the same volume of potassium hydroxide from the burette as he used the first time.

He uses heat to evaporate some of this second solution so that the volume is reduced then he leaves the solution to cool and form crystals.

Finally, Chris separates the crystals from the remaining solution by filtration and leaves the potassium nitrate crystals to dry.

▲ Crystals are separated by filtration

Questions

1. Write a symbol equation for the reaction Chris is using.
2. Why does Chris need to use an indicator?
3. Phenolphthalein changes from colourless in acid to pink when neutral. Why does this give a clearer indication of when enough alkali has been added than Universal Indicator?
4. Why does Chris not make crystals of potassium nitrate from the first solution he makes?
5. Why do you think he reduces the volume of the second solution by evaporation to make the crystals?

C4d Making ammonia – the Haber Process and costs

Reversible reactions

In this item you will find out

- how ammonia is made using the Haber Process
- how conditions used for the process affect the cost of the product
- how we use the ammonia that is produced

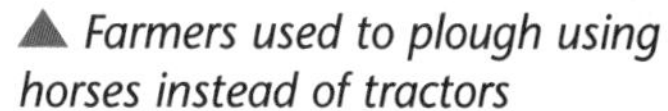

▲ *Farmers used to plough using horses instead of tractors*

For centuries farmers used manure and crop rotation (growing a different crop each year) to give their crops enough nitrogen for them to grow well. Simpler methods of agriculture were used than today. When the population of Europe was small, enough food could be grown this way.

During the nineteenth century the population in Europe increased at a fast rate.

To provide the nitrogen needed to grow enough food, guano (bird droppings) was imported from Chile and Peru. However, by the beginning of the twentieth century these supplies were used up.

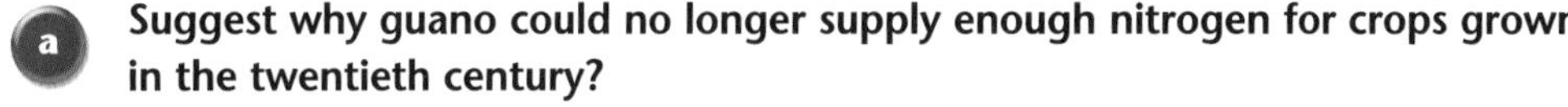

a **Suggest why guano could no longer supply enough nitrogen for crops grown in the twentieth century?**

The famous scientist Sir William Crookes warned that the exhaustion of these nitrogen-rich guano deposits would lead to worldwide starvation if no alternative could be found.

In 1908, the German chemist Fritz Haber found a way to combine nitrogen and hydrogen to make ammonia.

Ammonia made by this process is used to make nitric acid, which is used to make fertilisers (such as ammonium nitrate) and explosives. Ammonia is also used in household cleaning products.

b **Explain how Fritz Haber's discovery solved the problem of food supply in Europe.**

During the First World War, Fritz Haber's process supplied the materials needed to make munitions such as bombs. He also devised and manufactured poison gases, which he described as 'a higher form of killing'.

In recognition of his work, Fritz Haber was awarded the Nobel Prize for chemistry in 1918. At the presentation ceremony other scientists refused to shake his hand.

Thanks to Fritz Haber's discovery, it is now possible to grow more than enough crops to feed the population in the developed countries.

▼ *Fritz Haber*

Amazing fact

China now uses more synthetic fertiliser than any other country – over 40 million tons in 2004.

The Haber Process

In the Haber Process, ammonia is made from nitrogen and hydrogen.

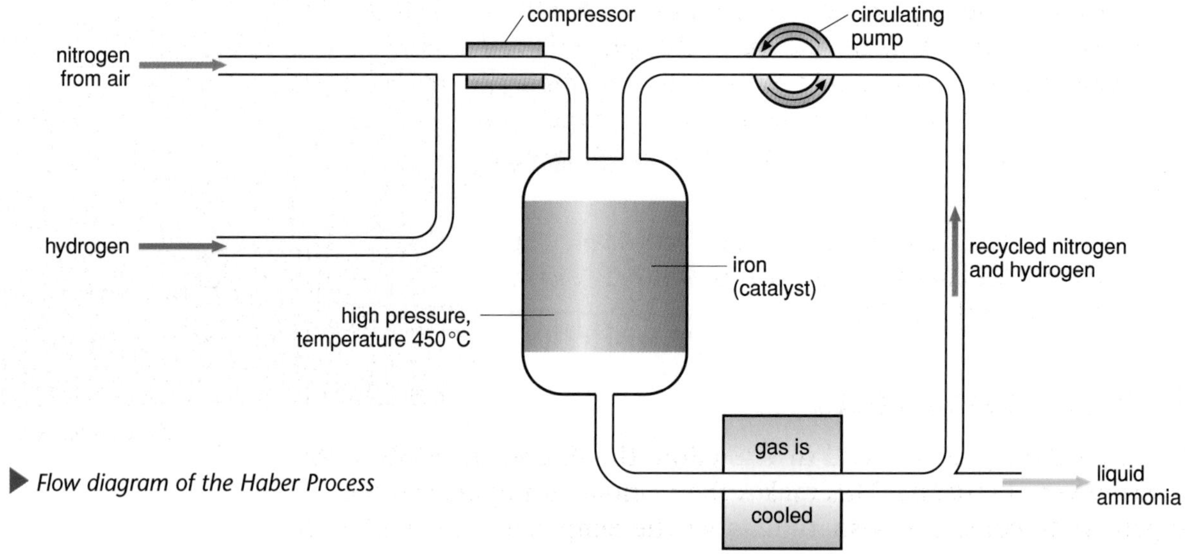

▶ *Flow diagram of the Haber Process*

Nitrogen gas is extracted from the air, and hydrogen is obtained from natural gas or the cracking of fractions from the distillation of crude oil.

 **The air contains about 78% nitrogen and is free. But nitrogen for the Haber Process is an expensive raw material. Suggest why.**

Nitrogen and hydrogen are reacted together under carefully controlled conditions:

- a temperature of about 450 °C
- a high pressure
- an iron catalyst

Using these conditions about 15% of the nitrogen and hydrogen are converted into ammonia as they pass through the reaction vessel.

$$N_2 + 3H_2 \rightleftharpoons 2NH_3$$

nitrogen + hydrogen ⇌ ammonia

This is a **reversible reaction**. It can go in either direction. As ammonia is formed it breaks down into nitrogen and hydrogen. This means that the reaction mixture always contains unreacted nitrogen and hydrogen. For this reason not all of the nitrogen and hydrogen form ammonia.

 **Why does the mixture of gases leaving the reaction vessel contain only 15% ammonia?**

Examiner's tip

In a reversible reaction there will always be some of each of the reactants present as well as the products.

Why certain conditions are used

So why does the Haber Process use a certain temperature and pressure, and a catalyst?

A high pressure encourages the formation of ammonia from nitrogen and hydrogen – the higher the pressure, the higher the yield of ammonia.

A high temperature encourages the reaction that decomposes ammonia into nitrogen and hydrogen. So the yield of ammonia decreases as the temperature increases. But, the higher the temperature, the faster the rate of reaction. This means that although the yield of ammonia is lower, it is produced more quickly. A compromise temperature of about 450 °C is used. This gives a reasonable yield with a fast enough rate of reaction.

An iron catalyst is used in the process. This speeds up the reaction. The catalyst alters the rate of reaction, but does not change the yield.

▲ A chemical factory

Manufacturing costs

The higher the pressure used in a reaction, the thicker the walls of the reaction vessel must be. This makes the manufacturing plant more expensive to construct. Also, the higher the temperature the higher the energy cost. However, a faster reaction makes more chemical in the same time and so reduces the cost.

Catalysts speed up the rate of a reaction. Although a catalyst costs money, a chemical can be made in a shorter time, saving fuel costs. When unreacted chemicals are recycled back into the reaction vessel, this reduces the cost of expensive raw materials. The chemicals can be passed through the reaction chamber several times which means that none is wasted.

The reaction process can be **automated**. This means that computers can be used to monitor and adjust the conditions, such as temperature and pressure, and the flow of chemicals. This reduces the number of people involved and so reduces the wages bill. It also enables the conditions to be controlled more accurately.

Computers are used to control conditions in the Haber Process. Explain the advantages of using them.

Chemical economics

To compete with other companies, a factory that makes a chemical product must do so as cheaply as possible.

The rate of the reaction used must be high enough to make a sufficient quantity of the chemical product each day. To achieve this, for most processes a high temperature is used. For most reactions a catalyst is also used to speed up the rate of formation of product.

Optimum conditions are a compromise to produce a good enough yield at a fast enough rate, and so make the chemical at the lowest possible cost.

Sometimes a low yield is acceptable if unused reactants can be recycled back into the reaction vessel. This means that expensive raw materials are not wasted.

Keywords

automated • reversible reaction

Building a Haber Process factory

Dr Jones works for a company that is going to build a new factory to make ammonia from nitrogen and hydrogen using the Haber Process.

$$N_2 + 3H_2 \rightleftharpoons 2NH_3$$
nitrogen + hydrogen ⇌ ammonia

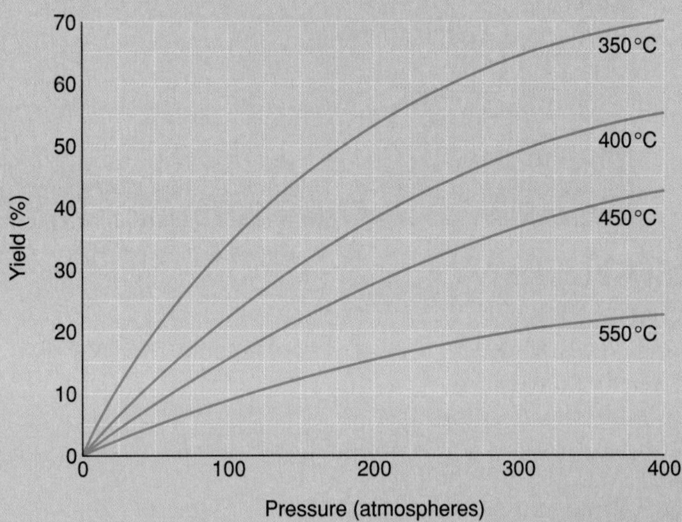

He must decide on the conditions that will be used in the reaction vessel of the new factory, so that it can be built using the correct materials and design.

He looks at this graph showing the effect of temperature and pressure on the yield of ammonia in the Haber Process using an iron catalyst.

From this data Dr Jones decides that the new factory will use an iron catalyst and will operate at 450 °C and 175 atmospheres pressure.

Dr Smith tells Dr Jones about a new catalyst that can be used for the Haber Process. He shows Dr Jones some experimental data about the new catalyst.

	Iron catalyst	New catalyst
Rate of ammonia formation (kg per min)	433	748
Cost of catalyst (£)	3800	12 600
Lifetime of catalyst (year)	12	4

Dr Smith says that they should use the new catalyst in their Haber Process factory.

Questions

1. What does the graph show about the relationship between percentage yield of ammonia and temperature?
2. What does the graph show about the relationship between the percentage yield of ammonia and pressure?
3. What yield of ammonia will be obtained in the new factory using the conditions proposed by Dr Jones?
4. Suggest why the new catalyst proposed by Dr Smith may be a good option for the new factory.
5. Dr Jones decides not to use the new catalyst. Suggest why he made this decision.

Whiter than white

In this item you will find out

- what goes into washing powders and washing-up liquids
- how these products clean
- how dry-cleaning works

Some clothes have a label that says 'Dry-clean only'. If you wash these clothes in a washing machine they will be damaged. Often they shrink, even if washed at low temperature. Sometimes clothes have stains that are very difficult to remove in a washing machine. Greasy stains such as lipstick or butter may still be visible after the clothes have been washed.

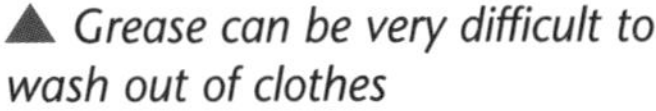

▲ *Grease can be very difficult to wash out of clothes*

These clothes are taken to a **dry-cleaning** company. Workers at the dry-cleaning company do not wash the clothes in water. They use an organic solvent. This is a compound obtained by the distillation of crude oil.

The solvents used in dry-cleaning are volatile (evaporate easily) and toxic. Suggest what precautions the workers at a dry-cleaning company should take.

▲ *A dry-cleaners*

Water is the most widely used solvent but it will not dissolve all substances. Some substances that are not soluble in water will dissolve in an organic solvent.

Water molecules have small positive and negative charges. This means that they will easily attract and dissolve other substances that also have positive and negative charges. However, they will not attract molecules that have no charge.

Oil and grease contain compounds with molecules that do not have any charge. Molecules of these compounds are not attracted to the charges on water molecules, but intermolecular forces of attraction are formed between the uncharged oil or grease molecules and the uncharged molecules of an organic solvent.

So, the organic solvents used in dry-cleaning dissolve oily and greasy stains that are difficult to remove in a washing machine. These solvents do not damage the fabric of the clothes. They are also quick to evaporate.

Why do you think it is important that the solvents used in dry-cleaning evaporate quickly?

Soap or not?

Washing powders are complex mixtures of ingredients. They are designed to get clothes clean even using water at temperatures as low as 30°C. This saves energy. It also avoids damaging some delicate fabrics, which would otherwise have to be dry-cleaned.

Each of the chemicals in a washing powder has a different job to do. The active **detergent** is the chemical that does the cleaning. Many of these detergents are made by the neutralisation of acids and alkalis.

The detergent in some washing powders is soap but most washing powders contain a synthetic detergent – also called a soapless detergent. Synthetic detergents clean better but soap is less damaging to delicate fabrics.

Synthetic detergents are designed to wash at low temperatures. This means that less energy is used to heat up the water. Also delicate fabrics are less likely to be damaged if washed at a low temperature. At a high temperature the dye in some clothing may 'run' as it is dissolved into the water, and the clothing may shrink.

Amazing fact

Evidence of ancient washing soap was found at Sapo Hill in Rome, where the ashes containing the fat of sacrificial animals was used as a soap.

Detergent molecules

Detergent molecules have a charged hydrophilic (water-loving) head and an uncharged hydrophobic (water-hating) tail. The tails of the detergent molecules are attracted to and stick into the greasy dirt. The heads of the detergent molecules are attracted to charged water molecules.

The force of this attraction between the heads and water molecules pulls the dirt off the clothes. The detergent molecules then surround the dirt. This keeps the dirt suspended in the water so that it doesn't go back onto the clothes.

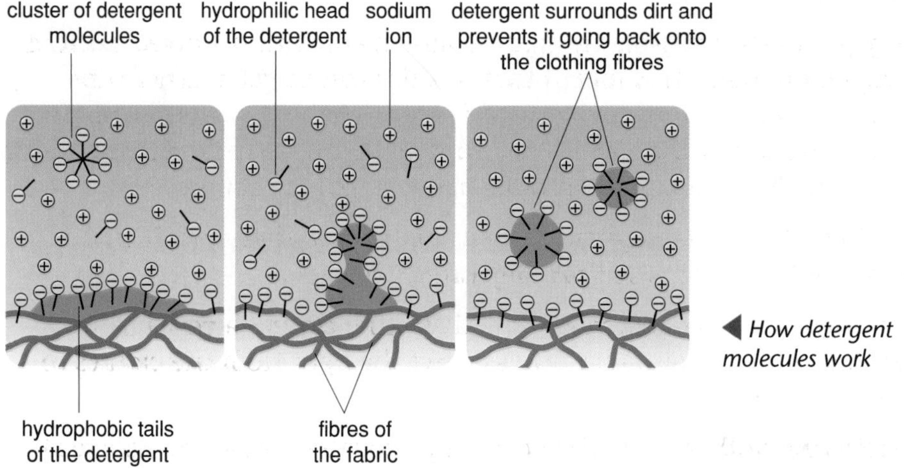

◀ *How detergent molecules work*

c **Why must a detergent have an uncharged tail and a charged head?**

Making soap and synthetic detergents

▲ *Making soap*

Soap is made by the neutralisation of fatty acids from animal fats or vegetable oils with an alkali such as sodium hydroxide. Fatty acids have long chains of carbon and hydrogen atoms which form the hydrophobic end of the detergent. In fats and oils the fatty acids are joined to glycerol in a complex molecule called a triglyceride. When the triglyceride reacts with sodium hydroxide, the sodium salt of the fatty acid is formed. This is soap and the reaction is called saponification. The charged end of the sodium salt is the hydrophilic end of the molecule.

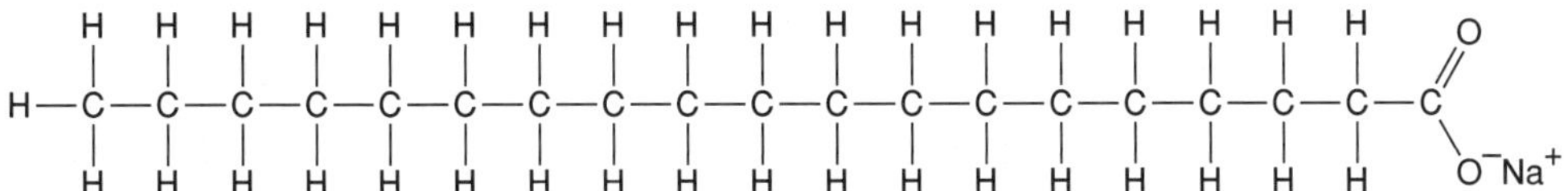

▲ *A soap molecule*

Synthetic detergents are made by the neutralisation of a synthetic acid that has a long hydrocarbon chain with an alkali such as sodium hydroxide. The result is a molecule similar to soap, but with much more powerful detergent properties.

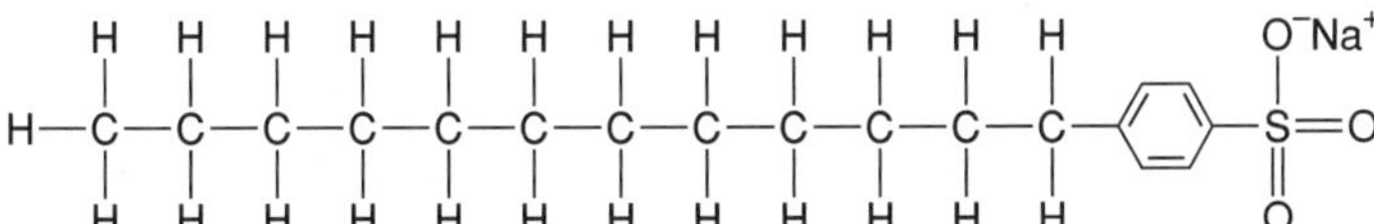

◀ *A synthetic detergent molecule*

d **What do the structural formulae of the soap and synthetic detergents have in common?**

More ingredients

In many places the tap water is hard because it contains dissolved calcium and magnesium salts. This means that it is difficult to get a lather with soap. Hard water also forms a scum with soap. Washing powders contain chemicals that soften the water. This stops clothes being covered with scum. It also means that you can use less detergent to get the clothes clean.

Some coloured stains are difficult to remove from clothes. Bleach takes the colour out of these stains so that they cannot be seen.

Optical brighteners are chemicals that give white clothes a very bright 'whiter than white' appearance. They reflect the light from the clothes to our eyes.

Food stains on clothes are broken down by enzymes. These are biological catalysts that speed up the reactions that break down some stains. They will only work in a low temperature wash, for example at 40°C. Enzymes are proteins and are destroyed at high temperatures.

e **Suggest why it may be an advantage to leave dirty clothing to soak for a while in a solution of washing powder containing enzymes, before beginning the wash cycle of the washing machine.**

Keywords

detergent • dry-cleaning

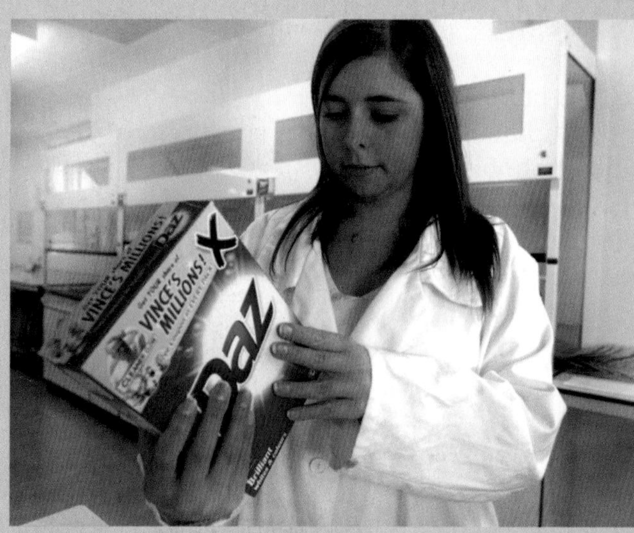

Which washes whiter?

Anita works for a company that makes washing powders. The company employs scientists to develop new and better washing powders. When a new product has been developed it needs to be tested to see if it is truly better than those already sold.

Anita's job is to test new washing powders to see if they are better than the washing powders that the company has made for some time.

She tests a washing powder containing a new synthetic detergent. For comparison she also tests a washing powder containing an old synthetic detergent and another containing soap flakes.

Anita takes 11 similar pieces of white cotton cloth. She stains 10 of these pieces using the same mixture of dirt and grease.

She dissolves the two washing powders and the soap flakes in water at different temperatures, and places one of the dirty cloths in each solution – putting the clean cloth and the remaining dirty cloth to one side.

She stirs each cloth in its solution. She leaves the cloths for 30 minutes. She then stirs again. Then she rinses and dries each cloth.

Anita scores how well each piece of cloth has been cleaned on a scale of 1 (very dirty) to 10 (very clean).

Her results are shown in the table.

	Washing temperature (°C)		
Washing powder	**30**	**60**	**90**
containing soap	3	5	7
containing 'old' synthetic detergent	6	9	10
containing 'new' synthetic detergent	8	9	10

Questions

1 Anita did not put dirt onto one piece of cloth, and put this and one dirty cloth to one side. Suggest why.

2 What do the results show about the effectiveness of soap and synthetic detergents in removing dirt from the cotton cloth?

3 In what way is the new synthetic detergent better than the old one?

4 Why may this experiment not simulate what happens in a washing machine?

5 What do the results show about the effect of temperature on the cleaning action of soap and synthetic detergents?

6 Suggest an explanation for this effect of temperature on cleaning action.

Making drugs

In this item you will find out

- about using batch or continuous processes to make chemicals
- about the cost of research and development of new medicines
- the differences in the production of bulk and speciality chemicals

▲ *Thalidomide can cause babies to be born with disabilities*

In the late 1950s and early 1960s, pregnant women across the world were prescribed a new remedy for morning sickness. At the time nobody had any idea how this would affect the lives of their unborn children. Around ten thousand babies were born with disabilities as a result of their mothers taking the drug thalidomide. Just under half of those have survived, including 456 of them in the UK.

Though the first child afflicted by thalidomide damage was born on 25 December 1956, it took about four and a half years before doctors suspected that thalidomide was causing these deformities. Thalidomide was withdrawn in the UK in 1961.

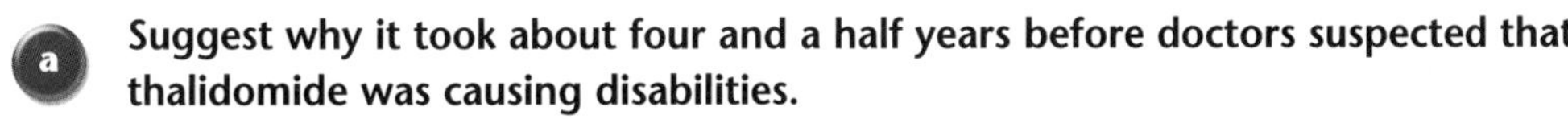

a **Suggest why it took about four and a half years before doctors suspected that thalidomide was causing disabilities.**

Two things are clear about the testing of thalidomide. First, thalidomide was never tested on pregnant animals before it was used in humans. Second, after thalidomide had been withdrawn, it was tested on pregnant mice, rats, hamsters, rabbits, macaques, marmosets, baboons and rhesus monkeys, and the same terrible effects were found.

At that time there was no legal requirement to test new drugs on pregnant animals before they were given to humans. If it had been tested in this way the disaster could have been avoided.

In the middle of the last century we did not know enough to prevent thalidomide being used by pregnant women. Today, laws on drug testing are much stricter. If thalidomide had been developed in the twenty-first century, rigorous testing on animals, including pregnant animals, would have been required, and this would have prevented the tragedy.

b **Why is it unlikely that a similar tragedy will occur in the future?**

Development costs

Developing a new medicine or **pharmaceutical drug** is a long and costly process. It may take 15 years and cost over £300 million pounds to develop a new drug. The flow chart shows the steps in the development of a new drug.

▼ *How a new drug is developed*

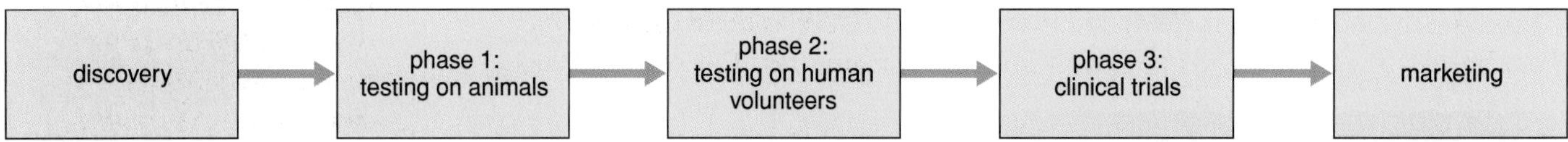

Thousands of new chemical compounds are made and tested to find one new product. When a promising chemical compound is found it has to be tested. This involves testing on animals and then on volunteers. Finally clinical tests are used to find out how effective it is at curing patients and to make sure that are no serious side effects.

THE SIDE EFFECTS OF THE CURE FOR BIRD FLU WERE UNEXPECTED

When the drug is proved to be effective, it has to have legal approval before it is sold.

Finally it can be marketed. This involves advertising and supplying the drug to hospitals and doctors.

Why do you think so few of the compounds tested are marketed as new drugs?

Production costs

The development of the drug is not the only expense that the drug company has. The company also has to meet very high costs during manufacture of the drug.

It takes a lot of people to make the new drug. Some of the processes involved cannot be automated, and many require highly skilled workers. Paying the wages of all these employees costs the company a lot of money.

The raw materials needed to extract or make the drug have to be purchased. Many of these raw materials are rare and expensive. To get some of the required materials from plant sources, costly extraction processes are required.

The manufacturing process for a drug uses a lot of energy. The company has to pay for the electricity, gas or oil used in manufacture.

Extracting chemicals

Many drugs are extracted from plants. This process follows several stages.

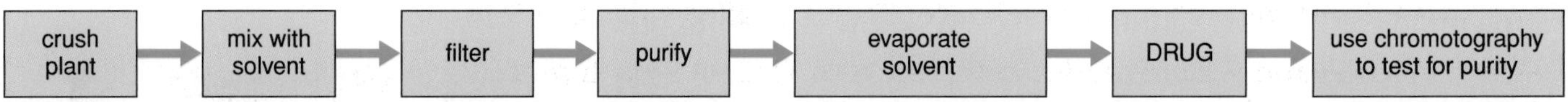

▲ *Extracting a drug from a plant*

Firstly the plant material is crushed. This breaks the tough cell walls in the plant and releases the chemicals contained in the plant cells. Most of the chemicals extracted from plants are not soluble in water so a suitable organic solvent is mixed with the crushed plant material to dissolve the chemicals. Solid plant material is then removed from the mixture by filtration.

The organic solvent dissolves other chemicals as well as the required drug so the drug must now be purified by removing it from the other chemicals. This is done by mixing the solution with another solvent that will dissolve the drug but not the other chemicals. This solvent is then evaporated off to leave the pure drug.

To make sure that the drug is pure it is tested using **chromatography**. This helps to identify both the drug and any impurities that may still be present.

Drugs extracted from plants are tested for purity using chromatography. Suggest how this will show whether or not the drug is pure.

Amazing fact

Aspirin is a pharmaceutical drug that is made in huge quantities. Worldwide, over 100 billion aspirin tablets are taken each year: about 20 tablets for each person living on the Earth.

Development decisions

Several factors have to be considered by a pharmaceutical company before making the decision whether or not to make a new drug:

- in terms of time and labour, what the cost of research and development for the new drug will be
- how long it will take to meet legal requirements, including testing, before the drug can be sold
- how much demand there will be for the new product
- how long it will take for profits from sale of the drug to repay the investment made by the company.

Pharmaceutical companies are some of the richest in the world. Suggest how they make such large profits when the expense of developing new drugs is so high.

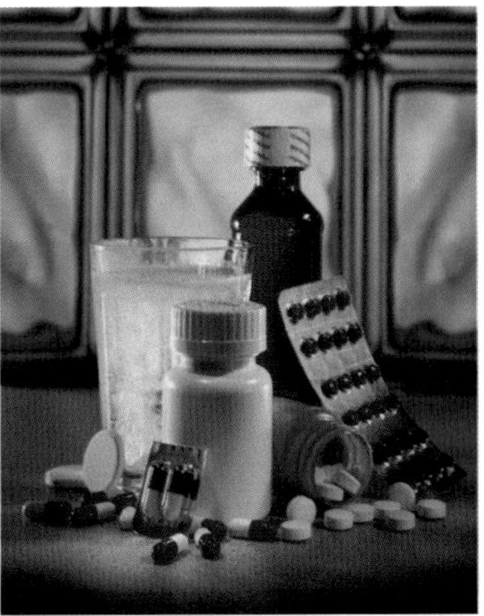

▲ *These medicines are made from speciality chemicals*

Batch and continuous processes

The chemical industry can produce products using two types of process: **batch process** or **continuous process**.

The Haber Process for the manufacture of ammonia is an example of a continuous process. Nitrogen and hydrogen are passed into the reaction vessel. Here they react to make ammonia. The ammonia gas is condensed into a liquid and collected as it is produced. This process can continue for 24 hours a day until the plant has to be closed down for maintenance.

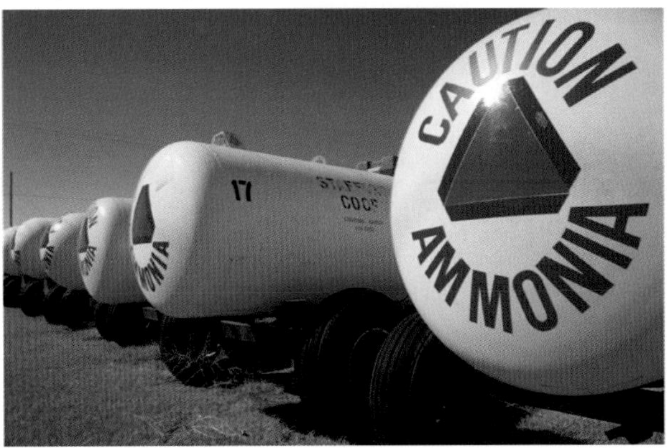

▲ *Ammonia is a bulk chemical*

Like other chemicals made by continuous processes, ammonia is used in the manufacture of many other products. Because they are so widely used, very large quantities of these chemicals are made. They are called bulk chemicals.

Many medicines and pharmaceutical drugs are produced by a batch process. Measured amounts of raw materials are mixed and processed to produce the drug. This happens only when a new supply is required. These chemicals are not made continually. Also, much smaller quantities of these chemicals are made. They are called speciality chemicals or fine chemicals.

Bulk chemicals are much cheaper to buy than speciality chemicals. Suggest why.

Keywords

batch process • chromatography • continuous process • pharmaceutical drug

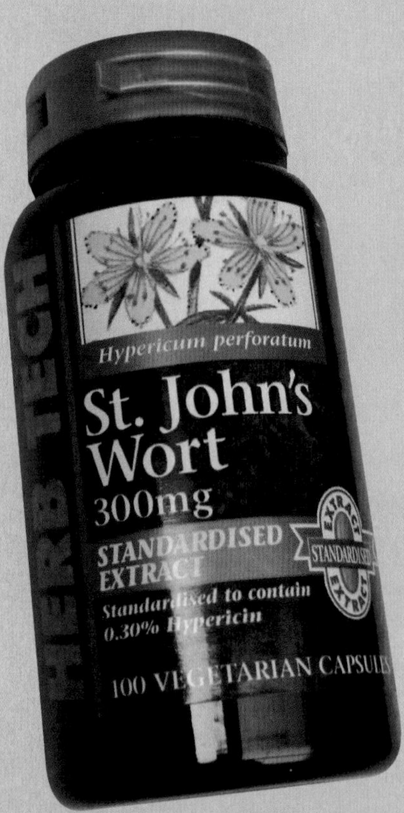

▲ St John's Wort

St John's Wort

St John's Wort, sometimes called the 'Sunshine herb', is a bushy perennial plant with numerous star-shaped yellow flowers. It is native to many parts of the world, including Europe and the United States, and has been used as a herbal remedy for about two thousand years.

St John's Wort is used by many people to treat mild depression, as an alternative to prescribed drugs such as Prozac (fluoxetine). Research shows that it is not the whole plant but an ingredient called hypericin that has anti-depressant activity.

Paul runs a small natural and herbal medicine company. One of the products his company sells is St John's Wort. Paul sells packets containing the dried stems and leaves of the plant.

Over the past year Paul's sales of this product have increased by 300%.

Paul has developed a process to extract the active ingredient, hypericin, from the stems and leaves of St John's Wort.

He sells this extract in tablets at a much higher price than the dried plant.

Paul produces small quantities of the extract by a batch process. This requires the work of several people for a whole day. The process uses standard equipment that Paul has in his factory.

Another way to produce the extract uses a continuous process. This involves the purchase of new, and very expensive, machinery. When this machinery is running, it requires only one person to look after the process.

Both processes require the plant St John's Wort as raw material. Paul can negotiate with his supplier to buy the plant in larger quantities at a lower price.

Questions

1 Describe an advantage and a disadvantage of Paul using a batch process to produce the extract from St John's Wort?

2 Describe an advantage and a disadvantage of Paul using a continuous process to produce the extract from St John's Wort?

3 Suggest what other costs Paul may have before his extract can be sold to the public?

4 What other information do you think Paul should obtain to help him decide which process to use to make this extract?

It's a small world

In this item you will find out

- about the three forms of carbon: diamond, graphite and fullerene
- about the properties and uses of these forms of carbon
- how fullerene has been used to create a miniature chemical world – nanochemistry

How is a pencil like a diamond ring?

They both contain carbon. The pencil 'lead' is made from graphite. The gemstone in the ring is diamond. Graphite and diamond are different forms (**allotropes**) of carbon. They contain only carbon atoms but these are arranged in different ways.

This gives these two types of carbon some different properties which you can see in the table below.

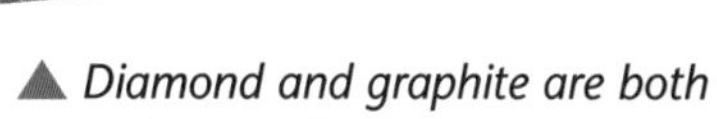

▲ *Diamond and graphite are both made from carbon*

Diamond is lustrous and colourless, making it ideal for use in jewellery. The fiery appearance of a diamond is caused by the separation of white light into the colours of the spectrum as it passes through the stone. This makes diamond the most sought-after gemstone.

 **Both diamond and graphite are lustrous. Why do you think only diamond is used as a gemstone?**

Diamond is also the hardest natural substance. Diamond can be cut only with another diamond, and is very resistant to wear. It is an excellent material for the cutting edges of industrial tools.

The properties and uses of graphite are quite different. Since graphite conducts electricity and has a high melting point, it is used as an electrode in electrolysis reactions. The graphite is used to pass an electric current through the molten material or solution to be electrolysed. An example is the manufacture of aluminium.

The softness and black colour of graphite make it useful for pencil 'lead'. The slipperiness of graphite means it is a good lubricator. It is used as an additive to oils and greases.

 **Diamond is much more expensive than graphite. Suggest why.**

Diamond	Graphite
colourless and transparent	black and opaque
very hard	soft and slippery
very high melting point	high melting point
does not conduct electricity	conducts electricity
lustrous with a brilliant shine	lustrous

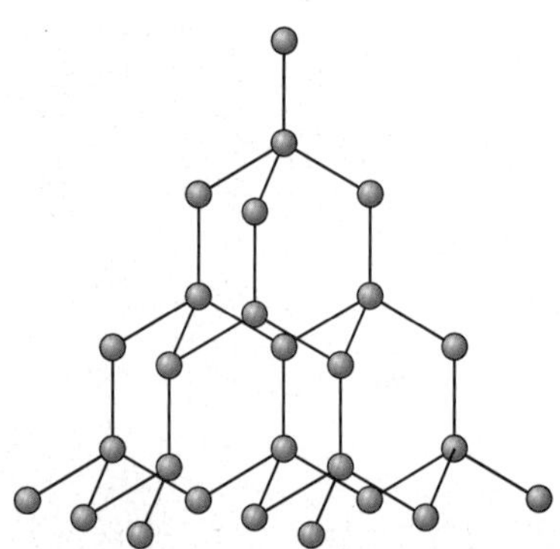

▲ *How carbon atoms are arranged in diamond*

Diamond

The differences in properties shown by diamond and graphite are caused by the different ways that the carbon atoms are arranged in the two allotropes.

In diamond, each carbon atom is joined to four others by strong covalent bonds. To separate the atoms these covalent bonds need to be broken. This requires a very large amount of energy. This explains why diamond is so hard and has such a high melting point.

The structure of diamond contains no ions or free electrons. There are no mobile charged particles to carry an electric current, so diamond does not conduct electricity.

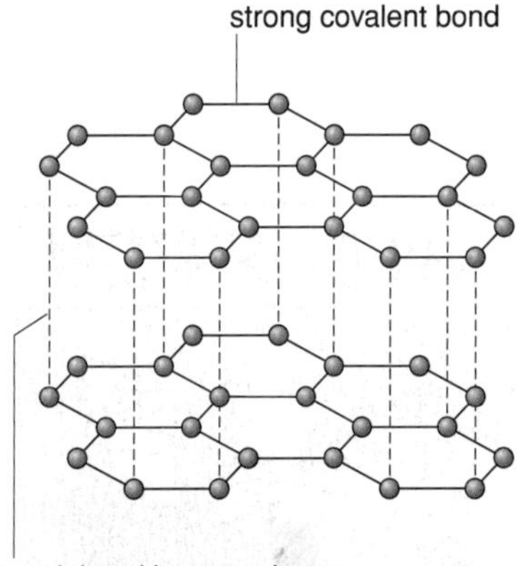

▲ *The layers of carbon atoms in graphite*

Graphite

In graphite the carbon atoms are arranged in layers.

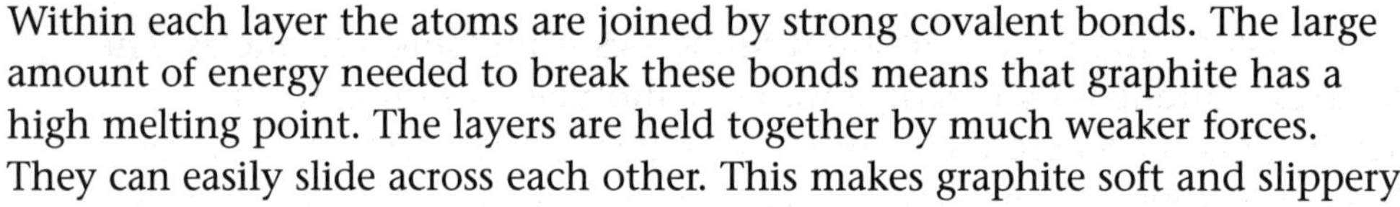

Within each layer the atoms are joined by strong covalent bonds. The large amount of energy needed to break these bonds means that graphite has a high melting point. The layers are held together by much weaker forces. They can easily slide across each other. This makes graphite soft and slippery.

The electrons between the layers of graphite are **delocalised**. This means that these electrons can move along in the space between the layers, carrying an electric current. So, graphite can conduct electricity.

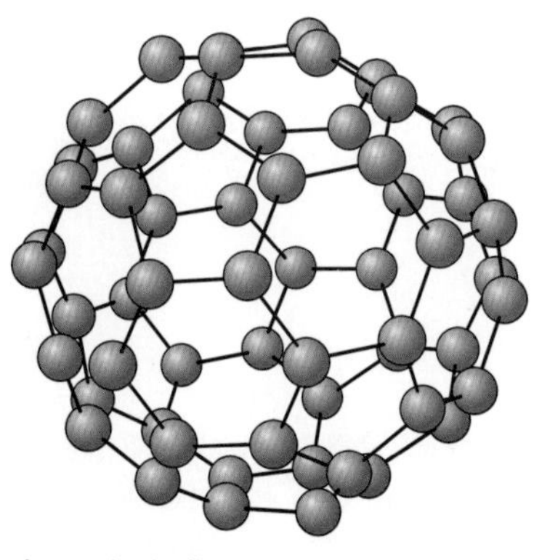

▲ *Bucky balls*

Buckminsterfullerene

A third allotrope of carbon, buckminsterfullerene, was discovered in 1985. Each molecule of this allotrope is made up of 60 carbon atoms joined to each other in the shape of a ball. These are known as 'Bucky balls'. Buckminsterfullerene has the formula C_{60}.

Since this first discovery, other **fullerenes** have been made with different numbers of carbon atoms in each ball. The number of atoms ranges from 32 to 600.

Nanotubes

Fullerenes can be joined together to make tube shapes called **nanotubes**. This has led to a whole new area of development called nanotechnology.

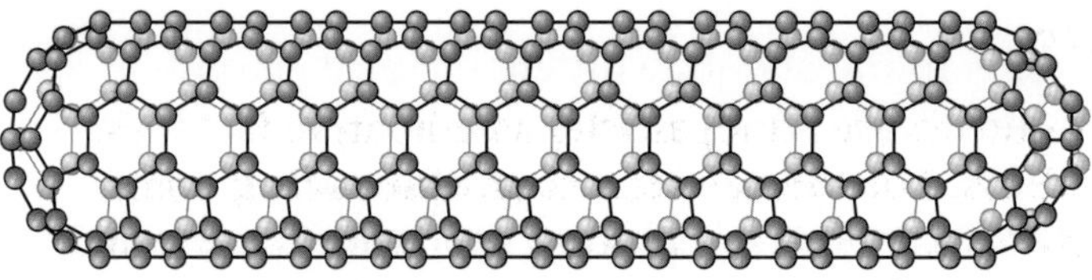

▶ *How carbon atoms are arranged in a nanotube*

Nanotubes are very strong and can conduct electricity. They have a number of uses as:

- semiconductors in electrical circuits
- industrial catalysts
- a reinforcement for the graphite in tennis racquets.

Catalyst atoms or molecules can be attached to the outside of nanotubes. This allows a wider variety of substances to be used as catalysts. Even though the nanotubes are so small, they have a very large surface area. This gives a very large area of contact for the catalyst. The nanotubes can be separated from liquid products, allowing re-use of the catalyst.

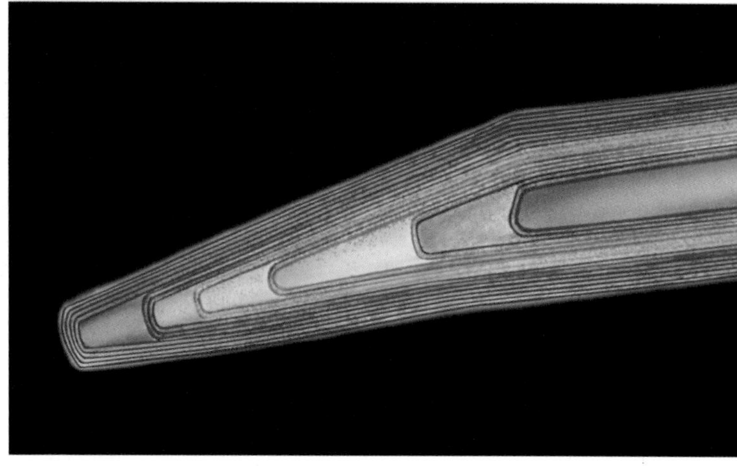

▲ *Electron micrograph of carbon nanotube fibres*

Nanoparticles

The discovery of nanotubes has created a new area of science called nanochemistry. Normally, chemistry works with materials on a large scale. Nanochemistry uses materials on a very small scale. It works with materials at the atomic level, with particles of incredibly small size, called **nanoparticles**.

These nanoparticles have different properties from 'bulk' chemicals. The electrical conductivity of single-walled nanotubes is similar to that of metals. This is because their unique structure means electrons can freely pass along a material made from nanotubes. They are the only known molecules that can electronically act as a true metallic conductor. By spacing and controlling the size of the nanotubes they can behave as semiconductors, similar to silicon.

NAN O'- CHEMISTRY

Caging molecules

It is possible to use fullerene nanotubes as 'cages' in which to trap other molecules. Just a few molecules can fit inside or be attached to the outside of a nanotube.

In the future, nanotubes containing drugs for the treatment of diseases such as cancer may be injected into the bloodstream. They will deliver the drugs straight to the tumour and not release them elsewhere in the body. This means that less of the drugs will be needed and there will be less damage to other cells in the body.

It is thought that drugs carried in fullerenes will be more effective in treating cancer tumours, and that they will have fewer side effects than those injected directly into the bloodstream. Suggest why.

Making molecules

It may ultimately be possible to use nanoparticles as miniature factories, producing chemical products. This **molecular manufacturing** could be achieved by nanoparticles assembling a product molecule by molecule, each nanoparticle bringing a different part, perhaps just a few atoms, to be precisely positioned in the assembly of a complete molecule. This is called **positional chemistry**.

Another possibility is to start with a larger structure, and remove part of it bit by bit until it has nanoscale features.

Keywords

allotropes • delocalised • fullerenes • molecular manufacturing • nanoparticle • nanotube • positional chemistry

Nanoparticles may cause brain damage

Nanotechnology – the science of incredibly small particles – may pose a real threat to human health, scientists have warned. Research shows that nanoparticles, the ultra fine powders produced by the nanotechnology industry, can build up in the brain if they are inhaled. Because the particles are so fine, they could remain in the atmosphere for some time. We could take them in with every breath, while being unaware of the danger.

In a study carried out on rats, researchers found that once the rats inhaled tiny carbon nanoparticles, the particles not only accumulated in the lungs but also found their way to parts of the brain. Although the rats appeared to be unaffected by the particles, scientists believe they could ultimately lead to brain damage.

Nanoparticles are among the most common materials to come out of the new science, being used in everything from sun block to plastic car bumpers.

Only small quantities of nanoparticles are currently produced in Britain. But it is a growing industry which is expected to be worth billions within a decade.

Scientists fear that the more companies start producing nanoparticles, the greater the risk that these particles may get into the atmosphere where they could be inhaled. Some nanoparticles are already widespread in the air we breathe, largely due to the burning of fossil fuels and vehicle exhaust fumes. In a busy street, each breath we take contains around 25 million nanoparticles. Scientists already suspect that nanoparticles from diesel fumes contribute to heart disease, asthma and other respiratory diseases.

They caution that this finding does not warrant a ban on the use of nanotechnology, but say we should be very careful when producing new nanoparticles. Further research is needed to find out if these tiny particles are likely to pose a big threat.

Questions

1. Why are we unaware of breathing in nanoparticles?
2. What discovery from the research on rats has worried scientists?
3. Nanotechnology is a very new science, yet scientists say that we have been breathing in nanoparticles for years. Explain this apparent contradiction.
4. Explain why scientists do not think that a ban on the use of nanotechnology is justified at the moment.

Water, water everywhere

In this item you will find out

- which chemicals may pollute our water
- about the processes used in the purification of water
- about ways of testing for some substances that may be dissolved in water

▲ *The water in this lake contains harmful chemicals*

Water is essential to all living things. Without water we cannot survive for more than a few days. Not only must we have water to drink, but that water must not contain chemicals or microbes that may harm us. The water coming out of your taps at home may come from a river, lake, reservoir or aquifer.

Tap water is not pure. It contains many dissolved chemicals. These include salts that dissolved as the water passed over rocks. These are harmless to us. Water may also contain pollutants, such as:

- nitrate residues – these get into the water when rain dissolves and washes fertiliser from fields into rivers and lakes
- lead compounds – these can dissolve into water from lead pipes in very old houses
- pesticide residues – if farmers spray a pesticide too near rivers or lakes, some may drift over, or be washed by rain, into the water.

a **The water pipes in some old houses are made of lead. Why should these pipes be replaced with new ones made of copper or plastic?**

▼ *Clean water is very important*

In many of the developing nations, people get their water directly from rivers or lakes, without any purification. Often this water is contaminated with sewage and contains disease-causing microbes. Aid agencies such as Oxfam are working to make clean water available to these people.

Not only is water essential for use in our homes but it is also a material vital to industry.

Water is used as:

- a cheap raw material in some manufacturing processes
- a coolant to prevent many industrial processes from overheating
- a solvent.

b **TV adverts are often used in a campaign to persuade people in the United Kingdom to use less water. This country has a high rainfall. Suggest why it is important for us to conserve water?**

Amazing fact

In the United Kingdom on average each person uses more than 150 litres of water each day.

Is it fit to drink?

When water is pumped from a lake, reservoir or river it contains a number of materials dissolved or suspended in it. These may include:

- dissolved salts and minerals
- microbes
- pollutants
- insoluble materials.

During water purification, those materials we do not wish to remain in the water supplied to our homes are removed.

Which of the substances in the list above would make the water unsafe to drink?

Water purification

Water from most sources contains small insoluble solid particles. The first job in the purification of water is to remove these suspended solids. Water is first passed into a **sedimentation** tank. Here the larger solid materials suspended in the water are allowed to settle. These include sand and soil particles.

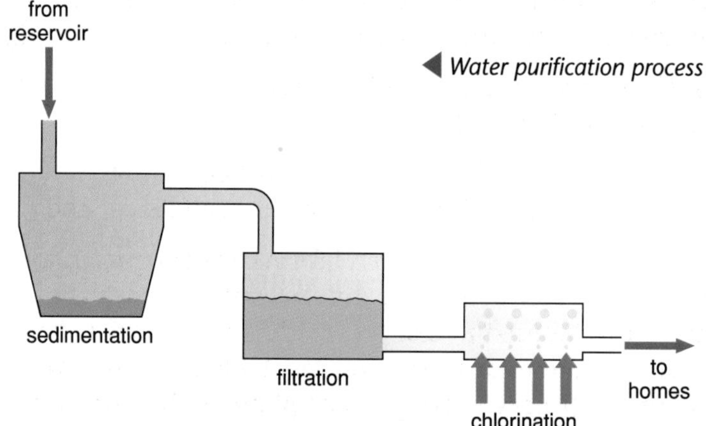

Water purification process

Next, water goes through **filtration**. It is passed through a filter made of layers of grit, coarse sand and fine sand. This traps finer suspended materials consisting of very small and light particles such as clay. These particles are too small and light to settle out in the sedimentation tank.

Finally the water undergoes **chlorination**. A very small quantity of chlorine gas is dissolved in the water. This kills microbes that might otherwise cause disease.

Chlorine is a very poisonous element. Suggest why it is not harmful to us when we drink chlorinated water?

The purification process does not remove all impurities from water. A number of dissolved chemicals remain. Soluble salts of calcium and magnesium cause water hardness. This is not harmful to anyone drinking the water but does cause damage to the heating elements in kettles and washing machines. Other chemicals dissolved in the water may include nitrates, pesticides, herbicides and metal salts. Some of these are poisonous. Though they are present only in very low concentrations, they may have an adverse effect on health.

Distilling seawater

In some countries, seawater is distilled to obtain drinking water. A little over 3% of the mass of seawater is dissolved salts, mainly sodium chloride. When seawater is distilled, these salts are left behind.

On a small scale, distillation can be used to provide enough water for use on long sea journeys in small yachts. On a large scale, the distillation process uses a lot of energy. The product is pure water, which has no taste.

Suggest why distillation of seawater is used to make large quantities of fresh water only in places where water cannot be obtained from other sources.

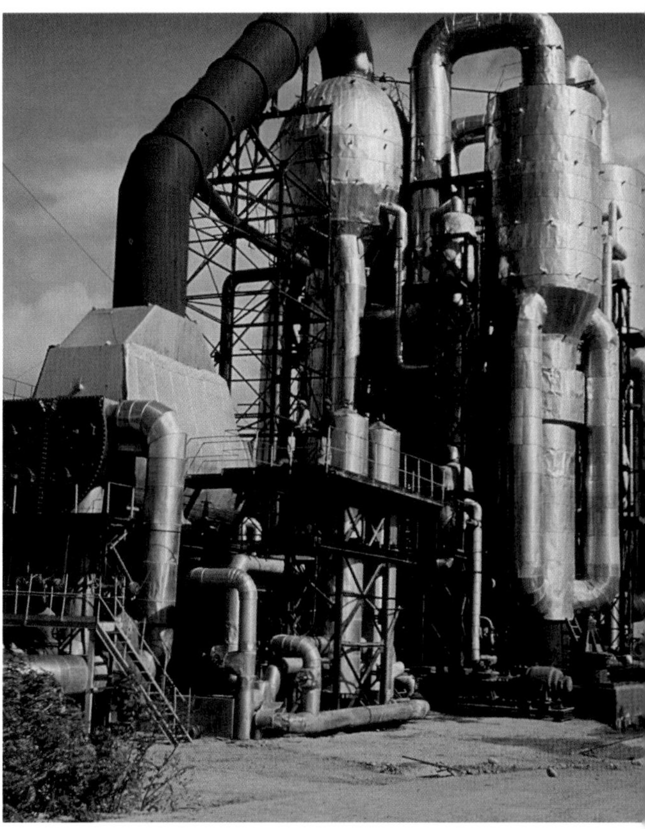

▲ *Seawater is turned into drinking water here*

Testing water

Water can be tested to identify some of the chemicals dissolved in it. These tests involve **precipitation** reactions. In these reactions, dissolved chemicals react to make an insoluble product. This is suspended in the solution to form a precipitate, making the mixture appear cloudy.

To test for sulfate ions, barium chloride solution is added. For example, with sodium sulfate:

$$Na_2SO_4 + BaCl_2 \rightarrow BaSO_4 + 2NaCl$$

sodium sulfate + barium chloride → barium sulfate + sodium chloride

Barium sulfate is insoluble in water and forms a white precipitate. This shows that there is a sulfate dissolved in the water. In a similar way, silver nitrate solution can be used to test for halide ions: chloride, bromide and iodide. Each of these ions forms an insoluble silver salt, which is precipitated out. Each halide forms a precipitate with a different colour.

Halide	Chloride	Bromide	Iodide
Name of precipitate	silver chloride	silver bromide	silver iodide
Colour of precipitate	white	cream	yellow

For example, with sodium halides:

$$NaCl + AgNO_3 \rightarrow AgCl + NaNO_3$$

sodium chloride + silver nitrate → silver chloride + sodium nitrate

$$NaBr + AgNO_3 \rightarrow AgBr + NaNO_3$$

sodium bromide + silver nitrate → silver bromide + sodium nitrate

$$NaI + AgNO_3 \rightarrow AgI + NaNO_3$$

sodium iodide + silver nitrate → silver iodide + sodium nitrate

Write word and symbol equations for the reaction between potassium bromide and silver nitrate.

Examiner's tip

A precipitate is formed only when the product of a reaction is insoluble in water. Soluble products do not form precipitates.

Keywords

chlorination • filtration • precipitation • sedimentation

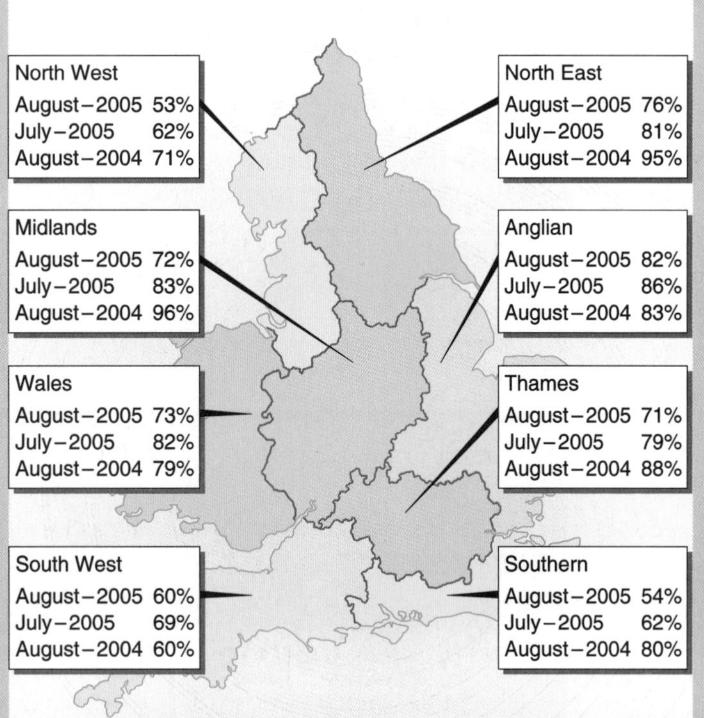

Monitoring water pollution

Dr White works for a water supply company. His company takes water from reservoirs, then purifies it and supplies it to customers in industry and in private houses.

Although the United Kingdom has a high annual rainfall, most of this rain falls during the winter. This fills up the reservoirs so that they give a good supply of water during the summer. If winter rainfall is a lot less than usual, the reservoirs are not filled, and water supplies may become very low during the summer.

When water levels are very low, water supply companies have to reduce demand. They can do this by banning the use of hosepipes for watering gardens and washing cars. They can also advise people of ways to reduce the amount of water they use at home, such as taking showers instead of baths and reducing the amount of water used each time a toilet is flushed.

The water supply companies monitor reservoir levels in their areas during the year. Part of Dr White's job is to predict whether there is likely to be a shortage of water supply in his area during the next summer. He works in the Southern region, which has the highest population density in England and Wales.

Dr White looks at the map above showing reservoir levels in the year from August 2004 to August 2005.

The map shows how full the reservoirs in each area were at three times: in August 2004 after high demand during the summer, in July 2005 when they still contained most of the water from winter rain, and again in August 2005.

Questions

1 The figures for Wales show that reservoir levels rose and then fell during this year. Suggest why this happened.

2 In none of the regions were reservoirs very near to 100% full during this year. What does this suggest about the amount or rain that fell during the winter of 2004–2005?

3 How is the pattern of reservoir levels in most of the other regions different from that in Wales? Suggest a reason for this difference.

4 Dr White looks at a long-term weather forecast for the winter of 2005–2006. This suggests that rainfall will be less than average. Suggest and explain the most likely prediction that Dr White makes for water supplies in his region during the summer of 2006.

5 Suggest what advice Dr White's water supply company will give to its domestic consumers during the summer of 2006.

C4a

1 An acid is slowly added to a solution of a base. The word equation for the reaction that takes place is:

acid + base → salt + water

a What is the term used to describe a base that is soluble in water? [1]
b Explain why the pH changes during this reaction. [1]
c Write a word equation for the reaction between an acid and a carbonate. [2]

2 When an acid is added to a base a salt is produced.

Copy and complete this table – fill in the empty boxes to show which salt is produced.

acid	base	salt
sulfuric acid	sodium hydroxide	
hydrochloric acid	magnesium oxide	
nitric acid	potassium carbonate	

3 **a** Which ions are always present in an acidic solution? [1]
b Which ions are always present in an alkaline solution? [1]
c Write a symbol equation to show the neutralisation reaction between these two ions. [2]

4 Copper(II) oxide is added to sulfuric acid. The word equation for this reaction is:

copper(II) oxide + sulfuric acid → copper(II) sulfate + water

Write a symbol equation for this reaction. [3]

5 Write word and symbol equations for the following neutralisation reactions.

a sulfuric acid and potassium hydroxide [2]
b hydrochloric acid and ammonia [2]
c nitric acid and calcium carbonate [2]

C4b

1 When calcium carbonate is heated it decomposes to form calcium oxide and carbon dioxide. 100 g of calcium decomposes to give 56 g of calcium oxide.

a What mass of calcium oxide is made when 10 g calcium oxide decomposes? [1]
b Write a word equation for the reaction. [2]

2 A student adds 5.6 g calcium oxide to some hydrochloric acid.

She evaporates some water from the solution, leaves the solution to form crystals of calcium chloride, filters off the crystals and then leaves them to dry.

She uses relative atomic masses to work out that the predicted yield of calcium chloride for this experiment is 11.1 g.

She finds that the mass of calcium chloride she has made is 8.0 g

a What is the percentage yield for her experiment? [2]
b Suggest two reasons why she did not get 100% yield. [2]

3 For any chemical reaction, the total mass of reactants is the same as the total mass of products.

Explain why. [2]

4 Copper(II) carbonate decomposes when heated.

$CuCO_3 \rightarrow CuO + CO_2$

3.1 g of copper(II) carbonate is completely decomposed by heating.

a What mass of copper(II) oxide is formed? [3]
b What mass of carbon dioxide is given off? [3]
(Relative atomic masses: C,12; Cu, 64; O,16.)

5 When aluminium is heated in chlorine, 6.0 g of aluminium chloride is made, according to this equation.

$2Al + 3Cl_2 \rightarrow 2AlCl_3$

What mass of aluminium reacted to make this aluminium chloride?
(Relative atomic masses: Al, 27; Cl, 35.5.) [3]

C4c

1 The compounds used in fertilisers are soluble in water.

Explain why this is important. [2]

2 The fertiliser potassium nitrate can be made by a neutralisation reaction between an acid and an alkali.

Name the acid and alkali. [2]

3 If the same type of crop is grown in the same field for several years, the yield falls.

If fertiliser is applied to this field each year, the yield does not fall.

Explain why. [3]

4 Describe the process of eutrophication. [6]

5 Ammonium nitrate, NH_4NO_3, and ammonium sulfate, $(NH_4)_2SO_4$ are popular fertilisers.

Calculate the percentage of nitrogen by mass in each. (Relative atomic masses: H, 1; N, 14; O, 16; S, 32.) [4]

6 A scientist studies the effect of nitrate pollution on the growth of algae to give an algal bloom.

He adds different amounts of ammonium nitrate to equal volume samples of the same river water.

After five days he measures the amount of light that can pass through the water, compared with a control.

His results are shown in the table.

Mass of ammonium nitrate added (g)	Percentage of light passing through (%)
0	100
1.0	88
2.0	64
3.0	41
4.0	25
5.0	18

a Describe the correlation shown in this data. [1]
b What is the connection between the percentage of light passing through the solution and the growth of algae? [2]
c What additional information is needed to decide whether ammonium nitrate is the cause of algal bloom? [1]

C4d

1 **a** State two conditions used in the Haber Process to give a good yield of ammonia in a short reaction time. [2]
b Describe how each of these affects the rate and yield of the ammonia produced. [2]

2 Explain why ammonia is important in relation to world food production. [4]

3 Explain how temperature and pressure conditions used in the Haber Process affect the cost of production of ammonia. [2]

4 Explain how temperature and pressure conditions used in the Haber Process are a compromise to produce ammonia at the cheapest cost. [4]

5 For many years iron has been used as a catalyst in the Haber Process.

A new catalyst is being tested. Here is a comparison of iron and the new catalyst.

	Iron	New catalyst
Cost of Catalyst	cheap	expensive
Percentage conversion to ammonia	15	25
Pressure and temperature used	pressure 100–140 atmospheres temperature 400–700 °C	pressure 80–100 atmospheres temperature 300–400 °C
Replacement interval	5 years	still unknown

Describe two advantages and two disadvantages of using the new catalyst instead of iron. [4]

C4e

1 Describe the function of the following ingredients in a washing powder:

a active detergent [2]
b water softener [2]

2 Some clothes are cleaned by a dry-cleaning process.

a How is this process different from using a washing powder? [1]
b What are the reasons for using this process instead of a washing powder? [2]

3 Describe the essential features of a molecule which functions as a detergent. [2]

4 Describe how a detergent molecule:

a removes dirt from clothing during the washing process [2]
b prevents dirt from going back onto clothing during the washing process. [2]

5 Sam uses a washing powder that contains enzymes.

The instructions on the packet say that she should wash clothing at 40 °C.

a What may happen to the enzymes in the washing powder if she washes the clothing at a higher temperature? [2]
b What other advantages are there for washing clothing at a low temperature? [2]

C4f

1 Making and developing a new pharmaceutical drug is usually much more expensive than producing a bulk chemical such as ammonia.

Describe three factors that make the drug so much more expensive. [3]

2 Describe the processes used in the extraction of chemicals from plant sources. [5]

3 It may take several years for a new pharmaceutical drug to move from first synthesis in a laboratory to marketing to the public.

Explain why this takes so long. [2]

4 Pharmaceutical companies carry out extensive market research to get information about the attitude of members of the public to a new product.

Market research is expensive. Why do the companies spend this money? [2]

5 A pharmaceutical company has developed a new drug.

The managing director of the company is given this data about the drug.

Cost of development (£)	120 000 000
Expected annual sales (kg)	15 000
Selling price (£/kg)	2 700
Cost of production by batch process (£/kg)	1 700
Cost of production by continuous process (£/kg)	700

a How long will it take before the company gets back the cost of developing the new drug:

i using a batch process [2]
ii using a continuous process? [2]

b The managing director decides to use a batch process.
Suggest why he made this decision. [2]

6 The drug fluoxetine is used to treat depression. Its development and testing took many years, and its side effects are well known. Some people drink tea made using leaves of the plant St John's Wort to treat depression. This is a herbal remedy which has not received the testing that is required by law for any new drug.

What are the advantages and disadvantages of using St. John's Wort to treat depression instead of fluoxetine?

C4g

1 Diamond and graphite are allotropes of carbon.

Use the properties of diamond and graphite to explain the following facts.

a Diamond is used in cutting tools. [2]
b Graphite is used to make pencil leads. [2]

2 Buckminsterfullerene is another allotrope of carbon. It can be used to make nanotubes.

Describe three uses for nanotubes. [3]

3 Use ideas about bonding to explain why diamond does not conduct electricity but graphite does. [4]

4 Explain how nanotubes can be used to increase the effectiveness of catalysts. [2]

5 Fullerenes can be used to 'cage' other molecules.

a Explain what is meant by this statement. [1]
b What advantage do caged molecules have in the treatment of diseases using drugs? [3]

6 Silicon can behave as a semi-conductor. Now silicon 'chips'are used in numerous devices from computers to washing machines. Nanotubes can also be made to act as semi-conductors.

Suggest what advantage nanotubes may have over silicon chips, and predict the effect their use may have on future computer design.

C4h

1 Describe two ways that pollutants can get into water sources in the United Kingdom. [2]

2 Write a word equation for the reaction of potassium sulfate with barium chloride. [2]

3 Water purification involves three processes: sedimentation, filtration and chlorination.

Explain why each of these processes is carried out. [3]

4 Explain why the purification carried out on the water that is supplied to our taps cannot guarantee that it is harmless to drink. [3]

5 Silver nitrate solution is used to test for the presence of halide ions in water.

Write symbol equations for the reactions that take place when silver nitrate solution is added to water containing the following halide ions.

a potassium chloride [2]
b sodium iodide [2]
c magnesium bromide [3]

P3 Forces for transport

- We live in a world that is more and more concerned about safety. Engineers are often involved in investigating how to make travel safer. For instance they use crash dummies in cars to investigate the effect of collisions on car passengers. Sensors and dataloggers record their measurements. They share their findings with other engineers, who check their results, and with the manufacturers who build in more safety features. The media publicise their findings by reporting on safety issues on TV, in magazines or over the Internet.
- Even theme park rides, which we go on for a thrill, are designed with safety in mind. Theme ride designers understand science and how to use it safely – but they also know how to scare us too.

What you need to know

- Forces are measured in Newtons.
- Forces can change the movement of objects.
- Energy is useful when it is transferred.

How fast? How far?

In this item you will find out

- how to measure and interpret time and distance
- how to calculate speeds, distance and time
- how to use distance-time graphs

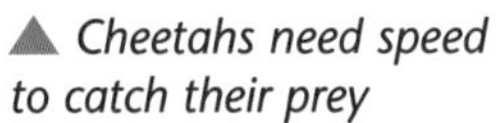

▲ *Cheetahs need speed to catch their prey*

Speed is very important to animals and humans. Animals need to move swiftly so they can catch their prey or escape from predators. Humans are always looking for faster ways to get to work or school on time. Sometimes you may drive to work too quickly and break the speed limit. Being able to measure, compare and estimate speeds is important for all road users. Motorists use their speedometers while the police sometimes use speed cameras to check your speed. Keeping within speed limits improves road safety. Police use accurate measurements of speed to convict speeding motorists.

Understanding speeds can help you plan a journey. Knowing how fast you will travel can help you calculate journey times and distances. Imagine the precise understanding of speeds needed to produce train timetables or airport schedules!

Speed is how far something moves in a certain time. To calculate speed you need to measure two things – distance and time. Distance is measured in metres (m) and time in seconds (s) and the result of the speed calculation is in metres per second (m/s).

If a fast object and a slow object set off together, the faster object will cover more distance in ten minutes than the slower object. The faster object will also cover the same distance as the slower object but in a shorter time. For example, a train is faster than a bicycle and covers more distance in ten minutes.

You can calculate speed using this equation:

$$\text{speed} = \frac{\text{distance}}{\text{time}}$$

a **A car travels 10 metres in 20 seconds. Calculate the speed.**

Amazing fact

Electromagnetic radiation travels at 300 000 000 m/s in a vacuum. That is about 186 000 miles in a second! Nothing else can travel this fast.

▲ *Speed camera*

Speed cameras

The next time you see a speed camera, look at the white lines on the road. When a car that is travelling too fast passes the speed camera, the camera flashes as the car reaches the start of the white lines. The camera then flashes again, by which time the car will have passed more white lines. The two flashes are a certain time apart and the white lines are a certain distance apart so the speed of the car can be calculated. The photographs also record the registration number of the car.

b **Explain how speed cameras help the police to work out the speed of a car.**

c **The speed limit is 12.5 m/s. The speed camera shows two pictures of a car taken 0.2 s apart. In this time the car crosses three marker lines on the road. This is a distance of 3 m. Calculate the speed of the car to find out if it was speeding.**

Rearranging the speed equation

As we saw earlier, you can calculate speed by using this equation:

$$\text{speed} = \frac{\text{distance}}{\text{time}}$$

By rearranging this equation you can also calculate time and distance if you know the other two variables.

$$\text{distance} = \text{speed} \times \text{time}$$

$$\text{time} = \frac{\text{distance}}{\text{speed}}$$

Examiner's tip

Don't give up when doing a series of calculations. If you make an error it will only be punished once. You can go on to gain full marks even though you've carried this error forward.

For example, a roller coaster ride lasts 50 s. The average speed is 10 m/s. We can calculate the distance of the ride in metres.

$$\text{distance} = \text{speed} \times \text{time}$$

$$\text{distance} = 10\,\text{m/s} \times 50\,\text{s}$$

$$\text{distance} = 500\,\text{m}$$

Or you can use the original equation:

$$\text{speed} = \frac{\text{distance}}{\text{time}}$$

$$10\,\text{m/s} = \frac{\text{distance}}{50\,\text{s}}$$

$$\text{distance} = 10\,\text{m/s} \times 50\,\text{s}$$

$$\text{distance} = 500\,\text{m}$$

d **Gita goes at 6 m/s on her skateboard. What time will it take to move 24 m?**

e **A car travels at an average speed of 60 mph. How many miles will be covered in a 4 hour journey?**

We can also measure speed in other units, for example in kilometres per hour (km/h), or centimetres per second (cm/s).

f **It is 750 kilometres to Glasgow. The train travels at an average speed of 150 km/h. Calculate the time needed for the journey.**

Distance–time graphs

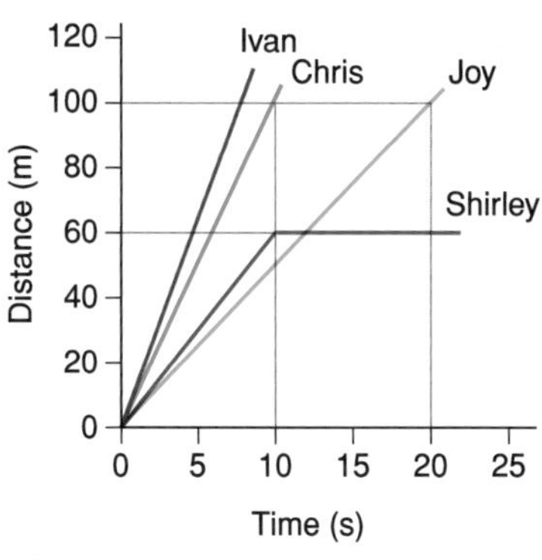

▲ *Distance–time graph*

We can use graphs to display data on distance and time. The shape of the graph can tell you how the speed varies.

Look at the **distance–time graph** for Chris, Joy, Ivan and Shirley's bicycle rides. We can calculate the speed of each cyclist from the graph by calculating each **gradient** (slope):

Ivan moves 100 m in 8 s: speed = $\frac{\text{distance}}{\text{time}} = \frac{100}{8} = 12.5\text{ m/s}$

Chris moves 100 m in 10 s: speed = $\frac{\text{distance}}{\text{time}} = \frac{100}{10} = 10\text{ m/s}$

Shirley moves 60 m in 10 s and then does not move for 10 s:
speed = $\frac{\text{distance}}{\text{time}} = \frac{60}{10} = 6\text{ m/s}$. When Shirley is not moving she has zero speed.

This tells us some important information about distance–time graphs:

- sloping straight lines show steady speeds
- horizontal straight lines show zero speed.

Look at the lines for Ivan and Chris. The gradient of Ivan's line is steeper and he is going faster. This means that on a distance–time graph, the steeper the gradient, the higher the speed.

 **Calculate Joy's speed from the gradient of the graph line.**

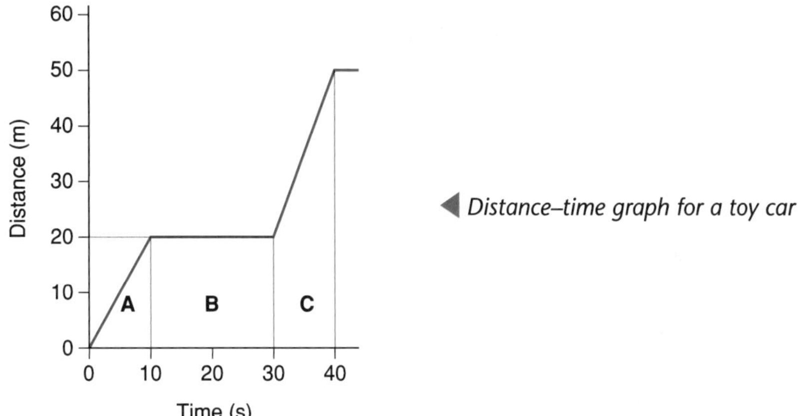

◀ *Distance–time graph for a toy car*

 **Look at the distance–time graph for a toy car. Describe the journey in detail. Think about time, distance and speed.**

Distance–time graphs are very useful. The shape of them can give you an overview of the journey. Comparing gradients can tell you about speeds. But looking at them carefully can tell you very accurate information indeed. Graphs are often a better way of communicating lots of data. That is why we use them.

Keywords

distance–time graph • gradient • speed

Heading for the planets

▲ Man taking first steps on the Moon

In 1969 men visited the Moon, stayed there for 21 hours, then returned safely to Earth. The Moon is 384 000 km from Earth and the spaceship travelled at an average speed of 39 500 km/h.

Some scientists are hoping to put people on Mars by the year 2030. Mars is about 7 834 000 km from Earth when it is closest to us. In January 2006 the *New Horizons* spacecraft was launched on its mission to Pluto, even though Pluto is about 5 764 000 000 km away when it is nearest to Earth. The journey is estimated to take 10 years.

The Sun is a large hot object 149 600 000 km from Earth. This distance is vast and it takes light about 8 minutes to travel from the Sun to Earth. So when you watch a sunset, in one sense you are watching it 8 minutes late.

Our nearest star (apart from our Sun) is about 4 light years away. It takes light from this star 4 years to get to us.

Questions

1 Calculate the approximate time it took the spaceship in 1969 to travel from the Earth to the Moon.

2 How long would it take this spaceship to travel to the Sun?

3 A 'light year' is the distance light travels in a year. Light travels at a speed of 300 000 km/s.

(a) Calculate how many seconds there are in 1 year (365 days).
(b) Calculate how many kilometres there are in a light year.

4 How long would it take the spaceship from 1969 to travel to Pluto?

5 How likely is it that humans will travel to the outer planets or even other star systems? Explain your answer using some of the facts and figures you have calculated.

High acceleration

▲ Dragster car

In this item you will find out

- how to calculate acceleration
- how to measure and interpret speed–time graphs

Dragster cars change their speed very quickly indeed. A dragster car has to start from rest and needs a very high **acceleration** to get it to a high speed in a short time.

The car in the photograph starts and accelerates from 0 to 60 miles per hour in 2 seconds. The driver will need a very strong seat and headrest! Many family road cars accelerate from 0 to 60 mph in about 12 seconds. This is six times less acceleration than the dragster.

Acceleration happens when the speed of an object changes. The speed can change to become faster or slower. When an object speeds up it has positive acceleration. When it slows down it has negative acceleration or deceleration.

▼ You can experience high acceleration at a theme park

Most of us will never drive a dragster but we may have the chance to experience high accelerations on a roller coaster.

Here are some of the details of the *Kingda Ka* roller coaster – one of the highest and fastest roller coasters in the world. It:

- has a maximum height of 140 m, 5 m taller than the London Eye
- sends riders horizontally from 0 to 202 km/h at an acceleration of 56 m/s^2
- climbs up vertically 90 degrees
- plummets straight down 148 m to the ground so that the next 41 m drop leaves riders feeling weightless.

On this roller coaster we would experience high accelerations when our speed increases or decreases quickly. We would also experience high accelerations when we changed direction quickly.

Calculating acceleration

Acceleration depends on two things:

- how much the speed of the object changes
- how long the change in speed takes.

We usually define acceleration as how much the speed of an object changes in one second and it is measured in metres per second squared, m/s^2. An acceleration of 10 m/s^2 means the speed increases by 10 m/s each second. You can do calculations about acceleration using this equation:

$$\text{acceleration} = \frac{\text{change in speed}}{\text{time}}$$

$$\text{metres per second squared (m/s}^2\text{)} = \frac{\text{metres per second (m/s)}}{\text{seconds (s)}}$$

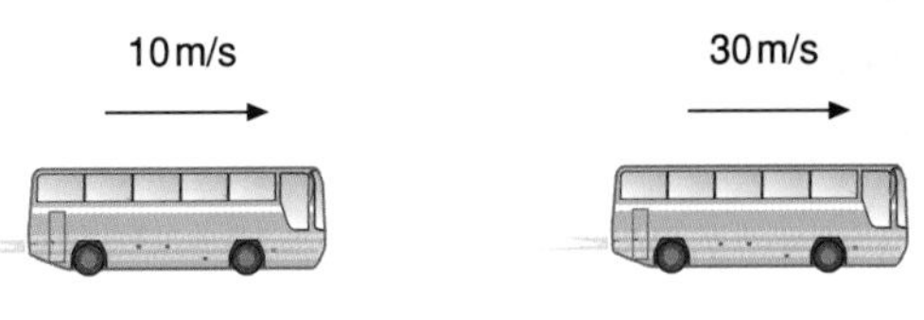

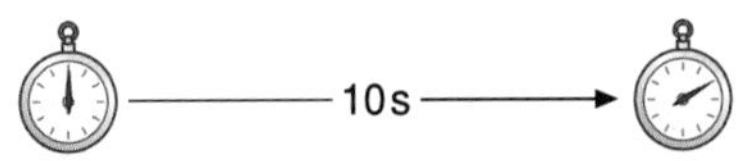

▲ *School bus accelerating*

For example, a school bus accelerates from 10 m/s to 30 m/s in 10 s.

To calculate the acceleration of the bus in m/s^2, we first find out the change in speed.

This is 30 m/s –10 m/s = 20 m/s.

Using:

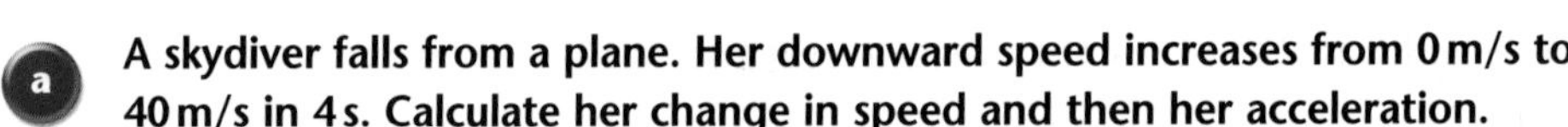

$$\text{acceleration} = \frac{\text{change in speed}}{\text{time}} = \frac{20\text{ m/s}}{10\text{ s}} = 2\text{ m/s}^2$$

a **A skydiver falls from a plane. Her downward speed increases from 0 m/s to 40 m/s in 4 s. Calculate her change in speed and then her acceleration.**

By rearranging the acceleration equation you can also calculate the change in speed or the time if you know the other two variables.

b **A car accelerates at 6 m/s^2 for 10 seconds. Calculate the final speed if the car's speed starts at zero.**

Speed–time graphs

Speed–time graphs can help us to understand acceleration. At a glance they can show us how the speed changes. If you look at them carefully you can work out exact speeds, times and accelerations.

Look at the speed–time graph for a toy car. You can use the graph to describe the journey of the toy car.

Part A the toy car accelerates from 0 to 20 m/s in 10 s.

$$\text{acceleration} = \frac{20\text{ m/s}}{10\text{ s}} = 2\text{ m/s}^2$$

Part B the toy car has a steady speed of 20 m/s for 20 s.

$$\text{acceleration} = \frac{0\text{ m/s}}{20\text{ s}} = 0\text{ m/s}^2$$

Part C the toy car accelerates from 20 m/s to 50 m/s in 10 s.

$$\text{acceleration} = \frac{30\,\text{m/s}}{10\,\text{s}} = 3\,\text{m/s}^2$$

Part D the toy car decelerates from 50 m/s to 0 m/s in 20 s.

$$\text{acceleration} = \frac{-50\,\text{m/s}}{20\,\text{s}} = -2.5\,\text{m/s}^2$$

c **If the toy car had decelerated at $4\,\text{m/s}^2$, how long would it have taken to stop?**

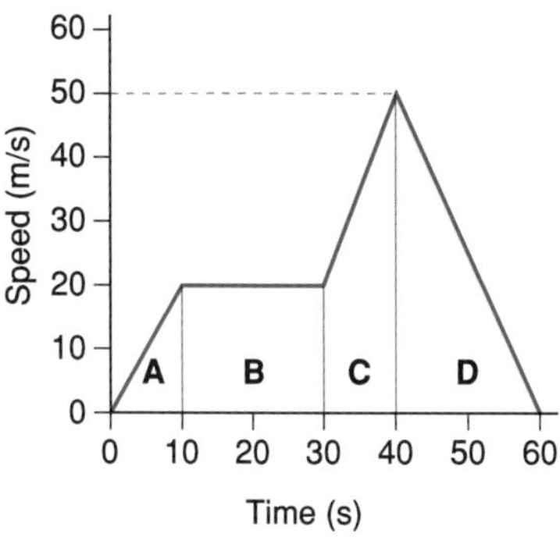

▲ *Speed–time graph for a toy car*

Gradient of a speed–time graph

Have another look at the speed–time graph for the toy car. The slope or gradient of the graph shows the acceleration.

In Part A, the toy car's speed is increasing which is shown by a straight line with a positive gradient. In Part B, the toy car's speed is constant. This is shown by a horizontal line. In Part C, the toy car's speed increases again. The acceleration in Part C is greater than the acceleration in Part A so the gradient of the line is steeper. In Part D, the toy car's speed is decreasing and this is shown by a straight line with a negative gradient.

Calculating distance

We can calculate the distance travelled from a speed–time graph by working out the area under the graph.

For example, in Part B of the toy car graph:

$$\begin{aligned}\text{distance} &= \text{average speed} \times \text{time}\\ &= 20\,\text{m/s} \times 20\,\text{s}\\ &= 400\,\text{m}\end{aligned}$$

We can also calculate distance from the area under the graph when speeds change.

For example, in Part A, the graph has a triangular shape. So using the area of a triangle, which is $\frac{1}{2}$ × base × height:

$$\begin{aligned}\text{area} &= \tfrac{1}{2} \times 20\,\text{m/s} \times 10\,\text{s}\\ &= 100\,\text{m}\end{aligned}$$

Keywords

acceleration • speed–time graph

d **Draw a speed–time graph for a sprinter. Use the same axes as for the speed–time graph for the toy car and show the following information:**

part A: increasing speed from 0 m/s at $6\,\text{m/s}^2$ for 10 s
part B: decreasing speed with an acceleration of $-3\,\text{m/s}^2$ for 10 s
part C: a steady speed of 30 m/s for 40 s.

e **Which part has zero acceleration?**

f **Calculate the distance travelled in each part.**

Sometimes acceleration is not constant. Look at the speed–time graph drawn for three objects. Object B has constant acceleration so the speed–time graph is a straight line. Object A has increasing acceleration so the speed–time graph is an upward curve – as the acceleration increases so the gradient of the line increases. Object C has decreasing acceleration so the gradient of the line decreases as the acceleration decreases.

▼ *Acceleration*

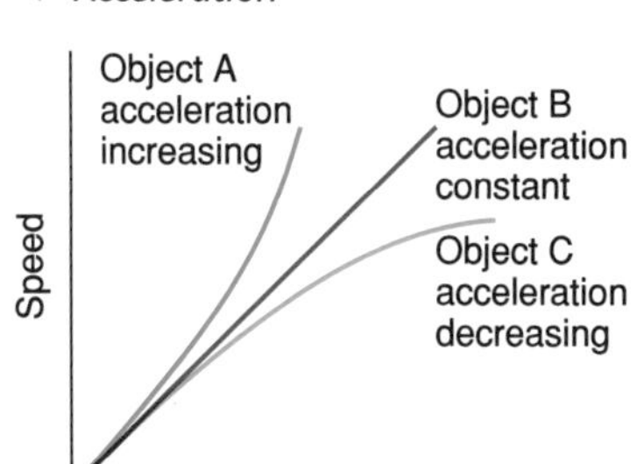

▲ *Space Shuttle launch*

The Space Shuttle

The Space Shuttle is a reusable spaceship. It is used for research and carrying satellites into space. When it is launched, it takes off from rest and accelerates at 0.0375 km/s^2. It must reach a speed of about 4.5 km/s by a height of about 226 km above the surface of the Earth so that it can then orbit the Earth.

After it reaches this speed the heavy solid rocket boosters are discarded. They fall to Earth where they are recovered and reused.

The remainder of the Space Shuttle climbs to attain a speed of 7.75 km/s at a height of 250 km. This is done by using only the Shuttle's engines. These engines are not as powerful as the solid rocket boosters.

Once in space the engines are not used very often. When they are used, very little fuel is needed.

When the Shuttle returns to Earth it approaches at a very high speed. The braking rockets are fired 65 minutes before landing. These slow down the Shuttle before it enters the Earth's atmosphere. The atmosphere slows it down a lot before it approaches the runway. The Shuttle lands and then comes to rest on the tarmac.

▼ *Space Shuttle releasing its solid booster rockets*

Questions

1. Why do you think the scientists use km/s rather than m/s or km/h?
2. Calculate the time it takes to accelerate from lift-off to 4.5 km/s.
3. After the Space Shuttle reaches 4.5 km/s, less powerful engines are needed to reach 7.75 km/s. Suggest reasons why.
4. The Shuttle travels at a steady speed of 7.75 km/s in space. The astronauts do not 'feel' that they are moving very quickly. Suggest why.
5. When the Shuttle returns to Earth, for the last 65 minutes of its journey it has a negative acceleration (deceleration) of –0.001 9871 km/s^2. Calculate its speed before it starts to decelerate.

Stopping safely

▲ *When you are driving you have to be prepared to stop at any time*

In this item you will find out

- about the relationship between force, mass and acceleration
- what affects thinking, braking and stopping distances

Before taking your driving test you need to pass a theory test. Part of this involves an understanding of driving safely and knowledge of car **stopping distances**. This will make you more aware of how quickly others can stop.

You need to be able to predict these things to have an appreciation of the dangers from other vehicles on the road. Stopping safely in an emergency is one of the most important skills in driving.

When cars move they have lots of energy. When cars brake, the energy is absorbed in the brakes as heat energy. The brakes get hot and the car stops safely.

When you need to stop, a small amount of time passes between you deciding to step on the brakes and actually doing it. The car travels several metres in this time. This is called the **thinking distance**.

After you put a foot on the brake the car slows down but it continues to travel until it stops. This is called the **braking distance**.

a **The stopping distance for a supertanker is huge but the thinking distance is small. Suggest why.**

b **It is important to understand stopping distances for road safety. Suggest reasons why.**

Many drivers think it is clever to travel too close to the car in front of them. This is particularly dangerous when it is a large vehicle in front which can restrict forward vision of the road ahead. If you are driving within your thinking distance and something happens you will not have time to react by braking or swerving.

Amazing fact

Some large ships can take 10 km to stop from a cruising speed of 13 km/h.

Stopping distances

The stopping distance for a car is the thinking distance + the braking distance.

▶ *Stopping distance of a car at 6 m/s or (15 mph) = 5 m + 4 m = 9 m*

The table shows the stopping distances for cars travelling at different speeds.

Speed of car (m/s)	(mph)	Thinking distance (m)	Braking distance (m)	Total stopping distance (m)
8	18	6	6	12
16	36	12	24	36
32	72	24	96	120

As you can see, the faster a car is travelling, the longer it takes to stop and the further it travels while stopping.

Explain why stopping distance increases with speed.

Examiner's tip

Be clear about what thinking, braking and stopping distances mean.

Can't stop!

People who drive while they are tired take longer to react to an emergency than people who are not tired. This means their thinking distance increases and they travel further before they stop.

Thinking distance also increases when drivers have drunk alcohol or if they have taken some types of drugs.

Driving faster does not affect your thinking time but it does increase your thinking distance. This is because a faster car moves further in this time. Thinking distance can also be increased if you are not concentrating or if you have distractions, such as small noisy children in the car with you.

Different road conditions will affect how long a car takes to stop once the brakes have been applied. Braking distance increases the faster you are driving, when the road is slippery, wet or icy. It also increases if your brakes are not working properly or if your tyres are bald.

Apart from speeding and poor road conditions, a major cause of accidents is driving too close to the vehicle ahead.

Many drivers drive so close to the car in front that they do not have time to react if it brakes. It is dangerous to drive within the thinking distance.

Changing braking distance

When road vehicles brake, a brake pad squeezes the disc on the wheel. The wheel slows down and a **friction** force between the road and the tyre slows the vehicle. This friction force needs to be large enough to stop the vehicle in a safe distance. The friction force may not be big enough if:

- the road is slippery (either wet or icy)
- the tyres have little or no tread
- the vehicle has a large mass or is carrying an extra load such as pulling a caravan
- the vehicle is speeding.

These things can increase the braking distance.

Large vehicles have brakes that can provide bigger **braking forces**. But large braking forces are useless if there is not enough friction between the road and the tyre. Cars have four wheels, but lorries may have six, eight or ten wheels. These extra wheels give more tyre contact with the road allowing bigger friction forces.

Keywords

braking distance • braking force • friction • stopping distance • thinking distance

Forces

Forces can speed things up (accelerate) or slow things down (decelerate). How much acceleration you get depends on two things, the mass of the object and the size of the force acting upon it. For an object of a certain mass if a greater force is acting on it, it will have more acceleration than if a smaller force is acting on it. So if you hit a golf ball with more force it will accelerate more.

In the same way, for a given force an object with a bigger mass will have less acceleration than an object with a smaller mass. So if you use your golf club to hit a golf ball and a football, the same force would give the football a very low acceleration compared to the golf ball.

You can calculate the force needed to accelerate an object using this equation:

force	=	mass	×	acceleration
kg m/s^2 or newtons (N)	=	kilograms (kg)	×	metres per second squared (m/s^2)

▼ *Force on a speedboat*

2000 N

For example, a 1 000 kg speedboat has a driving force of 2 000 N. We can calculate its acceleration.

force = mass × acceleration

2 000 N = 1 000 kg × acceleration

$$\text{acceleration} = \frac{2000\,\text{N}}{1000\,\text{kg}}$$

acceleration = 2 m/s^2

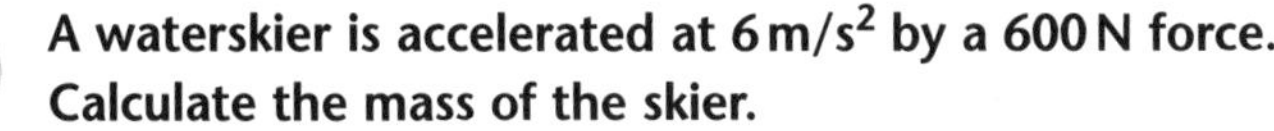

d **A waterskier is accelerated at 6 m/s^2 by a 600 N force. Calculate the mass of the skier.**

The boat pulling the water skier exerts a force on the water skier and the water skier exerts an equal but opposite force back on the boat. These are not balanced forces but just different ways of looking at the same interaction.

▲ *Force on a waterskier*

Testing stopping distance

Shaun is testing the total stopping distance of a car. He takes the car to a test strip and drives the car at different speeds then brakes. His colleague, Angela, measures and records the thinking and braking distances each time.

Shaun's reaction time is the time between him thinking about putting on the brakes and actually putting on the brakes. In this time, the car travels the thinking distance.

The braking distance is how far the car moves with its brakes on before stopping.

The table shows their test results.

Speed of car (m/s) (mph)	Thinking distance (m)	Braking distance (m)	Total stopping distance (m)
8 (18)	6	6	12
16 (36)	12	24	36
32 (72)	24	96	

Shaun then takes the car on one last drive. At the end he brakes and stops. The speed–time graph on the left shows the end of Shaun's journey.

Speed (m/s)
30
25
20
15
10
5
0
thinking distance
braking distance
0
0.75
1.0
2.0
3.0
3.75
4.0
Time (s)

Questions

1 Calculate the total stopping distance at 32 m/s.

2 Use the equation speed = distance/time to calculate Shaun's reaction times at the three speeds.

3 Look at the thinking distances in the table. Describe and explain the relationship between speed and thinking distance.

4 Look at the speed–time graph for Shaun's car. Shaun's reaction time is 0.75 s. Calculate his thinking distance in metres.

5 The braking time is 3.0 s. Calculate the braking distance.

6 Shaun knows that you should never drink and drive. If he had a drink of alcohol, suggest how and why this would affect his stopping distance.

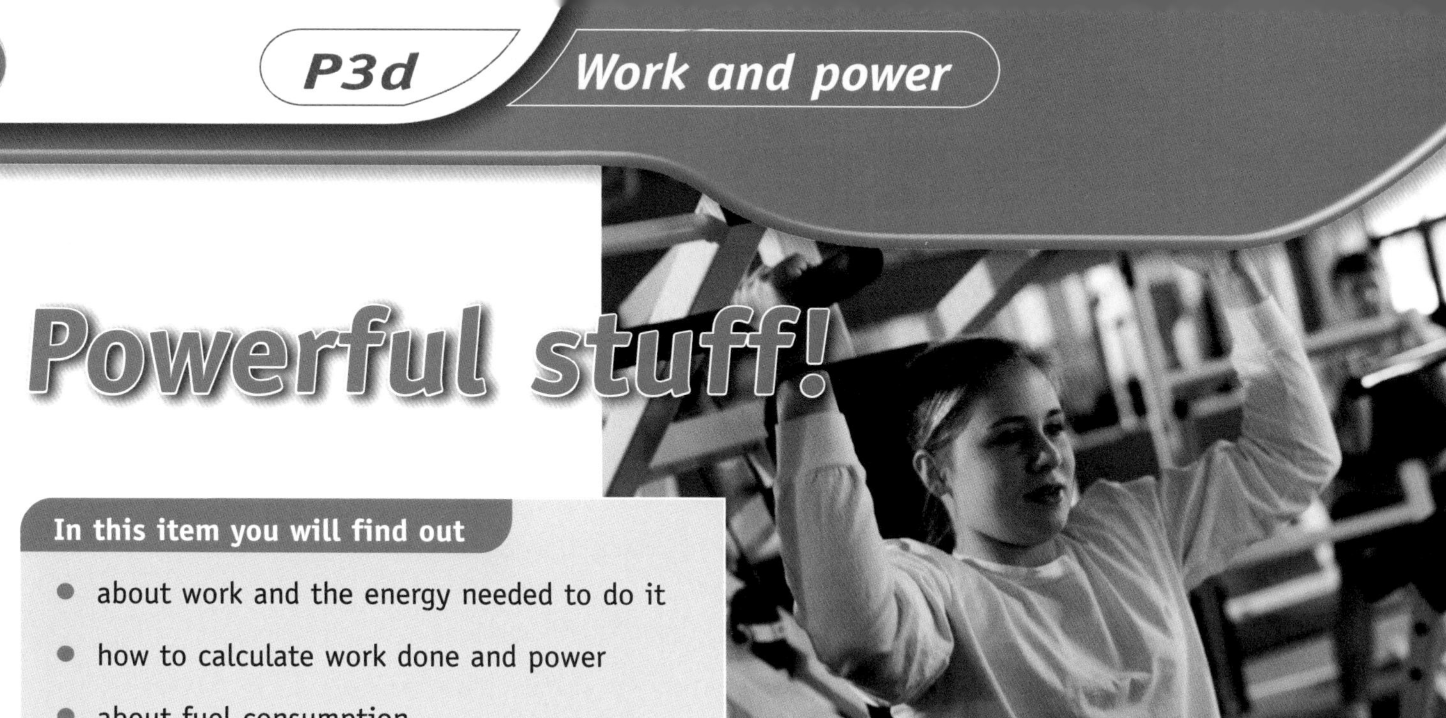

Powerful stuff!

In this item you will find out

- about work and the energy needed to do it
- how to calculate work done and power
- about fuel consumption

What do lifting weights, climbing stairs, pulling a sledge and pushing a shopping trolley have in common? They all involve **work**.

Work is not a popular word for many of us. Some people think of hard work as being difficult, for example doing homework, digging the garden, or decorating. But in science the word 'work' has a specific meaning. Work is done when a force moves an object and energy is needed to do work.

Dave can push against the wall but if the wall does not move he does no work. But if Dave pushes his broken-down car, he has to overcome the friction force between the car tyres and the road. He needs energy (from his food) to do this work.

Buying a car is one thing, paying insurance is another and, putting fuel in it tends to be expensive too. Using cars also has a cost to people and their environment. We drive our cars forgetting that they pump out carbon dioxide gas into the atmosphere. This can add to global warming.

All cars use **energy** but some cars use energy faster than others. These cars are generally more powerful. They will also use more fuel because it is this that provides the energy when it is burnt in the engine.

People produce a little carbon dioxide too. We do work when we lift weights and we develop high **power** when we do press-ups. These things can keep us fit and they all involve using energy.

When we drive, the car does the hard work for us. To do this hard work the car needs energy and we need to buy fuel. But how much fuel do cars use, and what are the costs to us and the environment?

a **Using cars is 'costly to the environment'. Suggest how cars may harm the environment.**

Amazing fact

Air travel produces:

- **19 times more greenhouse gases than trains**
- **190 times more greenhouse gases than a ship.**

Doing work

▲ *Pushing a car is hard work!*

When Dave is pushing his broken down car, two things will make him use up energy more quickly. These are:

- having to push with a greater force
- having to push for a greater distance.

So, from this you can see that work is connected to force and distance. Work done depends on two things:

- the size of the force (measured in newtons)
- the distance the object moves (measured in metres).

b **Suggest why Dave will do more work if he pushes his car uphill.**

You can calculate the work done using this equation:

work done	=	force	×	distance
joules (J)	=	newtons (N)	×	metres (m)

$$\text{force} = \frac{\text{work done}}{\text{distance}}$$

$$\text{distance} = \frac{\text{work done}}{\text{force}}$$

Work and energy are both measured in joules (J). By rearranging the equation we can also calculate the force and distance if we know the other two variables.

▲ *Car braking*

For example, 2 000 J of work is done to brake the car in the diagram. The braking force is 1 000 N. We can calculate the braking distance.

work done = force × distance

2000 J = 1000 N × distance

$$\text{distance} = \frac{2000\,\text{J}}{1000\,\text{N}}$$

distance = 2 m

If 4 000 J of work is done on the car. Calculate the braking force needed for a braking distance of 5 m.

The braking force and braking distance are crucial for safe braking. The brakes on road vehicles have to have the capacity to do work. These brakes need to produce a large force over a small distance. Powerful brakes do the same work as less powerful brakes – they just do the job quicker, which is a good thing!

Power

Power is a measure of how quickly work is being done and energy is being transferred. Power is measured in watts (W) and is:

- how much work is done in one second or
- how much energy is transferred in one second.

We can use this equation to calculate power:

$$\text{power} = \frac{\text{work done}}{\text{time}}$$

$$\text{watts (W)} = \frac{\text{joules (J)}}{\text{seconds (s)}}$$

By rearranging the equation we can also calculate the work done and the time if we know the other two variables.

$$\text{work done} = \text{power} \times \text{time}$$

$$\text{time} = \frac{\text{work done}}{\text{power}}$$

For example, a weightlifter develops a power of 50 W. She lifts a weight in 2 s. We can calculate the work done on the weights.

▲ *Work is done on these weights*

$$\text{power} = \frac{\text{work done}}{\text{time}}$$

$$50\,\text{W} = \frac{\text{work done}}{2\,\text{s}}$$

$$\text{work done} = 50\,\text{W} \times 2\,\text{s}$$

$$\text{work done} = 100\,\text{J}$$

d **The weightlifter develops a power of 100 W. She does 50 J of work on the weight. How long does it take her to lift the weight?**

Cars and energy

Cars are always on the move and are having work done on them. All cars use energy but some cars use energy faster than others. These cars are generally more powerful. They will also use more fuel.

When people think about buying cars the cost of fuelling them is an important factor. Car manufacturers have to give accurate and fair data on **fuel consumption**. This helps people make sensible choices about which car to buy. The fuel consumption tells you how many miles you can drive on one gallon (about five litres) of fuel.

The table shows the fuel consumption for four cars.

Car	Fuel consumption (mpg)
Car A	52
Car B	48
Car C	43
Car D	51

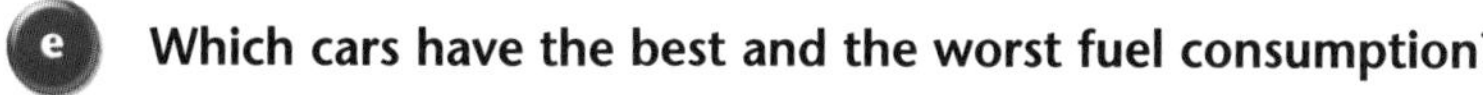

e **Which cars have the best and the worst fuel consumption?**

f **Car C has 10 gallons of fuel in its tank. Estimate how far it can travel before running out of fuel.**

More powerful cars use more fuel. This not only costs more money but it creates more pollution. Fumes from vehicles are unpleasant. But in cities and towns, these fumes can be a serious problem. Asthma sufferers are particularly affected by fumes and there is some evidence to suggest that they can encourage asthma attacks. Other respiratory illnesses have also been linked to this sort of pollution.

Keywords

energy • fuel consumption • power • work

Lifting boxes

Alice is measuring how much energy she needs to use before she feels tired. She does an experiment lifting boxes. She lifts a box up 0.5 m for each lift. The force she exerts on the box is 20 N.

She sees how many times she can lift up a box with each hand. Here are her results.

	Lift height (m)	Force on box (N)	Number of lifts	Total work done on box (J)
Left arm	0.5	20	150	
Right arm	0.5	20	90	

Alice decides to measure her power. She knows that power is how much work she does on the box in 1 s. She decides that she will lift the box as many times as she can in 100 s. At the end she has lifted the box 147 times in 100 s.

Questions

1 Look at the table. How much work is done on the box for one lift?

2 Calculate the total work done for each arm.

3 Calculate the work done on the box for 147 lifts in 100 s.

4 Calculate the power she develops.

5 This result seems very low for Alice. After all a 60 W light bulb has more power than she has! She feels she has been working much harder than a light bulb. Some of her energy has been wasted. Suggest how.

6 Alice holds a box still above her head.
(a) Does she do work on the box? Explain your answer.
(b) Holding the box stationary in this way is still tiring. Suggest why.

7 Escalators carry people up to higher floors in shops. They do work and use energy. The escalators continue to move even when they are empty. On busy days the escalators do even more work and develop more power. Explain why.

The cost of transport

▲ Most buses run on diesel

In this item you will find out

- how to calculate kinetic energy
- how kinetic energy affects fuel consumption and braking distance
- the advantages and disadvantages of electric vehicles

We all use transport to get around. This can be buses, bicycles, cars, trams, trains or walking.

All these need a source of energy that is changed into **kinetic energy** causing movement.

Most road transport, such as cars, buses and lorries, runs on diesel or petrol and these are made from **fossil fuels**. Fossil fuels are precious because they cannot be renewed. This means that one day in the future they will become scarce and very expensive. They may even run out altogether.

Some types of vehicle use more fossil fuels than others. This means that they are more expensive to run, use up resources more quickly and cause more pollution in our cities.

When people choose a family car it can be a difficult decision. It is not possible to say, scientifically, which is the best car. It depends on too many variables and preferences.

Amazing fact

A real electric sports car, which stars in a Hollywood film, achieves an impressive 0–60 mph in 4.5 seconds and has a top speed of 90 mph.

Car manufacturers produce facts and figures about their cars. Some of these facts, such as car fuel consumption, have been produced scientifically, but are they realistic in everyday driving?

But there are now other choices such as electric cars. They do not need petrol or diesel.

a **What do you think are the advantages and disadvantages of using electric cars?**

▶ Choosing a new car can be hard

▲ *Electric milk float*

Electric transport

Electric vehicles have been around for a long time. A milk float delivers milk and is powered by electricity. It is a 'very clean' vehicle and produces no fumes. This means that it does not pollute the atmosphere when you use it, unlike fossil fuel vehicles.

Each evening, after the milk is delivered, the milk float is plugged into the mains so the batteries can be recharged. This stores enough energy for a journey of about 35 km. But, the electrical energy from the mains is produced at a power station and most power stations burn fossil fuels which do cause pollution.

b **The electric milk float is supposed to be a very 'clean' vehicle. It can also be described as a 'polluting' vehicle. Explain both of these points of view.**

But there is a limit to how far electric vehicles can go between being charged at the mains. Most electric vehicles at the moment have a range of less than 100 miles before they need to be charged. This range will be even smaller if you:

- drive uphill a lot
- carry a large load
- drive at higher speeds.

If we drove electric vehicles every day, for example to go to work, this small range would be a problem. We might get to work, but we might not be able to get home again!

How much kinetic energy?

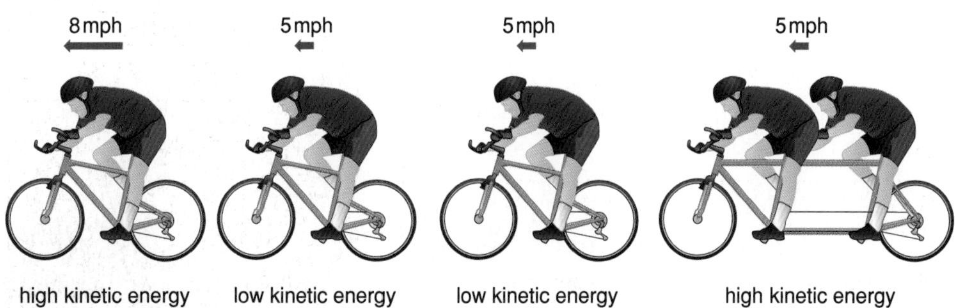

▲ *Kinetic energy depends on speed and mass*

When the bicycle moves it has kinetic energy. The amount of kinetic energy depends on two things: speed and mass.

As you can see from the diagram on the left, an object has greater kinetic energy if it is travelling at a higher speed or if it has a greater mass.

We can calculate kinetic energy by using this equation:

$$\text{kinetic energy} = \tfrac{1}{2} \times \text{mass} \times \text{velocity}^2$$
$$\text{J} = \tfrac{1}{2} \times \text{kg} \times (\text{m/s})^2$$

For example, if the speed of a bicycle is 5 m/s and the mass of the bicycle and rider is 80 kg, we can calculate the kinetic energy of the bicycle and rider.

kinetic energy = $\frac{1}{2}$ × mass × velocity^2

KE = $\frac{1}{2} \times mv^2 = \frac{1}{2} \times 80\,\text{kg} \times (5\,\text{m/s})^2$

KE = 1 000 J

c **Calculate the kinetic energy of the tandem and riders in the diagram on the right.**

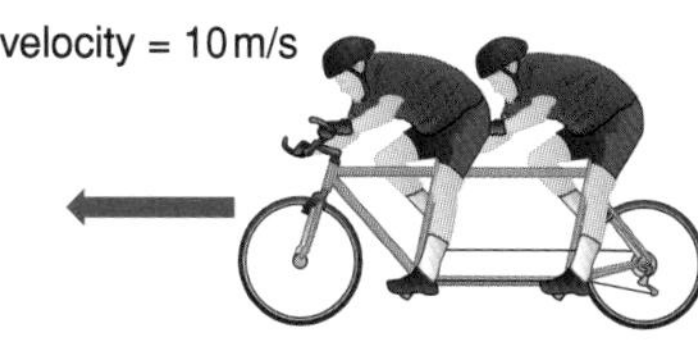

▲ *The greater the mass, the greater the kinetic energy*

Braking a car absorbs kinetic energy. If a car goes twice as fast, its kinetic energy quadruples (KE = $\frac{1}{2} \times mv^2$ and it increases with the square of the velocity). Cars going twice as fast may have four times the braking distance.

More about fuel consumption

The fuel consumption of a vehicle depends on the speed the vehicle is being driven at, the style of driving and different driving conditions. Once a vehicle is moving it needs a driving force to do work against friction and drag. This requires energy which comes from the fuel it consumes. When you go faster you are increasing the kinetic energy of the car. This also requires energy and more fuel is consumed.

▼ *Filling up a car with fuel can be expensive*

Some driving styles use more energy than others. Drivers that accelerate and brake a lot waste energy. The brakes transfer the kinetic energy into heat and this is energy wasted. Using gears more sensibly, driving smoothly and braking less can reduce fuel consumption.

Fuel costs can be reduced in two ways:

- reduce drag by streamlining – this means less driving force is needed for a given speed, so less power is needed, which in turn means less fuel is used
- drive slower – this needs less kinetic energy and results in lower friction forces and drag – less driving force is needed and so less power is developed, which in turn means less fuel is used.

The table shows some data on different vehicles and their fuel consumption. Liquid petroleum gas (LPG) is also a fossil fuel and produces carbon dioxide gas.

Vehicle	Petrol fuel consumption (mpg)	Diesel fuel consumption (mpg)	LPG fuel consumption (mpg)
Family car	43	57	61
People carrier	23	42	LPG version not available
Sports car	27	Diesel version not available	LPG version not available
Van	21	34	LPG version not available

▲ *Thirsty work*

c **Which version of the family car has best fuel consumption – petrol, diesel or LPG?**

d **Which vehicle has the worst petrol consumption?**

Keywords

fossil fuel • kinetic energy

Car solutions

Toyota makes a car with two engines called a 'hybrid' car. It has a petrol engine and an electric motor. In the countryside, where it is travelling quickly, it burns petrol as the fuel. This fuel gives the car the kinetic energy it needs. The petrol engine also drives a generator that charges batteries and stores energy. When the car enters the city, where it will travel more slowly, the driver turns off the diesel engine and switches on the electric motor. This petrol/electronic hybrid car is exempt from the congestion charge in London.

▶ *Toyota petrol/electric hybrid car*

Other manufacturers have thought of alternative ways of reducing fuel consumption and pollution from petrol and diesel fumes. Citroën has developed a 'Stop & Start' car. The electronics automatically stop the engine when the car is at a standstill. When the driver releases the brake the car automatically starts again.

Diesel cars are also popular as they usually have better fuel consumption than petrol cars. This is a good thing but there are other environmental concerns about how clean diesel vehicles are. The exhaust fumes contain particulates and these may be harmful to people. Diesel cars do burn less fuel for each mile, however, so less carbon dioxide is released into the atmosphere.

	Hybrid car	Stop & Start car	Diesel car
Cost to buy (£)	17 000	11 000	12 000
Fuel consumption (mpg)	65	51	67

Questions

1 Suggest how the hybrid car helps the city environment.

2 How do you think the 'Stop & Start' car may reduce fuel consumption?

3 Other factors need to be taken into account when choosing a more environmentally friendly car. Suggest and explain some of these factors.

4 Diesel cars help reduce global warming but are still a pollution risk. Explain why.

Crash protection

▲ *Testing the safety of a car*

In this item you will find out

- about how forces can be reduced safely when stopping
- about active and passive safety features of cars

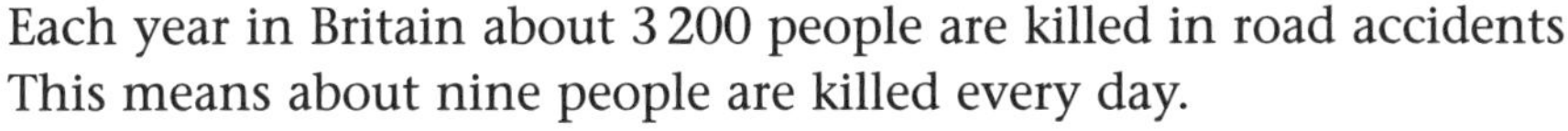

Each year in Britain about 3 200 people are killed in road accidents. This means about nine people are killed every day.

Often these accidents are caused by dangerous driving or by drivers who are drunk. Sometimes they are caused by driver error. We can get advice on how to drive safely from the Highway Code, driving instructors, TV and the Internet. But no matter how carefully you drive, someone else can always run into you or you may need to stop suddenly in an emergency.

When cars move they have lots of kinetic energy. When they stop they have no kinetic energy at all. Controlling this transfer of energy is crucial for passengers' safety. When the car brakes, the energy is transferred through friction into heat in the brakes. The more energy the brakes can transfer each second, the better the brakes are. In a crash the kinetic energy is transferred through work done in changing the shape of the car. It is also transferred to heat by friction and a small amount is transferred into sound.

Cars are fitted with many safety features. They help reduce injuries in a crash. They are also designed to reduce injury to pedestrians. We have **air bags**, **seat belts**, **safety cages** and **crumple zones** in our cars but how do they work?

Whether you choose to walk, ride or drive, vehicle safety is important and it could save your life.

a **Racing cars have ventilated disc brakes. The brakes can transfer heat more quickly to the surrounding air. Suggest why this is a good idea.**

Amazing fact

Rusty Haight survived 718 collisions as a 'human crash dummy' used for testing car safety. Luckily, nowadays the dummies are false and dataloggers collect the evidence!

▼ *Safety features can save your life in a crash*

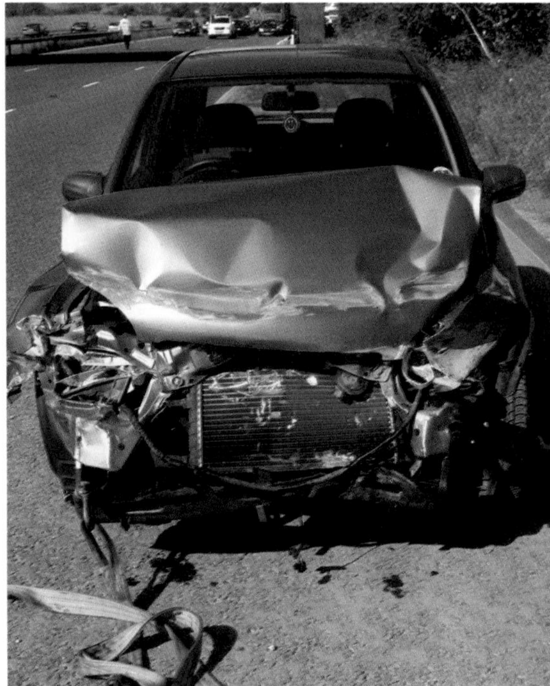

Reducing forces

When cars move they have kinetic energy. When cars stop suddenly, for example in a crash, the kinetic energy needs to be absorbed safely and slowly enough to reduce injuries.

The crumple zones in cars collapse in a crash. They help reduce injuries by changing shape and absorbing energy through progressive, controlled and reduced deceleration of the vehicle. A good crumple zone will mean that a car stops in a longer time and longer distance. The change in speed remains the same but the deceleration will be smaller. The forces needed for this lower deceleration will also be smaller and safer too. This is also true when braking gently. Less braking force is used and cars take longer to stop.

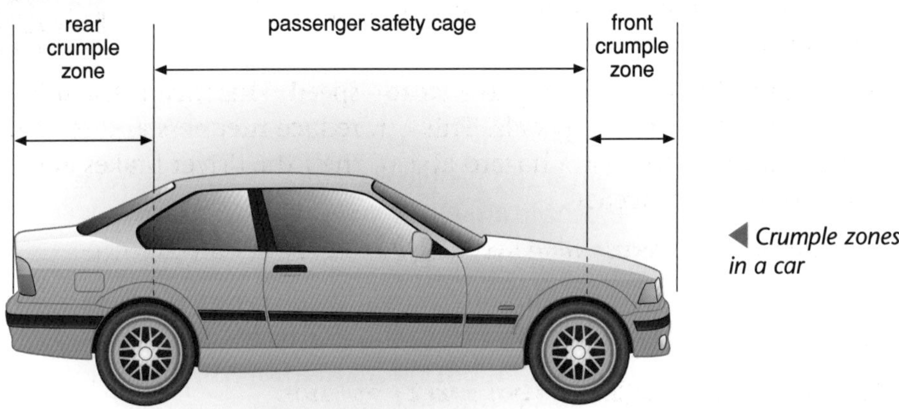

◀ *Crumple zones in a car*

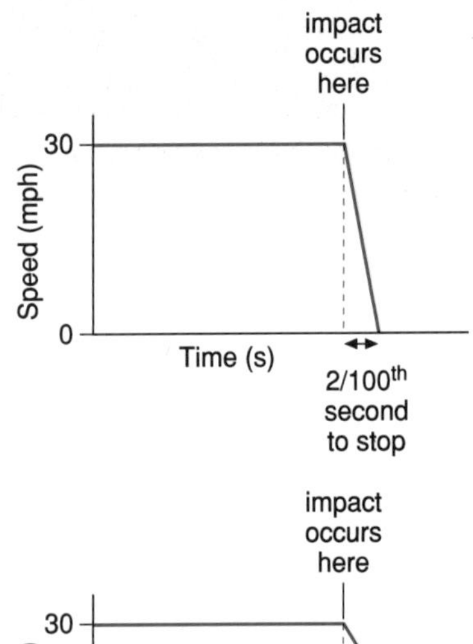

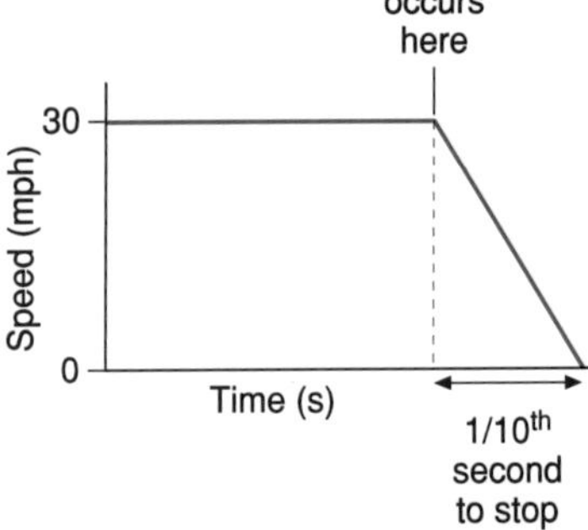

▲ *Speed–time graphs for cars with poor crumple zones and good crumple zones*

When there is a crash the car stops but the contents of the car keep moving. This includes the people inside. Seat belts help keep you in your seat. They change shape by stretching a little in a crash to absorb energy, but they cannot always stop you making contact with the steering wheel or dashboard.

Air bags can help prevent the driver or the front seat passenger hitting the dashboard. When a car is in a front-end collision at more than 10 to 15 mph, a sensor activates the control system for the air bag. A signal is sent to a small detonator system which produces gas to fill the air bag. The driver or the passenger then hits the air bag instead of the dashboard and the energy is absorbed more safely.

▼ *Motorway crash barriers*

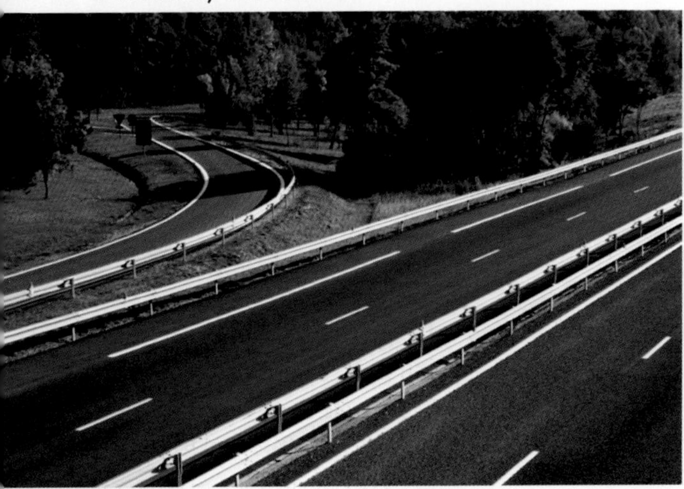

Both air bags and seat belts increase stopping distance and time. This reduces deceleration and the forces that go with it.

b **There are crash barriers at the sides of motorways. They collapse in a collision. Suggest how this increases stopping time and stopping distance.**

c **There are often escape lanes at the bottom of very steep hills. They are filled with deep sand and gravel. Suggest why they are needed and how they work.**

Passive safety features

Designers develop cars with many safety features to help prevent injuries. Some of these are called **passive safety** features.

Electric windows can be considered a luxury but they are also a safety feature. Winding down a window can be distracting. It involves taking one hand off the steering wheel. That means you are less in control of your car.

Many cars have paddle shift controls around the steering wheel, for example for gears or for music player controls. So, without taking a hand off the steering wheel, you can change gear or control the CD player. This can help you to concentrate on your driving and make you safer.

Making drivers more comfortable is important. Air conditioning keeps the inside of the car at a comfortable temperature. Adjustable seats reduce aches, pains and distractions.

▲ *Cars are built around safety cages*

Cruise control helps cars keep to a steady speed. This means the driver does not need to use the pedals. This can reduce tiredness and so improve concentration. If there is a hazard ahead, then the driver brakes and the cruise control is cancelled.

d **Explain how electric windows can help to prevent car accidents.**

Active safety features

Other features are called **active safety** features.

Anti-lock braking systems (ABS) help you stop without skidding. With normal brakes when you have to brake hard in an emergency the car wheels can lock and the car can skid. This is even more likely on wet or icy roads. When a car skids, friction is reduced. This is dangerous as it takes longer to stop and it is harder to steer properly.

ABS brakes prevent the car from skidding even when you brake hard. On hard braking when the wheel starts to lock, the braking force is automatically reduced to avoid skidding and increase friction. The driver is more in control, has a shorter braking distance and has steering control.

The table shows the difference in braking distance between normal brakes and ABS brakes.

Type of brakes	Braking distance 30 to 0 mph (metres)	Braking distance 70 to 0 mph (metres)
ABS brakes	8.5	46.6
Normal brakes	9.8	55.3

Traction control can increase or decrease forces to each wheel. This is really helpful on icy or muddy surfaces as it increases friction and grip. It also works on normal roads and reduces the chance of sliding out of control.

The safety cage is made of hardened steel. It keeps its shape in a crash unlike the crumple zones. This protects the passengers.

e **Explain why traction control is a safety feature.**

Keywords

active safety • air bag • anti-lock braking system (ABS) • crumple zone • passive safety • safety cage • seat belt

Lucky motorway escape

A car crash on the M6 this morning left a trail of destruction. The northbound carriageway was completely blocked for 6 hours. Queues of 30 km were recorded at one stage. There were 46 vehicles involved in rear-end collisions. 31 people were injured and taken to hospitals across the Birmingham area. Six had serious injuries but luckily none was life threatening.

People slowing down to look also caused some minor accidents on the southbound carriageway. This caused severe congestion which delayed ambulances and fire crews. Most minor casualties were suffering from neck injuries and shock. Police blamed a combination of thick fog, a wet road surface, and motorists driving too fast and too close to the driver in front.

PC Singh said, 'Before the crash we clocked one motorist travelling at 80 mph only 5 metres behind a large van. I am not surprised an accident occurred. One rear-seat passenger appears not to have been wearing his seat belt. The driver of this car, his wife, suffered head injuries and she is lucky to be alive. Three drivers were arrested – one for failing a breath test, another for having unsafe tyres with little or no tread and one lorry driver who appeared to have been driving for 7 hours without a break.'

Questions

1. Suggest how each of these factors may have caused the crash: thick fog; wet road; driving too fast; poor tread on tyres; tired driver; driving while drunk.
2. One car was 'travelling only 5 m behind a van'. This is very dangerous. Use information on stopping distances to explain why.
3. One rear seat passenger was not wearing his seat belt. Why do you think this was dangerous for him and for his wife who was driving?
4. The police take measurements after serious crashes. Suggest what measurements they take and why they take them.

What a drag!

In this topic you will find out

- about terminal speed
- about free fall

When you drop an object on Earth it always falls down. This is because the force of gravity (the object's weight) pulls the object towards the centre of the Earth. Objects accelerate as they fall so they get faster and faster. However, **drag** from the air in the Earth's atmosphere provides an opposing force which will reduce this acceleration.

▲ *Skydivers rely on gravity and drag*

We often forget about gravity because we are always under its influence here on Earth. However, we can clearly see its effect when people jump out of aeroplanes and then fall safely to Earth using parachutes. Skydivers need to understand forces to keep them safe and increase their fun.

Skydivers accelerate as they fall. Their speed increases until they get to their **terminal speed** where they stop accelerating and fall at a constant speed.

The Moon is the only natural body away from the Earth that people have travelled to. It has gravity so things fall downwards. But the force of gravity is less than on Earth. When you look at the Moon it is covered in numerous craters. Meteorites and other large objects hitting the Moon at very high speeds cause these craters.

Because there is no atmosphere on the Moon to stop things slowing down, a falling object would get faster and faster. There would be no limit to its speed – until it hit the Moon! The same would happen in outer space where there is no atmosphere either. Luckily meteorites have affected the Earth less. Many fail to reach Earth as they break up due to high temperatures caused by friction with the atmosphere. Others are slowed down and so make less of an impact. Also, on Earth weathering can remove traces of craters. With no atmosphere or water on the Moon, the craters are there to stay.

An 8 tonne meteorite will hit the Earth at a speed similar to that of a falling skydiver before he opens his parachute. Suggest reasons why.

Amazing fact

Meteorites can reach the Earth's outer atmosphere at 25 000 mph. Those that are less than 8 tonnes can slow to 200 mph in the atmosphere before reaching the Earth's surface. Larger meteorites are another story!

▼ *Forces on a parachute*

What is drag?

If a person jumps out of an aeroplane and opens a parachute, the parachute pushes air particles out of the way. This causes an upward frictional force called air resistance or drag. This slows the parachute down. Drag and other frictional forces always act against the movement of an object.

A fast moving parachute pushes more air particles out of the way. A wide parachute also pushes more particles out of the way. The drag forces increase with speed and with the surface area of the parachute.

Terminal speed

When objects fall through the Earth's atmosphere they get faster and faster until they reach a speed where the forces of drag and weight are equal. This is called the terminal speed.

Look at the diagram of the skydiver. Her weight is always the same. Her changing speed changes the drag forces. At the start of the dive, her speed is 10 m/s and is increasing because her weight is more than the drag. As her speed increases, she pushes more air particles out of the way per second, which increases the drag force.

Her speed continues to increase until her drag force becomes equal to her weight. When these two forces are equal there is no unbalanced force to accelerate her and she falls at a constant speed of 55 m/s. This is called her terminal speed and it happens when the forces balance.

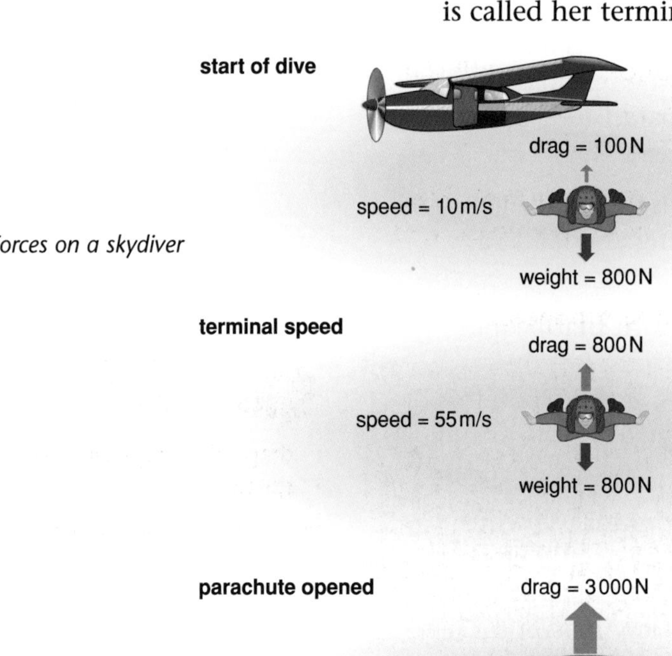

▶ *Forces on a skydiver*

When she opens her parachute it increases her surface area. She has to push more air particles out of the way per second and this increases the drag. Drag increases with surface area. With her parachute open her drag is much larger than her weight so she slows down very quickly.

As her speed reduces so does the drag force – until it equals her weight again. She then moves at a slower, safer constant speed.

b **Sometimes military vehicles are dropped by parachutes from aeroplanes. They usually need more than one parachute for each vehicle. Explain why.**

Free fall

A spaceship accelerates towards the surface of the Moon. The table shows how much the speed of the spaceship changes each second.

Time (s)	0	2	4	6	8	10	12	14	16
Speed (m/s)	0	3.2	6.4	9.6	12.8	16.0	19.2	22.4	25.6

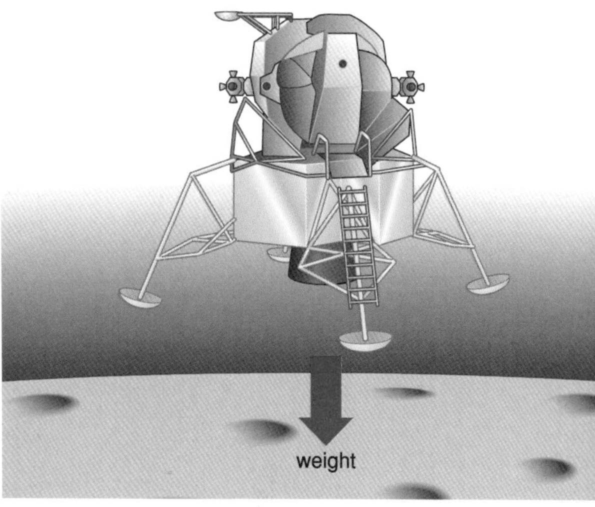

▲ *Falling spaceship*

The falling spaceship has only one force on it. This is the downward force of its weight due to gravity. There is no drag force because the Moon has no atmosphere. The speed increases steadily and the acceleration is constant. This is known as **free fall** (g) acceleration.

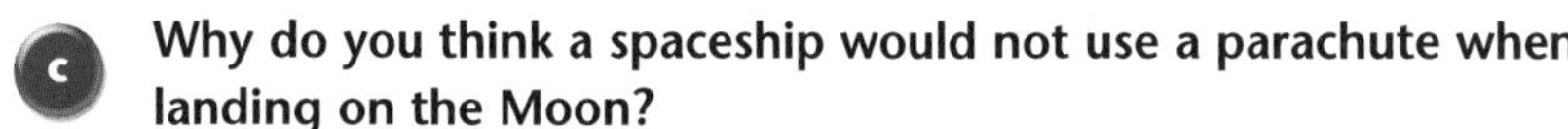

c **Why do you think a spaceship would not use a parachute when landing on the Moon?**

d **Suggest how a spaceship could reduce its speed.**

Unwanted drag

Drag can be useful if you are trying to slow down, but it can also be a nuisance when you are trying to go faster.

Racing cars need to be able to go as fast as possible to win, so they have a shape which allows air particles to flow more easily around them so the drag or air resistance is reduced.

Some high-speed sports find drag and friction a nuisance. A downhill skier reduces the drag of the air by wearing a tight smooth suit. He can also put wax on his skis. This wax lubricates the ski and reduces friction.

Lorries and caravans are not very streamlined so they can be slowed down by a lot by drag. Some have deflectors to help the air flow over them. This helps reduce fuel costs.

e **Suggest why the roof box on top of a car can reduce its top speed.**

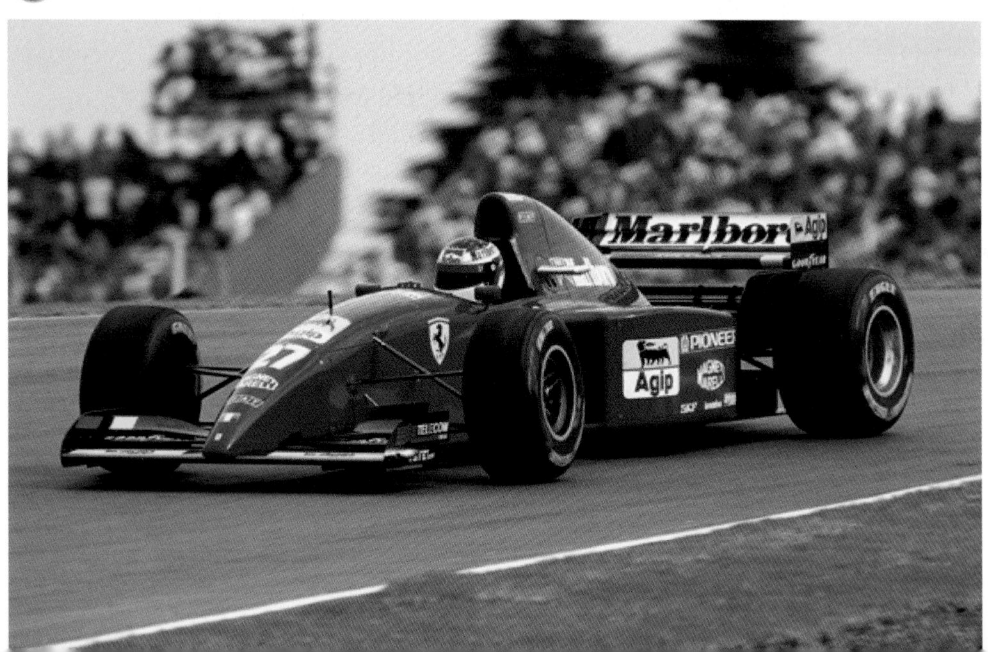

◀ *Racing cars need to reduce drag*

Keywords

drag • free fall • terminal speed

All fall down

Greg is investigating falling objects. He is interested in why some things fall faster than others. He collects some data from the Internet on the speed of skydivers when they are affected by air resistance or drag.

The table shows the downward speed of a skydiver as she falls.

Time (s)	0	2	4	6	8	10	12	14	16	18	20	24	26	28
Speed (m/s)	0	19	34	45	52	55	55	55	55	20	5	5	5	0

Greg also thinks about a falling ball. He knows that when a ball falls it accelerates because its weight pulls it down. But he wonders what would happen if there was no drag to slow it down.

He predicts what would happen and the table shows his predictions of the speed of the ball after each second.

Time (s)	0	1	2	3	4	5	6
Speed (m/s)	0	10	20	30	40	50	60

Questions

1 Look at the table of the falling skydiver. Draw these results on graph paper.

2 What was the skydiver's highest speed in m/s?

3 When in seconds do you think skydiver opened her parachute?

4 What was the skydiver's speed in m/s when she reached the ground?

5 When was her deceleration highest? (When did the speed change most quickly?)

6 Look at the table with Greg's predictions. Draw these results onto graph paper with the vertical axis from 0 to 60 m/s and the horizontal axis from 0 to 6 s.

7 How much does the speed increase each second?

8 What is the acceleration of the ball in m/s/s?

The science of fun

In this item you will find out

- about gravitational potential energy and what affects it
- about how gravitational potential energy is converted to kinetic energy
- about how energy is used in theme rides

▲ *Having fun with kinetic and potential energy*

Theme ride designers fool about with your kinetic and gravitational potential energy. You gain potential energy when the ride goes uphill. You gain kinetic energy as the ride falls towards Earth. Designers have a scientific understanding about the forces on you and how they can affect and scare you. They are experts on how far they can go safely. Most people are not experts on forces and so they can be scared.

On Earth we are always being acted upon by the force of gravity. When we are lifted off the ground by a roller coaster, we have potential, or stored, energy due to gravity. This is called **gravitational potential energy**.

The amount of gravitational potential energy objects have depends on their mass and position in the Earth's gravitational field. The more mass an object has, the greater its gravitational potential energy. The higher an object is, the greater its gravitational potential energy.

The gravitational potential energy of an object also increases when the force of gravity (**gravitational field strength** (g)) increases. On Jupiter, gravity is about three times stronger than on the Earth. This means if objects of the same mass were lifted to the same height on the Earth and Jupiter, the object on Jupiter would have greater gravitational potential energy.

After humans visited the Moon, they and the spaceship left the Moon's surface and returned to Earth. Because the Moon has such a low gravitational field strength it made the weight of the spaceship very low. This meant that less force and energy was needed to lift it away from the Moon. It needed relatively little fuel to leave the Moon and get into orbit. The spaceship can be six times higher on the Moon for the same potential energy as above the Earth. Also there was no atmosphere on the Moon to cause drag to slow it down.

a **If a spaceship visited and took off from another planet with a high gravitational field strength this would cause problems at lift-off. Suggest and explain reasons why.**

Amazing fact

Some of the world's roller coasters are higher than 130 m, longer than 2 km and move you at speeds that can be over 120 mph.

Kinetic energy

When objects move they have kinetic energy.

Speed of car (m/s)	Kinetic energy of small car (mass = 1 kg) (J)	Kinetic energy of large car (mass = 2 kg) (J)
0	0	0
1	0.5	1.0
2	2.0	4.0
3	4.5	9.0
4	8.0	16.0
5	12.5	25.0
6	18.0	36.0

The table shows the kinetic energy of two remote-controlled cars at different speeds. One car is twice the mass of the other.

As you can see from the table, the kinetic energy of the larger car is twice the kinetic energy of the smaller car. So doubling the mass, doubles the kinetic energy.

The cars have a lot more kinetic energy when they move faster. If the speed doubles, the kinetic energy quadruples.

b **The large toy car is twice the mass of the small toy car and the batteries run out about twice as quickly. Suggest reasons why. (Remember KE = $\frac{1}{2} \times m \times v^2$)**

c **At 2 m/s the batteries of the large toy car last about 1 hour. But at 4 m/s the batteries only last about 15 minutes. Suggest reasons why.**

Examiner's tip

Practice selecting the right formula from a list and make sure you can use it.

Calculating gravitational field strength

The gravity or gravitational field strength (g) of a planet is measured in newtons per kilogram (N/kg).

We can calculate the weight of an object using this equation:

weight	=	mass	×	gravitational field strength
N	=	kg	×	N/kg

We can also rearrange the equation to calculate mass or gravitational field strength if we know the other two variables.

For example, an astronaut in his suit weighs 160 N on the Moon. The gravitational field strength on the Moon is 1.6 N/kg. We can calculate the mass of the astronaut.

weight = mass × gravitational field strength

160 N = mass × 1.6 N/kg

$$\text{mass} = \frac{160\,\text{N}}{1.6\,\text{N/kg}}$$

mass = 100 kg

d **A 3 000 kg space probe weighs 15 000 N on a planet. Calculate the gravitational field strength on the planet.**

Calculating gravitational potential energy

▲ *Climbing stairs gives you gravitational potential energy*

We can calculate the gravitational potential energy of an object by using this equation:

potential energy	=	mass	×	gravitational field strength	×	height
joules (J)	=	kg	×	N/kg	×	m
PE	=	mgh				

For, example, Alice gains 1500 J of gravitational potential energy climbing a flight of stairs. She has a mass of 50 kg and g = 10 N/kg on Earth. We can calculate the height of the stairs.

$$PE = mgh$$

$$1500\,J = 50\,kg \times 10\,N/kg \times height$$

$$height = \frac{1500\,J}{(50\,kg \times 10\,N/kg)} = \frac{1500}{500} = 3\,m$$

A forklift truck lifts a 800 kg mass to a height of 3 m. Calculate the PE gained if g = 10 N/kg on Earth.

Converting energy

Most roller coasters take you to the top of a large slope to start. This gives you maximum gravitational potential energy.

From the top of the ride you roll downhill, converting gravitational potential energy to kinetic energy.

Halfway down the hill you will have both gravitational potential energy and kinetic energy. At the lowest part of the ride you will have maximum kinetic energy. Here you will be travelling the fastest. Sometimes this kinetic energy is used to allow you to climb up yet another slope.

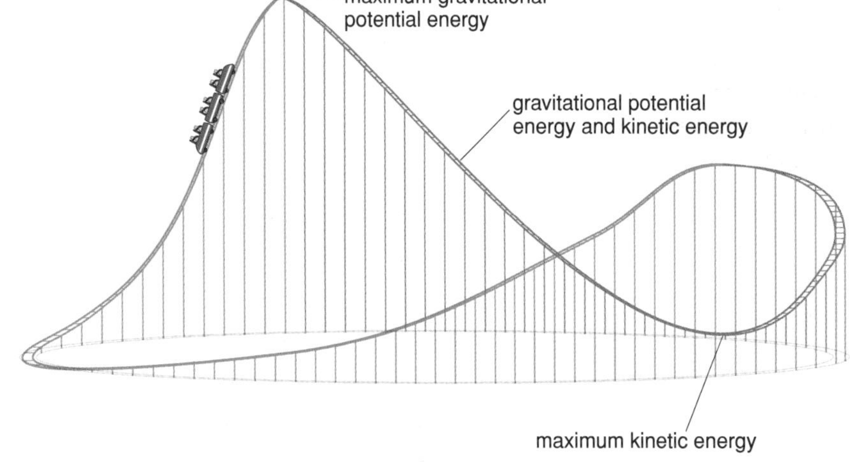

▲ *Changes in roller coaster energy*

The second slope is usually not as high as the first slope. Use the ideas of KE and PE to suggest why.

Falling down

When skydivers fall they convert gravitational potential energy into kinetic energy. Eventually they reach a terminal speed. This maximum speed means that the kinetic energy cannot increase any more. The gravitational potential energy they still have does work against air resistance (friction) as they fall.

Keywords

gravitational field strength • gravitational potential energy

On the roller coaster

Rachel and Ellie ride the giant roller coaster. An electric motor lifts their car up the slope to the highest point on the ride. Looking down looks really scary.

At the top of the ride the electric motor is switched off and the car starts to roll down 'Scary Hill'. Half-way down 'Scary Hill' the speed increases but gets even faster at the bottom.

Their car then rolls up 'White Knuckle Hill', which is not quite as high as the first one. Rachel is worried that the car will not reach the top but it just manages. Ellie can't understand why this smaller hill is supposed to be more frightening than 'Scary Hill'.

The next drop is called 'White Knuckle Cliff' which is almost a vertical drop and this accelerates them into the underground tunnel that is the lowest and fastest part of the ride.

Ellie is relieved to escape the tunnel as the car climbs a small slope before turning upside down around the 'Loop-de-loop'. The end of the ride is much less scary as they climb up a small hill back to the start.

Questions

1 Sketch a diagram of the roller coaster ride that Ellie and Rachel use and label the features.

2 The car starts to roll from the highest point of the ride. Why do you think this is important?

3 Explain the types of energy there are and the energy changes at these points on the ride.
   (a) At the top of Scary Hill
   (b) Half-way down Scary Hill
   (c) At the bottom of Scary Hill

4 The car just manages to climb White Knuckle Hill. Suggest why in terms of energy.

5 Why is the acceleration greatest falling down White Knuckle Cliff?

6 Why is the speed highest at the bottom of the tunnel?

7 Sketch a speed–time graph for your ride. Label the features on your graph.

8 Protection for passengers is essential in cars and roller coaster rides. They both have seat belts, padding and headrests. Suggest at what points in the ride these features would be used by the passengers.

P3a

1 Look at the distance–time graph for a cyclist.

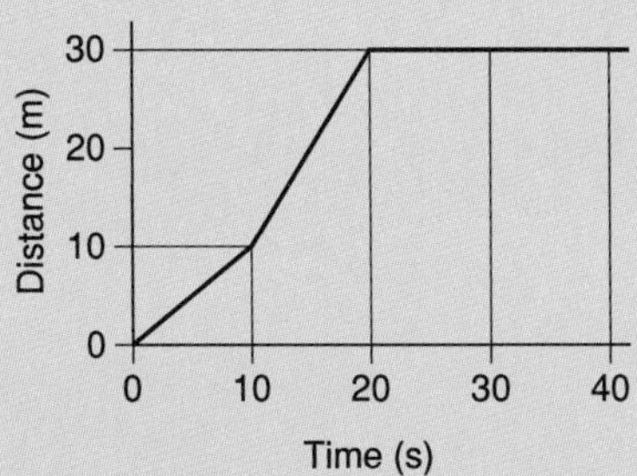

a The cyclist moves 10 m in the first 10 s. Calculate the speed for the first 10 s. [3]
b The cyclist travels a greater distance in the next 10 s. Explain why. [2]

2 A car travels at an average speed of 70 mph.

a Calculate how many hours it will take to cover 490 miles. [3]
b Calculate the distance it can travel in 90 minutes. [3]

3 A runner runs at an average speed of 10 m/s. Calculate the distance she travels in 20 s.

4 A car moves at 70 mph. Calculate the time needed to travel 420 miles.

P3b

1 Look at the speed–time graph of a motorbike.

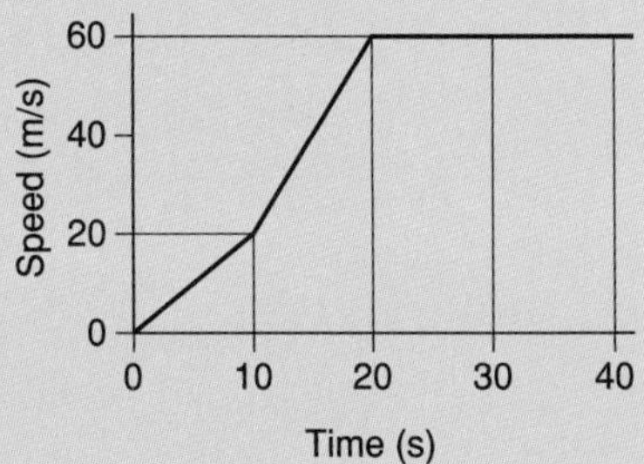

a When does the motorbike have the greatest acceleration? [1]
b When does the motorbike have zero acceleration? [1]
c Calculate the acceleration for the first 10 seconds. [3]
d How could you calculate the distance travelled for the first 10 seconds? [1]

2 Look at the speed–time graph of a car.

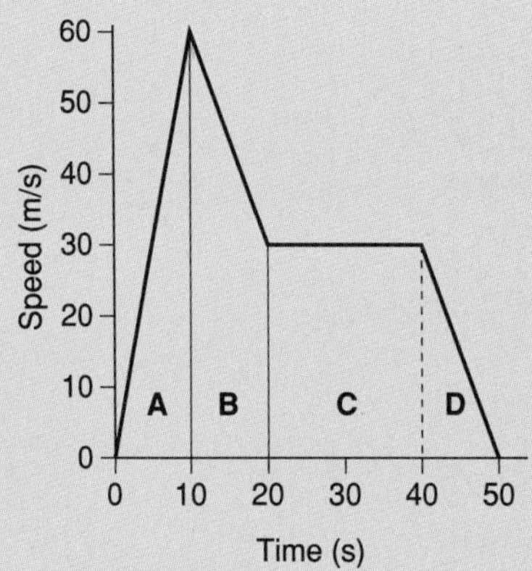

a Calculate the acceleration of the car in part A. [3]
b Calculate the distance travelled in part B. [3]
c In part D, the car brakes. Calculate the braking distance. [2]

3 Calculate the acceleration in m/s^2 of the following vehicles. Copy and complete the table.

Vehicle	Starting speed (m/s)	Finishing speed (m/s)	Change in speed (m/s)	Time (s)	Acceleration (m/s^2)
a	10	30	20	5	4
b	10	40	30	6	
c	20	60	40	4	
d	0	50		10	

4 Calculate the change in speed and the acceleration in m/s^2 of the following vehicles.

Vehicle	Starting speed (m/s)	Finishing speed (m/s)	Change in speed (m/s)	Time (s)	Acceleration (m/s^2)
e	20	100		2	
g	0	60		300	
h	4	9		10	
i	0	500		15	

P3c

1 Look at the diagram of the stopping distance of a car.

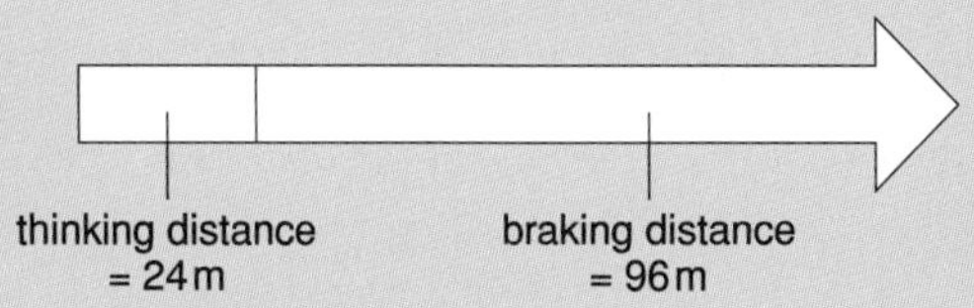

a *Write down two different factors that can increase thinking distance.* [2]
b *Write down two different factors that increase braking distance.* [2]
c *This car is moving at about 80 mph. The driver often travels about 10 m behind the car in front. Explain why this can be dangerous.* [3]

2 *A 1 000 kg car brakes with its maximum braking force of 4 000 N.*

a *Calculate the acceleration of the car when braking.* [3]
b *The car then pulls a trailer. The braking distance is increased. Explain why.* [2]
c *The car then pulls a trailer along a wet road. The car skids and the braking distance is increased a lot more. Explain why.* [2]

3 *A car accelerates on a dry road. It gets to 30 mph in 6 seconds. The same car attempts to accelerate on an icy road. The driving force is the same but the acceleration is reduced. Explain why.*

4 *Copy out and complete the table using calculations.*

	Force (N)	Mass (kg)	Acceleration (m/s²)
a	50	10	5
b		20	10
c	1000	100	
d	2000		20

P3d

1 **a** *A car has a driving force of 2 000 N. It moves 100 m. Calculate the work done.* [3]
b *The car does 400 000 J of work in 8 s. Calculate the power developed.* [3]

2 **a** *A lift has a power of 10 000 W. It takes 10 s to go to floor 3. Calculate the work done.* [3]
b *The lift does 200 000 J of work over a 40 m height. Calculate the lifting force.* [3]

3 *Look at the data for the fuel consumption of various cars, for use around town, on long distances, and for a combination of the two.*

Car	Fuel consumption (around town) (mpg)	Fuel consumption (long distance) (mpg)	Fuel consumption (combined use) (mpg)
Steve's car	25	37	30
Nafisa's car	40	55	46
Rebecca's car	40	60	52
Ryo's car	42	68	58

a *Whose car has the worst fuel consumption around town?* [1]
b *Whose car has the best fuel consumption on long distance journeys?* [1]
c *Ryo's car has only 12 gallons of fuel in it. How far should it travel if he does a mixture of town and long distance driving?* [2]

4 *Look at the table in question 3. Rebecca expects to be able to travel 400 miles around town when she has 10 gallons of fuel. Unfortunately her car runs out of fuel after 360 miles. Suggest why she runs of fuel sooner than she thought.* [2]

P3e

1 *Look at the information about the braking distances of a car.*

Speed of car (m/s) (mph)	Braking distance (m)
8 (18)	6
16 (36)	24
32 (72)	96

a *Describe the relationship between speed and braking distance.* [2]
b *Explain the relationship between speed and braking distance. (Hint: kinetic energy = $\frac{1}{2}$ x mass x velocity²)* [3]

2 *Sally and her bike have a mass of 100 kg*

a *Calculate her kinetic energy at*
i *2 m/s* [2]
ii *4 m/s* [2]
iii *6 m/s* [2]
iv *8 m/s* [2]
v *10 m/s* [2]
vi *12 m/s* [2]
b *Plot a lone graph of these results. Put the kinetic energy along the vertical axis.* [2]
c *What happens to KE when the speed doubles* [1]

3 *Simon and Denise talk about road accidents. Simon says 'a car crash at 60 mph is twice as bad as an accident at 30 mph'. Denise says if you double the speed of the car crash it will be four times worse'. Denise is more correct. Use your ideas about KE to explain why.*

4 *Car fuel consumption depends on several things. Explain how fuel consumption depends on*

a *the speed* [2]
b *work done against friction* [2]
c *different driving styles* [2]
d *different road conditions.* [2]

P3f

1 **a** Seat belts, crumple zones and air bags are useful in a crash. Explain why. [3]
b How can active safety features, such as ABS, make driving safer? [3]
c How can passive safety features, such as adjustable seating, make driving safer? [2]

2 **a** Explain in detail how crumple zones and safety cages can reduce injuries in a crash. In your answer use ideas about forces, acceleration, distance and time. [4]
b Write down two other safety features in cars that reduce injuries in a similar way. [4]

3 Cars are fitted with passive safety features. Explain how these safety features make cars safer:

a electric windows [1]
b cruise control [1]
c paddle shift controls on the steering wheel for the gears or stereo [1]
d adjustable steering. [1]

4 Escape lanes and crash barriers help cars to stop if they are out of control. They can improve safety. Explain how. [2]

P3g

1 Helen is a parachutist. She jumps out of an aeroplane.

a Her speed increases. Explain why. Use ideas about forces in your answer. [1]
b Before she opens her parachute she gets to a terminal speed. Explain why. Use ideas about forces in your answer. [1]
c She opens her parachute and her speed reduces very quickly. Explain why. Use ideas about forces in your answer. [1]

2 Simon drives his car. It has a top speed of 80 mph when he uses its highest driving force.

a He starts from rest and accelerates. What happens to the drag force as he gets faster? [1]
b He gets to a top speed (terminal speed) of 80 mph. What can you say about the driving force and the drag force at 80 mph? [1]
c He puts a large roof box on the top of the car. The car's new top speed is only 65 mph. Explain why. Use ideas about forces in your answer. [3]

3 Describe an experiment to work out the terminal speed of a falling shuttlecock in badminton. [5]

4 Describe how you could investigate changing the surface area of the shuttlecock to see its effect on the terminal speed of the shuttlecock. What would you expect to happen and why? [4]

P3h

1 Sally goes for a bike ride. She travels at 2 m/s.

a She fixes a child trailer on the back of the bike for her children to ride in. She puts her two children in it and goes for a ride again. This has doubled her mass and her speed is still 2 m/s. What happens to the amount of kinetic energy if she has doubled her mass? [1]
b She doubles her speed to 4 m/s. What happens to the amount of kinetic energy she has at double the speed? [1]
c She rides to the top of a hill and rests. What type of energy does she have here? [1]
d She rolls down the hill without pedalling. She gets faster. Explain what happens to her energy from the top of the hill to the bottom. [2]

2 Look at the table. It shows the weight of a 1 000 kg space probe in different places.

Place	Earth	Moon	Jupiter
Weight (N)	10 000	1 600	27 000

a Calculate the gravitational field strength on the Earth, Moon and Jupiter. [3]
b The space probe has 200 000 J of potential energy 100 m above the surface of a planet. Calculate the gravitational field strength on the planet. [3]

3 Look at the diagram of the rollercoaster ride.

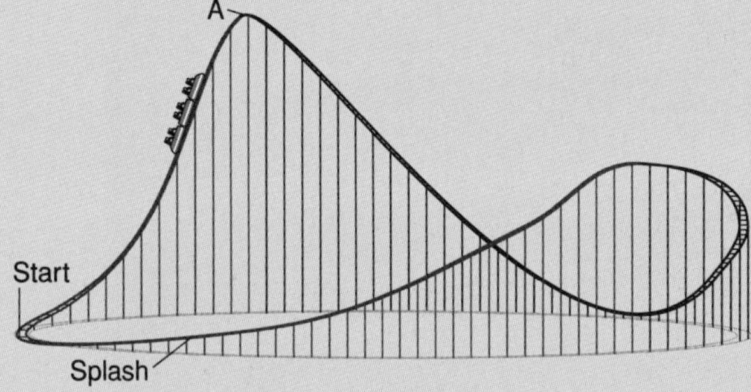

The car is lifted from the start to A, which is the highest point of the ride. The car rolls down the sloope, up and down the next slope and then comes to rest after a big splash. Describe the energy changes in the ride. [5]

4 Look again at the diagram of the rollercoaster.

a Explain why the second slope has to be lower than A. [2]
b The car has a mass of 2000 kg and its height at A is 90 m. On Earth $g = 10\ m/s^2$. Calculate the PE at A. [2]

P4 Radiation for life

- Electricity kills 10 people in their homes in the UK every year, often because DIY enthusiasts don't take the right precautions when wiring plugs and sockets. Electrostatic charge can cause explosions, but electrostatics can also clean up pollution and can even save your life when a paramedic uses a defibrillator to re-start your heart.
- Radiation frightens many people. Yet in hospitals radiographers inject radioactive liquid into people or make the patients swallow radioactive liquids. Why are these people happy to have radioactive substances in their bodies?
- We are running out of energy. Many people want renewable energy but some environmental groups are opposed to wind power because it causes climate disturbance and harms birdlife. Now nuclear power is in the news as the only way to save the environment.

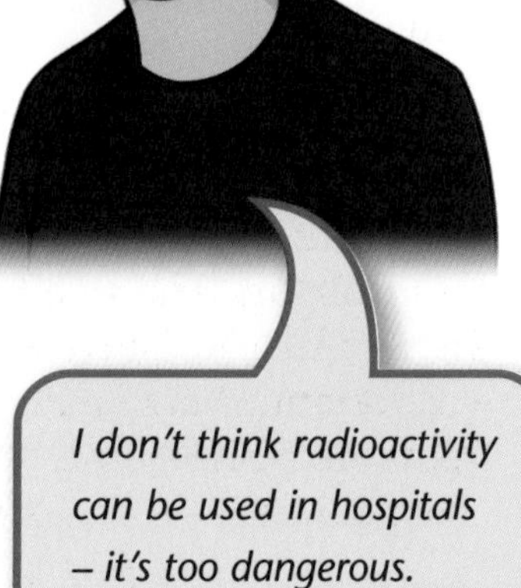

What you need to know

- What electrical current is.
- What electrical conductors and insulators are.
- What an atom is made of.

Static electricity can kill

In this item you will find out

- about new products that work because of electrostatics
- how static electricity can be dangerous and cause problems
- how to avoid a fatal electric shock

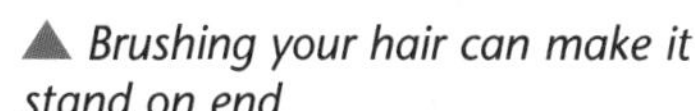

▲ *Brushing your hair can make it stand on end*

Are you shocked when you get out of a car?

Do sparks fly when you walk round an expensive shop?

These effects are due to **electrostatic** charges. They are caused by tiny negatively charged particles called electrons. If an object has too many electrons it is negatively charged. If it has too few electrons it is positively charged.

Two negatively charged objects will **repel** each other because like charges repel, but a **positive** and **negative charge** (unlike charges) will **attract** each other as they try to neutralise (cancel out) the difference in charge.

a **Make a list of things that happen in everyday life because of electrostatic charging. Explain why these things happen.**

Our clothes often cling to us because modern synthetic materials are insulators, and so electrostatic charge cannot flow through them. When we move and create friction between fabrics, electrostatic charge builds up on them as the electrons transfer from one fabric to the other, making them positively or negatively charged. Unlike charges attract, so the fabrics cling to each other.

Manufacturers of anti-static sprays, liquids and tumble drier cloths claim that their products will stop charge building up on the fabric and stop our clothes clinging.

Dust particles are made mainly of dead human skin and often carry electrostatic charge. When the dust lands on an insulator like a plastic container or TV screen, the charged dust particles stick.

Dusters can be made of special fibres called electret fibres that have positive and negative electric charge on them. As unlike charges attract each other, these new dusters attract and trap the dust instead of flicking it around the room.

▼ *Tumble drier sheets can reduce the static cling in your clothes*

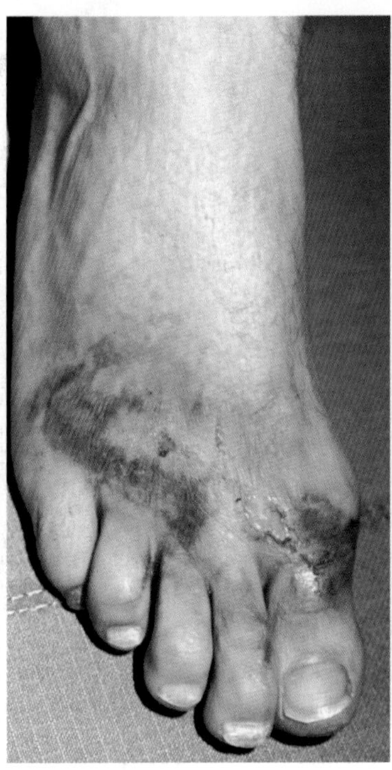

▲ An electric shock can cause burns through your feet as the charge bursts out to get to earth

A shocking experience

Empty oil tankers can explode! As the crews clean the empty ships the water droplets from the sprays can get an electrostatic charge on them. The heavier droplets with one type of charge will fall but the lighter ones with the opposite charge will float in the air.

Separating charges like this can create a spark because the separated charges can cause a discharge as they try to neutralise, a bit like lightning. This spark can ignite the flammable oil vapour, causing an explosion that rips the ships apart.

Similar problems can happen anywhere where there is a flammable gas or vapour, plenty of oxygen to help the burning and particles or droplets with electrostatic charge on them waiting to discharge and make a spark.

b Food manufacturers working with flour or sugar often suffer explosions. What do you think might cause these explosions?

Can you die of shock?

You can die of shock – especially if it is an **electric shock**. We are all good conductors of electricity. If you touch something that has a large electric charge on it, the charge will flow through you as the lowest resistance route to earth. This is an electric shock. It causes your muscles to contract and can stop your heart beating.

How to avoid death

An electric shock is caused by an electric current flowing through your body. The way to avoid a shock is to stop the current flowing. There are three ways to do this:

Ways to avoid an electric shock	How it works
Make sure the device (e.g. electric fire) is correctly earthed	The device is earthed if there is an earth wire connected between the metal casing of the electrical appliance and earth. If there is a fault and the casing gets a large charge on it, it becomes live. The current flows straight down the earth wire to earth instead of through you.
Stand on an insulating mat made of rubber or plastic	If you touch a charged object and you are standing on an insulating mat made of rubber or plastic, then the current cannot flow through the mat and so it will not flow through you and you will not feel a shock.
Wear shoes with insulating soles made of rubber or plastic	Rubber or plastic are insulators. Wearing shoes with rubber or plastic soles will stop the current flowing through you and so you will not feel a shock.

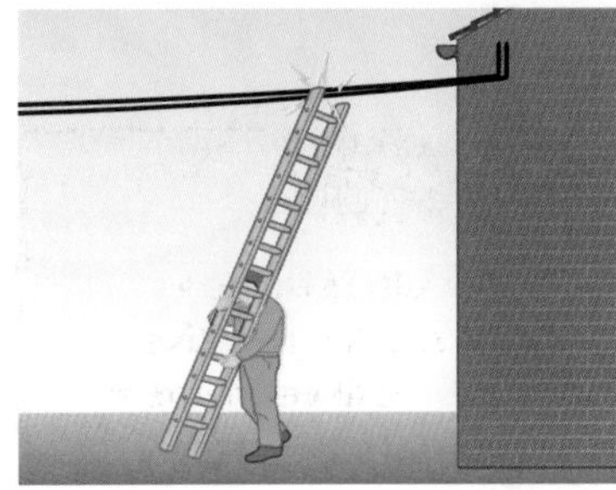

▲ Electric shocks can happen in all sorts of ways

Warning!

If you walk across a synthetic carpet or vinyl floor wearing shoes with insulating soles (plastic or rubber) you might become electrostatically charged due to friction. The charge on you will flow from you to earth as soon as you touch something that is connected to earth, such as a metal clothes rail or water pipe. This is why you often get a mild shock when you are out shopping.

c **Describe the different ways you can get an electric shock and what you can do to avoid getting a shock in each case.**

▲ *Stand on an insulating mat to make sure you do not get a shock from the van de Graaff generator*

Lorries need earthing too

Even a lorry can suffer from **static electricity**. Refuelling lorries (which pump aviation fuel into aircraft) often get an electrostatic charge because of friction between the fuel and the pipe. Years ago it was quite common for aircraft to go up in flames because of a spark setting fire to the fuel.

Now an earth wire is connected between the refuelling lorry and the aircraft to allow the charges to neutralise (cancel out). More recently all aviation fuel has had anti-static additives added to it so that it is less likely to charge up and generate a spark.

Lorries which carry flammable gases and powders also need to be earthed before they are unloaded.

d **Explain how an earth wire makes refuelling an aircraft safer.**

e **Explain how fuel additives make refuelling an aircraft safer.**

◀ *Refuelling an aircraft carried dangers of explosion before anti-static additives in fuels and earth connections were used*

Keywords

attract • electrostatic • electric shock • negative charge • positive charge • static electricity • repel

Static saves the world from burial under plastic

▶ The TriboPen

We should recycle more of our waste. The UK is near the bottom of the recycling league table in Europe with less than 10% of our waste being recycled. Germany and Holland recycle close to 50% of their waste.

Should we be worried? We throw out enough rubbish to fill the Royal Albert Hall every two hours. What we throw out has to be buried in landfill sites and we are running out of land in which to bury it.

Plastic is expensive to produce so it makes sense to recycle it. But plastic is a term that covers many materials (polymers) so we cannot simply mix them together. We have to sort the different polymers before we can recycle them into something else. Now the Ford Motor Company is working with the University of Southampton, UK to develop a way to identify polymers before they are stripped from scrapped cars.

Graham Hearn at the University of Southampton works on this project. This is what he has to say about it.

'We have come up with the TriboPen. It uses the "tribo effect", which is when two insulating materials are rubbed together and a static charge is produced. The size of the charge and whether it is positive or negative is different for each type of plastic that is used in a car. We can measure the charge, compare it with a table of values stored in the pen's memory and identify which polymer it is.'

Questions

1. Years ago we did not worry about recycling. Why do you think things are different today?
2. How much more of their waste does Germany recycle than the UK?
3. Why do we have to identify different plastics before we can recycle them?
4. The Tribopen uses the 'tribo effect' to identify different plastics. Explain what this effect is.
5. If the Tribopen nib is made of polypropylene and is rubbed on to another plastic the pen becomes positively charged. What charge would the other plastic have? Explain what has happened to the electrons to cause this.

Hearts, chimneys and paint!

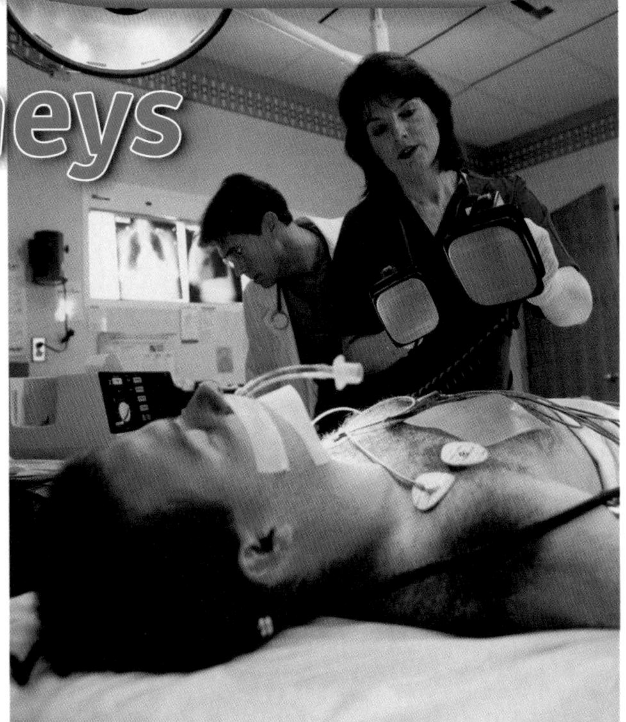

▲ *A heart defibrillator being used on a patient in A&E*

In this item you will find out

- how electrostatics saves lives
- how electrostatics can reduce pollution in the atmosphere
- how electrostatic charge on spray paints makes them more effective

'Stand clear!' the shout goes up and four nurses leap backwards. 'Charging, three, two, one.' The lifeless body on the hospital trolley contorts in a spasm as a huge electric current surges through him from the paddles pushed onto his bare chest.

'Going again. Stand clear.' The instruction is unnecessary as all the staff are well away. They know the drill: get too close and they will receive the same huge electric shock and it could kill them.

A nurse confirms that a slight flicker on the monitors shows that the patient has at last responded to the huge shocks that make his heart contract – this time his heart has continued contracting at its normal rhythm.

Heart attack!

Paramedics can use a **defibrillator** if your heart stops or is in fibrillation. There are two large paddles with insulated handles. One is laid over your heart area. The other is placed to the side of your chest. There has to be good contact with the body so that current can flow. This is why clothes are removed from the contact area. A sudden large charge is passed through the patient to make the heart contract strongly. No one should be in contact with the patient during the procedure as the current will flow through them to earth, possibly killing them in the process as the huge shock interferes with their own heart's rhythm. It is very important that the operator does not get a shock and the operator will tell any doctors or nurses standing by the patient to 'stand clear' as well. If the treatment is successful, the patient's heart will begin beating normally by itself.

a **Why do you think the huge electric shock is able to start the patient's heart beating?**

Amazing fact

A defibrillator pumps 360 J of energy into a patient's body. This is the same as the energy consumed by an electric light bulb in 4 seconds. However, the shock to the heart is delivered in only a fraction of a second.

▲ *Didcot Power station burns pulverised coal to produce electricity*

Charges suck

The ash that is produced at coal-fired power stations contains more radioactivity than is allowed in the low-level nuclear waste released from nuclear power stations. Didcot power station in Oxfordshire produces about 3 420 tonnes of ash per day; 80% of this ash flies up the huge chimneys and this is called fly ash. **Electrostatic dust precipitators** in the chimneys remove 99.9% of the fly ash.

b **From the information above, how many tonnes of ash fly up the chimneys at Didcot power station every day?**

c **How much ash, in kg, is *not* removed by the electrostatic dust precipitators and therefore flies out into the air?**

Amazing fact

280 million tonnes of ash is produced each year by coal-fired power stations in the UK.

How does it work?

In a simple electrostatic dust precipitator, opposite high voltages (positive and negative) are put on two grids, one above the other in the chimney. The fly ash is carried up the chimney by the hot air rising.

The positive grid gives the particles a positive charge by tearing the electrons off the dust particles. The negative grid attracts them because opposite charges attract. The dust particles clump together on the negative grid to form larger particles that eventually become heavy enough to fall back down the chimney into containers for collection.

Examiner's tip

Don't confuse positive and negative charge in electrostatics with north and south poles in magnetism.

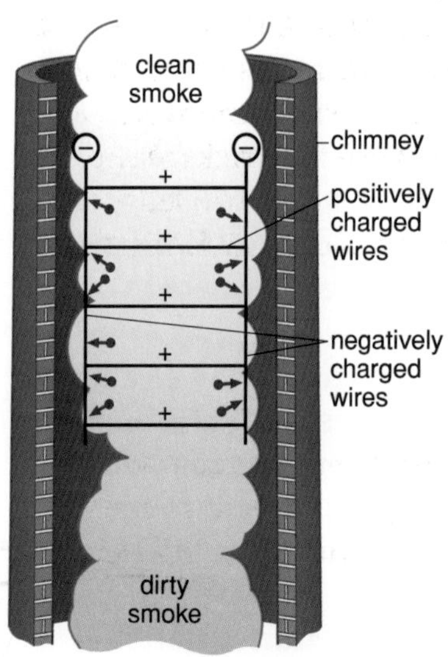

▲ *How an electrostatic dust precipitator works*

▲ *The waste from power stations can be made into building materials*

d **Why do the grids in an electrostatic dust precipitator need to be at high voltages?**

Charged orifices

Car manufacturers are saving money by using electrostatically charged paint sprayers. As the spray comes out it picks up an electrostatic charge. This means all the particles carry the same charge and repel each other, making a fine spray.

The car is charged opposite to the spray and so the spray is attracted to the car. This makes the whole process much less wasteful and more effective as the spray will find its way into cracks and crevices that the operator could not see.

▲ *Charging the spray means that the car attracts the spray to the car which is more efficient than using normal paint*

e **Why is it a good idea to put an electrostatic charge on paint?**

f **What would happen if the car and the paint had the same charge?**

Keywords

defibrillator • electrostatic dust precipitator

Electrostatic chemicals

One of the most polluting things in the countryside is the chemical waste from crop spraying. Farmers have to spray crops with fertiliser and with weed and pest killers. Thousands of litres of these toxic chemicals drain off the land into rivers each day. By electrostatically charging the chemical sprays, the spray will be attracted directly onto the plant and less will be free to land on the ground. This makes the process much less wasteful and much less polluting.

Lasers

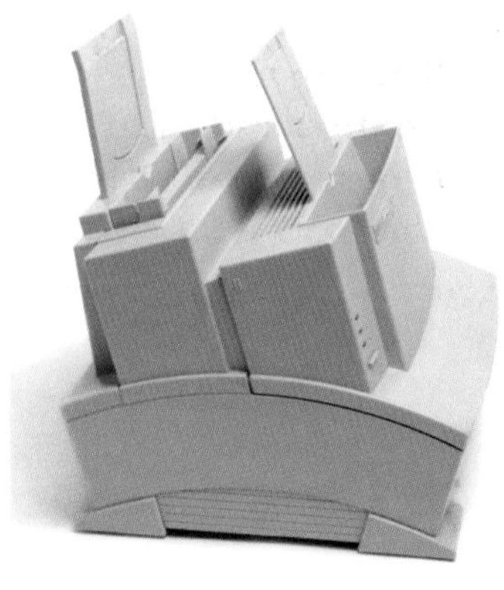

Laser printers and photocopiers rely on electrostatics too. A laser printer has a drum inside which can be electrostatically charged with a positive charge. When the laser hits the drum, it discharges – the laser writes the words as an electrostatic image which is negative compared with the background (which is positive). The toner is positive so sticks only where the letters are, leaving the background white. The page has to be heated to stick the toner to the page.

Photocopying

A photocopier works like a laser printer but the drum is discharged where light reflects onto it from the white parts of the original page. The drum stays charged where there is black on the original and the toner sticks to these parts.

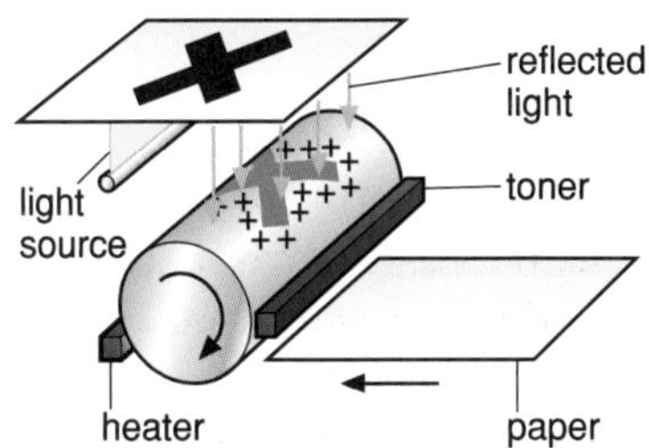

▲ *Electrostatics makes printers and photocopiers work*

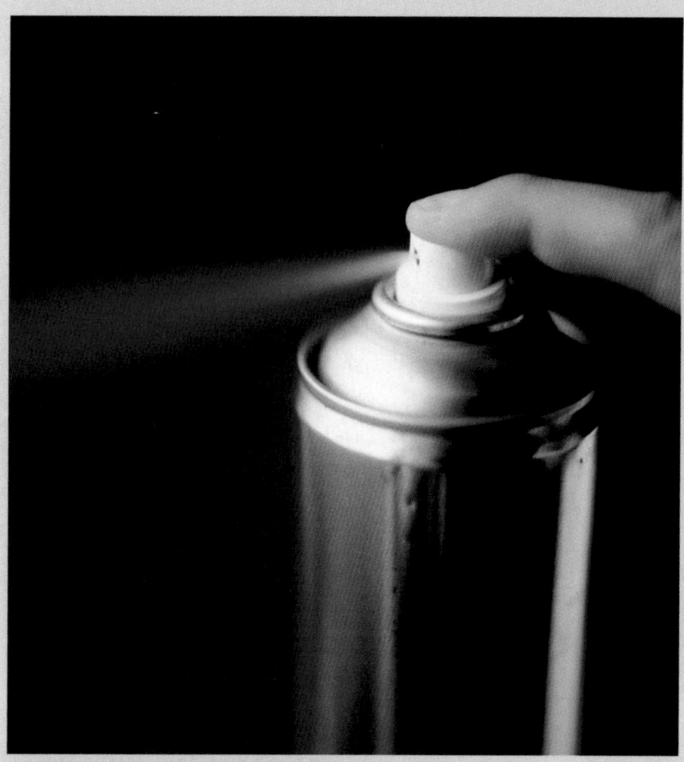

▲ *Electrostatic fly spray saves money*

Electrostatics and fly spray

Fly spray can get up your nose – and if it is up your nose, it is not killing flies. An Australian company is now paying Professor John Hughes, an electrical engineer, for his latest idea about how to make fly spray more efficient.

It works because of the shape of the hole in the aerosol can. Different shaped holes will cause the spray to come out with an electrostatic charge on it. If the spray is charged, it is attracted to the flies so it will target them instead of just floating round in the air.

An American company has created a metered fly spray dispenser as a way of ensuring maximum value for money. The can contains 170 g of fly-killer with 1% of the active ingredient Pyrethrin and they claim that it has 3 000 sprays.

Timers allow for sprays as often as every 5 minutes or up to 30 minutes, while photocells give the owner the choice of spraying only when lights are turned on, only when it is dark or 24 hours a day. They claim this option saves product and money.

Questions

1 Why does changing the shape of the hole in the aerosol make the fly spray work more efficiently than typical fly sprays?

2 If the amount of active ingredient Pyrethrin in the fly spray is 1% of the total contents of the spray, how many grams of Pyrethrin are there in a full can?

3 If the can will provide 3 000 sprays, how much product is in each spray?

4 The manufacturers claim that the spray will cover a volume of 140 m^3. How many grams of Pyrethrin will be in each cubic metre of space in the room if it is evenly dispersed?

5 The manufacturers claim that the can will last 30 days. How many sprays per day will this give?

6 If the can lasts 30 days and is only spraying during daylight hours, how often does it spray?

Keeping safe

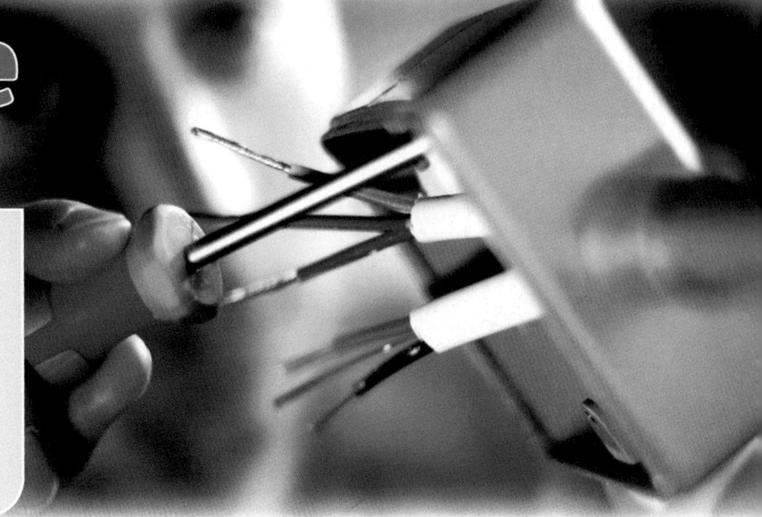

In this item you will find out

- how to do DIY electrical wiring safely
- why your hairdryer doesn't need earthing
- how fuses and residual current circuit breakers save lives

▲ *This person is risking a £5 000 fine*

Homeowners who tackle DIY electrical work could face fines of £5 000 and find they cannot sell their property. It is now illegal to do any electrical work in kitchens, bathrooms and gardens or to install electric floor or ceiling heating unless you can prove to the local authority Buildings Control that you are able to satisfy safety regulations. The reason is that water is a good conductor of electricity. If someone in the house has wet hands and touches faulty electrical wiring they are more likely to get an electric shock.

On average 10 people die and 750 are seriously injured each year as a result of unsafe electrical installations. It is essential to understand how basic electric **circuits** work if you are going to keep yourself safe when doing any electrical wiring.

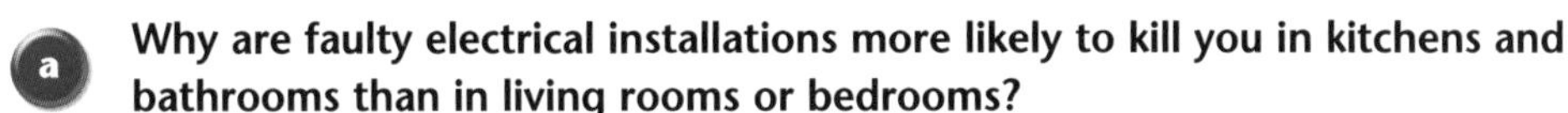

a Why are faulty electrical installations more likely to kill you in kitchens and bathrooms than in living rooms or bedrooms?

Amazing fact

In USA the voltage used is 120 volts compared with 230 volts in UK. This means the wires have to carry twice the current to make appliances work.

Static electricity is charge that does not move. As soon as the charge moves, it becomes an electric current. Charge can only flow through an electrical conductor such as metals or carbon. It cannot flow through insulators such as rubber and most plastics (polymers). To make a working electric circuit, you have to have a complete loop for the current to flow round.

Although all new appliances must have a 3-pin plug fitted, older appliances may need their plugs replacing if, perhaps, the casing cracks.

Colour of insulation	Name	Function
Brown	**live wire**	carries high voltage
Blue	**neutral wire**	completes the circuit
Yellow and green (if present)	**earth wire**	safety wire to prevent the casing of the appliance becoming live

Appliances with a plastic casing, such as a hairdryer or drill, do not need an earth wire. The casing is an insulator and cannot become live so you cannot get a shock from it. They are called **double insulated** appliances.

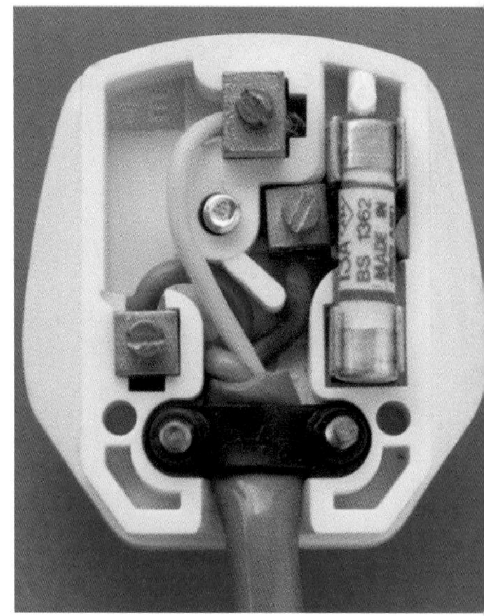

▲ *A correctly wired 3-pin plug*

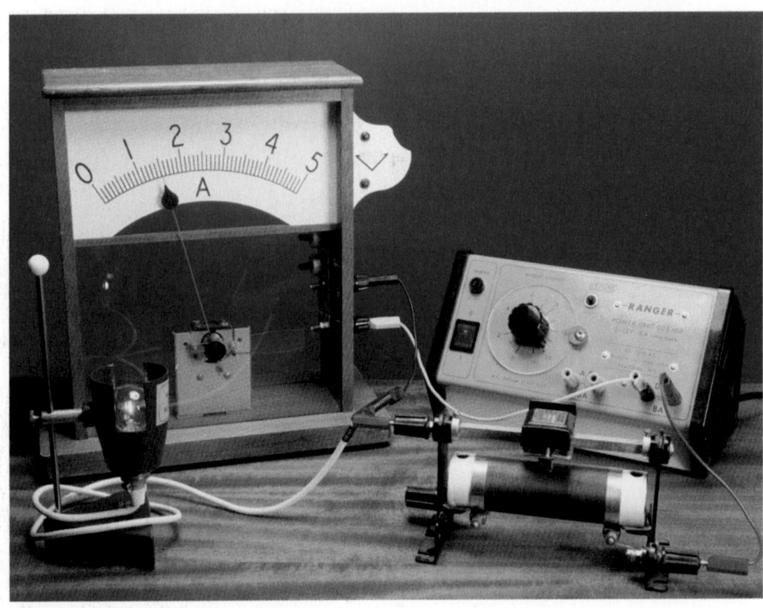

▲ *Moving the sliding handle changes the resistance of the rheostat*

b **Explain why some appliances do not have an earth wire.**

Your resistance is low

A **rheostat** can control the current that flows in a circuit. It does this by changing the **resistance** that the flowing current has to overcome. For example, increasing the resistance of a rheostat in a circuit means less current flows, so any bulbs in the circuit will be dimmed. A rheostat can be set to any resistance so it is called a **variable resistor**.

Putting up a resistance

The size of the current that flows in any circuit depends on what resistance there is in the circuit and the **potential difference** (pd) or voltage that is driving it.

	Cause	Effect
For given resistor	higher pd	higher current
	lower pd	lower current
For given pd	higher resistance	lower current
	lower resistance	higher current

c **If in a circuit, the pd remains at 12 V but the resistance is doubled, what effect would you expect this to have on the current?**

d **If in a circuit the resistance remains the same but the pd is halved, what effect do you expect this to have on the current?**

Examiner's tip

Write the units after your answer, for example 3.5 volts or 1.2 amps.

Working it out

For most circuits kept at a steady temperature you can work out the resistance you need to get a certain current.

$$\text{resistance} = \frac{\text{voltage}}{\text{current}}$$

Resistance is measured in ohms, voltage is the pd measured in volts (V) and the current is measured in amps (A).

For example, if the pd of the circuit is 12 V, and the current you require is 0.5 A, then the resistance you have to put into the circuit is:

$$\text{resistance} = \frac{\text{voltage}}{\text{current}} = \frac{12\text{ V}}{0.5\text{ A}} = 24\text{ ohms}$$

e Calculate the resistance needed in a circuit if the pd is 30 V and the current required is 2 A.

f Calculate the resistance needed in the circuit if the pd is 220 V and the current required is 10 A.

To work out the pd needed to drive a certain current, or to work out the current obtained in a circuit you have to rearrange the equation:

voltage = current × resistance

$$\text{current} = \frac{\text{voltage}}{\text{resistance}}$$

g Calculate the pd needed to give a current of 0.2 A in a resistor of 470 ohms.

h Calculate the current obtained when a pd of 220 V is applied to a resistor of 1 100 ohms.

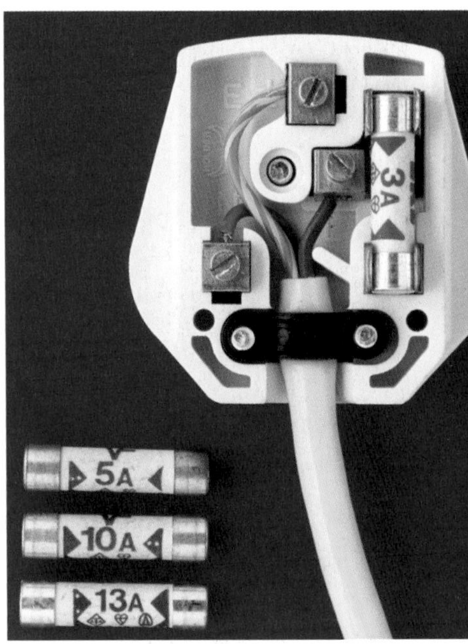

▲ *To keep an appliance and its wiring safe, the plug should have the correct fuse*

When the fuse blows

If an appliance develops a fault, the current in the wire between the plug and the appliance (the flex) might get too high. This would cause the flex to get very hot and might cause a fire. **Fuses** are put into circuits to prevent electrical devices causing fires. The fuse is a high resistance piece of wire which melts when the current gets too high, stopping the current flowing. This prevents the flex overheating and causing a fire and also prevents further damage to the appliance.

If the wrong fuse is in the plug, then it might not melt in time so may not protect your computer or TV.

Fuse 1 : electrocution 0

Fuses also prevent you getting electrocuted. If there is a fault on an appliance with a metal casing, the metal can become live and anyone touching it will be electrocuted when the charge flows through them to earth. These appliances have to have an earth wire (yellow and green) connected to their casing so that, if the casing becomes live, the charge flows to earth along the earth wire immediately. This current is huge and makes the fuse blow (melt).

Keywords

circuit • circuit breaker• double insulated • earth wire • fuse • live wire • neutral wire • potential difference • resistance • rheostat • variable resistor

Resetting... resetting... resetting

When the fuse in a plug blows it often causes the fuse in the fuse box of the house to blow as well. Older fuse boxes contain strips of metal fuse wire that melt. More modern fuse boxes contain resettable **circuit breakers** that 'trip' (switch off). These can be reset but it is sensible to check what tripped it in the first place to make sure no one is in danger.

i **Why is it a good idea to check why a resettable fuse tripped before you reset it?**

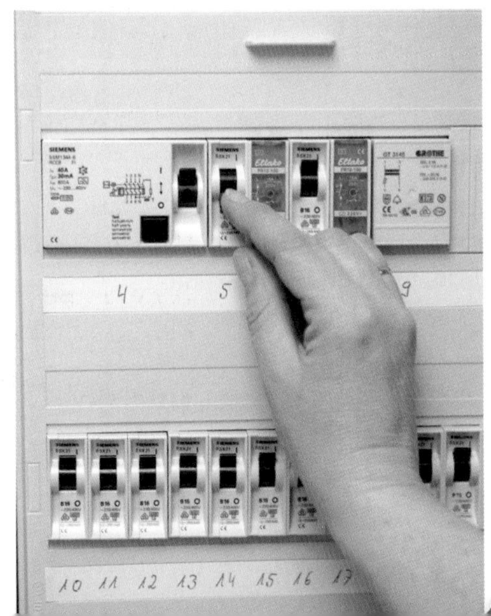

▶ *Modern fuses boxes have resettable circuit breakers*

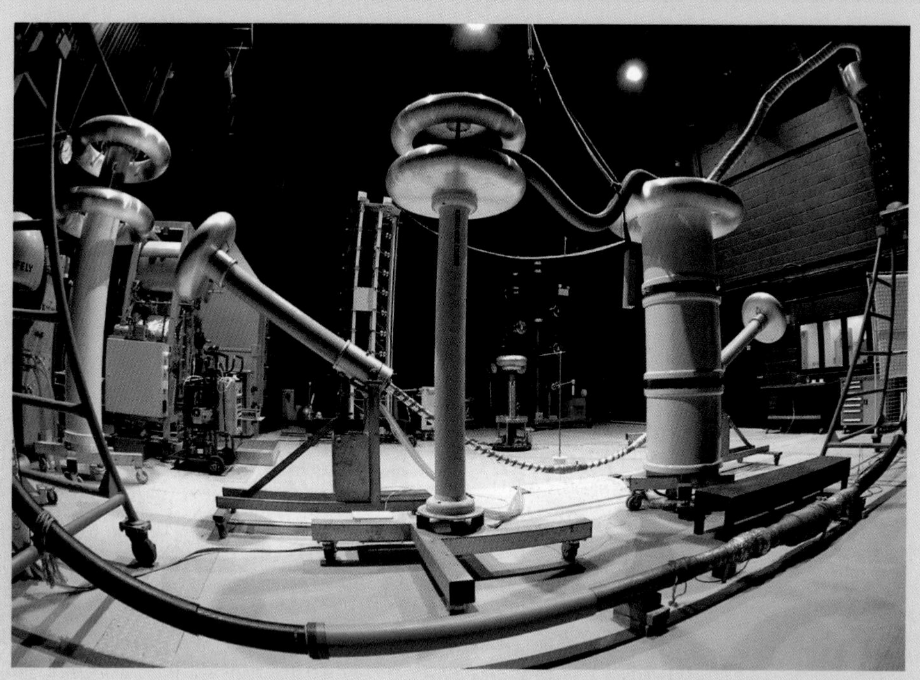

Paid to play with 30 000 volts

Neil Palmer is a Laboratory Engineer at the Tony Davies High Voltage Labs at the University of Southampton. His work involves testing devices at high voltages to check they work properly.

'We are testing some cable joints to check that they meet British Standards. Cable joints are where two high voltage electrical cables are joined – the type that feed electricity to your house for example. It is important that water doesn't get into them.

'I have to set up a testing rig. For safety I put the whole thing in a large cage with an interlock that switches the voltage off as soon as anyone unlocks the door.

'We apply 30 000 volts to the cable joint and then raise its temperature to 100 °C over 3 hours, maintain it for 2 hours then let it fall to room temperature over 3 hours. We repeat this for 123 cycles. We measure the resistance of the joint at the beginning and again at the end. The resistance must stay the same for the joint to pass its test.

'At the moment the engineers are trying to make reusable cable joints filled with gel as the insulator. So far all the ones we have tested have failed.

'Working in a high voltage lab can be dangerous. I remember when I got a shock from a new piece of equipment. Often these units are on rubber wheels so a charge can build up on them. They usually have an earth wire connected to discharge them but this one didn't. As I walked past I felt a jolt in my shoulder and my body tensed up. When I looked there was a red mark on my shoulder where the charge had gone in and another on my ankle where it had come out. I'm usually very careful to test things with an earth stick now to check it is fully discharged before I go near.'

Questions

1. Why does Neil need to test cable joints?
2. Working with high voltages is dangerous. What does Neil do to make sure the test rig is safe?
3. Describe the test that he does on the cable joints.
4. If the temperature of the rig is raised to 100 °C from 20 °C over 3 hours, what is the rate of temperature rise in degrees per minute?
5. How many days does it take to complete the 123 cycles?
6. Neil describes when he suffered an electric shock. Why did a charge build up on the new unit instead of flowing to earth?
7. What does he do to make sure he doesn't get an electric shock now?

Ultrasound is important

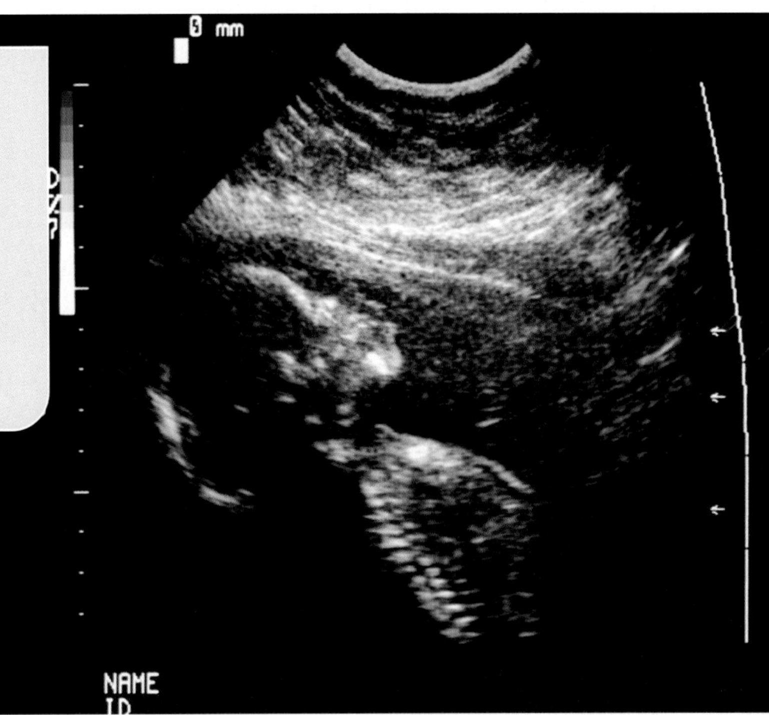

▲ *Ultrasound scan image of a baby at 20 weeks*

In this item you will find out

- how the ultrasound scan you received before you were born told your mother you were healthy
- why ultrasound is safer than X-rays
- how the shock waves from ultrasound can shatter kidney stones in your body

Doctors send every pregnant woman to the hospital to have an **ultrasound** scan to check that the baby is developing properly in the uterus.

Many other people have ultrasound treatment for kidney stones. The ultrasound pulse deliberately shatters the solid stone in the patient's kidney. A solid stone over 1 cm in diameter is shattered into thousands of tiny pieces that will pass out through the patient's urethra as they urinate.

But what are ultrasound scans? Should we use ultrasound on unborn babies when we know they are powerful enough to shatter kidney stones?

The difference is that very low power ultrasound waves reflect off a baby to show the outline of its body, but several strong beams of ultrasound waves will hit a kidney stone and make it vibrate so much it shakes itself apart and shatters.

Ultrasound is sound above about 22 000 Hz. It is so high pitched that humans cannot hear it. But many animals, such as bats, dogs and cats, can hear ultrasound.

The highest pitch sound anyone can hear is called the **upper threshold of human hearing**. It is about 20 000 sound waves per second (20 000 Hz) when you are young but gets lower as you get older. When you are about 15 it may be down to about 15 000 Hz, depending on how much loud music you have been listening to. Older adults have even lower limits.

a **Why are sounds above 22 000 Hz called ultrasound?**

Amazing fact

Mice can sing like birds – but usually at such high frequencies we don't hear. Scientists are now recording mice song at frequencies up to 70 000 Hz and changing the frequency down to levels we can hear.

Longitudinal waves

All sound waves, including ultrasound, are longitudinal waves. This means that they are caused by something vibrating which then puts pressure on the nearest molecules, pushing them closer together. As they bounce back to their normal position the molecules disturb surrounding molecules and this is how the pressure wave is passed on. All the time the air molecules are vibrating back and forth along the direction of the wave. This is most clearly seen in the waves travelling along a slinky spring.

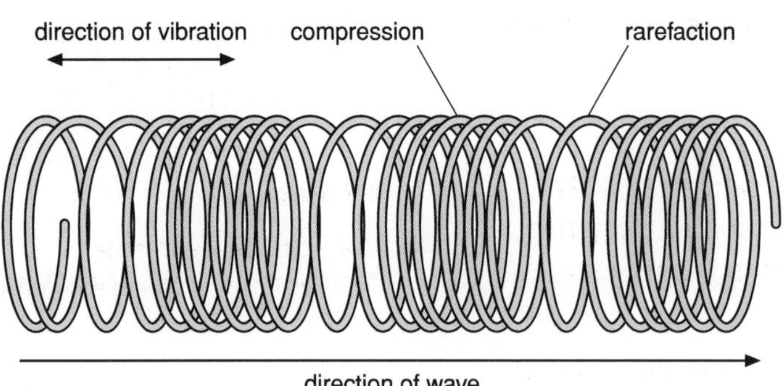

▲ *Longitudinal wave*

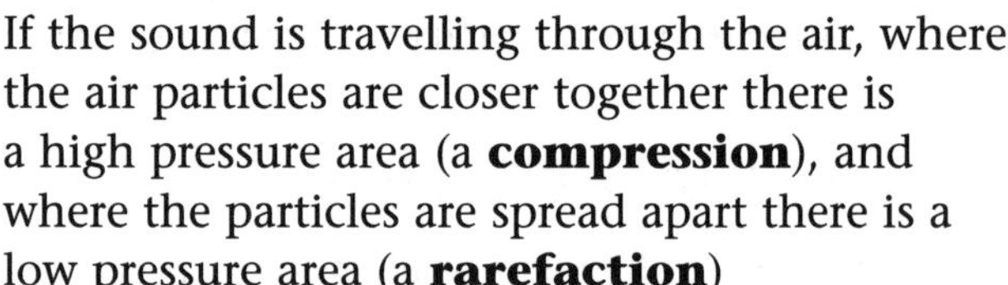

If the sound is travelling through the air, where the air particles are closer together there is a high pressure area (a **compression**), and where the particles are spread apart there is a low pressure area (a **rarefaction**)

Amplifying the meaning

In a loud sound the air molecules will move back and forth with more energy so they go further each time. This means that molecules hit your eardrum harder so you experience a louder sound. The distance moved by the molecules as they vibrate back and forth is the amplitude of the wave.

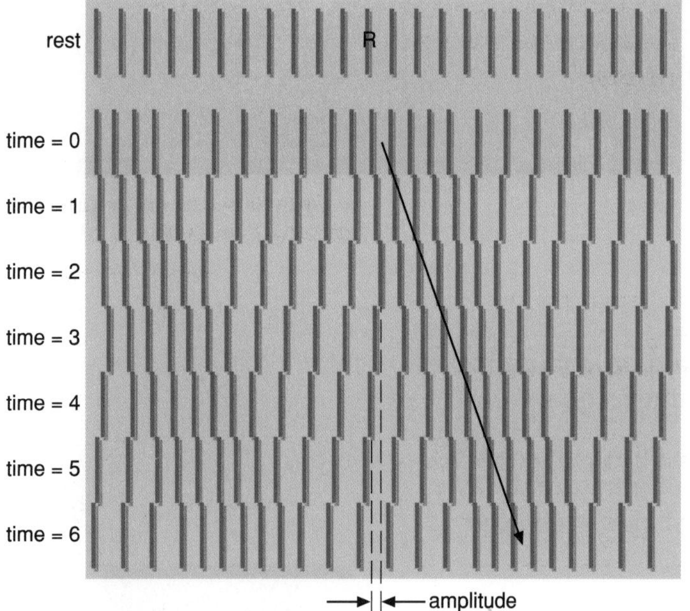

▲ *Amplitude*

On the right wavelength

The distance between one high pressure area (compression) and the next is called the wavelength. The wavelength is measured in metres and is often indicated by the symbol λ.

Hertz

If you count the number of waves hitting your eardrum each second, this is the frequency measured in waves per second (or hertz, Hz). A high pitch sound has a high frequency. Ultrasound is high frequency sound that is too high for us to hear.

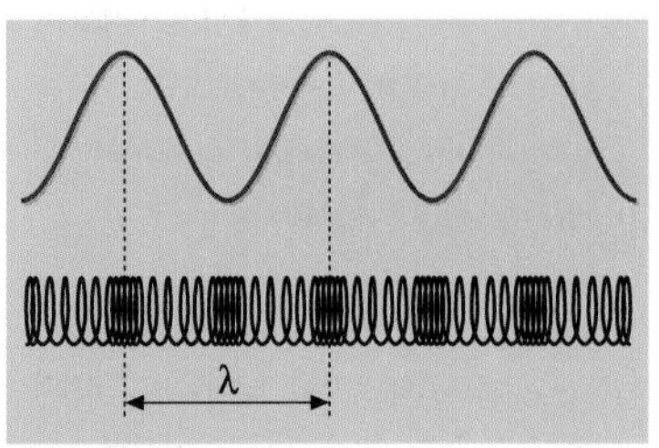

▲ *Wavelength*

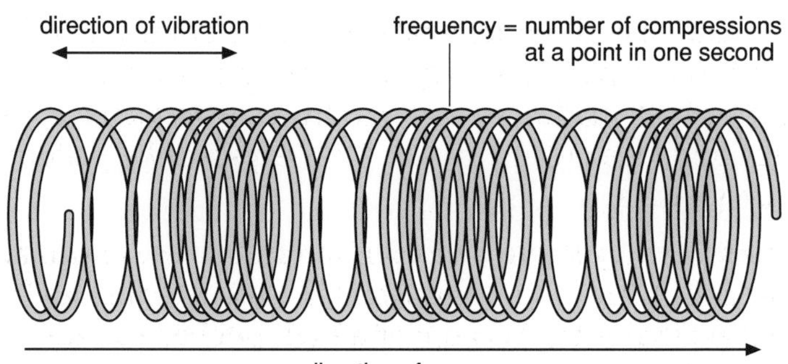

▶ *Frequency*

Going transverse

Sound is a longitudinal wave. But there is another type of wave called a transverse wave. A good example of a transverse wave is a ripple in a pond. For sound and other longitudinal waves the particles move along the same direction as the wave. For ripples in water and other transverse waves the particles go up and down as the wave goes along horizontally (the particles move at right angles to the direction the wave is travelling).

Make a table showing the meaning of ultrasound, longitudinal wave, transverse wave, amplitude, frequency, wavelength, compression, rarefaction.

ultrasound probe

fetus

▲ *A computer creates the ultrasound image from the reflected waves*

Babies and ultrasound

All sound can reflect off objects – an echo is the best example of this happening. Ultrasound behaves in the same way. In hospitals they use ultrasound waves with frequencies of about 1 000 000 waves per second (1 MHz) to create images of unborn babies.

The ultrasound waves used on babies are of very low energy (very small amplitude) so they do not cause any damage to the baby or to the mother. Ultrasound waves are entirely different from **X-rays**. X-rays are electromagnetic waves and can damage or kill human cells. Ultrasound waves reflect differently off different tissue types and they can produce images of soft tissues such as the organs in your body. X-rays create images of hard materials such as bones much better than soft tissues.

Why don't we use X-rays?

X-rays are very different from ultrasound.

Ultrasound	X-rays
high frequency sound waves	high frequency electromagnetic waves
reflect off baby	most pass through mother and baby
can image soft tissue and hard tissue such as bone	can image hard tissue better than soft tissue
not damaging to mother or baby	can cause damage to the growing fetus

▼ *The ultrasound wave causes the stone to shake itself to pieces*

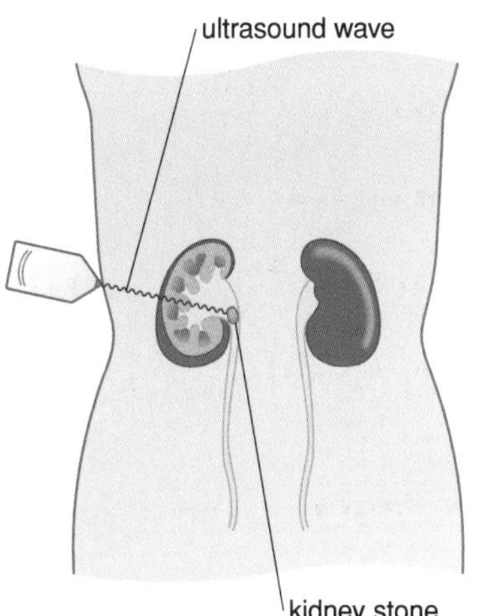

Smashing time

Ultrasound may be entirely safe for babies but it can also be used to smash stones inside a patient's body. Some people develop hard stones in their kidneys or gall bladders. Years ago the only treatment was to open up the patient and take out the stones. This required the patient to stay in hospital for several days.

Now several very strong pulses of ultrasound are aimed at the spot where the stone is lying. The stone vibrates until is shakes itself apart (a bit like a wine glass shattering because of a high pitched sound).

c **Summarise the two different ways that ultrasound is used in hospitals.**

Keywords

compression • rarefaction • ultrasound • upper threshold of human hearing • X-ray

Cleaning water with ultrasound

Keeping your drinking water clean could be putting you at risk. We use chemical disinfectants such as chlorine dioxide, sodium hypochlorite and chloramines to clean drinking water but they leave disinfectant by-products (DBPs) behind. Over 500 DBPs have been identified and some studies have found links between long-term consumption of water with high levels of DBPs and the risk of birth defects and cancers such as bladder cancer.

However, chemicals might not be needed to destroy water pollutants according to a new study. Instead ultrasound at just the right frequency might do the trick.

Ultrasound creates bubbles in water. The process is called cavitation.

'When the bubbles collapse, the gas inside them becomes highly pressurised and gets to a very high temperature for just a short amount of time,' said Inez Hua of Purdue University USA. 'These high temperatures and pressures can degrade the organic contaminants, such as bacteria, in the water.'

To work out which frequency of ultrasound would be most efficient for water purification the scientists placed a glass container of 1 litre of water on a steel transducer to vibrate the container and put an organic pollutant in the water. Then they zapped the mix with ultrasound of frequencies of 205, 358, 618 and 1 071 kHz. They found that at 358 kHz the pollutant reacted faster than at any other frequency. Inez hopes that ultrasound will become an alternative to chemical methods of purification.

'It's very easy to use,' she adds. 'You just turn on the switch and the cleaning process begins.'

Questions

1. Explain what the word cavitation means in the article above.
2. What two effects happen when the bubbles collapse?
3. Why does this effect help in cleaning up polluted water?
4. The frequencies tested were measured in kHz. What does kHz mean?
5. Why was it important to try different frequencies?
6. How did they decide which frequency was most effective?
7. Why do you think ultrasound might be a better way of cleaning water than using chemicals?

Radiation can kill or cure

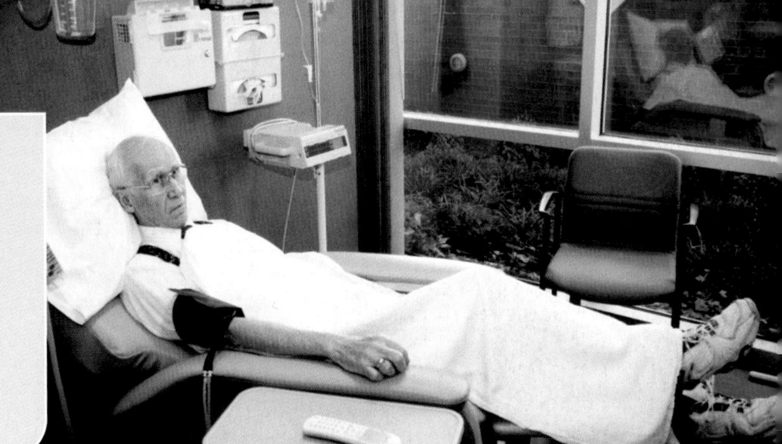

▲ *Gamma radiation can be deadly – especially to tumour cells*

In this item you will find out

- why we use gamma radiation to treat cancer
- the difference between X-rays and gamma rays and where they come from
- why beta and gamma radiation can get through your skin

Lots of people are concerned about nuclear waste and are frightened about having nuclear power stations near their houses. But then, they are quite happy to drink radioactive substances or have them injected into their bodies in a hospital.

Can it be true that something that we consider so deadly can also be a cure for a wide range of illnesses?

In fact you are much more likely to get cancer from smoking than because you live near to a nuclear power station. Cancer is the name given to tumours or growths that grow out of control in the body.

Lung cancer is a tumour in the lungs, while breast cancer is a lump or tumour in the breast. The tumour grows out of control and begins to take over the patient's body.

The only treatment for cancer is to get rid of the tumour. Some treatments rely on cutting out the tumour but this risks leaving a few cells behind that then spread and begin to form new tumours in other parts of the body.

Other treatments rely on giving the patient drugs that will kill the tumour. This is called chemotherapy. Radiotherapy uses **gamma radiation** to kill the tumour cells.

a **Suggest why a cancer specialist might prescribe both chemotherapy and radiotherapy rather than surgery to treat a patient with a brain tumour.**

Gamma radiation is essential in modern hospitals. Apart from cancer treatments, it is used for sterilising hospital equipment and as a **radioactive tracer** to see how the blood is flowing round the body or whether your lungs are functioning properly.

Amazing fact

The person with the lowest life expectancy is an unmarried male who smokes. The highest life expectancy is enjoyed by unmarried females who do not smoke and are not overweight.

Amazing fact

Alpha particles can't even get through something as thin as cigarette paper. However, if you eat or breathe them in they are deadly.

Alpha, beta, gamma

Gamma rays are only one type of radiation that comes out of the nucleus of a radioactive atom. The others are **alpha radiation** and **beta radiation**. Gamma rays and **beta particles** can travel through skin, but **alpha particles** cannot because they are much bigger and heavier than beta particles. They travel too slowly and they interact too much with atoms in the skin so they are quickly stopped before they have passed through the skin.

b **Where, within an atom, does gamma radiation come from?**

c **What is the main similarity between gamma and beta radiation?**

X marks the spot

Gamma rays and X-rays are often confused with each other because they have many things in common. They both travel at the speed of light and can pass through the human body, though they damage or kill every cell they hit on the way through. However, they come from different sources. Gamma rays are entirely natural and come out of the nucleus of some atoms. X-rays are manufactured by firing electrons at metals.

Examiner's tip

Remember the differences between X-rays and gamma rays.

Gamma rays	X-rays
are electromagnetic waves	are electromagnetic waves
have similar wavelength to X-rays	have similar wavelength to gamma rays
occur naturally from radioactive materials – they come from the nucleus of the atom	are generated by firing high-speed electrons at metal targets – they do not come from the nucleus of the atom
are not easy to control as they rely on natural emissions	have easily controlled intensity and can be aimed at a target
can travel through human skin	can travel through human skin
can damage or kill living cells	can damage or kill living cells
are used to treat cancer as they kill tumour cells	used by radiographers to create X-ray images because X-rays are stopped by bones
are used as a tracer to show progress of a drug around the body	
are used to sterilise hospital equipment as they kill bacteria	

d **List the main similarities and the main differences between X-rays and gamma rays.**

Kill the tumour not the patient

The danger of using gamma radiation to treat a patient is that the gamma radiation can kill any living cell that it hits – both tumour cells and healthy cells. The medical physicists have to kill as many cancer cells as possible without harming the patient.

They do this by aiming a beam of gamma rays at the tumour from all directions. The beam is rotated round the patient, keeping the tumour at the centre. This means that the tumour gets a higher overall dose than the rest of the body, and it is destroyed.

e **Explain why aiming at the tumour from different directions is better for the patient. (A diagram might help.)**

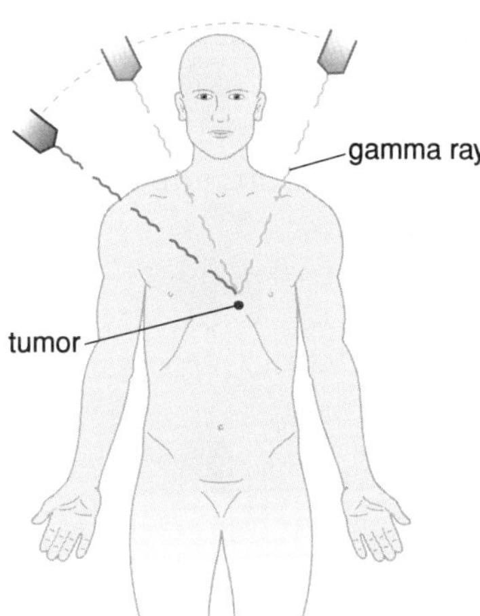

▲ *By aiming the gamma rays at the tumour from different directions the damage to the patient's healthy cells is limited*

Tracers

Gamma radiation is also a good way to diagnose a wide range of medical conditions. Medical physicists in hospitals use the fact that gamma rays and beta particles can pass through human skin to form an image of inside a patient, without cutting them open.

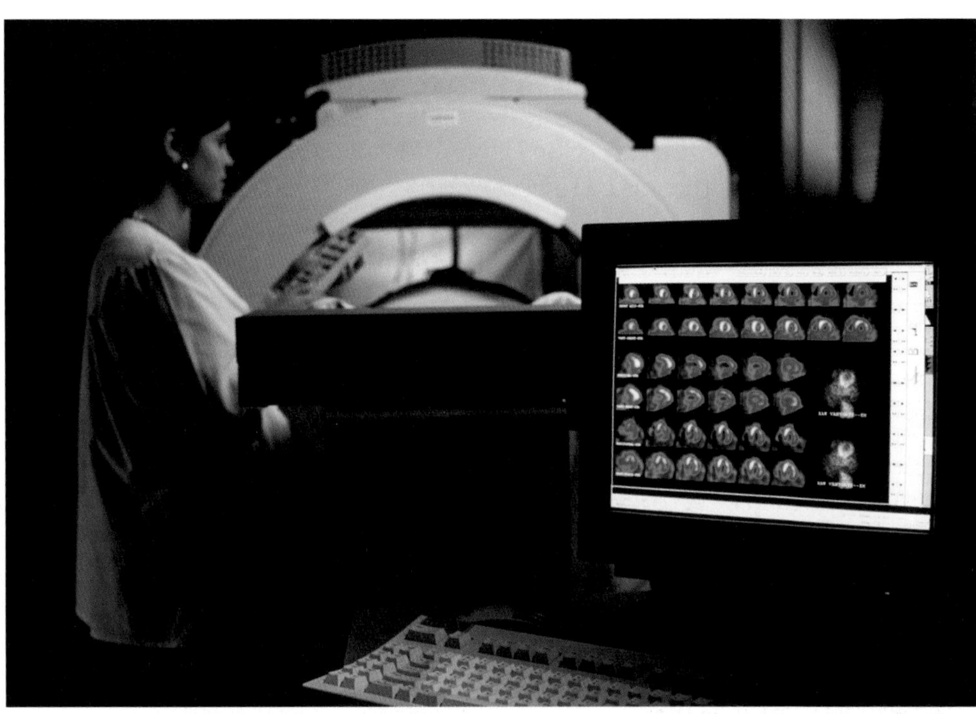

◀ *Patient being treated with radioactive tracer*

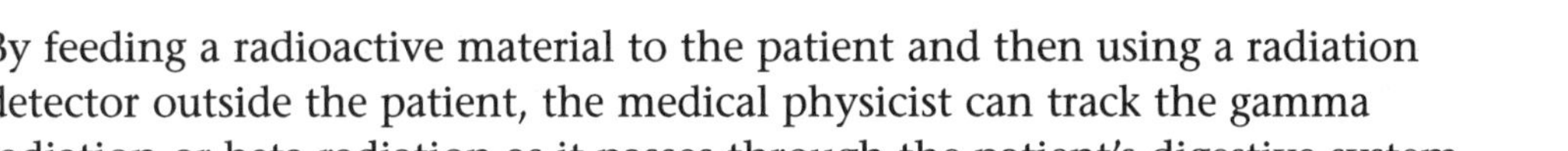

By feeding a radioactive material to the patient and then using a radiation detector outside the patient, the medical physicist can track the gamma radiation or beta radiation as it passes through the patient's digestive system.

If there is a blockage the radioactive material will not get through. If there is a leak the radiation will start coming from unexpected areas. The medical physicists call this technique tracing.

As well as radioactive liquids, which are drunk by the patient to investigate the digestive system, radioactive tracers can be gases breathed in to look at the lungs and they can be injected to look at the blood circulation.

In fact, without medical physicists and radiographers, hospitals would be unable to diagnose and treat hundreds of different illnesses.

f **Make a table to summarise the use of radioactive tracers – the form they are used in (liquid, gas), how they are put into the patient and what they are used to look at.**

Keywords

alpha particle • alpha radiation • beta particle • beta radiation • gamma radiation • gamma ray • radioactive tracer

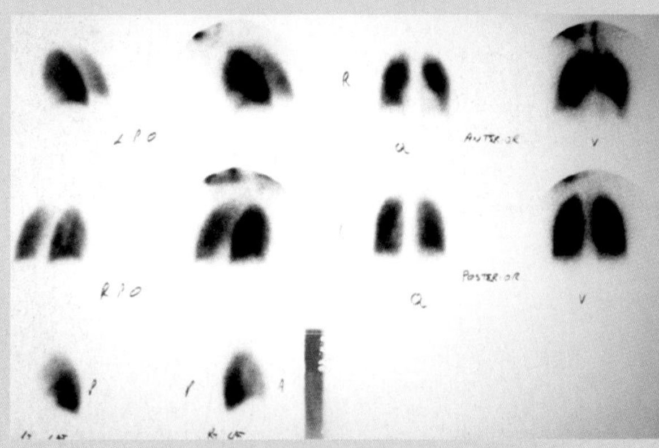

▲ Lung images from a ventilation perfusion scan

Deep vein thrombosis – the killer of the long haul holiday?

Malcolm Sperrin is a Medical Physicist at the Royal Berkshire Hospital in Reading. Here he tells us of a time he had to save the life of a woman who had developed DVT.

'The patient had gone to her doctor complaining of chest pains and shortness of breath. She was young so the doctor didn't think it was a heart attack. He found out she had been on a long flight and immediately suspected that she had developed a blood clot in the deep veins in her leg – called Deep Vein Thrombosis (DVT). These clots can move and if it got as far as her lungs it could form a blockage and kill her. He sent her straight to the hospital.

'In the hospital we had to check where the blockage was. We chose a "Ventilation Perfusion Lung Scan".

'First the patient sat against a gamma camera. She breathed through a special mouthpiece so that she could fill her lungs with a radioactive gas. This gas emits gamma radiation which we detect with the gamma camera. We got an image showing her lungs were working perfectly. The radioactive gas doesn't stay in the lungs very long so we had to be quick.

'Then we injected a solution of technetium into a vein to trace how it flowed through her blood system. As the image of her lungs appeared on the gamma camera screen, one part of her lungs wasn't showing up. We knew that there was a blockage in a blood vessel feeding that area.

'We didn't want to risk the blockage moving to her brain as this can kill part of the brain and leave the patient disabled or it can even be fatal. We prescribed "clot-busting" drugs. Fortunately there were no more complications and the patient was back home in less than

Questions

1 What symptoms did the woman have that made the doctor send her to the hospital?

2 Why did the medical physicists have to work fast?

3 What was the first treatment they applied? What did they find?

4 What happened next?

Is radioactivity really dangerous?

In this item you will find out

- that radioactivity is a natural phenomenon and how it happens
- that the radioactivity from a substance decreases with time
- how an element changes to a totally different element when it emits radioactivity

If you point a radiation detector at ground coffee beans you will see that the detector registers radioactivity.

You'll also get a reading showing radioactivity if you point a radiation detector at the kerbstones by the roadside.

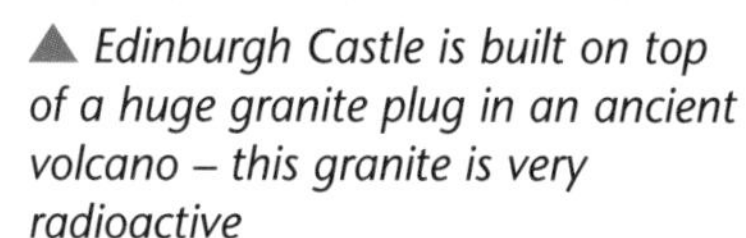

▲ *Edinburgh Castle is built on top of a huge granite plug in an ancient volcano – this granite is very radioactive*

In fact there are a huge number of natural things that give out radioactivity. There are even 'cosmic rays' from outer space hitting every one of us at a rate of about one per second. Because there are more cosmic rays higher up in the atmosphere, airline pilots who fly long-distance flights have to be checked to make sure that they have not received too high a dose of cosmic rays.

We, and other living creatures, have evolved to live in a world of radiation. In fact we could not exist without it. It is the radioactive materials in the Earth's core that keeps the Earth warm enough to sustain life.

Some people believe that radiation is made by people. But there are huge numbers of natural substances around us that **decay** naturally by giving out alpha radiation, beta radiation and gamma radiation.

The radiation comes from the nucleus of an unstable atom, where the protons and neutrons are. It has nothing to do with the electrons that orbit the nucleus. And when an atom emits radiation it can have a significant effect on the nucleus and even change it into a completely different element!

a **Explain why radioactivity can be described as a natural phenomenon.**

Breaking up is hard to do

When a radioactive material decays, its nucleus changes because it emits an alpha particle, or a beta particle or a gamma ray from its nucleus.

The table shows what happens when each of these types of radiation is emitted.

Type of radiation	What it is	Effect on nucleus	Effect on element
Alpha particle	two protons and two neutrons (same as helium atom)	two fewer protons and two fewer neutrons	new element formed with atomic number 2 lower and mass number 4 lower
Beta particle	fast moving electron	adds one proton and takes away one neutron	new element formed with atomic number 1 higher and no change to mass number
Gamma ray	high energy electromagnetic wave	reduces energy of nucleus	no new element formed

To summarise:

- Alpha radiation changes the element by reducing the mass number by 4 (2 fewer protons and 2 fewer neutrons) and the atomic number by 2 (2 fewer protons). This makes a new element that is lighter than the original atom.
- Beta radiation changes the element by increasing the atomic number by 1 (1 more proton) but it doesn't affect the mass number. This happens by changing a neutron (neutral particle) into a proton (positive particle) and an electron (negative beta particle).
- Gamma radiation has no effect on the nucleus of the atom and doesn't change it into anything else but it is the only way a nucleus can get rid of excess energy. Often gamma radiation happens after an alpha or beta particle has been emitted because the new atom has too much energy.

Examiner's tip

Know the difference between alpha, beta and gamma radiation.

Making it add up

Simple equations can summarise the effect of radioactive decay. For example, the equation below shows what happens when radon decays by alpha radiation to form polonium.

$$^{219}_{86}\text{Rn} \rightarrow {}^{215}_{84}\text{Po} + {}^{4}_{2}\alpha$$

▲ *An alpha particle is 2 protons + 2 neutrons coming out of the atom's nucleus*

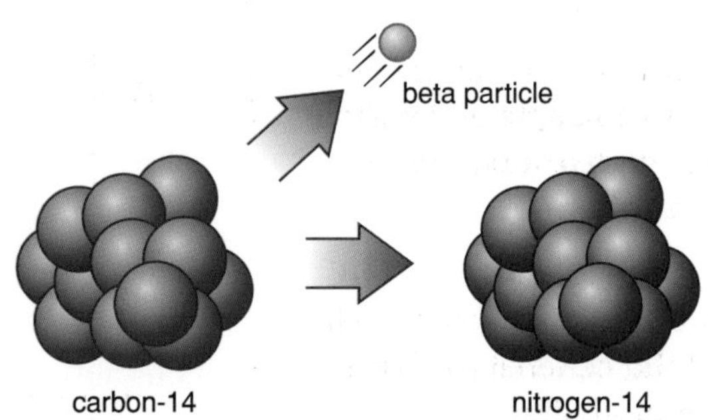

▲ *A beta particle is a fast moving electron coming out of the nucleus of the atom*

The next equation shows what happens when carbon decays by beta radiation to form nitrogen.

$$^{14}_{6}C \rightarrow {}^{14}_{7}N + {}^{0}_{-1}\beta$$

b **An element Y has a mass number of 234 and an atomic number 91. Construct an equation to show what happens to it when it emits an alpha particle.**

c **Construct an equation to show what happens to the same element when it emits a beta particle.**

Amazing fact

The half-life of uranium is exactly the same as the present age of the Earth, 4500 million years.

Half a life is better than none

All radioactive materials will continue to give out alpha or beta particles (or both) and gamma rays until every atom in the material has changed into a different element. In fact all of the heavier radioactive substances are changing slowly into lead by this process.

But not all the radioactive atoms change at the same time. Some materials change quickly, others change more slowly. It all depends on how many radioactive atoms you have that need to change and what the **half-life** of the material is.

Keywords

decay • half-life

What's a half-life?

If you have 1 million atoms of a radioactive material with a half-life of 2 years, then after 2 years, half a million will have changed (decayed) and a half a million will not. In the next 2 years a quarter of a million will change, and in the next 2 years an eighth of a million will change.

This is what half-life means. It is the time that it takes for half the radioactive atoms in your sample to decay. If you only have 10 radioactive atoms, then you have to wait two years for five of them to decay. A different material will have a different half-life – longer or shorter – but the same thing happens, just in a different time scale.

Usually scientists say that it takes about 10 half-lives for a radioactive sample to become non-radioactive.

d **How many atoms are left from a sample of 2 million radioactive atoms after 5 half-lives?**

e **For a material with a half-life of 30 days, how much of the material will have decayed after 150 days?**

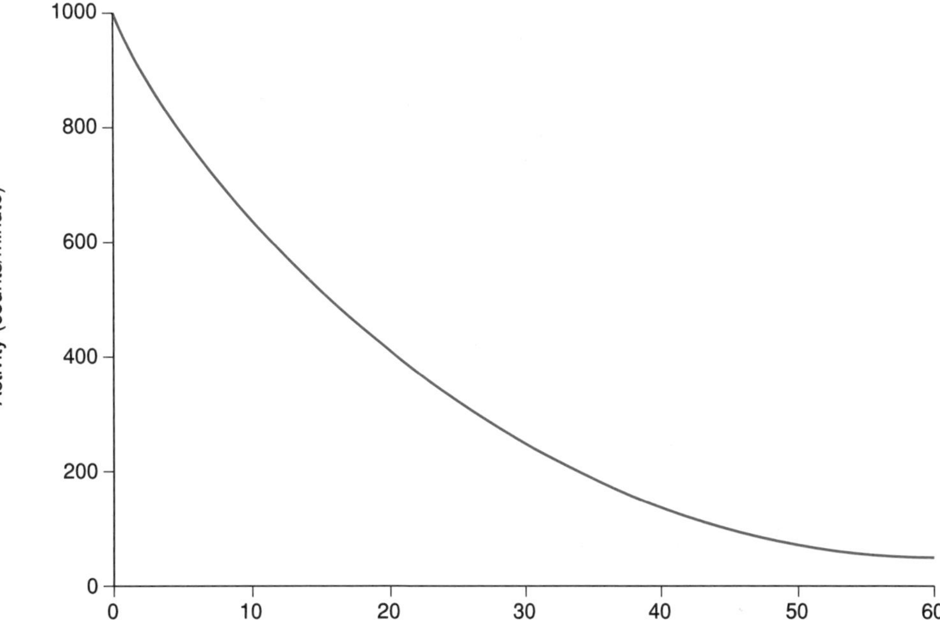

▼ *Number of radioactive atoms left after each half-life of 15 hours*

▲ Tower of London

Neutrons and the Princes in the Tower

Dr Roger Stewart works in the Physics Department at the University of Reading. As well as teaching students, he does scientific research projects where he tries to find out exactly what happens when neutrons hit other materials. Here he talks about some of the things you can do with neutrons.

'If you fire slow moving neutrons at a material, the nucleus of an atom will capture a neutron. This makes the atom unstable so it is radioactive and will soon emit a gamma ray. Measuring the energy of this gamma ray is a clever way to find out exactly which elements are in your material.

'As well as alpha, beta and gamma radiation, you can get neutrons from some natural radioactive materials. Because neutrons are neutral particles they aren't attracted to the negative electrons or the positive protons in materials so they can penetrate deep into a material. Because of this, fast moving neutrons can be better than X-rays for looking inside an object. You might use this to make a neutron radiograph (like an X-radiograph) of a submarine hull to see if there are defects in the hull.

'When archaeologists found a sealed lead coffin near the Tower of London, they thought it might be the coffin of the two young princes who were murdered in the Tower. They couldn't use X-rays because X-rays can't go through lead. Instead they used neutrons and saw that there were bones of young children inside.'

'When we want to do an experiment with neutrons we go to special laboratories. I often go to ISIS, at the Rutherford Appleton Laboratories near Reading, or the neutron reactor in Grenoble, France. When you are there you can find yourself having coffee with scientists from all over the world. This is one of the best things about this work.'

Questions

1 What are neutrons?

2 Why does firing neutrons at a material make it radioactive?

3 How can scientists work out what elements are in a sample after they have fired neutrons at it?

4 Why are neutrons so good at penetrating materials?

5 Why did the archaeologists use neutrons instead of X-rays to look inside the sealed lead coffin?

Detecting, tracing and dating

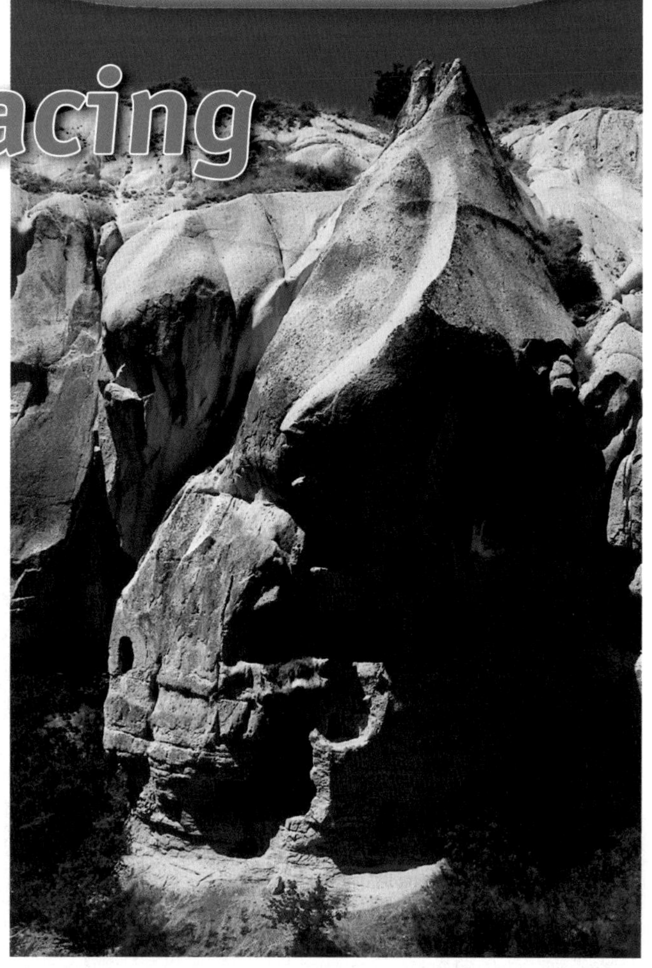
▲ *The oldest rocks on the Earth are about 4 000 000 000 years old*

In this item you will find out

- how we use radioactivity to work out the age of the Earth and things that were once alive
- how we use tracers to track waste and find blockages in underground pipes
- how we use alpha radiation to detect smoke

In medieval times Bishop Usher worked out that the Earth was created on 26 October 4004 BC. In the eighteenth century James Hutton noticed that some rocks had eroded far more than was possible if the Earth was only, according to Bishop Usher's theory, 5 700 years old.

In the nineteenth century Charles Darwin published the theory of evolution. His friend, Charles Lyell, dared to claim that the Earth was over 80 million years old based upon the time it would take marine molluscs to evolve.

By the end of the nineteenth century Lord Kelvin claimed the Earth was between 24 million and 40 million years old, based on how long it would have taken to cool down from a molten rock to its present temperature. Only 10 years later Ernest Rutherford used newly discovered radioactivity and claimed that the Earth was 500 million years old.

Now we know they were all very wrong. Scientists have calculated that the oldest rocks on the Earth are 4 000 million years old. So the Earth must be at least that old. But how can we be sure they are right? And how did the others get it so wrong?

Bishop Usher based his estimate on the writings in the Christian Bible. Charles Lyell had not realised that the Earth was around long before marine molluscs began to evolve and Lord Kelvin had failed to realise that the centre of the Earth is full of radioactive rocks which keep it warm so its temperature is much higher than he expected if it had just cooled normally.

Now we understand radioactivity and can use it to work out the age of the rocks on the Earth.

Make a time line to show the different techniques people used to work out the age of the Earth and the result each one obtained.

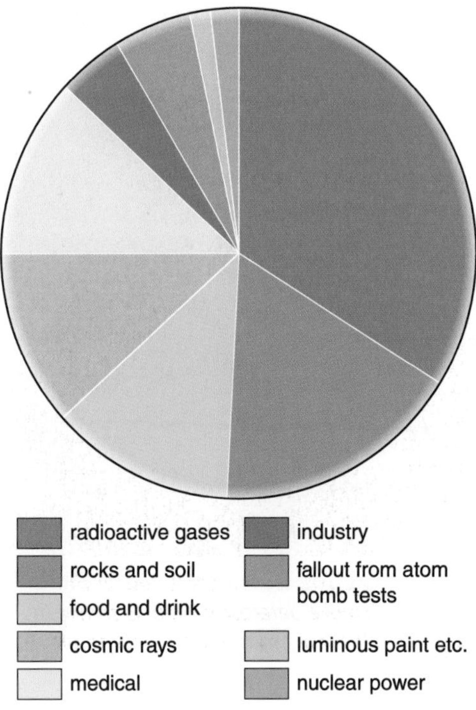

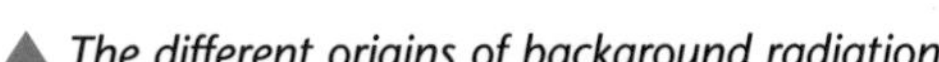

▲ *The different origins of background radiation*

In the background

There are huge numbers of natural materials, such as rocks and soil, that give out alpha, beta or gamma radiation. We are also bombarded all the time by gamma rays and high energy particles from outer space – called cosmic rays. Because this radiation is everywhere, we call it '**background radiation**'.

But we are also responsible for some of the background radiation ourselves. Around 10% of the background radiation is from waste products that come from hospitals and from industry.

Some of the background radiation comes from radioactive uranium. It is slowly decaying and turning to lead. By measuring the ratio of radioactive uranium to lead in a rock sample we can work out the age of the rock since it solidified. Younger rocks have more of their radioactive uranium left.

b **Explain why a young rock has more radioactive uranium in it than an older rock.**

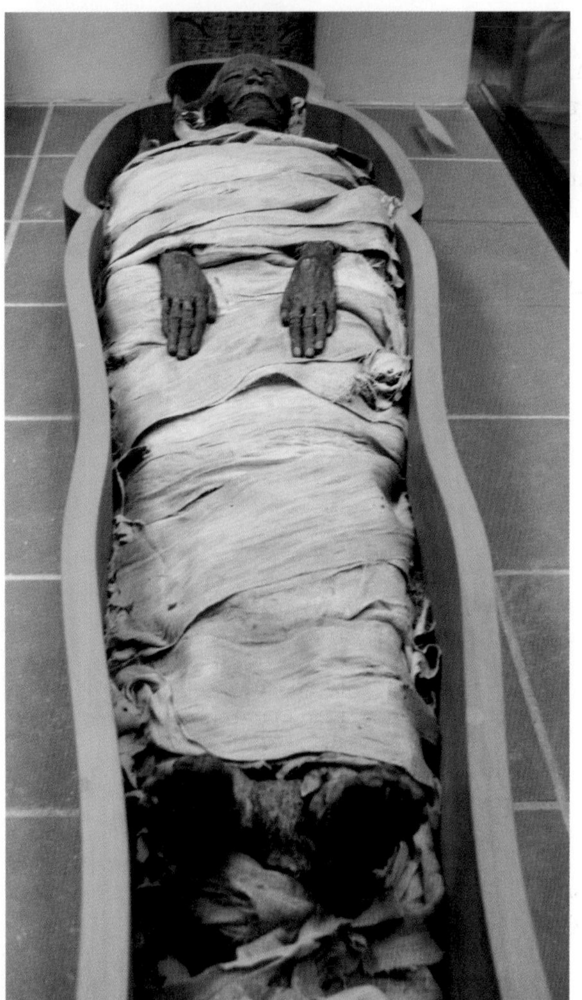

Dating an Egyptian

Living things do not contain uranium so we cannot use the same technique for working out how old different materials are, such as wood or an Egyptian mummy. Instead we use a radioactive isotope of carbon.

There is always the same ratio of radioactive carbon (carbon-14) to non-radioactive carbon (carbon-12) in the air so there is the same ratio in all living things. When something dies, it stops taking in air. The radioactive carbon-14 in its body will keep on decaying so the ratio of carbon-14 to carbon-12 will reduce.

By measuring the activity of the old material and comparing it with the activity of a living thing, we can work out the ratio of radioactive carbon to non-radioactive carbon in the Egyptian mummy. Knowing how fast the ratio reduces we can work out a reasonably accurate date for when it died. This is called **carbon dating**.

We cannot use carbon dating for very recent deaths as the half-life is too long (5 700 years). But it works perfectly for most of human existence.

c **If a human skeleton has only one quarter of the radioactive carbon-14 that you have in your body, approximately how long is it since that person died?**

◀ *We can measure the amount of radioactive carbon-14 in the body to work out when this ancient Egyptian person died*

Smoking you out

There should be at least one piece of radioactive material in your home if you want to keep safe from fire. **Smoke detectors** are an essential early warning system when there is a fire. Inside each smoke detector there is a tiny piece of radioactive substance (americium) that emits alpha particles.

The alpha particles collide with atoms in the air and ionise them (knock off electrons). The electrons are then attracted to a positive electrode while the positive ions go to the negative electrode. A sensor detects this tiny electric current. If smoke gets in the way the electrons won't get through, so the sensor detects that there is no current and the smoke alarm goes off.

d **Explain how smoke detectors work.**

▲ The current can't flow in the smoke detector if there is smoke in the way, so the alarm will go off

Going underground

Oil and gas companies lose huge amounts of money if their pipelines spring a leak. Simply digging up the whole pipeline to find the leak is not cost effective. Instead they mix the oil or gas with a radioactive material that gives out gamma rays. This is used as a tracer that they can watch to see how it flows along the pipe.

They use detectors to track the progress of the gamma radiation. Alpha and beta radiation will not work because they cannot get through the pipe to be detected above ground. When the technicians reach a part of the pipe where there is no radioactivity they know that the substance must have leaked out. This means they need dig up only the section of the pipe that needs repairing. The same technique is used to work out the route of underground pipes and to see where chemical waste is being dumped.

e **Explain why oil companies might use a radioactive tracer.**

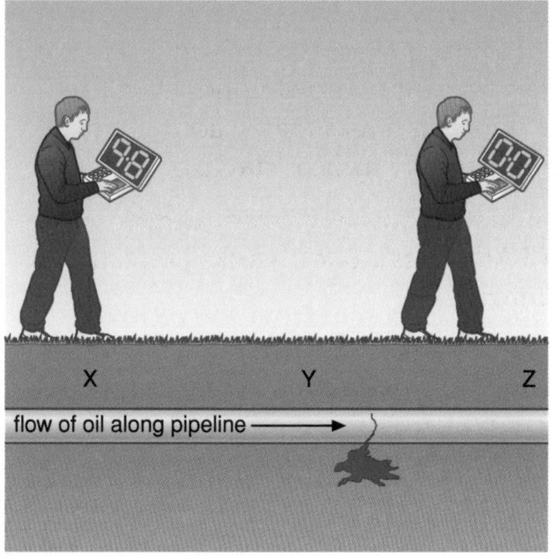

◀ Where there is a leak or a blockage, the radiation is not detected further along the pipe

Keywords

background radiation • carbon dating • smoke detector

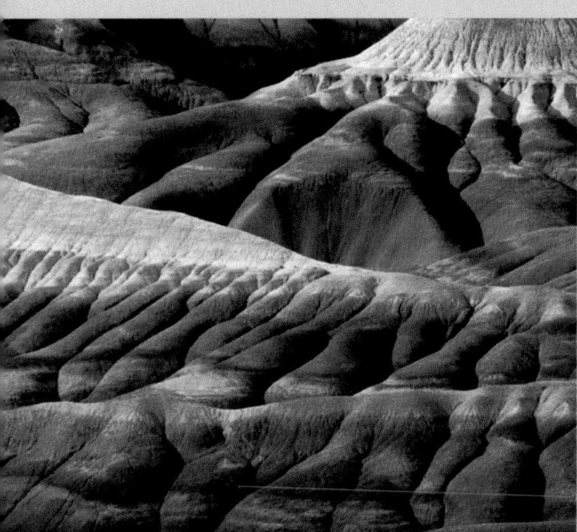

▲ *Some rocks are 4 000 000 000 years old*

The dating game

Most radioactive isotopes have rapid rates of decay (that is, short half-lives) and lose their radioactivity within a few days or years. Some isotopes, however, decay slowly, and these are the one used as geologic clocks to work out the age of rocks.

These parent isotopes are slowly turning into their corresponding daughter products. The most commonly used isotopes for working out the ages of ancient rocks are listed below:

Parent isotope	Stable daughter product	Currently accepted half-life value
uranium-238	lead-206	4.5 billion years
uranium-235	lead-207	704 million years
thorium-232	lead-208	14.0 billion years
rubidium-87	strontium-87	48.8 billion years
potassium-40	argon-40	1.25 billion years
samarium-147	neodymium-143	106 billion years

The proportion of parent isotope to daughter product tells us the number of half-lives that have passed, which we can use to calculate the age of the rock.

For example, if there are equal amounts of parent isotope and daughter product, then one half-life has passed. If there is three times as much daughter product as parent isotope, then two half-lives have passed.

The ratio of potassium to argon can be used to date rocks as young as a few thousand years old as well as the oldest rocks known. Potassium is found in most rock-forming minerals. The half-life of its radioactive isotope potassium-40 is short enough that sufficient argon (the daughter product) has accumulated in potassium-bearing minerals of nearly all ages. The amounts of potassium and argon isotopes can be measured accurately, even in very small quantities, to determine how many half-lives have passed.

So far scientists have not found a way to determine the exact age of the Earth directly from its rocks because the Earth's oldest rocks have been recycled and destroyed by the process of plate tectonics. The best age for the Earth comes from the ratio of lead-207 to lead-206. Uranium-235 decays slowly to lead-207 but uranium-238 decays to lead-206. As the half-life of uranium-235 is 704 million years and the half-life of uranium-238 is 4 500 million years, we can work out how old the rocks are by looking at how much of each type of lead there is.

Questions

1. Why do we need to measure the amount of two different elements in a rock to find out its age?
2. If we know that the amount of potassium is three times the amount of argon, how old is the rock?
3. Why can we not use isotope ratios to work out the age of the Earth?
4. What method do scientists prefer for working out the age of the Earth?

Are we destroying our world?

In this item you will find out

- how nuclear power provides electricity
- why nuclear waste is radioactive after it has been in a power station

▲ *Our environment is in danger from pollution*

Scientists agree that our climate is changing. The increased levels of pollution, especially greenhouse gases such as carbon dioxide, in the atmosphere seem to be raising temperatures across the globe.

The concentration of carbon dioxide in the atmosphere has increased by about a third since 1800. Before the Industrial Revolution the concentration of carbon dioxide in the atmosphere was quite stable at about 275 parts per million (ppm). Using fossil fuels has caused the level to rise to 370 ppm by 2000. Each year every coal-fired power station produces about 10 million tonnes of carbon dioxide.

Global temperatures changed very little, only about a quarter of one degree, over the thousand years to 1850. Since then temperatures have gone up by nearly 1 °C, and by 2100 they are likely to be between 1.5 °C and nearly 6 °C hotter.

Scientists are predicting devastating changes to weather patterns and rising sea levels. How can we change our lifestyles to reduce the level of greenhouse gases?

One way would be to move towards generating electricity using the so-called more environmentally friendly, renewable methods such as wind power. The problem is that we need far more electricity than these renewable sources can provide. Also, some people object to having wind farms built near to their houses because they say they are not attractive and take up too much space.

Now, many scientists are recommending nuclear power as the cleanest way to produce the electricity we need. But there are still many problems to be solved.

Amazing fact

To replace a single nuclear power station with a wind farm you would have to build one new wind turbine every day for 10 years.

a **Why are we now looking for new ways to generate electricity?**

b **Why are some people not happy with the idea of using renewable energy sources such as wind farms?**

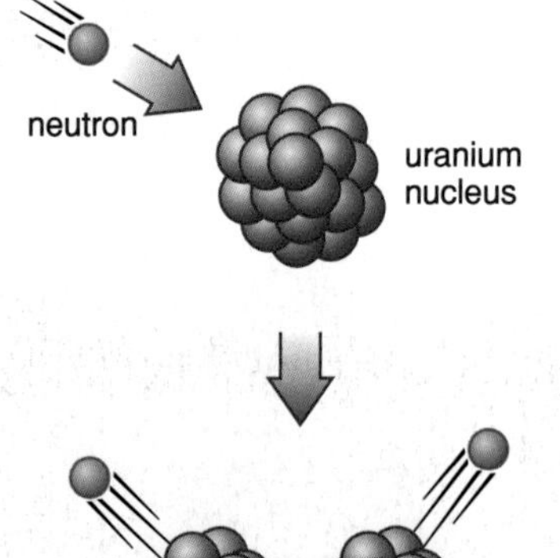

▲ *Firing a neutron at a uranium atom makes it split apart and release energy*

Uranium – the new coal

Uranium is a very dense metal that occurs naturally in the Earth's crust. Uranium is naturally radioactive. However, uranium-235 has a very special property. If neutrons are fired at the nucleus of a uranium atom at very high speed, they will enter the nucleus.

This heavier nucleus is unstable and cannot hold itself together so it splits into two unequal parts making two new atoms (two different elements), as well as firing out a few spare neutrons. The process of splitting apart is called **nuclear fission**. The fission process causes the uranium fuel rod to become very hot – and this is why it is useful. This heat energy can be used to generate electricity.

Making electricity

Coal-fired, oil-fired, gas-fired or nuclear power stations all use the same process to generate electricity. There are four stages:

- heat the water to make steam
- feed the steam into a huge turbine (like a water wheel)
- drive the turbine round to rotate a generator
- the rotating generator will create electric current in wires.

This is then fed into the national grid to supply our houses when we need it.

The only difference between power stations that work in this way is how the water is heated in the first place. In conventional power stations the fuel is burnt. In nuclear power stations the nuclear reactions, as uranium splits apart, generate heat. Scientists talk about burning nuclear fuel but there are no flames involved!

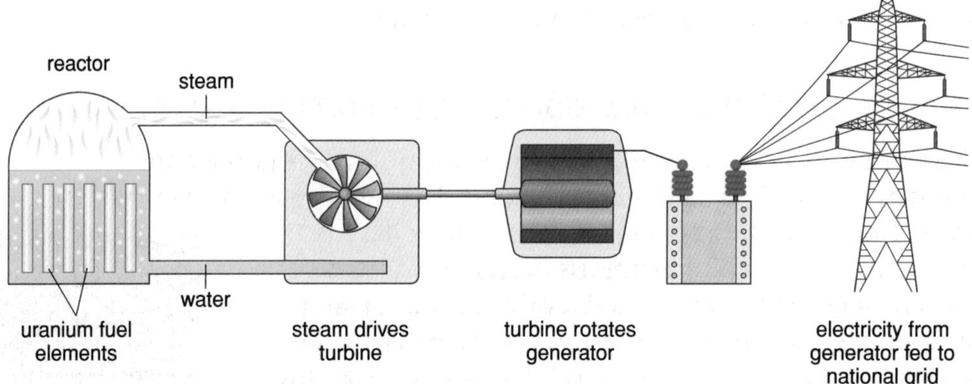

▶ *Generating electricity*

How is heat generated in a nuclear power station? Why is the phrase 'burning nuclear fuel' misleading?

Chain reactions

When each uranium nucleus splits, more than one neutron is given out so after a nuclear fission reaction there are spare neutrons left over.

If these neutrons hit more uranium atoms, you get a **chain reaction** so that each fission reaction makes another atom split apart and so on. If this chain reaction goes out of control, then you get an atomic bomb such as the ones used at the end of the Second World War. Nuclear power stations are built so that this cannot happen.

▲ *Atomic bomb*

Explain what a chain reaction is in a nuclear reactor.

Controlling nuclear reactions

Scientists control nuclear reactions in nuclear power stations. We need one of the spare neutrons produced at each fission reaction to go on and hit another uranium atom to keep the chain reaction going. The rest of the high-speed neutrons are captured by 'control rods'. These are often made of boron or cadmium because these materials are capable of capturing neutrons.

We can use these control rods to make sure enough spare neutrons are hitting new uranium atoms to get a chain reaction – but no more. If there is more than one, the chain reaction may generate too much heat and get out of control. The whole reactor core is monitored continuously and the control rods are raised and lowered, as required, to keep the reactor working at a controlled rate.

Keywords

chain reaction • nuclear fission

Explain what control rods do in a nuclear reactor.

What's so dangerous about radioactive waste?

The two new atoms made when each uranium atom splits apart are radioactive. It is these materials that are called radioactive waste or nuclear waste. Nuclear waste also contains other materials made radioactive by absorbing neutrons during the nuclear reaction such as the control rods and the metal jackets surrounding the fuel rods. Some of the materials in this waste have very long half-lives so it will take a long time for them to decay and stop emitting alpha, beta or gamma radiation and become safe.

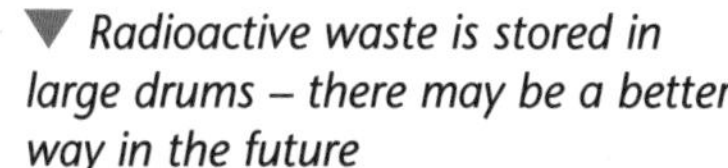

▼ *Radioactive waste is stored in large drums – there may be a better way in the future*

Until the waste has lost most of its radioactivity, it is toxic to humans and we have to be careful not to let people come into contact with it. Typically this means it has to be stored for 10 half-lives, which could be hundreds of years. Many people worry about whether we are able to store the radioactive waste safely for hundreds of years. Scientists are now working on ways to change the waste to less dangerous substances by a process called transmutation.

Can nuclear power save the environment?

Dr Michael Hudson works in the School of Chemistry at the University of Reading. His most recent project is to find a way to make nuclear waste safe.

Q: What has been the most exciting project you have done?

Michael: The one I'm doing at the moment. The idea that I can make nuclear waste safe is very interesting since it could make a huge difference to all our lives.

Q: Everyone believes that nuclear waste is dangerous. How can you possibly make it safe?

Michael: At the moment we have three possible ways of dealing with nuclear waste:

1 deep storage underground in geologically stable areas

2 surface storage in containers

3 chemical treatment followed by irradiation with neutrons.

In the UK we are probably going for deep storage. In France they prefer chemical treatment. I am working with French and other European colleagues to come up with new ways of treating the waste to make it safe.

Q: Why is it dangerous?

Michael: It's because the americium has such a long half-life. Its half-life is about 1 million years and it's not easy to keep things stored safely for several million years. Our project has created new molecules that pick up americium so that later it can be converted to its metal oxide. Then we bombard it with high-energy neutrons to convert it to different isotopes with much, much shorter half-lives – half-lives of only a few days! This means that soon after treatment the material is much safer.

Q: Why do you think this is a good project?

Michael: There are problems with every source of energy. I think nuclear power is the cleanest form of energy for the environment since it produces less greenhouse gases or other pollutants into the atmosphere. Once we can make nuclear waste safe, nuclear power is one of the best ways in which to generate electricity, especially if we want to reduce the problem of global warming.

Questions

1 What are the three ways that nuclear waste is treated at the moment?

2 What is the most dangerous material in nuclear waste?

3 How does Michael's work make this material safe?

4 Why is it important to try to make nuclear waste safe?

P4a

1 *A company has decided to manufacture a spray polish that is electrostatically charged. How will this be better than normal spray polish?* [2]

2 *Cars often have devices hanging off the back of the rear bumper that claim to stop you getting an electric shock when you get out of the car. They are supposed to discharge the car after it stops.*

- **a** *Explain why this device won't work if it is attached to a plastic bumper* [1]
- **b** *Explain why the car might need a device like this* [1]

3 *What will happen if two charges are brought close to each other if they are:*

- **a** *positive and positive?* [1]
- **b** *negative and negative?* [1]
- **c** *positive and negative?* [1]

4 *If you rub a balloon on your jumper, it becomes charged. Explain how the balloon gains a positive charge and work out what charge the jumper gains.* [2]

5 *Static electricity can be a nuisance. Explain how this is true by describing two different situations when static electricity causes problems.* [2]

6 *Explain how correct earthing of an electric fire can prevent you getting an electric shock.* [2]

7 *A lorry carrying flammable liquid will have an earth wire connected between the tank and the earth. Explain why the liquid becomes charged and why the earth wire is needed.* [3]

P4b

1 *If a defibrillator sends a charge through you which carries 360 joules of energy in 0.01 seconds. How much energy would there be in a second?* [1]

2 *If there are 8 coal fired power stations in an area of the UK each producing 3500 tonnes of ash each day, and 80% of this ash flies up the chimneys where 99.9% is removed by electrostatic dust precipitators, calculate:*

- **a** *How much ash is produced in total in this area of the UK* [1]
- **b** *How much ash flies up the chimneys of 1 power station on average per day* [1]
- **c** *How much is collected in the electrostatic dust precipitators* [1]

3 *Describe how a paramedic uses a defibrillator to restart a heart when it has stopped.* [4]

4 *Why can a defibrillator be dangerous?* [1]

5 *When paramedics use a defibrillator, they have to remove clothing from the patient's chest. Explain why.* [1]

6 *In an electrostatic dust precipitator the smoke passes a grid with a high positive pd (voltage) on it and then a grid with a negative pd on it.*

- **a** *Why is it important to have a high positive pd on the first grid?* [1]
- **b** *Why is it necessary to have a negative pd on the second grid?* [1]
- **c** *What makes the dust fall down the chimney?* [1]

7 *Crop spraying can be made more efficient by electrostatics. Explain why this is better financially and for our health.* [2]

P4c

1

Current (amps)	Voltage (volts)	Resistance (ohms)
0.2	4	
0.4	8	
0.6	12	
0.7	16	
0.8	20	
0.9	30	
1.0	40	
1.0	60	
1.0	100	

This table shows the current and voltage measured for a small heater.

Copy out this table and complete the final column to find its resistance

Plot a line graph of the current on the x-axis and the voltage on the y-axis. [3]

What do you notice about the gradient? [1]

2 *In a 3-pin plug describe what these parts do:*

- **a** *the live wire* [1]
- **b** *the neutral wire* [1]
- **c** *the earth wire* [1]
- **d** *the fuse.* [1]

3 *In an electrical circuit:*

- **a** *for a given resistance, if you increase the pd what happens to the current?* [1]
- **b** *for a given pd, if you increase the resistance what happens to the current?* [1]

4 *Explain why a double insulated appliance does not need an earth wire.* [2]

5 *If the current in a circuit is 0.5 A and the resistance is 5 000 ohms, calculate the potential difference.* [2]

6 *If the pd in a circuit is 12 V and the current is 0.2 A, calculate the total resistance in the circuit.* [2]

7 *If the pd in a circuit is 230 V and the resistance of an appliance is 500 ohms, calculate the current in the circuit.* [2]

P4d

1

Sound	Frequency (Hz)
Ultrasound scan in hospital	1,000,000
Upper threshold of cats' hearing	90,000
Mouse squeaking	70,000
Lowest level of ultrasound	22,000
Upper threshold of human hearing	20,000
Upper threshold of human hearing for older person	15,000
High pitched note on guitar	10,000
High pitch voice	1,000
Low pitch voice	100
Bass drum	20

Make a frequency line to show these frequencies [3]

2 *Sound waves are often used to work out how deep the sea is by sending a sound to the sea bed and waiting for the echo. This is called sonar. If the sound travels at 1,500 m/s in water and the echo takes 0.6 seconds to return to the ship, how deep is the water?* [2]

3 *From the list of words below, choose the correct one for each meaning:*

amplitude **wavelength** **frequency**
compression **rarefaction**

a *the number of waves per second measured in hertz* [1]
b *the area in a wave where the particles are closest together* [1]
c *the area in a wave where the particles are furthest apart* [1]
d *the distance between two compressions.* [1]

4 *Explain what 'the upper threshold of human hearing' means.* [2]

5 *What is ultrasound?* [1]

6 *The difference between transverse and longitudinal waves is based upon the way that the particles move. Using one example of each type of wave, describe how the particles move as the wave passes along.* [2]

7 *Why are ultrasound waves rather than X-rays used for creating images of soft tissue in the body?* [2]

P4e

1 *You need to find where there is a blockage in an underground pipe that carries waste water out to sea.*

a *What form of radioactivity would you choose if the pipe is made of plastic and is buried 1 metre below ground? Explain your answer.* [2]
b *Why would it be impossible to find the blockage if the pipe were made of lead?* [1]

2

Material	Half-life
A	1 minute
B	20 minutes
C	2 hours
D	20 hours

In a hospital the radiographers need to use a radioactve material to as a tracer to see if there is a blockage in the patient's blood supply to their brain. Which material would you choose? Explain why the other materials are less useful to you.

3 *Which types of radiation are able to pass through human skin?* [2]

4 *X-rays and gamma rays have similar wavelengths but are produced in different ways. Explain how they are produced.* [2]

5 *Substances that emit beta or gamma radiation can be used as tracers in hospitals.*

a *Explain what happens to a patient if they are treated with a tracer.* [1]
b *Why do the radiographers use beta or gamma but not alpha radiation?* [1]

6 *A patient may have a tracer injected into them, they may breathe it in, or they may ingest it. Which part or function of the body might they be testing in each case?* [3]

7 *If a patient is diagnosed with cancer they may be given radiotherapy. Explain how a radioactive source is used on the patient so that the tumour is killed but the patient's healthy cells are spared.* [3]

P4f

1 An experiment measured the radioactivity of protactinium

Time (s)	Counts in 10 s
0	68
10	63
20	49
30	40
40	38
50	29
60	25
70	19

Time (s)	Counts in 10 s
80	17
90	15
100	12
110	10
120	9
130	7
140	6

Plot these data as a line graph with the time on the x-axis and the counts on the y-axis. [3]

Work out the half life of this material. [2]

Why do some of the points not lie neatly on the line if the experiment was done very carefully? [1]

2 If a radioactive substance decays, it can give out three different types of nuclear radiation.

a What are the three types called? [3]
b Which two of these are particles and what are they? [4]

3 Why is radiation often called 'nuclear radiation'? [1]

4 When an alpha particle is emitted, what effect does this have on the nucleus of the atom? [2]

5 Copy and complete these equations to show what happens when the substance decays.

a $^{217}_{86}X \rightarrow {}^{213}_{84}Y + \_\_\_$ [1] **b** $^{213}_{84}Y \rightarrow {}^{\_}_{\_}Z + {}^{-1}_{0}\beta$ [1]

6 A substance begins with 100 000 000 000 000 unstable radioactive atoms in the year 2000. Its half-life is 2.5 years. Starting with the year 2000, plot a line graph to show how the substance decays up to the year 2050. Then read off your graph how many undecayed radioactive atoms are present in 2050. [3]

7 Scientists usually say that a substance will be safe after 10 half-lives. Looking at your graph, why do you think they consider 10 half-lives to be enough for the substance to become safe? [4]

P4g

1 In a factory that manufactures aluminium foil (kitchen foil) radioactive materials can be used to monitor how thick the foil is as it is rolled out. The radioactive material is placed above the foil and the detector is below the foil. If too little radiation gets through it means the foil is too thick.

a Would you choose alpha, beta or gamma radiation to monitor the thickness of the foil? [1]
b Explain why this form of radiation is suitable and the other two are not. [1]

2 Radiation can be used in industry as 'tracers'. What three things might a waste treatment company use radiation to do? [3]

3 Explain what 'carbon dating' is and what it is used for. [1]

4 From the list of ancient objects below, state which items can be dated using radioactivity. Of these, which can be dated using carbon dating?

a ancient cooking pot **b** meteorite
c skeleton **d** clothing [4]

5 If an oil company were using a radioactive source for tracing, why would it choose a gamma emitter and not a beta emitter or an alpha emitter? [1]

6 Explain why you cannot use carbon dating to work out the age of rocks. [1]

7 What do scientists use to find out the age of rocks? [2]

P4h

1 Nuclear waste contains many different elements. One of the longest lived radioactive elements is americium which has a half-life of 1 million years. If there is 10 kg americium in a sample, how long will it take for the americium to decay so that there is less than 10 g of radioactive americium in the sample? [4]

2 If the americium is transmuted so that its half-life is 5 days, how long will it take for the sample to contain only 10 g of radioactive material? [1]

3 Describe how electricity is generated in a nuclear power station. [4]

4 Explain what 'nuclear fission' means. [1]

5 What type of things become nuclear waste? [2]

6 How can materials become radioactive when they absorb extra neutrons? [1]

7 When a uranium atom splits more than one neutron is given out.

a What do these neutrons do if they hit another uranium atom? [1]
b Why is it important that only one of these neutrons hits another uranium atom? [1]
c What do the scientists do to make sure that only one neutron hits another uranium atom? [1]

8 How do scientists make sure that nuclear power stations do not go out of control? [1]

Research Study

If you have completed a Science in the News study for part of your GCSE Core Science course you will have written a report to answer a scientific question about science. To do this you probably used the information you were given and probably did some research.

The Research Study for the GCSE Additional Science award is very similar, but, instead of looking at a scientific issue, you will concentrate on the work of scientists. They may be scientists working today or they may be scientists who worked in the past.

Your teacher will have a bank of tasks they can choose from. You only have to do one. If you do more than one the best mark will count.

Stimulus material

At the start of your Research Study you will be given some stimulus material. You should read this carefully. There are five questions that you will need to answer.

You will then be asked to do some research to extend the information you have. This research can be from books, CD-ROMs, the Internet, etc. You should carefully reference where the information has come from. Your references can look like this:

1 www.webelements.com

2 Heinemann Gateway Science: OCR Science for GCSE, Foundation text book pages 75–77

3 Multimedia Science School 11–18 Alkali metals

Answering questions

In a later lesson, under the supervision of your teacher, you will have to write a report answering the five questions you were given. You can take in any notes you made doing research, but the questions must be answered in the lesson. Your notes may be collected by your teacher but they will not be marked. You should not answer the questions in advance.

The questions you are asked are graded in difficulty: the first one or two questions are straightforward and use the information you were given at the start. They are intended for candidates who will get a grade E–G. The last one or two questions will be much harder and often there are alternative acceptable answers. These questions are intended for candidates who will get A*–B overall.

The report you write to answer these questions should be between 400 and 800 words. Many of the best reports that are produced are brief, but they answer the questions clearly without including unnecessary material.

Your teacher will mark your report. A sample of these will be checked later by a Moderator from OCR to make sure the marking is fair. Your teacher will mark it against four criteria on a scale of 0–6. The total mark is 24.

The table summarises these criteria.

Criteria	Advice to you
The evidence you have collected	You should try to collect evidence from at least two sources.
How you have used the evidence to answer the questions	You should show how you have used the evidence to answer the questions.
How the evidence helps you to understand scientific ideas	You should show how the evidence helps to explain scientific ideas, e.g. how ideas have developed over time; how they are linked with socal, economic and environmental issues.
The quality of your report	You should be careful with your spelling, punctuation and grammar. Try to use correct scientific words.

Your teacher may give you a set of 'student speak' criteria to help you.

Scientific ideas and how they develop

Throughout the work you are doing you should be aware of how scientific ideas develop over time. You will find examples in this book. For example:

The development of radioactivity

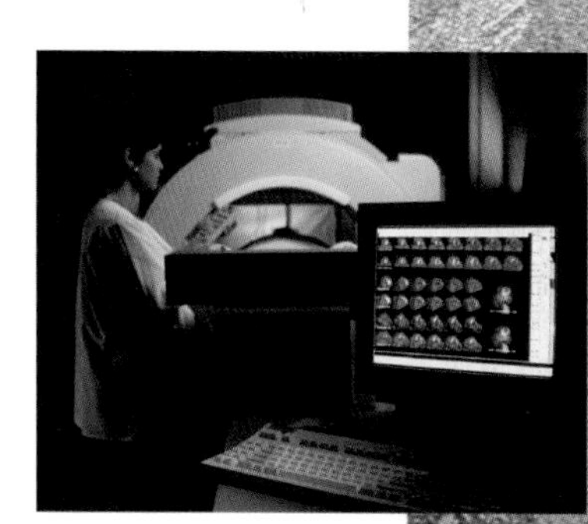

Radioactivity was discovered by Antoine Henri Becquerel in 1896 by accident. He left a photographic plate in a drawer in contact with some solid potassium uranium sulfate. When the plate was developed, he discovered a blackening on the plate corresponding to the position where the salt was. With his knowledge of phosphorescence, fluorescence and X-rays, he was able to conclude that the salt must be giving off invisible rays. He was able to examine these rays. These rays were not reflected like ordinary light and they discharged charged bodies. His experiments were confirmed by other scientists including William Thomson (Lord Kelvin). Later this discovery led to the discovery of new elements such as radium and polonium.

Where do you go from here? Having completed your courses in both GCSE Core Science and GCSE Additional Science, you might want to study the sciences further in the sixth form. It is important that you realise how scientific ideas have changed over time. It may well be that some of the ideas you have learned today may change as you study science in the future.

Science is not a set of known facts that must be learned and passed on to future generations. Science is a living subject that is likely to change as we find out more. Scientists have a responsibility to use this information for the good of everybody.

Good luck with your Research Study.

Data Task

What is a Data Task?

During your GCSE Additional Science course you will do a task that involves analysing and evaluating some real data from an experiment. This is called a Data Task. You will also then do some planning of a further experiment.

Your teacher will have a number of Data Tasks they can give you to do. You only need to do one. If you do more than one, your best mark will count.

An example of a Data Task is:

Is there a link between the height the ball is dropped from and the height to which it bounces? This links with the science in P3e Energy on the move.

Carrying out

You will be given instructions to follow to do a simple experiment. You can do this individually or as part of a group. Alternatively, you can watch your teacher do a demonstration, or get some data from a computer simulation. You will need to collect some results and record these in a table.

There are no marks for collecting the results, but later on you are going to suggest improvements to the experiment. You cannot really do this unless you understand what was done in the first place.

Your results should be collected in by your teacher to keep for the next lesson. If you didn't get any results, your teacher can give you a set of results. In the next lesson, your teacher will give you back your results and another sheet of instructions.

You can write your answers in the spaces given on the separate sheet from your teacher or you can write your answers on lined paper.

Writing up

This has to be done in a lesson supervised by your teacher.

The separate additional sheet will usually tell you to:

1. Average your results.
2. Draw a graph to display your results. Remember your graph should fill at least half the grid. Make sure you choose a suitable scale for each axis and label each axis clearly.
3. Look for any pattern in these results.

4 Make some comments about the accuracy and reliability of your results. Look back at the table. Are the results the most accurate results you could get with the apparatus you have used?
For example:

- If you are using a hand-held stop watch it might show the time to the nearest one hundredth of a second, e.g. 10.17 s. But you would be better recording this as 10.2 s because you cannot use it more accurately. There is a delay when you turn the stopwatch on and off and this makes a reading to more than 0.1 s wrong. When electronic timing is used, for example in the Olympic Games, there is not this delay because the turning on and off is done automatically by a computer. So times can be given accurately to 0.01 s.
- If you are using a burette to the nearest 1 cm^3, you are not using it to the maximum accuracy. You should be able to read to the nearest 0.1 cm^3. If you have three very similar results, e.g. 32.5, 32.4 and 32.5, this indicates that your results are reliable.
- Also, if you look at the graph you have drawn, are all the points you have plotted either on or close to the line or curve? Again, this suggests reliability. Any points that are away from the graph are called anomalous results. You should be able to identify anomalous results. You should show these clearly on the graph or in your writing. Remember that if the results you collected are, for example, 32, 33 and 154. 154 is an anomalous result and you should not include it. Instead you should ignore the 154 and average 32 and 33.
- Finally, you may be given the opportunity of suggesting what you could do to improve the experiment or get better results. This is called evaluation. Comments like 'take more readings' or 'do the experiment more carefully} are not worth credit. 'Take more readings' might be worthwhile if you can qualify it, e.g. take more readings between 10°C and 30°C.

5 At this stage, you should try to use some science to explain the pattern in the results you have found. In the bouncing ball example, you should know that when the ball is dropped it has potential energy and as it falls it transfers potential energy into kinetic energy. When the ball bounces it loses some kinetic energy. As the ball bounces up, the kinetic energy is converted back into potential energy. As the ball lost some energy when it bounced, it cannot reach the same height as before. If you are doing Higher tier you might try to use mathematical relationships such as: $PE = mgh$ and $KE = \frac{1}{2}mv^2$
(where PE = potential energy, m = mass, g = gravity, h = height, KE = kinetic energy and v = velocity).

6 Finally, you will be asked to do some planning for a further experiment. This may be either to improve the experiment you have done or to extend the experiment to investigate another variable. For example, 'How does changing temperature affect the height a ball bounces to?' You will not be expected to do this practically. The best way to do this is probably a series of bullet points, for example:

- Bounce the ball from the same height each time. Choose a height near the top of the range in your original experiment.
- Heat a large beaker of water (or better a thermostatic water bath) and put a thermometer in the water. Turn off the heat and put the ball into the water.

- After 10 minutes, when the ball has reached the temperature of the water, read the temperature of the water and take the ball out of the water.
- Bounce the ball and measure the height it bounces to.
- Put the ball back into water and repeat.
- Do the same thing again at five temperatures spread between room temperature and 70°C.

Marking your work

Your teacher will mark your Data Task against a set of criteria. Your teacher may give you a set of 'student speak' criteria. There are five things to be assessed by your teacher on a scale of 0–6. This makes the total for the Data Task a mark out of 30. This represents nearly 17% of the marks for the GCSE Additional Science award.

Interpreting your data	Can you draw a bar chart or, better, a line graph to display your results?
Analyse the data	Can you see a pattern? This should be expressed as, for example, As ______________ increases, ______________ increases. You might then be able to go further in explaining the relationship.
Evaluation of your data	Can you comment on the quality of the data and suggest any limitations to the method used.
Justifying your conclusions	Can you link your conclusions with science and understanding?
Ideas for further work	Can you give a plan which is detalied so another person can follow it up?

The Skills Assessment part of the course, (Research Study, Data Task and the Assessment of your Practical Skills) is worth one third of the marks available for GCSE Additional Science. By doing it should develop some practical skills which will be useful if you go onto further scientific studies. A sample of the Data Tasks from your school or college will be sent to a Moderator from OCR to confirm the marking.

Good luck with your Data Task.

Assessment of your Practical Skills

During your GCSE Additional Science course your teacher will have you make an overall assessment of your practical work. This is not based on any one practical activity, but it is a general view of your practical work throughout the course.

There are two things your teacher will be asked to look for:

How safely and accurately you carry out practical activities in science. How you collect data from an experiment, either individually or in a group with others.

They are asked to use a scale of 0–6 and are given some help to do this. They are told what is required for 2, 4 and 6 marks. They can give 1, 3 or 5 on their own judgement. If you have done no worthwhile practical work you may get 0.

The table summarises what is required for 2, 4 and 6 marks.

Number of marks	What is required?
2	You carry out practcal work safely and accurately, but you need a lot of help doing the work.
4	You carry out practical work safely and accurately, but you need some help doing the work.
6	You carry out practical work safely and accurately, but you do not need any help doing the work. Also you are aware of possible risks and take this into account.

This assessment is worth about 3.3% of the marks available for GCSE Additional Science.

Don't worry about asking for help thinking it might cause you to be marked down. The most important thing is you are able to complete the activity safely.

Enjoy the practical work in science. It is this that makes science different from other subjects you do.

Periodic Table

Key

relative atomic mass **atomic symbol** name atomic (proton) number

1	2											3	4	5	6	7	8
							1 **H** hydrogen 1										4 **He** helium 2
7 **Li** lithium 3	9 **Be** beryllium 4											11 **B** boron 5	12 **C** carbon 6	14 **N** nitrogen 7	16 **O** oxygen 8	19 **F** fluorine 9	20 **Ne** neon 10
23 **Na** sodium 11	24 **Mg** magnesium 12											27 **Al** aluminium 13	28 **Si** silicon 14	31 **P** phosphorous 15	32 **S** sulfur 16	35.5 **Cl** chlorine 17	40 **Ar** argon 18
39 **K** potassium 19	40 **Ca** calcium 20	45 **Sc** scandium 21	48 **Ti** titanium 22	51 **V** vanadium 23	52 **Cr** chromium 24	55 **Mn** manganese 25	56 **Fe** iron 26	59 **Co** cobalt 27	59 **Ni** nickel 28	64 **Cu** copper 29	65 **Zn** zinc 30	70 **Ga** gallium 31	73 **Ge** germanium 32	75 **As** arsenic 33	79 **Se** selenium 34	80 **Br** bromine 35	84 **Kr** krypton 36
85 **Rb** rubidium 37	88 **Sr** strontium 38	89 **Y** yttrium 39	91 **Zr** zirconium 40	93 **Nb** niobium 41	96 **Mo** molybdenum 42	[98] **Tc** technetium 43	101 **Ru** ruthenium 44	103 **Rh** rhodium 45	106 **Pd** palladium 46	108 **Ag** silver 47	112 **Cd** cadmium 48	115 **In** indium 49	119 **Sn** tin 50	122 **Sb** antimony 51	128 **Te** tellurium 52	127 **I** iodine 53	131 **Xe** xenon 54
133 **Cs** caesium 55	137 **Ba** barium 56	139 **La*** lanthanum 57	178 **Hf** hafnium 72	181 **Ta** tantalum 73	184 **W** tungsten 74	186 **Re** rhenium 75	190 **Os** osmium 76	192 **Ir** iridium 77	195 **Pt** platinum 78	197 **Au** gold 79	201 **Hg** mercury 80	204 **Tl** thallium 81	207 **Pb** lead 82	209 **Bi** bismuth 83	[209] **Po** polonium 84	[210] **At** astatine 85	[222] **Rn** radon 86
[223] **Fr** francium 87	[226] **Ra** radium 88	[227] **Ac*** actinium 89	[261] **Rf** rutherfordium 104	[262] **Db** dubnium 105	[266] **Sg** seaborgium 106	[264] **Bh** bohrium 107	[267] **Hs** hassium 108	[268] **mt** meitnerium 109	[271] **Ds** darmstadtium 110	[272] **Rg** roentgenium 111	Elements with atomic numbers 112–116 have been reported but not fully authenticated						

** The lanthanoids (atomic numbers 58–71) and the actinoids (atomic numbers 90-103) have been omitted.*

Glossary

ABS (acrylonitrile butadiene styrene) a low cost rigid thermoplastic
ABS (anti-lock braking system) prevents the wheels of a car locking when it is braking so preventing a skid
acceleration rate of increase of velocity
acrosome a structure in the head of the sperm that contains enzymes to digest a pathway into the egg
active safety features in a car that act to make it safer, for example, anti-lock braking and traction control
active site an hole or groove on an enzyme molecule where the substrate enters
active transport the movement of substances across a cell membrane using energy from respiration, usually occurring against a concentration gradient
actual yield the amount of product obtained in a chemical reaction
air bag car safety device that inflates on impact reducing injuries to passengers
algal bloom excessive growth of algae, for example, during eutrophication
alkali metal element in Group 1 of the Periodic table
allotropes different forms of the same element, for example, diamond and graphite are different forms of carbon
alpha particle particle made of 2 protons and 2 neutrons that is emitted when certain radioactive nuclei decay (resembles a helium nucleus)
alpha radiation low energy radiation, comprising alpha particles; it does not pass through skin into the body
alveoli (singular alveolus) small air sacs found in the lungs
anti-lock braking system (ABS) prevents the wheels of a car locking when it is braking so preventing a skid
aorta the main artery that carries blood from the heart, out to the body
artery blood vessel that carries blood away from the heart
artificially inseminate the placement of sperm in a female by non-natural means
aseptic technique a procedure that is performed under sterile conditions
atom smallest particle of an element
atomic number the number of protons in an atom of an element
atrium the left and right atria are the two upper muscular chambers of the heart; they pump blood into the ventricles
attract when two objects move towards each other, such as opposite poles of a magnet or objects with opposite charge
automated process not under direct human control
auxin a plant hormone that is produced in the growing points; it stimulates the growth of a shoot
background radiation radioactivity that is always present around us
base a metal oxide which reacts with an acid to form a salt and water only
batch process non-continuous chemical process to produce a small quantity of product
battery farming keeping animals in controlled conditions indoors
beta particle a high-speed electron emitted when certain radioactive nuclei decay; it can pass through skin
beta radiation radioactive emission comprising high-speed electrons
bicuspid a valve between the left atrium and left ventricle in the heart
biofuel fuels produced from natural sources that are renewable, for example, wood, alcohol from fermentation by yeast, and biogas from fermentation by bacteria
biological control the control of pests using living organisms
biomass the mass of living material
braking distance distance moved by a car in stopping after the brakes have been applied
braking force force applied to stop an object
capillary tiny blood vessel that carries blood to the tissues of the body; a human being has thousands of miles of capillaries
carbon dating method of determining the age of a once-living object by measuring the ratio of carbon-12 to carbon-14 currently present in the object
carbonates often insoluble salt containing carbon and oxygen; calcium carbonate occurs naturally in limestone and chalk rocks, and also in coral reefs
chain reaction process that occurs when the neutrons emitted from one atom hit other similar atoms causing them to decay and emit further neutrons that collide with other atoms, and so on
chlorination treatment with chlorine
chlorophyll a green pigment produced by plants that is used to trap light energy for the process of photosynthesis
cholesterol a fatty material mainly made in the body from saturated fat in a person's diet
chromatography technique used to separate dissolved substances in a mixture to identify them or test purity

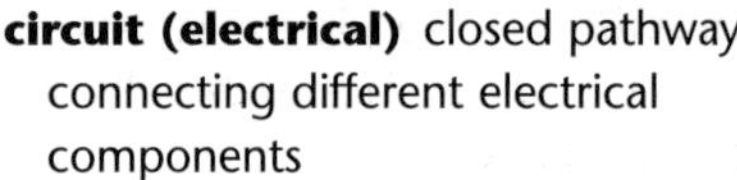

circuit (electrical) closed pathway connecting different electrical components

circuit breaker automatic switch which 'trips' (turns off) if the current exceeds a specified value; can be reset by turning the switch back on

clone two or more organisms that are genetically identical

complementary base pairing one type of base will always pair up with a particular other base in a DNA molecule

compression part of a longitudinal wave where the particles are closer together than normal

concentration gradient the variation in concentration of a substance in two different areas

continuous process chemical process that produces product all of the time

covalent bonding bonding in which a pair of electrons, one from each atom, is shared between two atoms

crenation shrinking of red blood cells due to their loss of water by osmosis

cross-breeding mating of two animals from different breeds

crumple zone the parts of a car that collapse and absorb energy in a crash, usually the front and rear parts

cuticle a waxy layer mainly on the top surface of leaves that reduces water loss

decay (plants and animals) breaking down of plant and animal matter

decay (radioactive) splitting of a radioactive nucleus with the emission of ionising radiation

defibrillator electrical device used following a heart attack to restore a normal rhythm to the heart

deficiency a lack of one or more minerals resulting in a lack of healthy growth

delocalised free to move, for example, delocalised electrons

denatured the change in shape of an enzyme molecule caused by high temperature or extremes of pH

denitrifying bacteria microbes that break down nitrates to nitrogen gas

detergent chemical that has a cleaning effect

detritivore animal that feeds on pieces of dead organic material

detritus pieces of dead and decaying material

dicotyledonous plant that has two seed leaves

differentiation the process by which cells become specialised for different functions

diploid when the chromosomes in a cell occur in pairs

displacement when a more reactive element takes the place of a less reactive one; moving from one position to another

distance–time graph graph showing distance moved by an object plotted against time; the gradient of the line at any point on the line gives the velocity of the object at that time

dormancy the state in seeds or buds where development or growth are occurring very slowly

double circulation a system that occurs in mammals where the blood passes through the heart twice on each circuit of the body

double helix the shape of a DNA molecule consisting of two chains twisted into a spiral

double insulated electrical device with plastic casing that does not require an earth wire as the casing can never become live

drag frictional force opposing the motion of an object through a fluid, for example, air

dry-cleaning cleaning of clothes carried out using an organic solvent

earth wire part of household wiring that only carries a current if there is a fault, breaking the fuse

egestion process by which material is ejected from an animal

electric shock symptoms resulting from the passage of an electric current through a body

electrode substance used to conduct electricity to an electrolyte during electrolysis

electron negatively charged sub-atomic particle which exists outside the nucleus

electrostatic stationary charged particles

electrostatic dust precipitator device fitted to the chimneys of power stations and factories to reduce pollution

electrostatically attracted attracted by the force between opposite (positive and negative) static charges

energy the ability to do work

essential elements elements that are needed by a living organism, for example, a plant

eutrophication the process by which excessive quantities of nitrate ions pollute lakes and rivers

fertilise/fertilisation the fusion of male and female sex cells

fetus an embryo that has developed to the point where it contains all the necessary structures needed to grow into a new individual

filtration technique used to separate an insoluble solid from a liquid

flaccid the state of a plant cell that loses shape due to a drop in internal water pressure in the vacuole

flame test test carried out by placing chemical in a Bunsen flame to determine the identity of the metal it contains

food preservation keeping organic matter such as food in conditions that stop it decaying

fossil fuel fuel produced by the slow decay of dead things

free fall when an object is falling under constant acceleration

friction contact force opposing the motion of one object sliding past another

fuel consumption the distance you can travel using a certain amount of fuel, usually measured in miles per gallon.

fullerenes isotopes of carbon discovered in 1985; they are made of ball-shaped molecules containing many carbon atoms

fuse thin piece of wire which melts if the current through it is too high breaking the circuit
gamete a cell involved in reproduction, such as an ovum or a sperm
gamma radiation high energy radiation emitted when certain radioactive nuclei decay
gamma ray most energetic and penetrating electromagnetic radiation, emitted when certain radioactive nuclei decay
genetic engineering moving genes from one organism to an other
geotropism a growth response in plants either towards or away from gravity
gestation period the period of time between fertilisation and birth
gradient measure of steepness; often related to graphs, taking two points that lie on a straight line, it is the difference in the *y*-coordinates divided by the difference in the *x*-coordinates; on a curve it is the slope of the tangent to the curve at a particular point
graphite one form of the element carbon where the carbon atoms are present in layers; these layers are only weakly held close to each other
gravitational field strength (g) the weight in N of every kilogram of mass; g is measured in N/kg.
gravitational potential energy the energy stored in a gravitational force field; the energy something has when it is lifted up against gravity (= mgh)
Group vertical column of elements in the Periodic table
guard cells two cells that control the opening and closing of a stoma
haemoglobin a red protein containing an iron atom that can combine reversibly with oxygen
half-life time taken for half of the nuclei in a sample of radioactive material to decay
halide compound containing the ions of halogen elements
halogen element in Group 7 of the Periodic table
haploid when each cell only has one copy of a chromosome from each pair
hydroponics growing plants without soil usually in water
inbreeding breeding between organisms that are closely related
indicator chemical used to test for acids and alkalis by change of colour
intensive farming trying to produce as much food as possible from a certain area of land
intermolecular force force of attraction between molecules
ionic bonding bonding involving the transfer of one or more electrons from one atom to another, forming positive and negative ions which are held together by electrostatic attraction
ionic compound compound containing an ionic bond
ionic lattice regular arrangement of ions in a solid ionic compound
isotope atoms of the same element and therefore with the same proton number, but with a different number of neutrons and therefore a different mass number
kinetic energy the energy possessed by a moving object ($= \frac{1}{2}mv^2$)
live wire a high voltage wire, with brown insulation, that carries electric current to mains appliances
lower epidermis cells making up the underside of a leaf
lumen central hollow cavity that allows the passage of water in the xylem vessels
lysis the bursting of cells such as red blood cells that have taken up too much water by osmosis
mass number sum of the number of protons and neutrons in an atom
meiosis cell division that occurs when gametes are produced; it reduces the number of chromosomes from 46 to 23
metallic bonding the forces that keep atoms together in a metal
microvilli microscopic projections found on the surface of the villi in the small intestine
minerals inorganic substances needed in small quantities by the human body and plants for good health
mitochondria (*singular* **mitochondrion**) microscopic organelles found in the cytoplasm of plant and animal cells; they are the site of many of the reactions of respiration
mitosis cell division that produces identical copies of cells
molecular manufacturing the molecule by molecule building up of a product
molecule particle with two or more atoms joined together
multi-cellular organisms comprising more than one cell, and having differentiated cells that perform specialised functions
nanoparticle very small particle, about one millionth of a metre in diameter
nanotube very small particles arranged in tube shapes
neutral wire wire, with blue insulation, kept at 0 V, which provides the return path for mains electricity
neutralisation reaction in which an acid reacts with a base or alkali
neutron neutral sub-atomic particle originating inside the nucleus
nitrifying bacteria microbes that convert ammonium compounds to nitrates
nitrogen-fixing bacteria microbes that convert nitrogen gas into nitrates and other nitrogen compounds that plants can use
nuclear fission the splitting of unstable nuclei to release energy
nucleon number sum of the number of protons and neutrons in an atom
organic farming growing crops or raising animals without the use of chemical assistance
osmosis the movement of water from an area of high water concentration to an area of low water concentration across a partially permeable membrane

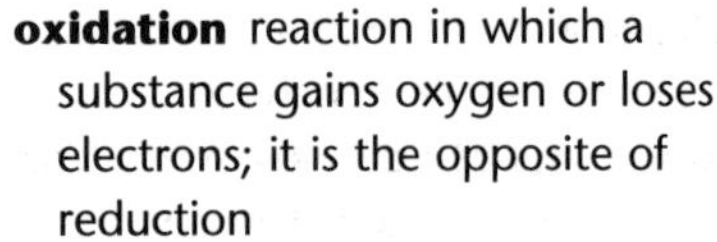

oxidation reaction in which a substance gains oxygen or loses electrons; it is the opposite of reduction

oxyhaemoglobin a chemical compound formed by the combination of haemoglobin and oxygen that takes place in the lungs

palisade mesophyll large rectangular cells in the leaf that are the main site of photosynthesis

partially permeable a membrane that allows small molecules like water to diffuse through but blocks larger molecules

passive safety features that make a car safe but do not actively affect how the car is driven, for example, cruise control and paddle shift controls

percentage yield the fraction of the predicted yield that is actually obtained, expressed as a percentage (= (actual yield/ predicted yield) ×100)

Period a horizontal row of elements in the Periodic table

permeable allowing substances to pass through

pesticide a chemical that will kill a pest on crops

pH a measurement of the acidity of a solution, on a scale from 1 to 14

pharmaceutical drug chemical that is made to be used as a medicine

phloem tissue that transports dissolved food substances (sugars) around a plant

phototropism a growth response in plants either towards or away from a light source

placenta a structure produced by the embryo that grows into the wall of the uterus to absorb nutrients for the growing baby

plant hormones chemical messengers that control how plants respond to stimuli – light, gravity and water; auxins are plant growth hormones

plaque a build-up of fatty deposits in blood vessels

plasma pale-yellow liquid that forms the fluid part of the blood

plasmolysis shrinking of plant cells that have lost water leading to the cell membrane coming away from the cell wall

positional chemistry placing molecules in the molecular manufacturing of a product

potential difference voltage in an electric circuit (voltage = current × resistance)

power the rate of transfer of energy

precipitate solid that appears when two solutions are mixed together

precipitation separation of a solid from a solution; the solid usually settles out

predicted yield the maximum amount of product that could be made during a chemical reaction, calculated using the chemical equation for the reaction and the relative atomic masses of the products

proton positively charged sub-atomic particle originating inside the nucleus

proton number the number of protons in an atom

pulmonary relating to the lungs, for example, pulmonary artery and pulmonary vein

pyramid of biomass a diagram showing the relative mass of organisms at each trophic level of a food chain

pyramid of numbers a diagram showing the relative number of organisms at each trophic level of a food chain

radioactive tracer a radioisotope introduced into a system so that its path can be followed

rarefaction part of a longitudinal wave where the particles are further apart than normal

recycling process by which materials are broken down, reprocessed and then reused, rather than being disposed of

red blood cell blood cell that contains the red pigment haemoglobin, which carries oxygen from the lungs around the body

reduction reaction in which a substance loses oxygen or gains electrons; it is the opposite of oxidation

relative atomic mass the mass of an atom measured on a scale where one atom of the isotope carbon-12 is exactly 12 units

relative formula mass mass obtained by adding together the relative atomic masses of all the atoms shown in the formula of a compound

repel when two objects move away from each other, such as like poles of a magnet, or objects with like charge

resistance opposition of a circuit component to the flow of electricity (= voltage/current)

reversible reaction a chemical reaction that can move in either direction, forwards or backwards

rheostat electrical device that allows you to change its resistance and control the current in the circuit

rooting powder a treatment containing plant growth hormones that is used to encourage cuttings to produce roots

saprophytes bacteria and fungi that feed on dead organic material

saprophytic nutrition feeding on dead organic material by releasing enzymes and then taking up the soluble food

seat belt restraint on the occupant of a vehicle to reduce injury in case of accident

sedimentation settling out of solid particles from a suspension

selective breeding a way of improving stock by selecting and breeding from those animals and plants that have the desired characteristics

selective weedkiller artificial plant hormones that kill some plants but not others

semilunar a half moon shaped valve at the beginning of each of the arteries leading from the heart

smoke detector device used to detect the presence of smoke

speed rate of change of distance (distance/time)

speed–time graph graph showing the velocity of an object plotted against time; the gradient of the line at any point on the line gives the acceleration of the object at that time; the area under the line gives the distance travelled

spongy mesophyll a layer of cells in the leaf that have large airspaces between them to allow gases to diffuse

stable octet full shell of eight electrons formed when atoms bond together

static electricity build up of stationary charge

stem cells cells that have not differentiated and can still produce different types of cells or tissues

stomata (*singular* stoma) small pores on the underside of a leaf that regulate the release of water, and allow the release of oxygen and the absorption of carbon dioxide

stopping distance distance a vehicle travels from the time the driver sees a hazard to when the vehicle comes to rest (= thinking distance + braking distance)

substrate a substance acted upon by an enzyme

superconductor material that conducts electricity with very little or no resistance

surrogate a person or animal that acts as a substitute mother for another

synapse an exceedingly small gap between two neurons

terminal speed the speed of an object where the forces balance

thinking distance distance travelled by a vehicle in the time it takes the driver to start braking once he has seen a hazard

tissue culture using small pieces of organisms to grow genetically identical organisms

transition element element in the central block of the Periodic table

transition metal metallic element in the central block of the Periodic table

translocation the movement of sugars and other food materials through the phloem in plants

transmitter substance a chemical that is released and diffuses across the gap between two neurones in a synapse

transpiration the loss of water from plant leaves

tricuspid a valve between the right atrium and right ventricle in the heart

trophic level a feeding level in a food chain

turgid the state of a plant cell when it is held in shape by water pressure in the vacuole causing it to press against the cell wall

ultrasound sound of a high frequency above 22 000 Hz which cannot be heard by humans

upper epidermis the top layer of cells in a leaf; it does not contain any chloroplasts

upper threshold of human hearing highest frequency of sound that can be heard by the human ear

urea a component of fertiliser and animal feed

variable resistor resistor whose resistance can be changed

vascular bundle strands of vascular tissue made up of xylem and phloem

vein (animal) a blood vessel that returns blood to the heart

vein (plant) the part of a leaf that carries water to the leaf cells

vena cava the large vein that returns blood from the body to the heart

ventricle the lower two muscular chambers of the heart; the left ventricle pumps blood around the body; the right ventricle pumps blood to the lungs

villi (*singular* villus) small finger-like projections in the small intestine that increase the surface area for absorption

white blood cell found in the blood and forms part of the body's defence mechanism; they produce antibodies and engulf bacteria

wilting what happens to a plant that does not take in enough water by osmosis

work the energy transferred when a force moves an object (= force × distance)

X-ray high energy, penetrating electromagnetic wave of short wavelength; it can penetrate skin but will not pass through bones

xylem tissue that transports water and dissolved minerals around a plant

zygote the single cell produced when two gametes join

Index